MW00345320

Shared Entrepreneurship

Dear David,

I hope some ideas in this book are useful in your future entrepreneurial endeavors!

Richard (Dick) Hoffman

Shared Entrepreneurship
A Path to Engaged Employee Ownership

Stephen B. Adams
Marvin O. Brown
Thomas J. Calo
Wayne H. Decker
Richard C. Hoffman
Charles C. Manz
Karen P. Manz
Olivier P. Roche
Frank Shipper
Marc D. Street
Vera L. Street
Christy H. Weer

Edited by Frank Shipper

palgrave
macmillan

First published in 2014 by
PALGRAVE MACMILLAN®
in the United States—a division of St. Martin's Press LLC,
175 Fifth Avenue, New York, NY 10010.

Where this book is distributed in the UK, Europe and the rest of the world,
this is by Palgrave Macmillan, a division of Macmillan Publishers Limited,
registered in England, company number 785998, of Houndmills,
Basingstoke, Hampshire RG21 6XS.

Palgrave Macmillan is the global academic imprint of the above companies
and has companies and representatives throughout the world.

Palgrave® and Macmillan® are registered trademarks in the United States,
the United Kingdom, Europe and other countries.

ISBN: 978–1–137–33221–9

Library of Congress Cataloging-in-Publication Data

Shipper, Frank.
    Shared entrepreneurship : a path to engaged employee ownership /
by Frank Shipper [and 11 other contributors] ; edited by Frank Shipper.
        pages cm
    Includes bibliographical references and index.
    ISBN 978–1–137–33221–9 (hardback :alk. paper)
    1. Management—Employee participation. 2. Employee ownership. I. Title.

HD5650.S484 2014
658.3'152—dc23   2014009689

A catalogue record of the book is available from the British Library.

Design by Newgen Knowledge Works (P) Ltd., Chennai, India.

First edition: August 2014

10 9 8 7 6 5 4 3 2 1

Contents

Tables, Figures, and Box

Tables

Figures

Box

Acknowledgments

We have many people to thank. First, we would like to thank the worker-owners of the companies that appear in this book, who generously shared their time and viewpoints to ensure that the cases accurately reflected the companies' practices and culture. They provided many resources, including internal documents, data, and stories of their personal experiences.

Second, we would like to thank Mary Ann Beyster, president of the Foundation for Enterprise Development; Joseph Blasi, J. Robert Beyster Professor of Employee Ownership at Rutgers' School of Management and Labor Relations (SMLR); Corey Rosen, founder and former executive director, and Loren Rodgers, current executive director of the National Center for Employee Ownership; and Michael Keeling, president of the ESOP Association, for their encouragement and support.

We would also like to thank the Booth Company of Boulder, Colorado, for collecting and providing the thousands of comments from worker-owners regarding leadership that served as a basis for chapter 2, "Shared Leadership, The Do's and Don'ts in Shared Entrepreneurship Enterprises." The comments provided us with concrete examples of what leaders do in such firms.

There were some people who worked behind the scenes on this book. They include Steve Adams, Karen Manz, and Frankie Shipper. Without their assistance, I can assure you that this book would not be what it is. Karen both edited individual chapters, and reviewed and edited across chapters to ensure consistency of content and terminology.

Preface

Initially, my colleagues and I (Frank Shipper) did not set out to write a book; we set out to write some case studies. We did not aim to write about employee-owned companies. However, that is exactly what we did. What follows is a brief history of how this book came about and why.

Charles Manz and I have been writing about W. L. Gore & Associates for over 20 years. Through Karen Manz, we obtained access to Herman Miller to conduct interviews and write articles. Both of these companies, coincidentally, have some degree of employee ownership. Then with other colleagues, we began to study other companies that were employee-owned. Along the way, my colleagues and I received a Kelso Fellowship, a Robert W. Smiley, Jr. Fellowship, a Kevin E. Ruble Fellowship, a National Center for Employee Ownership (NCEO) Rosen Ownership Opportunities Fund (ROOF) Grant, and Foundation for Enterprise Development Grants to fund our research on employee ownership. With this funding, some Perdue School Research Grants, and personal funds we were able to conduct interviews inside 12 companies. As we progressed and talked to each other, we learned that these companies had certain things in common. We surveyed the textbooks used commonly to teach management and found that what we observed going on in these companies was not covered in most texts. From our interactions as Kelso, Smiley, and Ruble Fellows with Joseph Blasi, Doug Kruse, and others, we learned that companies that had similar practices to the ones that we were studying outperformed other companies on both financial (e.g., return on assets and revenue growth) and humanistic (e.g., lower turnover and fewer layoffs) criteria. Thus, we decided that a book to fill the void was worthwhile and we should do it.

This book is an example of shared entrepreneurship. It is a collaborative effort. We worked on it for over six years. It would not have been possible for any one of us to do it alone.

The case studies were executed in various teams of researchers who went on site to a company for observation and interviews, and then followed up with further data collection and clarification. Therefore, different chapters have different authors. We practiced shared leadership of the writing so that the cases that are included in this book all have different first authors with two exceptions. Most of the decisions about this book were made by consensus. Thus, the authorship of the book is shared.

We are practicing shared ownership also in that the profits (royalties) will be used by the team that authored this book to continue work on shared entrepreneurship. Our goal is to become a sustainably funded research center. Our primary purpose is to develop educational materials for both students and the business community on how to develop companies that practice shared entrepreneurship. If someone would like to help fund such a center, please contact the book's lead author, Frank Shipper.

Introduction

What is "it" that an enterprise should be trying to do in a volatile and expanding global workplace? The "it" is creating a sustainable business model for both employees *and* society. The twenty-first century has been witness to millions of lost jobs worldwide, many never to return, and the related increasing social and governmental costs of unemployment and lost tax revenue which impact budgets for education, health and public safety. In modern society, one of the worst things that can happen to an employee is losing a job through no fault of his or her own. Perhaps even more serious is the loss or near-loss of a business enterprise which could have been sustained—but it was not—because of either outmoded or unethical practices and decisions which were given higher priority over employee or even social considerations. Again, the twenty-first century has been witness to the large-scale injurious effects of leadership at large corporations such as Enron and Tyco and within whole industries such as US banking and the American automotive industry.

Historically, management of workers was dominated by top-down thinking consistent with traditional military and religious models of order and influence. Well into the twentieth century, this command and control approach was increasingly infused into the fabric of organizations. The Industrial Revolution marked the beginning of the formal study of leadership and the importance of administration and supervision. The railroads symbolized the advent of enterprise on a large scale prompting new and more systematic methods for controlling and coordinating large workforces. Leading thinker Daniel C. McCallum introduced a set of management principles including one that emphasized that leadership should flow in a top-down manner and incorporate unity of command (essentially each employee reporting to only one boss). In the early 1900s, scientific management emerged to further reinforce separation of responsibilities of workers and managers and the dominant top to bottom view of influence and related command and control approaches. In general the role of managers was to carefully dictate expected work behaviors to employees who were to follow these dictates without question. It was nearly unthinkable to view workers as part of the leadership and decision-making process.

General Motors perhaps best serves as a symbol of the hierarchical top-down organization of the past. GM relied on a highly engineered corporate structure, under the leadership of former CEO Alfred Sloan, to become the largest corporation in the world. It struggled as a centralized, bureaucratic, and hier-archically managed firm (a recipe for success at the beginning of the twentieth century but not at the end) making it ill equipped to navigate the challenges of twenty-first-century business. This difficult truth became all too apparent when GM entered bankruptcy.

Today, views of leadership and management have significantly expanded and incorporate a variety of elements such as rewards, visions, and worker par-ticipation. However, most perspectives still view leadership as something that is assigned to a designated person who exercises influence downward toward subordinate followers. In many ways the persistent top-down command and control theme that still undergirds much of leadership thought and practice prevents organizations from fully tapping their human resources and having the flexibility to meet the challenges of increasingly dynamic, complex, and competitive environments.

The recent Great Recession and financial shenanigans have exposed the vul-nerabilities of the command and control model. The decline of AT&T, GM, Kodak, and many others attest to the need for new ways to do business in a vastly changed marketplace. What was good for business 100 or even 50 years ago is now unacceptable if an enterprise wants to survive and thrive; times have changed and we have a workforce and a marketplace with a different set of expectations. The new wave of unemployment is coming from global competi-tion. The new economic and political global challenges are felt locally.

Replacing the top-down approaches of the past and adopting new approaches that draw strength and innovation from collaboration and sharing are gaining importance. This also means that the goals of businesses have to change. The new goals need to create a business that can (1) find opportunities as global competitive changes occur, (2) sustain employees, and (3) sustain society. As will be documented in this book, the model *shared entrepreneurship* (SE) has been doing all three for over 50 years.

This book contains two main parts: "Understanding and Developing Shared Entrepreneurship" and "Shared Entrepreneurship in Action." The first consists of six chapters that provide an in-depth overview and discussion of shared entrepreneurship. The second consists of eight case study chapters. In part I, chapter 1 introduces the concept of shared entrepreneurship and the model of its four principal components: shared leadership (SL), shared collaboration (SC), shared ownership (SO), and the core value of freedom (to engage and innovate). Chapters 2–4 go into greater detail on the first three components and draw upon the cases presented in part II of this book as well as from other organizations that practice elements of shared entrepreneurship. Chapter 5 dis-cusses the critical role of culture in shared entrepreneurship organizations and in particular, identifies the principal core value of freedom and other core val-ues that contribute to the establishment and nurturing of a collaborative work environment or sense of ownership. In addition, the facilitating role of human resource development in shared entrepreneurship is examined. Chapter 6 will discuss lessons learned from our research and challenges for going forward with the practice of shared entrepreneurship.

The second part of this book, "Shared Entrepreneurship in Action," contains eight case studies of shared entrepreneurial organizations (table I.1). All of these companies were visited onsite by a researcher/author team of this book. Observations, interviews, and follow-up data collection and clarifications were the primary basis of each case study. The companies vary in scale from a small company with less than 200 employees, such as Equal Exchange, to large corporations employing many thousands, such as Herman Miller. Some of these businesses operate worldwide and have offices internationally. These companies represent a diverse array of industries and services; several operate with worldwide recognition of products or brand. The following lists the companies with website, home office location, number of employees, and type of products or services.

In addition to these eight companies, interviews were conducted in four other companies, and we have included examples from those companies in the first six chapters, too. In addition, we have benefitted from conversations with Dave Parker, former president of Southwest Airlines, and Jody Hofer Gittel, author of *The Southwest Airlines Way*.[1] Finally, Bill Nobles, former executive at Exxon, shared with us his insights from interviewing Ken Iverson, former

Table I.1   Profiles of companies featured as case studies

• SRC Holdings srcholdings.com Springfield, MO	Over 1200 employees; remanufactures products for agricultural, industrial construction, truck/automotive markets
• W. L. Gore & Associates www.gore.com Newark, DE	Over 8,000 employees worldwide; product applications in the medical, fabric (GORE-TEX®), and industrial markets
• TEOCO www.teoco.com Fairfax, VA	Over 280 employees; a leading provider of assurance and analytics solutions to communications service providers worldwide
• Herman Miller, Inc. www.hermanmiller.com Zeeland, MI	Over 6,000 employees worldwide; commercial furnishings and design services
• Equal Exchange equalexchange.coop W. Bridgewater, MA	120 employee ESOP/co-op members; fair trade importer/distributor of gourmet coffee, tea cocoa, bananas, and other foods produced by farmer cooperatives in Latin America, Africa, and Asia
• KCI Technologies www.kci.com Sparks, MD	1000 employees; largest employee-owned engineering firm headquartered in MD
• HCSS www.hcss.com Sugar Land, TX	130 employees; national pioneer and leader in software development for construction companies
• MBC Ventures Inc. www.marylandbrush.com www.skylouversystems.com Baltimore, MD	Less than 100 employees; manufactures industrial-use brushes and solar modules

president of NUCOR. Thus, we have incorporated examples from Southwest Airlines and NUCOR into the first six chapters, too. There are also examples in the first six chapters from companies that wish to remain anonymous.

Three of the learning points that should be takeaways from this book are: (1) there is more than one way to do "it," (2) no one person can do "it" alone, and (3) shared entrepreneurship welcomes and deserves examination as a proven model of an ethical, dynamic and freedom-based process of collaborative innovation for the twenty-first century.

Note

1. Gittell, J. H. 2005. *The Southwest Airlines way*. New York: McGraw-Hill.

PART I

Understanding and Developing Shared Entrepreneurship

This section focuses first on understanding what shared entrepreneurship (SE) is, its success in organizations, and why other organizations may need to adopt it. Second, it focuses on what are the common elements in SE enterprises relative to leadership, governance, innovative processes, and culture. The culture chapter also covers the progressive human resource management processes found in SE enterprises. What becomes clear in this section is that SE represents a paradigm shift in how firms are led and operated, and that firms that are to survive and thrive in the twenty-first century cannot operate as traditional command and control firms.

CHAPTER 1

Shared Entrepreneurship: Toward an Ethical, Dynamic, Empowering, Freedom-Based Process of Collaborative Innovation*

Frank Shipper, Charles C. Manz,
Karen P. Manz, and Bill Nobles

Shared entrepreneurship (SE) is becoming recognized as an organizational model that can succeed in a rapidly changing global marketplace where the hierarchical command and control model cannot.[1] Hierarchical command and control stifles innovation and often fails to reward those who are responsible for an innovation.[2] Innovation, whether product, process, or organizational, is the driver of success. This has always been true, but it is more critical today than ever before because of rapidly changing technological advances and consumer preferences. The academic evidence is sketchy because shared entrepreneurship is an emerging and growing practice although a limited number of organizations have been using it for 50 or more years. Those that do practice shared entrepreneurship appear to have a better chance of survival than those that don't.[3]

Shared entrepreneurship organizations do not give up control, they just do it differently. As will become evident in this book, shared entrepreneurship is a fundamental paradigm shift from the traditional command and control organization. Peter Drucker in his classic 1954 book, *The Practice of Management*, wrote about self-control and responsibility when hierarchical control was the preeminent model of management.[4] Herzberg identified responsibility as a key motivator.[5] Studies of shared entrepreneurship organizations, including ours, found frequent use of peer control via peer monitoring and social reinforcement.[6] Sometimes this is done through formal peer-to-peer mentorship programs, other times informally. In addition, vision-led freedom, a shared compelling vision of success, inspires people to achieve their potential and clarifies when self and peer control should be exercised. Control in shared entrepreneurship organizations substitutes the use of self, peer, and shared vision for mechanistic and hierarchical forms of control.

Organizations that practice shared entrepreneurship such as Southwest Airlines, the fourth largest airline in the United States, and NUCOR, the largest steel producer in the United States, are forcing some of their competitors into bankruptcy in their respective industries. Others are developing new product lines, such as W. L. Gore & Associates or are reviving failing plants as SRC Holdings has done. All of these companies practice *shared entrepreneurship* (SE), but none of them do it the same way. SE is simply a term that captures the key operating components of these firms and other companies featured in this book that has allowed them to survive and thrive in the rapidly changing global marketplace. *Shared entrepreneurship is an ethical, dynamic, empowering, freedom-based process where all are encouraged to share innovative ideas and then are supported with appropriate resources to develop these ideas and enabled to share in the rewards of success.* The key operating components will be defined later in this chapter and illustrated throughout the book.

As Thomas Friedman observed in his book *The World Is Flat*, global competition is forcing companies to do things cheaper, quicker, and/or better worldwide.[7] Price competition is moving jobs that make low value-added products from high-wage to low-wage countries. Low value-added products are those where the operating profits margin is low such as in the manufacturing of apparel sold at low-end department stores and discounters. The movement of such jobs to low-wage countries is evident when you look at figure 1.1, which reports the United States Balance of Payments from 1960 to 2011. The imbalance has grown since the early 1970s, but a breakdown between goods and services shows that the imbalance has been driven by goods such as raw materials (e.g., oil) and consumer goods (e.g., clothing and consumer electronics), products typically with low embedded value-added. In contrast, for services, the United States had a positive balance of payments during the same time period. Services by their very nature have a higher value-added. There are products such as the latest microprocessors that have high value-added. Organizations that practice SE are better prepared to participate in the global economy because they tend to be more innovative than hierarchical command and control organizations.[8] Thus, the former offer higher value-added products or services more than the latter.

The converse has also become apparent in that high-wage countries cannot compete well based on incremental productivity changes against low-wage countries. For example, the labor costs in manufacturing for the Philippines, Mexico, Poland, and Taiwan are 5 percent, 18 percent, 23 percent, and 24 percent, respectively, of the United States' according to the Bureau of Labor Statistics in 2010.[9] China's and India's are probably equal to or less than those of the Philippines. Thus, it is hard to conceive how companies in high-wage countries that focus on incremental productivity improvements can compete against those in low-wage countries. Incremental productivity changes should not be ignored;

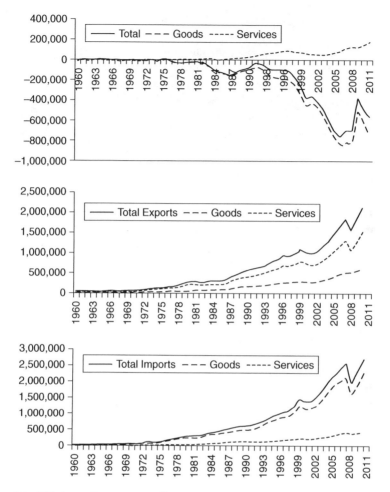

Figure 1.1 US balance of payments in millions, 1960–2011.
Source: US Census Bureau, Foreign Trade Division.

they just should not be the focus of global competitors based in high-wage countries. They cannot compete on how much they produce; they must compete on the added value embedded in their products, processes, or services. Germany is a high-wage country that has done this and become the financial savior of the European Union.

Companies in high-wage countries must compete on brains, not brawn. To do this they must innovate; they must compete on disruptive process, product, or service innovations. For example, NUCOR has developed numerous process breakthroughs including "Castrip" technology that produces solid sheets of steel while consuming 84 percent less energy than the traditional steelmaking facility.[10] Through its development of innovative processes both in production and in human resource management, NUCOR has grown in the US market and expanded overseas. It is an example of how a company that practices SE can compete in the global market place while producing a commodity priced product.

Silicon Valley was built and continues to grow based on disruptive product innovations. SE is widely practiced there (e.g., Google). Continuous improvement has been displaced by continuous innovation as the key to surviving and thriving. For example, distributive computing displaced mainframes, iPods displaced Walkman, and smart phones have displaced personal digital assistants (e.g., PalmPilots) and are displacing iPods plus both still and video digital cameras. In this competitive environment, mistakes are tolerable, such as Intel's Pentium 5 floating point decimal errors, as long as they are corrected; stagnation is not. Every innovation that yields a competitive advantage has a life cycle of introduction, growth, maturity, and decline just as markets have a parallel life cycle. For organizations to grow or even maintain market share they must continuously innovate or they will experience decline.

Some may argue that the preceding are isolated examples of companies that practice SE and have success. To the contrary, a three-year study of 780 mostly large companies found that those that practiced SE had lower voluntary turnover, increased intent to stay among employees, and higher return on equity than other companies.[11] Another study of 41,206 employees in 14 companies at 323 work sites found that SE improved firm performance.[12] In addition, there are studies of multiple companies that suggest that those that practice SE can weather economic recessions better than those that do not.[13] Thus, there are a number of studies of firms that suggest that those that do practice SE are more successful than those that don't.

Technology and the global market are evolving and co-evolving, but many organizations are not.[14] Technology as it has evolved allows outsourcing without any time lag. In some cases, such as with medical transcriptions, on-time performance is improved because the transcriptions are frequently done in India while the West sleeps.[15] As the standard of living improves for people in India, the companies and employees buy more equipment and services from the West. Macro input/output can track the gross economic changes, but what will coevolve at the micro level is unpredictable. For example, who knew that the overabundance of bandwidth created by the bursting of the technology bubble would lead to phone centers abroad or that phone centers abroad would lead to unprecedented demand for consumer products and electricity within a country such as India? The failure of organizations in India to respond to increased electrical consumption due to greater use of consumer products has resulted in unprecedented power outages. Some will say that this is an unfair example because power is a regulated industry. The failure of Kodak, Sears, IBM, AT&T, Xerox, US Steel, General Motors, United Airlines, and others to evolve is just as apparent. Some of them are mere shadows of their former selves, others taken over, and still others bailed out by the government. Companies that practice SE, contrary to the view of some of their critics, do respond faster than hierarchical command and control organizations.[16] Thus, they are more likely to evolve and coevolve in step with technological and marketplace changes.

Shared Entrepreneurship

The four components of SE are illustrated in figure 1.2: shared leadership (SL), shared ownership (SO), shared collaboration (SC), and freedom. The first three components are more complex entities and can be viewed as processes or loose structures. The fourth component, freedom, is a principal core value that is expressed through the first three components. The next five chapters will expand on how these principles operate in greater detail. In addition, they will illustrate the role freedom, the fourth component, plays in creating and sustaining SE throughout the organization.

Shared Leadership

SL can be described as an ongoing mutual influence process where both designated and emergent leaders participate in the influence process.[17] That means everyone is potentially a leader, at least some of the time. Who leads at any given moment depends on the capacities and experiences of the people involved and the immediate requirements of the situation. SL is related to many other concepts, including distributive leadership, freedom-based management, shared governance, industrial democracy, employee involvement, employee engagement, and employee participation. SL is the term we choose because it denotes clearly the opportunity for all employees to engage actively in a full range of responsibilities, including leadership, innovation, and ownership, throughout the organization. W. L. Gore & Associates has anchored the manner in which employees are encouraged to engage though its four guiding principles, which will be addressed later. Other SE organizations encourage SL through

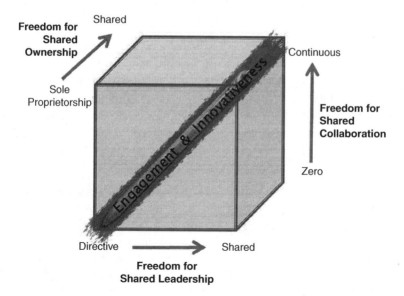

Figure 1.2 The four components of shared entrepreneurship.

values statements. For example, at one minority employee stock ownership plan (ESOP) company any proposed action can be questioned by anyone based on the corporate values. In an organization practicing SL, everyone has the freedom and the responsibility to emerge as a leader.

Leadership can be viewed as a performance art. As Douglas McGregor pointed out, individual leaders take their cues from their underlying assumptions about the nature of people. He labeled two common set of assumptions Theory X and Theory Y.[18] People who adopt one or the other have a certain mindset and this is going to carry over to the way that they attempt to lead people. To practice SL will require leaders to have a Theory Y mindset. In other words, these leaders believe employees can contribute far more to organizational success if given the freedom to fully develop and utilize their potentials and if they share in the rewards of their success through stock ownership and profit sharing. In reality, long-term studies have found that 60 to 75 percent of managers have probably a Theory X, command and control mindset relative to their employees.[19] Thus, those who want to be leaders in a firm that practices SE will have to make a conscientious effort to adopt a Theory Y mindset and exhibit role-appropriate behaviors.

For example, at Mondragon Corporation, a federation of worker cooperatives based in Spain, the roles of the central leaders are defined in terms of facilitation and coordination and not based on more typical top-down executive roles. With over 270 cooperatives participating in industries as diverse as supermarkets to the production and servicing of high-tech computer aided design and manufacturing equipment, it would be foolish to concentrate decision-making power in the hands of a few. For SL to be effective on a wide scale, it has to be embedded throughout the organization. In other words, the corporate mindset has to change as to what is an effective leader. The old mindset of command and control that stresses employees to get results has to change to an SL model that stimulates and engages employees to make and keep commitments. A description of SL in action from an ESOP company is discussed in chapter 2. Shared governance is covered with illustrative examples in chapter 3. In addition, a strong collaborative culture that inspires entrepreneurial activities has to be infused throughout the organization. How that might occur is discussed in chapter 5. Without the SL that facilitates SO, encourages a strong collaborative culture that inspires entrepreneurial activities, and upholds freedom for the worker-owners to exercise self-direction and self-control, an enterprise will not reach its potential. These four elements of SE work together in systematic harmony so a firm can achieve optimal results.

Shared governance is complementary and essential to the long-term survival of SL. We have seen this more than once when a leader that practiced SE left the organization without changing the formal structure and processes. During their time as the CEO (chief executive officer), they ignored the formal structure and processes. When they were replaced by a traditional leader, the organization reverted to command and control because there was no check on the new CEO's power that would have been created by formalized shared governance. In at least one case, we observed an organization that practiced shared governance reject a traditional leader hired by the board. As will be seen in chapters 2 and 3, it changes the role of leaders from planning, organizing, managing, directing, and controlling to motivating, facilitating, and coordinating. Shared governance is not something a company has or does not have. Rather, it is a matter of degree. Cooperatives such as Mondragon and egalitarian ESOPs such as at Equal Exchange tend to have a high degree of SL where all members of the cooperative have one vote. The members of these firms can literally vote out the president or change the strategic direction of the company. In one diagram of its organizational structure, Equal Exchange places its members at both the top and the bottom to signify that they have the ultimate authority and are workers too. At Mondragon, the term "worker-owners" is used to indicate the dual roles of employees. There are other elements to the practice of shared governance within an SE environment, and they are discussed in chapter 3. However, it can be easily seen from this brief description that shared governance complements SL because authority and responsibility are merged. In contrast, in hierarchical organizations authority and responsibility are often separated.

Shared Ownership

SO consists simultaneously of two parts. The duality of this concept has been described previously as a "dual creation, part attitude, part object, part in the mind, part 'real.'"[20] The first part is the formal structure that Kruse et al. refer to as "shared capitalism."[21] The second part is "intellectual financial engagement." This is also referred to as "psychological ownership." The former can occur in a number of forms including ESOPs, cooperatives, profit sharing, and gain sharing. Other terms such as "employee owned businesses" (EOBs), "democratic capitalism," and "mutual companies" are sometimes used to refer to companies that practice SO. It is the preferred term because multiple forms of financial participation can be encompassed by this term plus the idea that for it to be present employees must be actively involved. As with SL, there is no one way to do it.

SO can vary by degree from one organization to another. For example, ESOP companies are sometimes broken down by the percentage of stock held by employees. In one study, the breakdown was 1 to 50 percent, 51 to 99 percent, and 100 percent owned by employees.[22] Another important way to measure employee ownership is the average amount of value each employee has in their individual stock account. For example, the average employee in the largest 100 percent employee owned company, Publix Super Markets, had $48,000 in their individual stock account in 2010. According to a 2010 NCEO (National Center for Employee Ownership) analysis of ESOP company government filings, the average ESOP participant had an account balance of $55,836 in 2008. This analysis included approximately 2,500 companies. Within a company the value of stock held in an individual's account can vary widely by both longevity and organizational level. New employees start with little or no stock in their individual accounts. Long-term employees approaching retirement have exceeded $1 million in their ESOP accounts at some companies. In some cases, these were production or floor level employees. Jack Stack, president of SRC

Holdings, maintains that all employees who have been with the company for 25 years have more than $400,000 in their ESOP account including those who began and still work on the shop floor.

Not all companies that have the first part of SO have employees who experience psychological ownership primarily because they do not practice the second part of SO, intellectual financial engagement. For example, some companies set up ESOPs to take care of financial issues such as assisting the founders in getting money out of the firm, or to take advantage of special tax provisions. Financial information is infrequently shared and no attempt is made to have employees understand the financial statements, how what they do impacts them, or how they could improve them. SO does not exist because the employees in such a situation have no meaningful participation relative to uses and sources of funds. In this type of organization, firm performance is probably no greater than their rivals. They are just another company in the industry. They are missing intellectual financial engagement. Until that occurs, employees do not see how their work impacts their rewards.

The need to instill psychological ownership through intellectual financial engagement has been recognized by some companies practicing SO for decades. At SRC Holdings, the employees are taught to understand financial statements, including the income statement, the balance sheet and the funds flow statement, and such concepts as "net contribution to overhead." There is even the SRC Financial Quiz that everyone takes. Each week, workers in an operational work unit come together to review these statements and learn how well they are doing. Such meetings are common in companies that practice SE. Another common practice is open book management, which was developed at SRC Holdings. Open book management means that the financial statements are open for review by all employees. In practice, management more often reviews financial statements with the employees at quarterly, monthly, or weekly meetings than employees seek out this information. This is one of the major premises for success at what SRC Holdings refers to as the "great game of business" (GGOB).[23]

When SO is combined with SL, there is a synergistic effect, and psychological ownership is heightened. Feelings of "possessiveness and of being psychologically tied" to the firm and its success occurs.[24] As previously mentioned, such companies do not suffer as drastically in a recession and then recover faster from the recession than companies that have neither or just one of the two—SL or SO. The reason for their success has to do with a third concept underlying companies that practice SE—shared collaboration. When employees have psychological ownership, they believe that what benefits the company benefits them and vice versa. They believe that there is something in it for them and stop asking, "What's in it for me?"

Shared Collaboration

The third attribute of SE is SC. The term "shared collaboration" may seem redundant, but what is called collaboration in many organizations is at best cooperation.[25] SC "can obtain results that far exceed what could be achieved either by any person working alone or by the" individual inputs of many people.[26] Our use of this term denotes the *embeddedness* of the SE core value "freedom to engage and innovate." Everyone shares in the practice of SC and thereby creates a widespread sense of freedom. When freedom is deeply distributed within the organization, it energizes and directs effort in both challenging times as well as during periods of extraordinary opportunity.

On the careers page of the Herman Miller website, the need for all to collaborate in the development of innovations is emphasized to prospective employees by the following: "We're all challenged to design solutions."[27] Why innovations will occur more readily when knowledge is shared can and has been explained through NK diagrams.[28] NK diagrams look like topographical maps. They have peaks and valleys. The peaks can be considered potential competitive advantages through differentiation, and the valleys can be considered potential competitive advantages through low cost. For firms to be successful, they must find either peaks or valleys that they can dominate. Economists hypothesize that a rational human being when considering the landscape (containing the peaks and valleys) will tend to conduct only local searches and identify negative slopes leading to a low-cost position or positive slopes leading to a differentiation position. Since there can be multiple positions of low cost and differentiation, an individual will miss other opportunities and likely the optimum opportunity. To make the problem even more difficult, the landscape is not static. The peaks and valleys are constantly changing. An individual acting alone has little chance of maintaining competitiveness. Even a group of individuals acting in a hierarchical command and control structure has little chance of being responsive enough to remain competitive due to communication issues such as overload, filtration, and delays.

The alternative is an organic structure that is self-organizing. For example, one of the firms in Silicon Valley meets the challenge of short product lifecycles in a number of ways. First, it dispenses with hierarchical command and control structure. It does not even attempt to have an organizational chart because it "would be obsolete before the ink was dried."[29] Second, the most common form of structure is a task force. A task force is formed to pursue a new opportunity. In the beginning the task force will be loaded with scientists and engineers with a few production and marketing people. They are assigned an open office area and allowed to arrange themselves as they see fit. Additional people are asked to join the task force as needed by other task force members. As the new product advances from the development stage to the production stage, some of the scientists and engineers go on to new task forces and additional production and marketing people are added. Sometimes such task forces are referred to as sand dune teams. "Just as sand dunes change in number and shape as winds and times changes, (sand dune) teams...form and reform...as external demands and requirements change."[30]

Individuals no longer needed on a task force and who have not been asked to join another one will be declared surplus. They then have a fixed amount of time to find a new position within the company or they will be terminated.

This may sound harsh, but in reality forced turnover is very low. Everyone knows from the beginning that they must contribute and build their skills and reputation. What this firm has done is develop an organic, self-organizing, self-correcting organization. So have most of the other firms that will be featured as case studies in this book.

Another analogy that is used to explain why SC occurs more frequently in an organization that practices SE rather than hierarchical command and control is how common integrated computer chips can be wired together to produce a super computer. They can be either wired in a parallel or series configuration. When wired in parallel, simultaneous processing of information can occur whereas in serial, sequential processing occurs. This is roughly equivalent to a group of individuals receiving all the information at the same time versus having all the information pass from one individual to another without distortion. Most of us recall this rarely worked well when attempted in the childhood game of telephone (whispering a message in the ear the first person, who then whispers the message he/she heard to the next, and so forth), and there is little evidence that it works well in a hierarchical organization. To make matters more complicated, the game of telephone required only one-way communication, whereas, organizations at a minimum require two-way communication to achieve a common understanding. Thus, in organizations where information is shared collaboratively, innovation is fostered, rapid implementation is encouraged, and decentralized decision-making is the norm. They will outperform hierarchical command and control organizations where bureaucratic delays in information processing, decision-making, and implementation are typical.[31] The failure of hierarchical command and control companies to innovate was criticized extensively in 1982 in the best-selling business book *In Search of Excellence*, but an alternative business model such as the SE model was not offered at that time.[32]

Freedom—The Fourth Component of Shared Entrepreneurship

As indicated in figure 1.2 freedom is essential to each of the other three components. It is the freedom to examine the financial statements, the freedom to lead, and the freedom to develop ideas and much more. Freedom to engage and innovate means the freedom to make decisions on how to pursue objectives, the freedom to communicate without being restricted by hierarchical silos, the freedom to make decisions on such mundane things as travel and purchases, and so on. Freedom can also be defined more broadly as:

- Freedom to develop
- Freedom to make mistakes and to fail
- Freedom to question and to investigate
- Freedom of access to information
- Freedom from boundaries
- Freedom from arbitrary limitations such as work hours, location, dress, etc.[33]

In essence, freedom is the right to be treated like an adult, to be able to develop as an adult, to make decisions like an adult, and to be trusted. For example, an engineer who left IBM to go to work for W. L. Gore & Associates was amazed that he could purchase items without approval by others. At IBM, he had to get approval from a vice president to purchase any software package regardless of cost and whether IBM made a comparable product. He could also purchase precious metals such as gold without having to justify the expenditure to anyone. All employees at Gore can use "dabble" time to develop new products and all employees at Equal Exchange are encouraged to use "10 percent time" to develop new products or new skills. Freedom is not an abstract concept at these companies; it is encouraged and practiced by the employees every day. At the same time, the employees are held responsible for making good use of the resources they expend. It is still OK to make a mistake, but there is an expectation that overall there will be a payoff.

Some will argue that freedom in organizations is analogous to empowerment. Conceptually, we do not disagree. Unfortunately, "empowerment" is bantered about in command and control organizations without any real significant changes in authority. Fred Herzberg and Gary Hamel, writing over 40 years apart, both lamented that discretionary power has not increased.[34] To distinguish our use of the word "empowerment," we use it to describe what we have observed in the companies that practice SE—the freedom to make decisions without running it up the hierarchy. As David Marquet wrote, "Don't empower, emancipate!"[35]

With this freedom comes the expectation that worker-owners will make good decisions, act responsibly, and use company resources wisely, even frugally every day. During Andy Grove's time as CEO of Intel, he did not have a private secretary or a conference room; and he and everyone else who needed an office could have one as long as it was a cubicle. Among the company jokes was that it was alright to fly any class domestically as long as it was coach and that the Intel limo was a Ford Escort. In addition, Andy Grove followed the first rule of good leadership—be a good role model by going above and beyond these expectations.

A president of a typical company who was considering making the transition to SE was visiting in another SE enterprise. What pushed him into making the change were not all the good things that he was hearing from the upper-level worker-owners, but what he observed the lower-level worker-owners doing. A driver had carelessly wrecked a truck. The other worker-owners were mad and they were letting the driver know about it. One had already made a quick calculation about how the cost of the repairs was going to decrease their profit sharing. The visiting president was astounded. He realized that at his own company the driver and the employees "would all be standing around laughing." The driver might receive some razzing, but it would all be treated like a joke. The impact on the company would never be considered.

Another expectation that must come with freedom is absolute honesty. For example, all employees at one company can turn in their travel expenses directly via the Internet for reimbursement; no approvals or documentation is required. The bank account of the employee is immediately credited. In other words, no employee has to float the company a loan waiting for approval and processing of the expense report. On occasion, the employee will be asked for documentation. If the employee is found to have falsified the expense report, firing is immediate. At another company, it came to the president's attention that reports were being falsified. The person falsifying the reports was a long-time friend of the president and a vice president. When the president called in the vice president to fire him, the president said how much it hurt him to have to do this. However, the president had been given no choice because if he was going to expect absolute honesty from lower-level employees, he had to hold upper-level managers to the same standard. Again, this president recognized that the first rule of good management is to be a good role model.

Shared Collaborative Culture

As mentioned previously, a strong collaborative culture is also part of shared entrepreneurial organizations. A strong collaborative culture can be thought of as the binding force that keeps an organization together and focused on its mission. *Organizational culture typically includes values, beliefs, common practices, communication, rituals, and corporate symbols that help create an organization's identity and sense of employee affiliation to the company.*

In traditional organizational theory literature, cultures are often classified as weak and strong. The problem is that some organizations have strong negative cultures that perpetuate "we-they" and not collaborative behaviors. For example, in labor-management environments, the strongest predictor of union certification is peer communications.[36] The more acrimonious the history between management and labor, the stronger the negative culture, and the higher the strong negative binding force will be. Strong negative binding forces will contribute to the dissolution of the organization. For example, when employees of a company with strong positive culture are interviewed, they will proudly identify themselves as a member of the organization such as, "I am an associate at Gore." In contrast, when an employee of an organization with strong negative binding forces is asked, they will respond, "I am an engineer." The difference can also be seen in clothing. In the former, the employees will proudly wear clothes with the company logo on them. In the latter, they will proudly wear clothes with the union logo on them often devoid of the company logo.

Binding forces as used here can be thought of as being analogous to the binding forces in particle physics. Organizations with strong shared collaborative cultures will have strong positive binding forces. Such forces translate into higher stability, lower turnover, lower absenteeism, and greater sharing of innovative ideas as cited earlier. The converse is true for organizations with negative binding forces either weak or strong. Both the strong positive and negative binding forces in organizations are embedded in the culture of the organization and the weak binding forces stem from the structure and governance processes. The strong binding forces are reinforced intrinsically and sometimes socially. Weak binding forces depend on extrinsic reinforcement.

Fred Herzberg, among others, recognized intrinsic motivation as stronger than extrinsic motivation.[37] He went on to also say that organizational structure and processes had weaker influence on behavior than intrinsic forces. Fred Fiedler shared this position in his contingency theory of leadership as he stated that formal power derived from organizational structure and processes had relatively little ability to influence employee behavior in comparison to group cohesiveness.[38] In addition, Herzberg stated that intrinsic and extrinsic motivation should be aligned to achieve optimal effectiveness. Similarly, we think that the examples used in this book argue for organizations aligning positively both weak and strong binding forces to achieve optimal effectiveness. As noted earlier, organizational structure and processes are addressed in chapter 3 on organizational governance. Developing cultures with strong binding forces is addressed in chapter 5.

The Goal of Shared Entrepreneurship

The goal of creating SE within a firm is to create an ethical, dynamic, empowering, freedom-based organization. A manager that increases the productivity of the organization or a portion of it without an increase in resources could be considered a catalyst. In a firm that practices SE, all members of the organization have the opportunity and responsibility to serve as catalysts to make products, processes, and service better, faster, cheaper. As more and more members of the organization take advantage of the opportunity, the organization becomes autocatalytic, self-sustaining, self-renewing. It takes advantage of the wisdom of the crowd both within and without the organization; the autocatalytic organization is an open organization. The fuel that keeps it running, that prevents disintegration due to negative entropy, is the importation and development of ideas throughout the organization. These organizations innovate and reinnovate products, processes, and services that have high value embedded into them. They try to make their own products, processes, and services obsolete before their competitors do. Some well-known companies have followed this strategy and also practiced SE. For example, Intel, a minority ESOP, has followed this strategy with its microprocessor. Instead of an organization that tries to function as a closed system with rigid hierarchies and fixed channels of communications, an autocatalytic organization welcomes and cultivates new ideas and innovations from anywhere. These organizations practice crowd sourcing both within and without the organization.

This description may sound like some theoretical utopia of SE, but it is going on in organizations as diverse as Equal Exchange (EE), the largest fair trade firm in the United States, and W. L. Gore & Associates, the world's largest manufacturer of breathable fabrics and vascular grafts. At Equal Exchange every employee is encouraged to participate in "Exchange Time" every Thursday morning for an hour and a half. Exchange Time lectures and discussions cover topics such as fair trade, co-op history, or issues affecting their farmer partners. New employees are strongly encouraged to participate. The discussions are recorded and shared via EE's intranet with remote employees and regional offices. Cody Squire, who joined EE right out of college, enthusiastically described "Exchange Time" as: "It's one structured thing that you can depend on having every week just to learn about something new, to look deeper into something you already know about, or to hear from somebody who has just returned from working with farmer co-ops in Peru."

In addition to Exchange Time, EE has "10 percent time." Employees can use 10 percent of their work time for purposes unrelated to their core functions. This time can be used to cross-train, work on governance committees, or learn more about the product. From these efforts there developed a program called "Brew Crew," which made every participant a potential quality control inspector for its largest product—coffee.

Within W. L. Gore & Associates, all associates are encouraged to set aside some "dabble" time. Dabble time is when people have the freedom to develop new products and evaluate their viability. For example, after about nine or ten months of exploring the possibility, a team of excited and passionate associates developed a set of GORE™ products for the bike market. In their exploration, the team learned that the road bike market is larger than the trail bike market, and there might potentially be a product for the racing market.

A presentation, referred to within Gore as a "Real-Win-Worth" presentation, was prepared and presented to the Industrial Products Division (IPD) leadership team. Real-Win-Worth is a rigorous discipline that Gore uses to help hone in on the most promising new opportunities. The three issues that must be addressed in "Real-Win-Worth" are: (1) Is the idea real? (2) Can Gore win in the market? (3) Is it worth pursuing? Gore, through its associates and processes, actively seeks out multiple peaks of product differentiation to dominate, as described in the discussion of NK diagrams. After listening to and questioning the presenters, the IPD leadership team responded, "You know what? You do have some really good ideas. Let's do a market study on it. Let's see if the market is interested." The market study indicated that the market was interested and now there is a whole series of GORE™ products, from the recreational biker to the serious competitor.

These are just two examples of how companies that practiced SE tapped the innovative potential of the crowd within their organizations. More examples will be found in the case studies presented in later chapters. There is no one way to do it.

These organizations also practice tapping the crowd outside for innovative ideas. For example, W. L. Gore & Associates depends on internal organic growth as its primary way to increase sales, but a second source of growth can come from external acquisitions. Gore evaluates opportunities to acquire technologies and even companies based on whether they offer a unique capability that could complement an existing, successful business. The leadership at Gore considers this strategy a way to stack the probability deck in its favor by moving into market spaces its associates already know very well. To facilitate this growth strategy, Gore has a few associates who evaluate acquisition opportunities at the enterprise level. They do not do this in isolation, but in concert with leaders within each division.

Herman Miller recognized the significance of importation of outside ideas from as far back as 1930 when D. J. De Pree struck a deal to produce and sell a bedroom suite designed by Gilbert Rhode based on a 3 percent commission. It was not until 1942 that Herman Miller produced its first office furniture—a Gilbert Rhode design. Throughout Herman Miller's association with Gilbert Rhode and later Charles and Ray Eames, designers of the famous Eames Lounge chair, they were never employed within the organization. Furthermore, Herman Miller never had exclusive rights to their designs. Herman Miller continues to this day to have contracts based on sales commission with outside designers.

At the same time Herman Miller does not ignore the crowd within. For example, a team within was charged with developing the "Thrive Collection." Products included in this collection are the Ardea® Personal Light, the Leaf® Personal Light, Flo® Monitor Arm, and C2® Climate Control. All of these are designed for improving the individual's working environment. Continuing Herman Miller's tradition of innovative design the Ardea Personal Light earned both Gold and Silver honors from the International Design Excellence Awards (IDEA) in June 2010.

Herman Miller was one of only four organizations, and the only nonhigh-technology one, selected to *Fortune*'s *100 Best Companies to Work For* and *Most Admired Companies* and *FastCompany*'s *Most Innovative Companies* in both 2008 and 2010. The three high-technology organizations selected were Microsoft, Cisco, and Google, not usual company for a firm in a mature industry and definitely not for an office furniture company. The use of internal and external crowd sourcing while committing to other practices compatible with SE has at least partially contributed to the creation of a company where the unusual is usual.

What organizations that practice SE have discovered is the need to create permeable organizations. Information and ideas flow freely within the organization. Open book management discussed earlier is just one example of shared information. Innovations come frequently from shared ideas. In an SE environment, many employees participate in free-form brainstorming without any formalized structure or facilitation. Every employee has the potential to be either a node or tendril on the corporate neural network. This happens both internal to the corporation as with "10 percent time" at Equal Exchange and "dabble time" at W. L. Gore & Associates, and external to the organization as at Herman Miller use of external designers. Worker-owners at other companies such as HCSS and TEOCO serve informally as boundary spanners. As they work with their clients, they look for new product ideas that can provide both additional services for their clients, additional revenue streams for the company, and additional rewards for the worker-owners. Organizations that practice permeability try to prevent organizational silos and ceilings. They build their buildings with alcoves and other design elements that naturally foster informal meetings, and minimize the use of organizational structure and titles to foster the free exchange of information and ideas. They build offices that are open so worker-owners are aware of what others are working on and to have egalitarian public areas such as cafeterias to foster camaraderie and communications and parking lots with no priority spaces except for customers. The goal of creating a permeable organization is to expedite the development of new products, processes, and services.

Developing Intellectual Capital

Organizations that practice SE also engage in practices to enhance the intellectual capital of the worker-owners. For example, Mondragon has its own accredited degree granting university. Equal Exchange has an extensive library of which the worker-owners are justifiably proud. Increasing the intellectual capital of worker-owners is in the best interest of the firm because it will enhance SC.

Continuously increasing the intellectual capital of the worker-owners is linked to the organization's ability to continuously innovate. For example, one employee-owned firm did not pay for additional training for any of its worker-owners including its engineers. The justification was that since not all worker-owners could or would take advantage of this benefit, it should not be available to any worker-owners. When robotics became a major competitive force in the industry, it fell behind. The firm changed its policy to support work-related training. In addition, it has participated with multiple universities providing grants and speakers, and has developed its own technology center to ensure the company's leadership position in product development. Today, it is recognized as an industry leader both domestically and overseas.

Developing intellectual capital can be thought as a four-step process—attracting, selecting, retaining, and increasing. The large companies that appear in this book are well known for their advanced human resource management policies that underlie SE, such as Herman Miller and W. L. Gore & Associates, which attract a large number of applicants anytime they are hiring. Even the small companies such as Equal Exchange attract many applicants in their geographic areas of operation when they are hiring. Sometimes it appears that it is harder to get a job at a company that practices SE than to get into an Ivy League school. Effective human resource management strategies are critical to the success of these companies. The leaders of these companies don't just mouth the words that "people are our most important assets"; they assure that their companies operate that way, every day. This will be elaborated on in chapter 5 when we detail how a corporate culture of SE can be developed.

SC and SO go hand in hand with worker-owners' willingness to share their intellectual capital with the organization. Approximately 30 years ago, two large organizations were introducing elements of SL into their organizational processes. Both successfully introduced autonomous teams with documented results. In one of the organizations, they decided to tie the results to a profit sharing scheme. The results increased even further. In the other, the executives were frequently citing the results of the autonomous teams. At one large meeting, a worker asked, "What's in this for us?" The executive answered gruffly, "Your jobs." The program died. When employees have a tangible financial stake in the outcome, they are more willing to contribute their labor and brains, the essence of SE, and extraordinary results can be achieved.

Why Is Shared Entrepreneurship Successful?

Why are firms that practice SE more successful than ones that don't? There is no one or easy answer to that question. However, just as functional magnetic resonance images of brains are discovering that the brain has greater plasticity than previously believed, ethnographic studies of firms in this book that practice SE suggest that they have greater plasticity than firms that don't. Such a finding makes eminent sense in that, if a firm is dependent on the plasticity of the mind to continuously innovate, the firm must also have a high degree of plasticity in its structures and processes to enhance innovation. In studies since the early 1960s, structures and processes with a high degree of plasticity (aka organic[39]) have been recognized to be more effective in turbulent environments than hierarchical command and control (aka mechanistic) ones. A high degree of plasticity in their structures and processes may explain why, through constant innovation, such firms can respond better to recessions than those that have hierarchical command and control structures and processes.

For example, W. L. Gore and Associates as well as Mondragon will move people from one business area to another depending on the demand for the various products rather than laying people off. At Herman Miller, all employees will and did take a 10 percent cut in hours to preserve jobs during a difficult time such as the 2008 Great Recession. When the company recovered, the workers did not have to be recalled and retrained. Therefore, the company was able to respond to orders quicker than if it had to hire and train new employees or recall laid off employees. Thus, time to ramp-up production and cost of training were reduced.

Earlier we discussed how teams (i.e., task forces) are formed and evolved in an organization that practices SE. In traditional organizational theory, there are no terms to describe such transformations. Drawing on inspiration from biologist Stuart Kauffman's book *At Home in the Universe: The Search for the Laws of Self-Organization and Complexity*, concepts such as permeability, self-organizing, co-evolving, autocatalytic, and plasticity have been used to describe what happens in organizations that practice SE.[40] One other concept that can describe how these organizations operate is chaining, as in molecular chaining that occurs in organic compounds. The properties of organic compounds can be varied widely by increasing or decreasing their molecular length. For example, polytetrafluoroethylene (PTFE) is used by DuPont to produce Teflon©, and by W. L. Gore & Associates to produce Gore-Tex© fabric, vascular grafts, industrial seals, and a host of others products. Teams (aka task forces) can be formed by linking individuals together to achieve its current goals. As discussed earlier, scientists and engineers are linked together in the early stages of product development to move from the ideation to the prototype stage at another employee-owned company. At that point, production specialists are linked to the team to move to the production stage and some of the scientists and engineers may link together to develop other new products while still being available when needed by the first team. Marketing specialists are linked to the team when a marketing strategy becomes imperative. In reality, some production and marketing people will be linked to the team early in the development stage. However, the nucleus, the leadership, of the team is changing over time; members with different expertise share in the leadership as the essential functional know-how changes. At Gore, knowledge-based decision-making is practiced. As a team undergoes its metamorphosis, knowledge-based SL occurs. To optimize the expertise of its members, arguably, the team has to be as pliable as a polymer molecule and ready to change to meet different needs as they arise.

Other arguments for why SE has been successful in the organizations that we have studied can be given. By identifying the components that are common, we hope to advance the understanding of why SE firms are successful.

Summary

To summarize, we have defined SE and introduced its four major components in this chapter. They will be explored more thoroughly in the following four chapters. The contribution that this book hopes to make is to describe how the four principles of SE—SL, SO, SC, and freedom—have been observed in practice in a variety of highly successful companies. Through multiple qualitative studies, we have observed that the worker-owners need to have multiple forms of meaningful engagement and that the engagement has to occur in a nonthreatening egalitarian atmosphere. To emphasize this point, three of the four components begin with *"shared"*—SO, SL, and SC. The fourth and equally important component *freedom*—freedom to grow and develop, freedom to go for the brass ring—has to be emphasized. Through the implementation of these four components, employees are engaged; ideas and innovation bubble-up continuously throughout the organization; rewards are shared; a collaborative ownership culture develops; and a self-perpetuating system of SE is created. In the competitive, global knowledge-based economy, innovation is the global competitive advantage. It is not enough to be as good as the competition. Companies must leap-frog the competition, expect to be leap-frogged by the competition, and be ready to respond. The mantra of the 1980s of continuous improvement has changed in the twenty-first century to continuous innovation. To make this happen every employee must have the skills and freedom to think and act like an entrepreneur, and this will not happen unless every employee has both a financial and psychological stake in the action. There are many others better qualified to discuss the pros and cons of various forms of worker-ownership and how they can be setup. The focus of this book will be to describe multiple ways worker-owners can be engaged individually and in teams in the finances, leadership, and innovations of the firm. It is our belief that readers of this book will wonder why more firms do not practice shared entrepreneurship.

Notes

* See Shipper, F., Manz, C. C., Nobles, B., & Manz, K. P. 2014. Shared entrepreneurship: Toward an empowering, ethical, dynamic and freedom-based process of collaborative innovation. *Organization Management Journal*, 11(3).

1. Alperovitz, G. 2013. *What must we do? Straight talk about the next American revolution*. White River Junction, VT: Chelsea Green Publishing; Hamel, G. 2007. *The future of management*. Boston: Harvard Business School Press; Hamel, G. 2011, December. First let's fire all the managers. *Harvard Business Review, 89*: 48–60; Kinicki, A. 2008. *Organizational behavior: Core concepts*. New York: McGraw-Hill; and Kruse, D. L., Freeman, R. B., & Blasi, J. R. 2010. *Shared capitalism at work: Employee ownership, profit and gain sharing and broad-based stock options*. Chicago: The University of Chicago Press.

2. Shipper, F., & Manz, C. C. 1993. W. L. Gore & Associates, Inc.: A case study. In Hill, C. W. L., & Jones, G. R. (Eds.), *Cases in strategic management* (pp. 429–444). Boston: Houghton Mifflin.

3. Olson, E. 2013. The relative survival of worker cooperatives and barriers to their creation. *Advances in the Economic Analysis of Participatory & Labor-Managed Firms, 14*: 83–108.

4. Drucker, P. 1954. *The practice of management*. New York: Harper & Row.

5. Herzberg, F. 1966. *Work and the nature of man*. Cleveland: World Publishing.

6. Freeman, R. B., Kruse, D. L., & Blasi, J. R. 2010. Worker response to shirking under shared capitalism. In *Shared capitalism at work* by Kruse, D. L., Freeman, R. B., & Blasi, J. R. Chicago: University of Chicago Press.

7. Friedman, T. L. 2005. *The world is flat*. New York: Farrar, Straus and Giroux.

8. For evidence of the innovativeness of firms that practice shared entrepreneurship, see Lampel, J., Bhalla, A., & Pushkar, J. 2010. *Model growth: Do employee-owned businesses deliver sustainable performance?* London: Employee Ownership Association; and Knell, J. 2008. *Share value: How employee ownership is changing the face of business*. Herts: The All Party Parliamentary Group on Employee Ownership, pp. 11–12.

9. http://bls.gov/fls/home.htm#compensation. Accessed: August 14, 2012.

10. http://www.nucor.com/responsibility/environment/leadership/benefits/. Accessed: August 14, 2012.

11. Kruse, D. L., Blasi, J. R., and Freeman, R. B. 2012. Does linking worker pay to firm performance help the best forms do even better? Working Paper 17745, National Bureau of Economic Research, Cambridge, MA.

12. Hsueh, J. C. 2011. *Dynamics of Shared Capitalism Policies in a Startup Company*. Doctoral dissertation, Massachusetts Institute of Technology.

13. Blair, M., Kruse, D., and J. Blasi, J. 2000. Is employee ownership an unstable form? Or a stabilizing force? In Kochan, T., & Blair, M. (Eds.), *The new relationship: Human capital in the American corporation* (pp. 241–298). Washington: The Brookings Institution.

14. Kauffman, S. 1995. *At home in the universe: The search for the laws of self-organization and complexity*. Oxford: Oxford University Press.

15. Freidman, T. L. 2005. *The world is flat: A brief history of the twenty-first century*. New York: Farrar, Straus and Giroux.

16. Pierce, J. L., & Furo, C. 1990. Employee ownership: Implications for management. *Organizational Dynamics, 18*, 32–43; and Lampel et al., *Model growth*.

17. Pearce, C. L., Manz, C. C., & Sims, Jr., H. P. 2014 *Share, don't take the lead*. Charlotte, NC: Information Age Publishing; Pearce, C. L., & Conger, J. A. 2003.

Shared leadership: Reframing the hows and whys of leadership. Thousand Oaks, CA: Sage.

18. McGregor, D. 1960. *The human side of enterprise.* New York: McGraw-Hill.
19. Hogan, R., Raskin, R., & Fazzini, D. 1990. The dark side of charisma. In Clark, K. E., & Clark, M. B. (Eds.), *Measures of leadership* (pp. 343–354). West Orange, NJ: Leadership Library of America.
20. Etzioni, A. 1991. The socio-economics of property. *Journal of Social Behavior and Personality, 6*: 466.
21. Kruse et al., *Shared capitalism at work.*
22. Pendleton, A. "The three forms of employee ownership" extract from inaugural lecture "When workers own business: What happens, and why," University of York, December 14, 2009. http://www.youtube.com/user/ProfAndrewPendleton#p/a/u /1/vNoA-oYVEkk. Accessed: August 23, 2012.
23. Stack, J. 1994. *The great game of business.* New York: Currency Doubleday.
24. Pierce, J. L., Kostova, T., & Dirks, K. T. 2001. Toward a theory of psychological ownership in organizations. *Academy of Management Review, 26*: 299.
25. Hackman, J. R. 2011. *Collaborative intelligence: Using teams to solve hard problems.* San Francisco: Barrett-Koehler.
26. Ibid.
27. http://www.hermanmiller.com/about-us/careers.html. Accessed: August 10, 2012.
28. Kauffman, *At home in the universe*; and Afuah, A., & Tucci, C. L. 2012. Crowdsourcing as a solution to distant search. *Academy of Management Review, 37*: 355–375.
29. Identity of the speaker and the company is withheld at the request of the company.
30. Hackman, *Collaborative intelligence*, p. 34.
31. See Kruse et al., Does linking worker pay to firm performance help the best firms do even better? Working Paper 17745; Hsueh, J. C. 2011. *Dynamics of shared capitalism policies in a startup company.* Doctoral dissertation, Massachusetts Institute of Technology; Blair et al., Is employee ownership an unstable form?.
32. Peters, T., & Waterman, Jr., R. H. 1982. *In search of excellence.* New York: Harper & Row.
33. Nobles, B., & Staley, P. 2010. *Freedom-based management: Building a culture that enables and encourages fully empowered employees to produce awesome business success.* http://www.42projects.org/docs/FreedomBasedManagement.pdf. Accessed: December 21, 2011.
34. Herzberg, F. 1976. *The managerial choice.* Homewood, IL: Irwin; and Hamel, G. 2007. *The future of management.* Boston: Harvard Business School Press.
35. Marquet, D. 2013. *Turn the ship around!: A true story of turning followers into leaders.* New York: Portfolio Hardcover.
36. Davy, J., & Shipper, F. 1993. Voter behavior in union certification elections. *Academy of Management Journal, 36:* 187–199.
37. Herzberg, *The managerial choice.*
38. Fiedler, F. E. 1967. *A contingency model of leadership.* New York: McGraw-Hill.
39. In this book, we have chosen to avoid the use of the term "organic" because as it was conceptualized by T. Burns and G. M. Stalker in 1961 (in *The management of innovation* [London, Tavistock]) organic organizations were the opposite of mechanistic. In the ethnographic studies on which this book is based, the authors found that shared entrepreneurship firms do have some opposite characteristics to mechanistic, but they are also different. Trying to describe them as opposite to mechanistic organizations was a limiting way of characterizing them.
40. Kauffman, *At home in the universe.*

CHAPTER 2

Shared Leadership: The Do's and Don'ts in Shared Entrepreneurship Enterprises

Frank Shipper and Charles C. Manz

When visiting shared entrepreneurship (SE) enterprises and studying them through formal interviews, conversations, and questionnaires, it became apparent that leadership in such enterprises is different than in traditional hierarchical command and control organizations. For example, Fred Freundlich of the University of Mondragon explained that the roles of the central leaders are defined in terms of facilitation and coordination and not based on typical top-down executive roles. At W. L. Gore & Associates such terms as "manager," "management," "employee," and "employer" are taboo. When employees have the ability to influence who their leader is either through a democratic process such as at Mondragon or Equal Exchange, or through the administrator of the employee stock ownership plan (ESOP) trust, leadership has to be different.

In some large companies such as Herman Miller the largest stockholder is the ESOP trust with more than 1,000,000 shares than the next largest stockholder. Even though the employees hold only 9.1 percent collectively in their ESOP trust, they are Herman Miller's largest stockholder.[1] Thus, the employees have significant power through the plan's administrator, who has the legal obligation to vote the shares in the best interest of the worker-owners. When the employees have such power executives must find a way to lead the enterprise other than through intimidation. Jack Stack, founder, president, and chief executive officer (CEO) of SRC Holdings, is adamant that intimidation, the quintessential command and control style of leadership, is an ineffective way to lead an organization.[2]

The primary difference that became apparent in visiting SE enterprises and studying them is the importance of leadership. The leaders create and sustain the business side of the enterprise, and they also create and sustain what Douglas McGregor identified as the human side of the enterprise.[3] It would be easy to argue that there would not be a NUCOR without Ken Iverson, a W. L. Gore & Associates without Bill Gore, an SRC Holdings without Jack Stack, and a Herman Miller without D. J. De Pree. The importance of leadership is true for the large well-known companies, and also for the small companies that practice SE. There would not be a TEOCO, which is no longer small, without Atul Jain or an MBC Ventures without Steve Mullan. The Employee Ownership Association of the United Kingdom maintains that to sustain an SE organization good leadership is required at all levels.[4] If it is, however, not sustained by the CEO, it will not be sustained at the operational level.

Another difference that became apparent in the interviews and conversations was the use of the descriptive term "worker-owner" to describe their leaders. Words not commonly part of the leadership theory vocabulary were used, such as "honest," "sincere," "cares for others," "intense," "integrity," "trust," and "puts others first." A search of over 100 hours of transcribed interviews did not identify one leader described as charismatic. Some, but not all leaders, could probably be described as charismatic, but this was not reported by the worker-owners as an important attribute. One could argue that the "leaders' honesty, sincerity, caring for others, intensity, integrity, and putting others first" overcame any lack of charisma that they might have.

Overall, the difference in terms of leadership practice for these companies can best be described via the concept of *shared leadership* (SL)—a dynamic interactive influence process, typically in some kind of team context, where members lead one another to reach group and organization goals.[5] The core of SL is a commitment to involving organization members in the central decision-making and influence process of the organization. It is not consistent with an emphasis on hierarchy and having a small set of central top-down oriented leaders hoard power, keep tight control, and make all the important decisions themselves. Rather, as we indicated in the previous chapter, with SL, the organizational context allows for individual employees to have meaningful input and to step forward and lead when their abilities or experience is needed. They also learn that other times they need to step back and allow those who are better equipped to meet requirements of the immediate work process to lead. There are many potential benefits provided by an SL approach relative to more traditional top-down leadership practices and it is an essential ingredient of SE.

In biological terms, when leadership operates from a command and control mindset, cortisol is released into the bloodstreams and brains of the employees inhibiting the innovativeness of the enterprise. In contrast, where leadership operates under an SL mindset, endorphins are released that stimulate innovativeness. Leaders operating with an SL mindset share successes with others, which in turn releases endorphins that stimulates more innovativeness. As has been observed for many years, success breeds success. Up until recently why this happens was unknown, but fMRI (functional magnetic resonance imaging) studies are providing us with biological understanding of how the brain works. When these studies are combined with our observations in organizations that practiced command and control versus those that practiced SE, the need for abandoning hierarchical command and control becomes even clearer.

For example, Scott Adams, in the *Dilbert* comic strip, had the Pointy-Haired Boss approach Dilbert and ask, "How is your creativity coming along?" Dilbert responds, "I don't have any. Your management style makes me focus all my energy on staying out of trouble," to which the boss responds, "Your insubordination is unacceptable." Dilbert concludes, "And there it is."[6]

The popularity of the *Dilbert* comic strip is probably due to how day-after-day it reflects what many people are experiencing in the workplace. Cartoonist Adams draws (pardon the pun) on his experience working at some well-known command and control companies. Apparently, many people can relate because of their own working experiences.

For the past 20 plus years, much has been written about transformational leadership. Some may ask, why not that mindset for leaders? Unfortunately, it has not lived up to its proponents' predictions. In a review of approximately 90 studies, it was found that "transformational leadership failed to predict leader performance."[7] Whether any of these studies were done in organizations that practice SE is unknown. Thus, how much we know about effective leadership in any company much less those that practice SE is at best limited.[8] Therefore, in keeping with an underlying principle of SE that the best people to help us understand are the worker-owners, we asked them.

Specifically, we asked the worker-owners in a large, high-tech, minority employee-owned company that practices SE to describe their leaders. The individuals identified as leaders by the company typically had responsibility for many people in managerial, staff, and operational positions. We used a 360-degree approach to learn what effective leaders do and what they do not do. To get responses and ensure that the direct reports and peers felt safe in providing answers, they were asked to respond online to a third-party administered survey and were assured that only aggregated responses from five or more direct reports or peers would be reported to leaders. In addition, everyone was assured that the information would be used only for development purposes, and no one inside the company would have access to individual profiles except the participating leader. To solicit the needed information the direct reports, peers, and the leaders' superiors were asked the following three questions:

1. What does this leader do that should be continued?
2. What should this leader do more of to be more effective?
3. Does this leader have any traits or characteristics that inhibit his or her success?

Leaders were asked the same three questions relative to themselves.

In total, 3,701 "continue" comments were collected, 2,419 "more of," and 1,404 "inhibit." Each set of comments was analyzed separately. A free association computer protocol analyzed the data based on cluster analysis of words in n-dimensional space. Common words such as articles, conjunctions, and prepositions were ignored. Words of the same root origin were treated as the same word. For example, "motivate" and "motivation" would be treated as the same word. In addition, words that do not have specific meaning, such as "very," and proper names were excluded. Other words that did not relate to the questions were excluded such as technical terms, references to the company or units within the company, and acronyms. After the program had grouped responses, additional checks were done by an outside expert to ensure that the groupings were appropriate.[9]

Once that analysis was completed, the average number of "continue," "more of," and "inhibiting" comments per respondent was computed per leader. Then the average number of each type of comment per respondent was tested against the leadership effectiveness as rated by the leader's superior. The only set of comments that turned out to be predictive of leadership effectiveness was the "continue" one. These results presented a conundrum—how could a set of comments predict performance, whereas a well-developed questionnaire for transformational leadership used in the meta-analysis referenced earlier could not? There are probably a number of reasons that could partially explain these results. First, the transformation of an organization from a command and control to SE does not happen due to a single leader as noted earlier. For leadership to be transformative, it must be infused and shared throughout the organization.[10] Thus, if one focuses on only those who hold formal leadership positions in a command and control organization, what motivates employees everyday may be missed. For example, Admiral Elmo Zumwalt was the youngest person to be chosen as chief of US Naval Operations. He was widely praised for trying to reform a number of the personnel practices of the US Navy. After retirement, he described his experience "as riding a bicycle pedaling like hell and steering like hell, but no one had told him that the chain had been disconnected and the handlebars loosened."[11] Outsiders focusing on his initiatives failed to see the lack of inside support. Obviously, Zumwalt's leadership was not infused through the organization, and therefore, no significant transformation occurred.

Second, the worker-owners who work with and observe their leaders everyday may be better able to describe effective leadership practices than others.[12] Peer and direct report observations of leaders' behaviors have often been found to correlate better with their performance than even the observations of the superiors. Therefore, the descriptive terms in a questionnaire may not describe effective leadership as well as the descriptions provided by peers and direct reports.

Third, there was agreement on the behaviors that the leaders should continue to use among the direct reports, the superiors, the peers, and the leaders themselves. This was not true of the "more of" or "inhibit" comments. In other words, the frequency with which the "continue" comments were mentioned by each group was statistically the same at the .007 level or lower. Therefore, it can be safely said that in this organization there is agreement among all groups on what effective leaders do.

Fourth, the seven behaviors listed in table 2.1 were identified by the worker-owners as ones leaders should continue. They are listed according to the frequency with which they were mentioned. All of the behaviors are positive; not one of them could be seen as a negative behavior as frequently used in command and control organizations.

Table 2.1   Leader behaviors that should be continued

Leader Behaviors that Should be Continued
1. Inspire People to High Results
2. Build Motivated Teams
3. Take Innovative Risks
4. Fulfill Commitments
5. Think Strategically
6. Communicate Openly
7. Listen Effectively

B. F. Skinner hypothesized and found in his studies that positive reinforcement was more effective than punishment.[13] Recent research on positive and punitive interactions between the leader and subordinate has found that the higher the ratio between the two the higher the unit's performance.[14] The research also suggests that it takes approximately four positive interactions to overcome one negative interaction, and that such interactions continue to negatively impact performance three years later.[15] Research using fMRI has found that during positive interactions a person is "open to new ideas and new emotions, and able to scan the business and social environment."[16] In contrast, during negative interactions a person's "social network was significantly deactivated or suppressed... and their minds are closed to new ideas or emotions." Others have reached the same conclusions by working with or observing leaders at work. For example:

> Jim Mallozzi, former CEO of one of the Prudential Financial Services businesses, turned around the financial performance in his organization by providing his top team "the latitude to experiment on being positively deviant leaders." Financial results changed in one year from a $140 million loss to a $20 million profit through applying practices of positive leadership.[17]

This example reinforces the need for positive leadership that encourages freedom in actions. Prudential is also a minority ESOP firm.[18] Thus, one can conclude that effective individuals rely on positive interactions to lead whether they occupy formal positions of power or not.

Exploring Positive Leader Behaviors (the Do's) through the Eyes of Others

The seven behaviors listed in table 2.1 were titles given to each group of behaviors as categorized together by the computer program. Although they provide some idea as to what effectively leaders do, they are not as descriptive as the actual comments. For example, a verbatim comment for the first category,

"Inspire people to high results," is "High energy, delivered for the organization inspires others to raise the bar. Expects a lot of herself and therefore of others." This comment reinforces what was identified a number of times in the first chapter as the first rule of effective leadership and that is to be a good role model. Not surprisingly, leading by example is an extremely effective way to lead. In addition, this behavior corresponds partially to what Nobles and Staley refer to as a "vision-led freedom" where everybody is "encouraged to achieve their potential."[19]

Build motivated teams: "Keep inspiring the organization through partnership, team work, and a positive atmosphere."
A number of behaviors can be seen in this comment. First, a leader is expected to be a team member on multiple teams. Second, maintaining a positive atmosphere is important for effective teams. Leaders who create a positive atmosphere cause mirror-neuron networks to be activated within each group member that in turn causes them to mimic the leaders' and others' actions, and sense how they feel.[20]

Take innovative risks: "Analysis and decision-making, informed risk taking, commitment to quality."
This comment lays out some of the steps to taking risks—analysis and decision-making, and that risk taking should be informed. In addition, any risk that is taken should ensure that quality is maintained or enhanced. Although these comments came from only one organization where the employees are the largest, but minority owners, each of the organizations featured in this book has a reputation for quality and protecting that reputation. This comment basically outlines an acceptable strategy for innovative risk taking—inform, analyze, commit to quality, and focus on making a decision.

Fulfill commitments: "She has a laser focus to execution. I can rest assured she will do what she commits to do."
Although this organization has a system of goal setting, people are asked to make personal commitments to either achieving the goal or some element needed for the accomplishment of a department or task force goal. At W. L. Gore & Associates, not the source of the data, one of its four guiding principles is "Make your own commitments, and keep them." In many, if not all, organizations that practice SE the worker-owners are encouraged and given the freedom, within broad guidelines centered on quality of products or services, to commit to achieving explicit outcomes. The one thing that they are not given the freedom to do is to fail to pursue their chosen outcomes. Yes, failure is tolerated, but failure to pursue is not. Multiple failures may, however, indicate that the individual was not committing to informed innovative risks, the prior behavior that leaders should continue as discussed earlier.

Think strategically: "Be strategic. Identify and engage with a variety of stakeholders who have impact to overall business."
This comment goes beyond the normal advice given on strategic management—identify your stakeholders. It tells the leaders to engage with a variety

of stakeholders. It is asking the leaders to be boundary spanners to a variety of stakeholder that have impact on the overall business. It is asking them to model the need for the organization to be permeable and actively seek to import ideas. When the leaders of companies that practiced SE were asked, "Where do you get your ideas for new products?" a common response was, "From our customers." The leaders of the organizations that initially brought these ideas to the corporation were often sales or technical representatives that had contact directly with customers. The practice of SL within these companies allowed the ideas to percolate through the company and become viable products. The results are that multiple stakeholders were engaged—customers, sales or technical representatives, product developers, and others.

WorldBlu, an organization that promotes the use of democratic practices and freedom in the workplace, echoes the importance of thinking strategically in its list of principles. Its principle labeled "Purpose and vision" states, "A democratic organization is clear about why it exists (its purpose) and where it is headed and what it hopes to achieve (its vision). These act as its true North, offering guidance and discipline to the organization's direction."[21] In *Alice in Wonderland*, Alice asks the question, "Which road do I take?" "Where do you want to go?" responds the Cheshire Cat. "I don't know," Alice answers. "Then," the Cat says, "It doesn't matter."[22] In a company that practices SE, where the organization is going matters and all the worker-owners should know it, too, as the next two behaviors confirm.

Communicate openly: "Continue to be open to suggestions and be approachable and available."
This comment encompasses three attributes of open communication. First, a leader must be physically available. How many times are the leaders of command and control organizations ensconced on the top floor of the headquarters building behind layers of receptionists, administrative assistants, and secretaries? All the leaders at the SE organization from which this data came worked at offices without doors. Herman Miller practices SE and designs office furniture. It is famous for having developed the first open office, the Action Office, which led to a whole host of Dilbert cartoons. Robert Probst, its designer, said about the way the Action Office was being used, "Not all organizations are intelligent and progressive; they make little bitty cubicles and stuff people in them, barren rat hole places."[23] In 2013, Herman Miller introduced a new open office design called the Living Office. It was designed to foster open communications and collaboration. Brian Walker, president and chief executive officer of Herman Miller, works in a Living Office. It is hardly recognizable as an executive office. It has no walls, partitions, or private conference rooms. On its website, Herman Miller states, "Encourage collaboration where it happens most: at the desk."[24] The Living Office is designed to make worker-owners, regardless of rank, available to each other. It is difficult, if not impossible, to communicate openly if people are not available.

W. L. Gore & Associates has to tackle this problem differently because members of its product teams are often on three or more continents. Thus, it uses multiple forms of communication including conference calls, video conferencing, and its own digital voice exchange called Gorecom. Because the associates at Gore do not believe that there is any substitute, team members and leaders are expected to meet face-to-face regularly. For team members and especially leaders, this can mean lots of travel. As one technical associate joked, "Probably, in the last 12 years, I spent 3 years traveling internationally, a couple weeks at a time." Thus, availability is assured.

Second, leaders in an SE organization must be approachable. Leaders are expected to use MBWA (management by walking around). Leaders engage employees when doing this by asking questions. This is where training in communications on how to ask, for example, nonleading, nonthreatening questions plays an important role. They are trained also to praise good things that are happening. The realization here is that if the only time a leader interacts with another employee-owner is when something is wrong, the leader will not be seen as approachable. In fact, just the opposite will happen and the leader will be seen as someone to avoid.

Since communications is at least a two-way process, worker-owners are expected to ask questions. They are also taught to ask nonthreatening questions at HCSS (Heavy Construction Systems Specialists, Inc.). The realization here is that as soon as either party asks a threatening question, stress goes up, the rational thinking portion of the brain begins to shut down, and communications begin to break down. If this pattern continues, the leader will not want to approach the other worker-owners.

Third, the leader must be open to suggestions. Leaders must hear and respond to the suggestions. A curt "Thank you for your suggestion, let's move on" will not do. When a suggestion is made, it needs a response. Sometimes the response can be immediate; other times the response will need more exploration and consideration. When this happens at one high-tech company that practices SE, the standard phrase is "Let's take that off-line." That phrase signals to both the employee-owner making the suggestion and the others in the room that the suggestion is going to explored and considered in detail. At Gore, there is a defined process for new product suggestions called "Real-Win-Worth" to help hone in on promising opportunities. If the suggesting associate or associates are inexperienced, they will be coached through the process by an experienced associate. At another company, worker-owners can make suggestions online to leaders of the company. They guarantee responses within 48 hours. In contrast, one command and control organization made a monetary award posthumously to an employee's widow some 17 years after a suggestion was made. Lack of openness to suggestions can come in many forms. Failing to respond in Skinnerian terms is putting the employee on an extinction schedule of reinforcement, meaning that open communication will be extinguished and suggestions will cease to come forward. Delayed responses have a similar effect over the long run. Under both scenarios the organization will miss out once again on the collective wisdom of the employees.

Listen effectively: "Listens, learns, executes."
That the computer program ranked "Communicate openly" and "Listen effectively" in juxtaposition may indicate how important they are to each other.

The experts on communication will tell you that open communication cannot occur without effective listening. That same message can be found in the juxtaposition of the two sets of comments by the computer program. There is much that has been written about active listening, but this comment goes beyond the act of listening—learning and executing. How do the worker-owners know that they were heard? The answer provided is that the leader must execute. Tangible action is the most concrete response confirming that the leader was listening. In Skinnerian terms, this is positive reinforcement. When taken together "Communicate openly" and "Listen effectively" are probably synergistic. Leaders may do both as defined in communication literature, but if they do not execute, that is unacceptable in a company that practices SE. Without execution there is no entrepreneurship, no new products, services, or processes, and no increase in equity to be shared. Thus, execution is confirmation of effective listening by the leaders.

WorldBlu echoes the importance of both communicating openly and listening effectively in its list of principles for democratic organizations. Its principle labeled "Dialogue + Listening" states, "Instead of the top-down monologue or dysfunctional silence that characterizes most workplaces, democratic organizations are committed to having conversations that bring out new levels of meaning and connection."[25] In organizations that practice SE, the same was found to be true.

As you review the suggestions given by peers and subordinates relative to effective leadership, you may wonder why leaders should bother to attend executive training seminars or executive MBA programs. The wisdom contained in the comments is another illustration of what James Surowiecki, writer for the *New York Times,* the *Wall Street Journal,* and other publications, refers to as *The Wisdom of Crowds.*[26] In some SE organizations, training is not conducted by specialists in training. It is conducted by worker-owners who have demonstrated their effectiveness. One organization conducted a long-term study of this model and found it to be effective and also useful in training future leaders.[27]

Individually, only one leadership attribute differentiated between high and low performing leaders, "Fulfill commitments," but collectively all of them do. Obviously, fulfilling commitments is extremely important in an SE organization. Someone who failed to do so would not remain as a leader for long in such organizations. To be an effective leader requires a complete set of attributes, a full toolbox. This has been found in other research, too.[28] Expecting any one attribute to be the answer to effective leadership is naïve.

Exploring the Leader Behaviors That Others Want More Of (More Do's)

When the comments were analyzed for the question, "What should this leader do more of to be more effective?" ten groupings of responses were found. They appear in the right-hand column of table 2.2 listed in the frequency with which they were reported. As can be seen, there are seven leader behaviors that should be continued, and ten that should be increased. That can be explained in that there is greater agreement on what an effective leader does than on what a leader needs to do to improve. Given that the advice is individualized to specific leaders, that there are a greater number of suggested ways to improve should not be surprising. That these suggestions were tailored to an individual leader was borne out further in the statistical analysis, in that the frequency with which they were mentioned by the direct reports, superiors, peers, and self was statistically different.

Another observation that is obvious from table 2.2 is that four of the behaviors overlap, but six new behaviors are introduced. This once again shows that no single behavior is sufficient to be an effective leader. Since the four overlapping behaviors have been discussed in some depth, the focus in this section will be on the six new behaviors.

The comments derived from the question, "What should this leader do more of to be more effective?" seems to be more specific than those for the question, "What does this leader do that should be continued?" The statistical results may support this supposition. For the "continued" question, only seven categories were identified, but for the "more of" question, ten categories were identified. The specificity of the responses will become evident in the discussion of these new categories.

Improve organizational skills: "To improve his organizational skills in planning and tracking operations."
This particular skill is identified in Clark Wilson's Task Cycle Theory. Others have identified it as a transactional model.[29] Notwithstanding that categorization, it has been found to correlate with managerial effectiveness.[30] The worker-owners are suggesting that the leader should become more effective at planning and tracking. They are not specifying how it is to be done, just that it needs to be done better.

Table 2.2 Comparison of leader behaviors that should be continued vs. those that should be increased

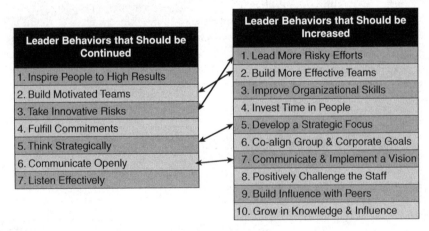

Leader Behaviors that Should be Continued	Leader Behaviors that Should be Increased
1. Inspire People to High Results	1. Lead More Risky Efforts
2. Build Motivated Teams	2. Build More Effective Teams
3. Take Innovative Risks	3. Improve Organizational Skills
4. Fulfill Commitments	4. Invest Time in People
5. Think Strategically	5. Develop a Strategic Focus
6. Communicate Openly	6. Co-align Group & Corporate Goals
7. Listen Effectively	7. Communicate & Implement a Vision
	8. Positively Challenge the Staff
	9. Build Influence with Peers
	10. Grow in Knowledge & Influence

Invest time in people: "Effective meetings especially face-to-face. Use this time to its maximum."
The need to meet face-to-face to develop positive relationships has been researched and documented at Southwest Airlines, a minority employee-owned company.[31] The importance of face-to-face meetings has also been found at W. L. Gore & Associates, a 100 percent employee-owned company.[32] As with the prior comment, the respondents are offering a specific technique for the leader to improve effectiveness. In contrast, the "continue" comments were more global in nature.

Co-align group and corporate goals: "He can gain more insight (into) corporate-wide business directions and challenges."
In this comment, the employee-owner wants to ensure that what the group is doing is in line with the corporate goals. Apparently, the respondent does not feel that what the group is being asked to do fulfills the directions and challenges in which the organization is going. The word "challenges" is interesting in that the respondent is seeking work that would provide personal growth. Organizations that are practicing SE need people who seek such work and leaders who present such to them for the organization to be entrepreneurial.

Positively challenge the staff: "Get staff to commit to consensus."
Again the word "challenge" appears in this category, but here the need for challenge is expressed as a need for the leader to positively challenge the staff. The verbatim comment indicates a technique for that to happen—for the leader to get the staff to commit to consensus. The tone of this category is significantly different than in the third category. Here the leader is being asked to challenge the worker-owners, whereas in the prior one the worker-owners are asking for challenging work. Ideally, the latter is preferred and was the more common comment in this organization. In contrast, the former recognizes that sometimes individuals do need to be challenged, but it must be done positively. This indicates the respondents are aware that positive motivational efforts are more effective than punitive ones, as discussed earlier.

Build influence with peers: "Influence and secure buy in and collaboration with peers."
In this category, the respondents are asking the leaders to work more effectively with their peers. They see that the leader needs to be more than an informational boundary spanner. Leaders must secure buy in and collaboration from their peers. In other words, the leaders are being urged to develop these attributes so that they and the group can be more effective, more in harmony with others in the organization. The worker-owners recognize the importance for all to be working as one team toward a common meta-goal, corporate success.

Grow in knowledge and influence: "He needs to expand his network and knowledge about the other areas of the company, to increase his breadth and impact as well as to develop new opportunities for future growth."
Here the respondents are asking the leader to go beyond building influence with peers. They are asking the leader to increase both knowledge and influence

across the company. In addition, they are asking for new opportunities to grow. The respondents have switched back to seeking opportunities for growth.

The statements made by the worker-owners in response to "What should this leader do more of to be more effective?" maintain a positive tone similar to the responses to "What does this leader do that should be continued?" It appears that the worker-owners have tacit knowledge that positive behaviors on the part of leaders are more effective than negative/punitive behaviors. Quantitative research has found that negative leadership behaviors can be detrimental to team performance and that it takes multiple positive behaviors to offset one negative behavior.[33]

Exploring the Traits or Characteristics That Inhibit Leader Success (the Don'ts)

When the comments were analyzed for the question, "Does this leader have any traits or characteristics that inhibit his or her success?" ten groupings of responses were found. They are listed in table 2.3 in the frequency with which they were reported with a typical verbatim comment.

Review of the categories and verbatim comments that inhibit leader success leads to two conclusions. First, they seem to fall into three broad categories. The first broad category could be labeled that "vision thing." It is evident in the third, eighth, and ninth response categories. The person occupying a formal leadership position appears to the respondents not to be able to develop a clear vision or to be able to communicate one. Obviously, if one does not have a clear vision, they cannot articulate a vision. So this issue may be intertwined. This

Table 2.3 Leader traits or characteristics that inhibit success

	The Don'ts	Typical Verbatim Comment
1.	One-sided communications	Interrupts people, doesn't let people finish their train of thought.
2.	Inability to build a team	Team building through consensus not intimidation.
3.	Lack of clarity of vision	Needs to speak directly to his own personal vision of where the organization should go.
4.	Inapproachability	Very reserved demeanor, does not invite interaction.
5.	Lack of involvement	Employees would like to see him own topics and bring to resolution.
6.	Flawed decision-making	My impression is that he makes decisions based on instinct/feelings more than facts.
7.	Unvarying emotional tone	She needs to adjust her style and tone based on the audience.
8.	Inability to change	He needs to increase his long-term planning and be more open to change.
9.	Lack of strategic focus	Her biggest area of growth is on the strategic setting/ formulation front combined with more market/customer focus.
10.	Failure to constructively engage	He needs to open up his investigation and interest to other's agenda that might not be clear or articulate to his.

broad category is approximately opposite of what the respondents identify in the first, "Inspire people to high results," and fifth, "Thinking strategically," response categories for what leaders should continue to do.

The second broad category could be labeled that communication thing. It is evident in the first, fourth, fifth, and seventh response categories. An individual who does not listen to others, is unapproachable, lacks involvement, and is unemotional is almost the archetype of a manager who arouses defensive communications.[34] This broad category is approximately opposite of what the respondents identify in the sixth, "Communicate effectively," and seventh, "Listen effectively," response categories for what leaders should continue to do.

The third broad category could be labeled that "command and control thing." It is evident in the first, second, and tenth specific categories. A leader who cuts people off in mid-sentence and shows a lack of interest in others' agendas can be seen as intimidating. Such a projected persona is opposite of what a leader who wants to stimulate growth and freedom would want projected in the second response category "Build motivated teams" of what leaders should continue to do.

The one remaining category of traits or characteristics that inhibits leader success is "flawed decision-making." It is approximately opposite to the verbatim comment, "Analysis and decision making, informed risk taking, commitment to quality," for the "Take innovative risks" category of what leaders should continue to do.

Conclusion

An overall conclusion is that successful shared entrepreneurial organizations tend to set aside traditional top-down command and control practices in favor of an SL approach. In the way of teasing out more specific lessons, one way to conclude is to compare the responses to "Does this leader have any traits or characteristics that inhibit his or her success?" with "What does this leader do that should be continued?" From that comparison one can see that the former is close to the polar opposite to those of the later, which one might expect because of the way the questions are framed. In addition, the responses to the former question are mostly stated in the negative in response to the question whereas the responses to the latter are invariably stated positively. Based on what we have learned from the work of Skinner, Boyatzis, and Cameron, the seven categories of what leaders should continue to do should be emphasized as model behaviors for leaders to emulate to stimulate growth, freedom, risk taking, and innovation.

What also becomes apparent in reviewing these behaviors is a focus on leaders who can build an emerging vision through listening effectively and communicating openly and thus, build a motivated team. The vision must be strategic, but risky. It cannot be bland if it is to inspire others to high results.[35] Also, the leader must keep commitments to others. In other words, much is expected of the leader, but not in isolation, and the leader has responsibilities to those who are below not just those above, or the stockholders as often occurs in a command and control organization. By focusing on developing an inspiring vision, freedom of action is achieved throughout the organization.

Interesting enough, the comments did not mention setting goals or objectives as behaviors of effective leaders except for co-aligning group and corporate objectives as one behavior leaders should do more. Obviously, there are objectives in these highly successful organizations, but they are found predominately at the operational level and not at the strategic level. Group leaders are expected to align their objectives with the strategic vision and not have them imposed on those in operations by strategic level leaders.

As Hamel has observed in a command and control organization, the imposing of rigid objectives can deter innovative efforts.[36] For example, in one organization, a new product division was established because it was felt that it should have huge potential. It was a drag on overall corporate profitability for a number of years. Eventually, the vision for this division proved to be correct. It's what Andy Grove would call a 10X change.[37] It was a game changer. Major competitors in the industry were driven into mergers with others and the value proposition for the industry changed. The profitability of the company zoomed. Under a rigid command and control organization, this division would have never been allowed to develop.

Google is another notable and successful company that practices SE. It conducted an internal study based on qualitative analysis of effective leader behaviors.[38] In table 2.4, the "Leader behaviors that should be continued" as identified in this study and "Effective leader behaviors" identified at Google are compared. It is readily apparent from the comparison that there is significant overlap between the two sets of leader behaviors. If the "Effective leader behaviors" at Google were compared also to the "Leader behaviors that should

Table 2.4   Leader behaviors to continue vs. behaviors of effective leaders at Google

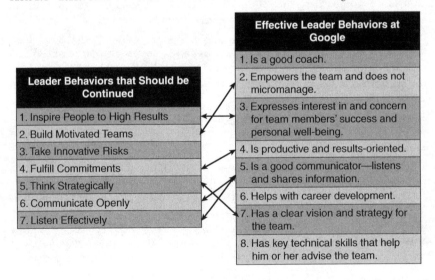

be increased," the overlap between the behaviors of effective leaders identified by these two qualitative studies would be even greater. Thus, the effective leader behaviors found in these studies apparently hold across multiple organizations.

Before closing, a note of caution should be sounded. To our knowledge, these are the first two studies in which such an exploration of leader behaviors in SE companies has occurred. Although the advice given in the comments made by the worker-owners makes sense, in other words they have face validity, additional such work may reveal other leader behaviors that need to be continued, increased, modified, or ceased to create an environment in which individuals have the freedom to develop their full potential, that is, where everyone not only has a chance to make meaningful genuine contributions but can share in significant ways in the ongoing leadership process.

Notes

1. http://investors.morningstar.com/ownership/shareholders-major.html?t=MLHR. Accessed: September 11, 2013.
2. Stack, J. 2013. *The great game of business* (revised edn). New York: Crown Books.
3. McGregor, D. 1960. *The human side of enterprise*. New York: McGraw-Hill.
4. www.employeeownership.co.uk. Accessed: November 21, 2013.
5. For more on shared leadership, see Pearce, C. L., Manz, C. C., & Sims, H. P. Jr. 2014. *Share, don't take, the lead*. Charlotte, NC: Information Age Publishing; Pearce, C. L., & Conger, J. A. (Eds.). 2003. *Shared leadership: Reframing the hows and whys of leadership*. Thousand Oaks, CA: Sage; and Pearce, C. L., & Manz, C. C. 2005. The new silver bullets of leadership: The importance of self and shared leadership in knowledge work. *Organizational Dynamics, 34*: 130–140.
6. Dilbert Comic Strip, November 21, 2013.
7. Judge, T. A., & Piccolo, R. F. 2004. Transformational and transactional leadership: A meta-analytic test of their relative validity. *Journal of Applied Psychology, 89*: 755–768.
8. Pearce, C.L., & Manz, C. C. 2013. The leadership disease...and its potential cure. *Business Horizons, 57*, no. 2: 215–224.
9. A more detailed and technical explanation of how the analysis was performed can be found in Shipper, F., & Davy, J. 2006. Probing qualitative 360 feedback for insights on leadership. Abstract published in the *Proceedings of the Academy of Management*, Atlanta, Georgia, August 11–16, 2006.
10. Ibid.
11. Shipper, F., & Jennings, M. M. 1984. *Business strategy for the political arena*. Westport, CT: Quorum Books, p. 25.
12. Bernardin, J., & Beatty, R. S. 1987. Subordinate appraisals to enhance managerial productivity. *Sloan Management Review, 28*: 63–74.
13. Skinner, B. F. 1970. *Walden two*. Toronto: Macmillan.
14. Losada, M., & Heaphy, E. 2004. The role of positivity and connectivity in the performance of business teams: A nonlinear dynamics model. *American Behavioral Scientist, 47*: 740–765.
15. Shipper, F., & Weer, C. 2011. A longitudinal investigation of the impact of positive and negative coaching on team effectiveness. Abstract published in the *Proceedings of the Academy of Management*, San Antonio, Texas, August 12–16, 2011.

16. Boyatzis, R. 2012, January/February. Neuroscience and the link between inspirational leadership and resonant relationships. *Ivey Business Journal*, http://iveybusinessjournal.com/topics/leadership/neuroscience-and-the-link-between-inspirational-leadership-and-resonant-relationships-2, p. 2.

17. Cameron, K. 2013. *Practicing positive leadership: Tools and techniques that create extraordinary results.* San Francisco: Berrett-Koehler Publishers, p. 2.

18. http://www.brightscope.com/401k-rating/90372/The-Prudential-Insurance-Company-Of-America/91697/The-Prudential-Employees-Savings-Plan/. Accessed: November 20, 2013.

19. Nobles, B., & Staley, P. 2010. *Freedom-based management: Building a culture that enables and encourages fully empowered employees to produce awesome business success.* http://www.42projects.org/docs/FreedomBasedManagement.pdf. Accessed: December 21, 2011.

20. Boyatzis, Neuroscience and the link between inspirational leadership and resonant relationships.

21. http://www.worldblu.com/democratic-design/principles.php. Accessed: November 13, 2013.

22. Carroll, L. 1865. *Alice's adventures in wonderland.* New York: Random House, Chapter 6, p. 26.

23. http://www.cbsnews.com/video/watch/?id=50147137n. Accessed: October 11, 2013.

24. http://www.hermanmiller.com/solutions/work/products/workspaces.html. Accessed: October 11, 2013.

25. http://www.worldblu.com/democratic-design/principles.php. Accessed: November 13, 2013.

26. Suriwiecki, J. 2005. *The wisdom of crowds.* New York: Anchor Books.

27. Shipper, F. 2009. Investigating the sustainability of a sustained 360 process. Published in the *Best Papers Proceedings* of the Academy of Management, Chicago, Illinois, August 7–11, 2009.

28. Shipper, F., & Davy, J. 2002. A model and investigation of managerial skills, employees' attitudes and managerial performance. *Leadership Quarterly, 13*: 95–120.

29. Bass, B. M. 1990. *Bass & Stodgill's handbook of leadership.* New York: The Free Press.

30. Shipper & Davy, A model and investigation of managerial skills.

31. Gittell, J. H. *The Southwest Airlines way: Using the power of relationships to achieve high performance.* New York: McGraw-Hill.

32. Shipper, F., Manz, C. C., & Stewart, G. L. 2013. Developing global teams to meet 21st century challenges at W. L. Gore & Associates. In Hill, C. W. L., & Jones, G. R., *Strategic management: An integrated approach* (10th edn) (pp. C148–C161). Mason, OH: South-Western, Cengage.

33. Shipper & Weer, A longitudinal investigation of the impact of positive and negative coaching.

34. Gibb, J. 1961. Defensive communication. *Journal of Communication, 11*: 141–148.

35. Hickman, G. R., & Sorenson, G. J. 2014. *The power of invisible leadership: How a compelling common purpose inspires exceptional leadership.* Thousand Oaks, CA: Sage.

36. Hamel, G. 2007. *The future of management.* Boston: Harvard Business School Press.

37. Grove, A. 1996. *Only the paranoid survive: How to identify and exploit the crisis points that challenge every business.* New York: Currency Books.

38. Garvin, D. A. 2013, December. How Google sold its engineers on management. *Harvard Business Review*, pp. 71–82.

CHAPTER 3

Shared Governance:
Structures and Processes

*Olivier P. Roche, Richard C. Hoffman, and
Marvin O. Brown*

In this chapter we explore various issues pertaining to the governance of organizations practicing some form of *shared entrepreneurship* (SE). For the purpose of our discussion, "governance" refers to the structures and processes that regulate the interactions among the senior management team, the board of directors, and the owners of the organization as well as the results of these interactions on the organization's social and financial performance. Shared governance refers to the governance structure and process of firms practicing SE. Some of the questions this chapter seeks to partially answer regarding the governance of SE firms include the following: Who are the firm's key stakeholders? Who oversees the stakeholders' interests? How are the interests of the board aligned with those of the stakeholders? What roles does the board of directors play in the firm's governance? What is the nature of management authority in such firms?

Corporate governance is a difficult issue to address within an SE framework because as frequently conceptualized it has been associated with hierarchical command and control. It, however, must be addressed because traditional corporate governance and its subordinate issues such as corporate policies and procedures have been identified as dissatisfiers and demotivators, the exact opposite of what is desirable in an organization trying to create an SE environment.[1] In addition, as corporate governance has been applied traditionally, employees' jobs have been fragmented and functional silos built. These practices limit individuals' freedom of action, access to information, and transparency. Again, this is in opposition to what is desirable in an organization trying to create an SE environment.

There are many theories seeking to explain the role/purpose of governance mechanisms in organizations, such as agency theory,[2] resource dependence theory,[3] and stakeholder theory,[4] among others. We agree with recent authors who suggest that the use of multiple theories for examining the complexities of corporate governance is more advantageous.[5] Indeed, the study of the extant literature shows that even, if one limits the scope of his/her observations to the basic for-profit corporations, the complexity and diversity of governance issues are extensive. For example, governance structures and processes are impacted by the characteristics of the organization's industry, the organization's stage of development, its ownership structure, and so on.[6] Furthermore, the present analysis focuses on atypical organizations having various types of ownership/ leadership relations and multiple stakeholders. Thus, the variety of possible governance structures and processes increases. The main objectives of this chapter are to share our views on what is so special and different about these organizations, to assess if there are common traits, and to provide guidance for those using SE in the management of their firms. Consequently, considering our limited portfolio of cases, our approach is more descriptive than prescriptive.

The chapter is organized as follows. After providing a brief overview of some traditional concepts of corporate governance, we examine the nature of shared governance in a small sample of SE firms. A profile of the firms is provided and then their governance structures and processes are described using specific research questions pertaining to the firm's stakeholders, the selection and composition of the board, and the primary roles played by SE boards. Finally, some brief observations on management authority in SE firms are presented. In the final section we summarize the major findings of our investigation and offer some nonprescriptive implications derived from the study.

Corporate Governance: An Overview

Corporate governance is concerned with ensuring that the goals of the organization are achieved in a manner consistent with the desires of the owners or members of the organization. A review of the work on corporate governance suggests that most organizational governance systems seek to balance the interests and responsibilities of shareholders, the board, and management. A useful lens for examining corporate governance is agency theory. In their pioneering work *The Modern Corporation and Private Property*, Berle and Means observed that the separation between corporate ownership and control resulted in the delegation of management control to a small group of managers within the company.[7] The result being that the shareholders or owners of capital lost not only their management functions, but also most of their rights to exercise control or to modify the terms of the initial delegation of authority. In this model managers serve as agents of the owners of the firm, and the role of the board is to interface between management and the shareholders to insure that the latter's wishes are carried out.

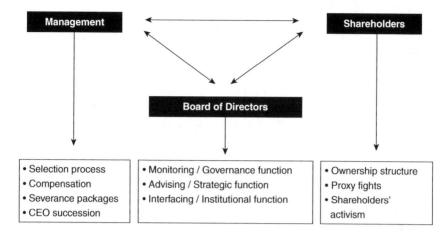

Figure 3.1   Corporate governance: key participants and issues.

Source: Originally printed in O. P. Roche. *Corporate governance and organization life cycle: The changing role and composition of the board of directors* (Amherst, NY: Cambria Press, 2009).

In general, the field of corporate governance has been concerned with three sets of participants and their issues. The first concerns the senior management team in terms of its selection, compensation, severance packages, and chief executive officer (CEO) succession plans.[8] A second set of participants and their issues pertains to shareholders,[9] for example, proxy fights,[10] shareholders' activism, as well as ownership structures.[11] The third set of participants/issues concerns the composition and role of the board of directors, including the three main board functions: monitoring, advising, and interfacing with external stakeholders. These key governance participants and their issues are depicted in figure 3.1.

In the typical corporate setting, governance seeks to balance the interests of owners with those of management. The traditional corporate model sees the governance role as a mechanism to insure that the firm is run primarily for the benefit of the owners or investors.[12] At the other end of the spectrum, one can examine collaborative forms of organizations (e.g., cooperatives)[13] in which governance seeks to mediate between the needs of organizational members and management. Some of the key characteristics in the governance processes of the traditional public corporation and the collaborative form of organization are displayed in table 3.1.

In table 3.1, we can view these two models of governance as a continuum describing the range of governance systems. This perspective was first articulated in chapter 1 regarding SE. While most of the characteristics described in the table are self-explanatory, a couple of points are worth noting. The traditional corporate model is hierarchical, wherein the board as a group of experts and experienced professionals oversees management to ensure they are running the organization to maximize returns to investors. At the other end of the spectrum, the essence of the collaborative form of governance is an adherence to democratic principles, wherein the board is selected to be representative of

Table 3.1 A range of governance models

	Corporate	*Collaborative*
Nature of decision-making process	Top down	Top down/bottom up
Selection criteria	Board members selected for expertise/independence.	Board representatives selected for expertise and representativeness.
	Top management team members are recruited within or outside the organization.	Recruitment process tilted toward internal promotion.
	Emphasis is on aligning the interests of the manager with the interests of investors.	Emphasis is on the sharing of the organization values.
Interest represented	Investors/owners	Co-op members/owners
Board role	Emphasis on the monitoring function and interface with key external stakeholders.	Emphasis on the advising function and interface with key internal stakeholders.

Source: Compiled from: J. D. Hunger and T. L. Wheelen. *Essentials of strategic management*, 5th ed. (New York: Pearson, 2011); and D. McDonnell, E. Macknight, and H. Donnelly. *Democratic enterprise: Ethical business for the 21st century* (UK: Cooperative Educational Trust, 2012).

those whom they stand for. The co-op is to be governed in the interest of its members, and the board works collectively with management to see that member goals are fulfilled.

In the ensuing sections we describe our observations of some of the characteristics of the governance systems of firms who practice SE. Before proceeding, we provide a brief profile of the sample firms practicing SE that serve as the basis for our observations of shared governance.

Firms Practicing Shared Governance

Over the past couple of years, in-depth case studies of close to a dozen firms practicing some form of SE were conducted. Seven of these firms, which range from those using a governance system closer to a typical corporate model (e.g., Herman Miller) to those using a hybrid form of governance (e.g., Equal Exchange), provided information on their system of governance. Three are manufacturers of furniture, diversified specialty products, and wire brushes. Three are in the technology and engineering fields and one is a wholesaler of fair trade products. The firms vary in size from 63 to 8,500 employees with annual sales ranging from $5 million to $2.5 billion. The average age of these firms using some form of SE is 33 years, with a range of 18 to 62 years. Three of the firms are older, having been founded earlier as more traditional firms before converting to some form of SE: MBC Ventures, 1851 (ESOP in 1989); Herman Miller, 1905 (Scanlon, 1950); and KCI, 1955 (ESOP in 1988). Despite the small number of firms, they are diverse in size, industry, and age and, therefore, provide varied examples of governance systems. Complete cases studies of eight of these firms are provided in the case studies section of this book.

Shared Governance: Structure and Practices

Our analysis of the shared governance is based on the model of the main participants in the governance process depicted in figure 3.1 presented earlier. We begin our analysis of shared governance by identifying the firm's key stakeholders, whose interests the governance structure is designed to protect. Then we examine the board, both its composition and the roles it performs for SE firms. Finally, we discuss a few issues pertaining to management authority and decision processes as they relate to the governance of our SE firms (see chapters 2, 4, and 5 for a more complete discussion of SE management practices). Our observations of the governance of these SE firms are guided by the research questions presented in our introduction. The reader is also advised to keep in mind the range of governance models depicted in table 3.1 as it helps to provide the range of options regarding the governance practices of our SE firms. Finally, where possible, we draw on prior work on corporate governance to provide both a starting point and a way to contrast the governance practices observed among our sample of firms with those observed elsewhere.

Key Stakeholders: In Whose Interest Is the Organization Governed?

We seek to answer this question by identifying who are the key stakeholders among our sample of SE firms. In the corporate view of governance,[14] it is clear who the key stakeholders are—the owners or shareholders. However, in recent years, others[15] have noted a wider array of interest groups having an economic impact on the firm such as employees, suppliers, customers, and the community. These so-called stakeholders have interests that need to be taken into consideration if the firm is to remain a legitimate institution in society. The picture of who comprises the key stakeholders in SE firms is also not so straightforward. For example, in four of the SE firms we studied, the employees are the key stakeholders as the main investors. Employees own 100 percent of the voting stock at Equal Exchange and KCI Technologies; employees are the primary investors at MBC Ventures (MBC) with 75 percent owned by nonmanagement employees while the remainder of the shares are held by company managers, so in effect all employees are also investors in the firm. HCSS has three groups of stakeholders holding roughly an equal proportion of the stock: the CEO owns 34 percent of the shares, the employees about 30 percent in an ESOP trust, and the majority of the remaining 34 percent is owned individually by employees and former business associates who received them in the company's early years. In the case of TEOCO, the founder currently holds more than 67 percent of the firm with the remaining shares evenly split between employees and an equity firm. Only Herman Miller seems to follow a traditional corporate model with the majority of their stock held by outside investors.

Three important points can be made regarding who benefits. In all cases it is the owner-investors, be they insiders or outsiders. This reflects the fact that governance models are based, in part, on the corporate model. Second, where firms practicing SE depart from the corporate model (see table 3.1), we find that most of them practice some form of shared capitalism. Ownership is shared with employees or members of the organization. The term used by Equal Exchange best reflects this stakeholder group: they are known as "worker-owners." Even among those firms without 100 percent employee ownership, employees own a significant part of the firm. In TEOCO's case the founder owns the majority of the shares, but he is also a major contributor to the firm's success on a daily basis. In addition, some of the early employees have already cashed out and left the company. In HCSS's case over two-thirds of the firm's stock is held by employees and family, many of the latter are also employed by the firm. Finally, as these examples reveal, these firms provide a range of focus on who the key stakeholder in the firm is from outside investors (Herman Miller) to employees (KCI). Thus, firms practicing SE do appear to recognize the need to balance the needs of owners with that of other relevant stakeholders in the firm.

Board Selection: Who Oversees the Stakeholders' Interests?
In most models of governance, the board plays a critical role in brokering the relationship between shareholders and management. According to table 3.1, the board primarily insures that management carries out the wishes of owners. In more collaborative forms,[16] the board brokers relationships between management and a defined set of stakeholders. Thus, in most governance models, it is the board's duty to insure that stakeholder interests are addressed. Consequently, selecting the board is crucial to its ability to carry out this mandate.

Among the key issues regarding board membership are the method of selecting board members, the composition of the board, and the primary role and incentives provided for the board. Again our firms offer a range of answers to the questions posed earlier. In the traditional corporate model, shareholders vote for the members of the board. Nominees are usually sought by a subcommittee of the board, by other board members, company managers, or some combination of these.[17] In the collaborative model, the members of the co-op, who are often employees, nominate some of their own members to serve and represent them on the board.[18] In both models, board members are usually selected for a term of one or more years and staggered in such a way that not all members are voted in the same year to provide for continuity. Two of our SE firms, W. L. Gore and Herman Miller, follow the corporate model in board selection. Departing from the traditional corporate model, KCI Technologies reserves one board position for an employee representative. Candidates for that position must obtain signatures from at least 35 employees to get on the ballot. This position is filled by an open ballot of all employees. The other positions are filled following a more typical corporate model with the employee stock ownership plan (ESOP) trust casting the votes for those positions. MBC also has one board member who is elected by employees. The remaining board members are "appointed," three members appointed by management, two appointed by the union, and a "neutral" seat is appointed with both union and management approval. This is truly a hybrid form of board selection and representation.

Finally, board selection at Equal Exchange also represents a hybrid model, but one that is closer to the collaborative model than the other firms we have discussed. The nine-member board is selected as follows: worker-owners nominate and vote for six candidates who represent co-op members—inside board members. Three positions are reserved for outside representatives. These latter board positions are selected by a three-member nominating committee consisting of a worker-owner (employee), a current board member, and a manager. All board positions at Equal Exchange are elected by the worker-owners following the democratic principle of one member one vote.

Board Composition: How Are the Board's Interests Aligned with Those of the Key Stakeholders?
Traditional corporate governance research has paid less attention to this issue. The emphasis has been on aligning management's incentives with those of shareholders through selection and compensation practices (see figure 3.1). Aligning board members' interests with those of shareholders has received little attention. Board members are elected by shareholders, and shareholders often approve paying fees for attendance at board meetings, and board members sometimes may even be required to own stock in the firm.[19] Thus, it is assumed that shareholders choose board members who have their interests in mind, but there are no guarantees.

The SE firms in our study appear to use two processes to coalign board and stakeholder interests. First, they rely on selecting board members who represent the interests of different stakeholders, and second, they use incentives to help align the board with their stakeholders' interests.

Our previous discussion provided insights into board selection methods. In the traditional corporate model, the main role of the board is to monitor management to insure that they maximize the shareholders' returns.[20] Indeed, the board of directors "is the ultimate center of control…The control…is exercised frequently through the ability to hire and fire the chief executive officer."[21] As a result, board members are sought for their expertise on management and perhaps the industry so that they can monitor successfully. Some studies[22] have noted that increasing board size and diversity becomes a way to link the organization to its external environment, to secure critical resources, and to build prestige and legitimacy. One way to insure objective monitoring is to reserve certain board seats for outsiders. According to theories of corporate governance, outsiders are perceived as more independent in their monitoring role of management.[23] Inside members on the other hand are usually managers and, therefore, insiders tend to provide only self-regulation as opposed to independent oversight. In the collaborative model, the role of the board member is to represent the members' interests to management; hence, the board would be composed primarily of co-op members.[24] However, some research casts doubt on the efficacy of using board composition to insure a co-alignment of board with stakeholder interests.[25]

Again our firms reveal an eclectic approach to board composition. Interestingly enough the firms adhering closest to the corporate form of board selection and those using more of the collaborative form of governance both have the greatest proportion of outside members. Herman Miller appears to follow a corporate form of board selection and has the greatest number of outside board members with nine of eleven being outsiders. These include board members representing the industry, but also other fields of use to the firm such as insurance, finance, and even education. The firm also has three women on the board including one minority to further diversify its composition. Equal Exchange, which is patterned more on the collaborative form of governance, has the second highest proportion of outside members with three of nine positions designated for outsiders. TEOCO and MBC each reserve two of seven seats for outside board members. Equal Exchange, the firm closest to the collaborative model, reserves two-thirds of their seats for employees while KCI and MBC each reserve at least one seat for employees. In addition, these latter two firms reserve seats for critical stakeholders of specific importance to their firms. In KCI's case two seats are reserved for members of the equity firm that has recently invested a 12.5 percent stake in the firm. For MBC one seat is reserved for the union that represents their largely blue-collar workforce. The union was instrumental in aiding MBC to convert to an employee-owned company in the early 1990s. Thus, SE firms also largely rely on board selection and the composition of membership to help insure the alignment of board interests with that of the firm.

Our SE firms also use incentives to align board interests with those of the firm and its key stakeholders. For example, Herman Miller tends to follow the corporate model and requires all of its board members to own an equity stake in the firm, thereby tying their interests directly with those of their shareholders. At the other end of the spectrum is MBC that prevents nonemployee directors from owning company stock; they are paid a fee instead. In this manner each group of directors at this firm has different incentives commensurate with their stake in the firm. MBC believes this practice permits the outside directors to remain more independent and as such provide more objectivity in their decisions. These board incentives are fairly similar to those found among public corporations.

Board Roles: What Purpose(s) Does the Board Serve?
As noted earlier, there are three primary roles that the boards of directors may perform for the organization including: monitoring management, serving as a strategic advisor, and interfacing with the firm's environment. By far the most prevalent role of the corporate form of governance is the monitoring role as described by Berle and Means and others who followed.[26] Furthermore, there has been renewed interest in the board's monitoring role in the wake of the recessions of the early 2000s and 2008 and the occurrence of major scandals such as Enron, Tyco, AIG, Countrywide, and Parmalat. A common thread through many of these scandals has been the perceived failure of the board to fulfill its fiduciary duty with regard to its control and supervision obligation. This has been the subject of the regulatory reforms in recent years.[27]

Prior research on corporate governance suggests that having some diversity in the composition of its members is believed to enhance the board's capability to serve as a source of information for the firm. Having a board that is diverse in terms of inside/outside members, industries, and job titles provides a variety of perspectives and information sources. This information may aid the board not only in their monitoring role[28] but also in their advisory role to management on major strategic changes such as acquisitions, mergers, divestment, and the like.[29] The board is then considered to be a good resource for management especially in the case of strategic decisions.

Resource dependence theorists define the institutional or interfacing role of the board as a way to link the organization to its external environment for the purpose of securing critical resources and to build prestige and legitimacy for the firm.[30] By the same token, however, "as boards increase in size and diversity to fulfill their institutional and governance functions, they may not be ideally suited to making timely strategic actions in response to critical environmental changes."[31]

In reviewing the role of the boards among our SE firms, we observed that they do not appear to consider the board's role as simply monitoring management. Instead, these SE firms tend to emphasize the strategic and interface roles of their boards. For example, the diversity of fields, genders, and races that appear on Herman Miller's board suggests the importance of having the firm interface with a variety of groups outside the firm and the industry. The best examples of using the board to assist management with strategy are TEOCO and MBC. In the case of TEOCO, the nonmanagement members of the board are persons with experience in the telecom industry that the firm serves or persons representing the equity partner that possesses a substantial stake in the firm. The CEO expects the new equity partner to take an active interest in assisting the firm to determine new avenues of future growth. As an example, TEOCO's CEO noted that the equity partner had an "impressive network of relationships" suggesting their role in assisting the firm in interfacing with broader groups in their environment. In addition, TEOCO's most recent acquisition would not have been possible without the backing and reputation of their equity partner. In MBC's case, the board actively participates with management in making strategic decisions. In part because the firm has a very lean management team, MBC's board meets monthly. According to the CEO, the board played a crucial role in assisting the firm to find a new product line to help diversify away from its slow growth niche in industrial brushes. MBC also uses the board to interface with its key stakeholder, the union, as discussed earlier. The board that most closely represents the interests of employee members is that of Equal Exchange with two-thirds of the positions held by elected employee representatives. The board in turn selects the executive directors (top managers) who attend board meetings, but have no voting power. Thus, in practice SE firms appear to use boards to represent key stakeholders at the top, to participate in the strategic direction of the firm, and to assist the firm in interfacing with key players in their environment.

It seems clear from this discussion of board selection, composition, and roles that SE firms emphasize the board's advisory and interface roles rather than the monitoring role. The various practices we have outlined reflect the unique set of circumstances each firm faces. In all cases the SE firms are all attempting to use the board to mediate countervailing forces between key stakeholders (these vary by firm) and management.

Management: What Is the Nature of Management Authority?

In the traditional corporate model managers are separate from ownership, therefore, the focus has been on using management selection, compensation, and other factors to align managerial interests with those of shareholders (see figure 3.1). Furthermore, in the corporate model, management's authority and decision-making process is usually top down (see table 3.1). However, because management is usually not completely separated from ownership in firms practicing SE, special selection and compensation practices are not needed to coalign management's interests with that of owners. Moreover, many SE firms use a combination of top-down and bottom-up decision processes by permitting input by nonmanagement employees in the decision-making process. In other words, SE firms usually seek to practice some form of shared leadership (SL) within their firms; this is more consistent with the democratic ideals[32] of the governance of collaborative firms. In this chapter we only highlight some broad leadership themes as they pertain to the shared governance of the firms in this study. A more detailed discussion of SL as practiced by these firms is provided in chapter 2.

Central to SL practiced by SE firms is the sharing of information between management and other employees. W. L. Gore holds monthly technology meetings where engineers and scientists discuss various developments in their fields of interest with other firm associates. TEOCO holds monthly "all hands" meetings for general business updates and announcements. It also has an advisory team to interface between management and employee-owners on topics throughout the year. Equal Exchange has a ten-member worker-owner cabinet to oversee education programs and elections. KCI has an Employee Committee that meets annually to discuss employee issues of concern. Consistent with their ESOP status, virtually all of the firms practice open book management where employees have access to the firm's financials, and these are discussed monthly or quarterly, for example, MBC and TEOCO. Equal Exchange publishes the financials on the company website for anytime access.

This sharing of information allows employees to be involved in the decision-making process. Even more important, since employees are the interface between the organization and their customers/clients, the organization's strategic and operational decisions are both bottom up and top down. Indeed, some of the best insights for new products and/or new markets come from the engineers/employees at both TEOCO and HCSS. These new ideas are then shared (i.e., bottom up) with the senior management team, which ultimately (i.e., top down) makes the decision on whether and how to proceed.

Firms practicing SE usually do not suffer from a separation of management from ownership. Consequently, their authority and decision-making processes reflect the tangible relationship that exists between management and employee-owners.

Summary and Implications

In summary we have examined in some depth the governance of a small sample of firms practicing SE, wherein all employees usually share in both the management and rewards of their firm. Using prior research on public corporations, where a separation of management from ownership exists, we have endeavored to describe some of the prevailing views of governance and presented some evidence of how SE firms differ from the typical model of corporate governance. We provide a brief overview of our findings by summarizing the answers to the questions posed regarding the governance practices of the SE firms examined here.

In whose interest is the organization governed? Governance of SE firms or shared governance appears to represent the interests of stakeholders not merely shareholders. The range of stakeholders varies but usually includes owner/employees.

Who oversees the stakeholders' interests? Firms practicing SE use a board of directors either elected or appointed by stakeholders to oversee the interests of the various parties having a stake in the firm.

How do firms insure that the board members' interests are aligned with those of the key stakeholders? In addition to the selection process, the coalignment of board interests with those of stakeholders is further insured by two factors among the SE firms studied: (1) paying close attention that the composition of board membership represents key stakeholder groups or interests; and (2) providing board members with incentives such as paying board member fees or requiring them to own stock in the firm.

What purpose(s) does the board serve? Because there is little separation of ownership from management, boards of SE firms tend to emphasize their role as advisor to management on strategic matters. Boards of SE firms also interface with key actors or institutions in their firm's environment. The board role of monitoring management is relegated to a minor activity among the SE firms studied.

What is the nature of management authority? Authority is more diffuse within SE firms. Management and employees tend to share a lot of information. This results in the use of reciprocal management among different levels of the organization, a hybrid consisting of top-down/bottom-up decision processes.

Despite some of the unique aspects of shared governance practiced by the firms in this study, their form of governance also shares some similarities with the corporate model. For example, similar to the corporate model, shared governance relies on the board to mediate the relationship between the management and stakeholders. To insure an alignment between management and stakeholder interests, SE firms use similar methods such as the board selection process, the composition of the board, and incentives. However, SE firms tend to use a combination of these more frequently than appears to be the case in traditional corporate settings. The key participants in the governance process depicted in figure 3.1 are also applicable to firms practicing shared governance with one exception. In the SE model "shareholders" are replaced with "stakeholders" suggesting the need to address the interests of a broader group of participants having an economic stake in the firm. Furthermore, this study suggests that the issues to be examined for each participant group in the governance process will likely differ for SE versus traditional firms. For example, management issues of SE firms are likely to involve forms of participation, delegation, and reciprocal decision processes rather than proxy fights and shareholder activism found among public corporations.

Shared governance of the firms in our sample varied. Some practiced extremely high shared governance (e.g., Equal Exchange). However, even those with low levels of shared governance still practiced it well beyond that found in traditional companies. The emerging model of shared governance reflected in the typical firm in our sample appears to be a hybrid of both the corporate and collaborative model depicted in table 3.1. As more firms adopt SE management and more research on the governance modes used by these firms occurs, a stronger dichotomy between the corporate and collaborative modes may emerge. For now, all we can conclude is that shared governance appears to be a hybrid of both corporate and collaborative models.

Although our observations are based on a small sample, the firms represent a variety of industries (from low to high tech), sizes, ages, and degrees of internationalization. As a result, our findings can be deemed to have implications that suggest guidelines for others to consider. Of course studies of shared governance using larger samples of firms are warranted before any definitive set of prescriptive recommendations can be offered.

The collective decision-making process of firms practicing SE has profound implications regarding strategy implementation for firms. Even though employees may not be the actual owners of the shares of the organization, they do actually feel ownership in the decisions that are made in the best interest of the organization. Information is shared with the senior management team, and decisions must be discussed and argued with the employees in charge of the subsequent implementation of the decision. Therefore, there is less opportunity for the senior management team to behave contrary to the best interests of the organization and its legitimate owners. This, in turn, has important consequences with regard to the role of the board. The board of directors can afford to spend less time monitoring top management and more time discussing and probing the strategy proposed by top managers. Therefore, less monitoring and more advising from the board seems to be an important outcome among SE organizations.

Finally, the governance experience of SE firms also has implications concerning the composition of the board. As noted earlier, most of these organizations tend to promote their senior managers from within the company. In addition, a few of these organizations have employees or middle managers who are also board members. Thus, in terms of access to information, there is less "asymmetry" between the senior management team and the board. Information asymmetry between the senior management team and the board of directors, which meets only a few times a year, has been a recurrent problem in the corporate world.[33] In the case of SE firms, there appears to be less risk of information asymmetry but, on the other hand, the risk of "group think" increases. This would imply a greater need for the appointment of more outsiders possessing different backgrounds to the boards of SE firms.

These are just some possible suggestions to help improve governance processes that may warrant further investigation. It is worth noting that some of these management/governance mechanisms (such as the sharing of information or the greater involvement of the employees in the decision-making process) have a considerable impact on an organization's corporate culture (discussed more fully in chapter 5). It is, therefore, conceivable that the governance processes of an organization can possibly be improved even though the employees are not the actual owners of the organization because employees have given their inputs to the decision-making processes of the firm.

Notes

1. Herzberg, F. 1966. *Work and the nature of man.* Cleveland: World Publishing.
2. Berle, A., & Means, G. 1932. *The modern corporation and private property.* New York: Macmillan; Eisenhardt, K. M. 1989. Agency theory: An assessment and review. *Academy of Management Review, 14*: 57–74.
3. Pfeffer, J., & Salancik, G. 1978. *The external control of organizations: A resource dependence perspective.* New York: Harper & Row.
4. Freeman, R. E. 2010. *Strategic management: A stakeholder approach.* Cambridge, UK: University of Cambridge Press.
5. Conforth, C. 2002. Making sense of co-operative governance: Competing models and tensions. *Review of International Co-operation, 95*: 51–57; and Lynall, M., Golden, B., & Hillman, A. 2003. Board composition from adolescence to Lynall maturity: A multitheoretic view. *Academy of Management Review, 28*: 416–431.
6. Roche, O. P. 2009. *Corporate governance and organization life cycle: The changing role and composition of the board of directors.* Amherst, NY: Cambria Press.
7. Berle & Means, *The modern corporation.*
8. Finkelstein, S., & Hambrick, D. C. 1989. Chief executive compensation: A study of the intersection of markets and political processes. *Strategic Management Journal, 10*: 121–134; Zajac, E. J. 1990. CEO selection, succession, compensation and firm performance: A theoretical integration and empirical analysis. *Strategic Management Journal, 11*: 217–230.
9. Tkac, P. 2006. One proxy at a time: Pursuing social change through shareholder proposals. *Economic Review: Federal Reserve Bank of Atlanta, 91*: 1–22; Becht, M., Franks, J., Mayer, C., & Rossi, S. 2007. Returns to shareholder activism (Finance working paper No. 138/2006). European Corporate Governance Institute. http://ssrn.com/abstract_id=934712. Accessed: December 3, 2007; Romano, R. 2001, Summer. Less is more: Making institutional investor activism a valuable mechanism of corporate governance. *Yale Journal on Regulation, 18*: 174–252.
10. Proxy fights are a strategy generally used in a takeover context. The acquirer and the targeted firm solicit proxy votes from the target's shareholders. Ultimately, the majority owner of these votes effectively controls the targeted company.
11. Denis, D. J., Denis, D. K., & Sarin, A. 1999. Agency theory and the influence of equity ownership structure on corporate diversification strategies. *Strategic Management Journal, 20*: 1071–1076.

12. Hunger, J. D., & Wheelen, T. L. 2011. *Essentials of strategic management* (5th edn). New York: Pearson.

13. McDonnell, D., Macknight, E., & Donnelly, H. 2012. *Democratic enterprise: Ethical business for the 21st century.* UK: Cooperative Educational Trust.

14. For example, Roche, *Corporate governance and organization life cycle.*

15. Freeman, *Strategic management*; Preble, J. F. 2005. Toward a comprehensive model of stakeholder management. *Business and Society Review, 110*: 407–431.

16. McDonnell et al., *Democratic enterprise.*

17. Hunger & Wheelen, *Essentials of strategic management.*

18. Conforth, Making sense of co-operative governance; McDonnell et al., *Democratic enterprise.*

19. Roche, *Corporate governance and organization life cycle.*

20. The board also advises the senior management team on key strategic decision but many board members complain that the advisory role is limited by time constraint. See ibid.

21. Mizruchi, M. S. 1983. Who controls whom? An examination of the relation between management and boards of directors in large American corporations. *Academy of Management Review, 8*: 426–435.

22. Pfeffer, J. 1972. Size and composition of corporate boards-of-directors: The organization and its environment. *Administrative Science Quarterly, 17*: 218–228; Pfeffer, J. 1973. Size, composition, and function of hospital boards of directors: A study of organization-environment linkage. *Administrative Science Quarterly, 18*: 349–364.

23. For example, Zahra, S. A., & Pearce, J. 1989. Boards of directors and corporate financial performance: A review and integrative model. *Journal of Management, 15*: 291–334.

24. McDonnell et al., *Democratic enterprise.*

25. Daily, C. M., Dalton, D. R., & Cannella, A. A. 2000. Corporate governance: Daily decades of dialogue and data. *Academy of Management Review, 28*: 371–382; Goodstein, J., & Boeker, W. 1991. Turbulence at the top: A new perspective on governance structure changes and strategic change. *Academy of Management Journal, 34*: 306–330.

26. Berle & Means, *The modern corporation*; Eisenhardt, Agency theory; Mizruchi, Who controls whom?.

27. Finegold, D., Benson, G. S., & Hecht, D. 2007. Corporate boards and company performance: Review of research in light of recent reforms. *Corporate Governance. Journal Compilation, 15*: 865–878.

28. Eisenhardt, Agency theory.

29. Golden, B. R., & Zajac, E. J. 2001. When will boards influence strategy? Inclination x power = strategic change. *Strategic Management Journal, 22*: 1087–1111; and Zahra & Pearce, Boards of directors and corporate financial performance.

30. Pfeffer, Size and composition of corporate boards-of-directors; and Pfeffer, Size, composition, and function of hospital boards of directors.

31. Goodstein & Boeker, Turbulence at the top.

32. Ibid.

33. For example, Eisenhardt, Agency theory; and Roche, *Corporate governance and organization life cycle.*

CHAPTER 4

Innovation through Shared Entrepreneurship

Marc D. Street, Vera L. Street, and Frank Shipper

Aperusal of the popular business press or any standard strategic management text quickly reveals the tremendously important role innovation plays in the strategic management decision-making processes of organizations. Much of the emphasis involves conceptualizing innovation as a potential source of competitive advantage for the firm, resulting in the ability to produce superior financial returns.[1] But establishing a competitive advantage via innovation is an extremely difficult thing to do: the research evidence on innovation suggests that only 10 to 20 percent of all major R&D projects result in a commercially viable product or service.[2] Thus, understanding the factors that lead to success in innovation is of critical importance to both academicians and corporate executives.

Beyond the obvious interest in innovation from an individual organization's perspective, the topic has received an increasing level of attention at a more macro level of analysis, particularly over the past ten years or so. Indeed, the importance of innovation to the future health of the overall US economy has been the subject of much discussion among economists, financial experts, policymakers, investors, corporate chief executive officers (CEOs), as well as academicians. Although there are some exceptions, the vast majority of scholars and business experts believe that in the coming years continued innovation and technological advances will be the primary drivers of economies globally. In the *International Journal of Business and Social Science* management scholar Alper Erturk comments on this global perspective:

> In the last decades, innovation has captured a significant attention of the international business environment, as scholars, policy makers and investors believe in its crucial role for economic prosperity. Innovative companies have become the building blocks of strong economies in different regions of the world (Ujjual, 2008). Companies that have innovation capability are among the organizations,

which are assumed as the key sources of innovative ideas, products, and processes that are essential to obtain and maintain economic and especially technologic competitiveness (Kodama, 1991).[3]

In contrast, Professor Robert Gordon of Northwestern University views the United States as not achieving its historical levels of economic growth in the future because of "faltering innovation," which therefore does not portend well for the United States' ability to compete globally.[4]

With this brief background in mind, the purpose of this chapter then is to examine the nature of the relationship between the concepts of shared entrepreneurship (SE) and innovation. Although limited, research suggests that firms that practice SE are more innovative than command and control organizations.[5] Thus, we suggest here that this relationship can and should be fruitfully viewed from two distinct, though not mutually exclusive, themes.

The first theme suggests that the adoption of SE ideas and policies—shared ownership (SO), for example—can be viewed as the result of an organization's commitment to an innovative, entrepreneurial human resource (HR) philosophy. Throughout this book, the four components of SE have been examined. Of particular interest here is that each of these components—SO, shared leadership (SL), shared collaboration (SC), and freedom—has been identified by HR scholars as leading to positive organizational outcomes, such as increased organizational commitment, lower employee turnover, and higher productivity.[6] Thus, organizations that want to gain a competitive advantage via their human resources should be very interested in SE since, as this volume makes clear, when properly implemented SE captures the positive benefits of SO, SL, SC, and freedom. In other words, from this HR perspective, SE is viewed as an *outcome* of entrepreneurial strategic thinking and progressive human resource management (HRM). To reinforce this first theme, consider this quote from management guru Jeffrey Pfeffer, the Thomas D. Dee II Professor of Organizational Behavior at the Graduate School of Business, Stanford University, Stanford, California:

> Achieving competitive success through people involves fundamentally altering how we think about the workforce and the employment relationship. It means achieving success by working with people, not by replacing them or limiting the scope of their activities. It entails seeing the workforce as a source of strategic advantage, not just as a cost to be minimized or avoided. Firms that take this different perspective are often able to successfully outmaneuver and outperform their rivals.[7]

The second theme in our examination of SE–innovation relationship suggests that the characteristics of an SE firm are important variables in the development and maintenance of innovative processes and products within the organization. In other words, SC is an antecedent factor that is an essential contributor to the overall level and quality of innovation within the organization. Thus, to summarize the first overall purpose of this chapter: to examine the nature of the SE–innovation relationship by employing these two themes as expository vehicles. In the first, a commitment to innovative and strategic

HRM leads to adoption of SE initiatives such as employee stock ownership plans (Esops), whereas in the second, the presence of an ESOP positively affects organizational innovation.

A second purpose of this chapter is to interact with a variety of qualitative studies of firms that practice SE. The authors of the chapters in this book were also responsible for the studies, and in addressing the first purpose, we draw on our own experiences as well as those of our colleagues. Specifically, our methodology is to present our viewpoint on the SE–innovation connection based on our understanding of the research literature and to reinforce our assertions with anecdotal information taken from various ethnographic studies. In a sense, we are using a "deductive → inductive" approach. First, based on a study of the literature, general findings and assumptions are derived, forming the foundation of the two perspectives on the SE–innovation relationship we present here. Next, we apply these general concepts to the individual ethnographic studies, noting instances where they are consistent with our case research experiences.

Before we end this introduction and move on to more substantive considerations, a brief word on the structure of this chapter. In the following section, we provide a discussion on the term "innovation," focusing particularly on its definition. The definition of this term has a wide scope in research literature, which, not surprisingly, has led to some confusion. Thus, we think it wise to provide a clear picture of what we mean by "innovation." After this, we present our discussion of the SE–innovation relationship, which is accompanied by an illustrative diagram (figure 4.1) of the various factors and processes involved and supported with illustrative examples. Finally, the chapter concludes with summary comments.

Innovation: A Definition

The term "innovation" has a wide range of definitions in the scholarly literature. Perhaps the most common usage of the term holds that innovation involves the development of new or improved products and services in the marketplace. Some scholars have expanded that perspective by noting that innovation can include "the successful idea being implemented," and that innovation is an important tool for entrepreneurs in creating new value for consumers and wealth and profits for themselves.[8] But as management consultants and ESOP experts Martin Staubus and Robert Porter Lynch advise, it's important to

> beware of the confusion about the word innovation. Most people think innovation means conjuring up a new technology. But the vast majority of innovation is not technical—it's unique solutions to problems, rearrangements of how we deliver products and services, improving the customer experience, making the flow of goods and services more efficient, reducing waste, getting rid of non-value-added effort or creating new business models.[9]

Of particular value to this chapter is the classification scheme for innovation identified by Avermaete and colleagues in a 2003 article published in the *European Journal of Innovation Management.* In this piece, the authors suggest

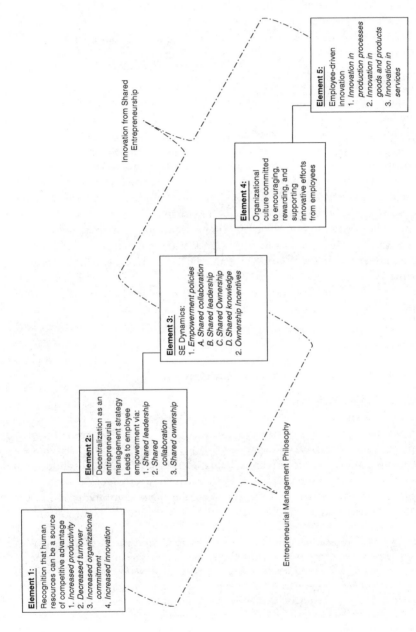

Element 1:
Recognition that human resources can be a source of competitive advantage
1. *Increased productivity*
2. *Decreased turnover*
3. *Increased organizational commitment*
4. *Increased innovation*

Element 2:
Decentralization as an entrepreneurial management strategy Leads to employee empowerment via:
1. *Shared leadership*
2. *Shared collaboration*
3. *Shared ownership*

Element 3:
SE Dynamics:
1. *Empowerment policies*
   A. Shared collaboration
   B. Shared leadership
   C. Shared Ownership
   D. Shared knowledge
2. *Ownership Incentives*

Element 4:
Organizational culture committed to encouraging, rewarding, and supporting innovative efforts from employees

Element 5:
Employee-driven innovation
1. *Innovation in production processes*
2. *Innovation in goods and products*
3. *Innovation in services*

Innovation from Shared Entrepreneurship

Entrepreneurial Management Philosophy

Figure 4.1   Shared entrepreneurship and innovation from an HR perspective.

that innovation can be categorized into four distinct classes, thus making it easier for managers (and scholars) to understand and manipulate resources in the most effective and efficient manner possible. The four categories are:

1. Product innovation—consists of products, services, and ideas
2. Process innovation—the technology and infrastructure in the organization
3. Market innovation—the ideas or inventions exploited and diffused to other market segments
4. Organizational innovation—refers to management and organizational policies[10]

Our discussion of the two themes underlying the SE–innovation relationship has implications for our use of the term "innovation." In the first, we argue that innovation—here, adopting SE—is the outcome of a progressive entrepreneurial-type HRM philosophy. As such, we view this theme as consistent with category four listed earlier—organizational innovation. As an interesting side note, consider that Gary Hamel, professor at London Business School and recognized innovation expert, asserts organizational innovation creates the most long-lasting competitive advantage.[11] Indeed, in our studies of companies that practice SE, organizational innovation was critical to their success.

Our second theme suggests that an existing SO with supportive HR practices, as an embodiment of SE, can be expected to contribute significantly to the development of innovative workplace processes as well as external goods and services produced by the firm. In this more traditional understanding of the term, our use of innovation is consistent with the first two categories of innovation.

The Shared Entrepreneurship–Innovation Relationship

Figure 4.1 consists of five elements and two themes. The first theme, entitled "Entrepreneurial management philosophy," consists of elements 1 through 3, while the second, "Innovation from shared entrepreneurship," consists of elements 3–5. In this portion of the chapter, we examine each of the five elements with reference to the academic literature while concurrently providing illustrative examples taken from various ethnographic studies.

Element 1: Recognition That Human Resources
Can be a Source of Competitive Advantage

The term "entrepreneurism" is commonly defined as "the process by which firms notice opportunities and act on those opportunities."[12] Thus, to the extent that the firm identifies and acts on perceived opportunities, it can be said to be acting in an innovative, entrepreneurial manner. One very important though frequently overlooked or ignored source of opportunity involves the organization's own worker-owners.

Over the past 25 years or so, there has been a growing awareness among both academicians and business executives that an organization's HR, if properly managed, can be a source of competitive advantage for the firm.[13] An important reason for this awareness has been the growth in both academic research and business world examples illustrating the power of various human resource policies to produce organizationally beneficial outcomes. Scholars have, for instance, determined that outcomes such as increased employee productivity, reduced turnover, increased organizational commitment, and increases in innovation can be attributed partially to the successful implementation of employee-motivating HR efforts.[14]

Thus, firms that recognize the tremendous opportunity inherent in their HR and consciously structure a management philosophy designed to exploit that opportunity are exhibiting entrepreneurial and innovative characteristics. And if our personal experiences in the development of qualitative studies are indicative, business managers and executives definitely understand this viewpoint.

As our figure indicates, the first step is recognizing and building a philosophy around the fact that human resources represent a potential source of competitive advantage for the firm. This raises the question of how an organization turns this potential into reality, the answer to which takes us to the second component in our model.

Element 2: "Decentralization" as an Entrepreneurial, Innovative Human Resource Strategy

One of the more innovative management philosophies in the past 25 years involves the concept of "decentralization"; indeed, both management scholars and business executives have given this powerful idea considerable attention over this time period. Broadly speaking, the term refers to a spreading of organizational authority to lower levels of the organization and thus, increasing individual freedom in decision-making. In terms of structure, it suggests a movement away from the traditional, "tall," centralized organizational hierarchy to a "flatter," more decentralized arrangement. As Hill and Jones note, "When authority is decentralized, it is delegated to divisions, functions, and employees at lower levels in the company."[15] Decentralization has implications for virtually all organizational functions, but for our purposes, it is particularly relevant in terms of the organization's management of its HR. From an HR perspective, the major benefit of decentralization is that it can lead to a sense of *empowerment* on the part of the worker-owners, which, in turn, can have positive implications for the organization. When done well empowerment provides worker-owners with greater freedom. In turn, additional freedom has been associated with higher corporate performance.[16] Empowerment is supposed to be common among employees working in a decentralized work environment; however, some scholars do not believe that it is that common in organizations.[17] Ed Lawler and his colleagues at the University of Southern California found that *only 10 percent* of employees are given the freedom to make decisions and receive extensive training and information on the business performance, especially relative to competitors.[18]

In contrast, consider a rather typical example from firms that practice SE based on comments from Ruth, a team leader at the employee-owned MBC

Ventures, a Maryland-based manufacturer of stock and custom brushes for industrial applications:

> The first thing...It's a small company now, so I get to do a lot of different things. I'm always busy. So, for me it's the work. The diversity of the work, and the fact that I can be involved in so many different things. [Second,] I would say that it is the flexible environment...The fact that you don't have a lot of supervision is good for self-directed people...[Third,] I would say the fact that we are employee owned...I think I have a big influence.

So how does an organization go about empowering its worker-owners? We answer that question by drawing on the relevant research and combining it with our personal experiences with the companies.

Empowering Worker-Owners via Shared Ownership,
Shared Leadership, and Shared Collaboration
Management scholars have spent considerable effort in recent years examining whether increasing worker-owners' sense of empowerment over their job conditions results in positive organizational outcomes. The work on *empowerment*—also referred to as employee "participation" or "engagement"—indicates that, in general, increases in employee empowerment (i.e., freedom) result in increases in employee satisfaction, employee commitment, employee productivity, and innovative processes, goods, and services.

Decentralization tends to empower employees because, as both research and experience indicate, the more responsibility and control people have over their work environments, the more engaged and empowered they feel.[19] Scholars have identified three prominent, critical characteristics of a successful employee empowerment initiative: SO, SL, and SC among worker-owners. We look at each next.

Increasing employee incentives via shared ownership. Generally speaking, efforts to increase employee productivity, for example, by increasing incentives, have fallen under the compensation aspect of the HR function. They typically range from pay-for-performance plans to profit-sharing to bonus plans; but what they have in common is the assumption that worker-owners believe their own personal productivity gains will result in overall firm productivity gains. But for reasons beyond the scope of this chapter, older research in this area has shown this belief to be, at best, questionable. On the other hand, recent scholarship and anecdotal business accounts suggest that increasing SO in the organization can, under the right circumstances, lead to both individual worker-owner and firm-level productivity gains. In fact, a growing body of research in this area has bolstered earlier work showing that companies with a significant percentage of SO tend to outperform similar non-employee-owned firms on a variety of performance measures.[20]

The benefits to and the logic behind SO is straightforward: by aligning the interests of the worker-owners with the shareholders—indeed, making them shareholders—all the benefits of ownership will be brought to bear on worker-owner workplace behavior. If the firm does well, they do well; hence the incentive to help the firm do well. By aligning the interest of employee and owners by creating worker-owners, one overcomes the principal-agent dilemma of agency theory where the interests of the employees and owners are not aligned. In some cases this leads to abuse of authority and in extreme cases results in criminal activities such as Enron and Bernie Madoff. A second important benefit is that ownership tends to shift the worker-owners' time horizon outward. In other words, worker-owners tend to think longer-term than do non-worker-owners.[21] For example, Dave, one of the earliest and longest-serving employees at TEOCO, captured this aspect nicely when asked what employee ownership meant to him: "I've got a stake in the game. My kid's college education is riding on this whole thing. There are no two ways about it...I think a lot of people in the company think that way." Third, employee ownership has beneficial effects on the employee–management relationship. By shifting employees into the ownership column, the "we-they" dynamic often turns into an "us together" dynamic.[22] Finally, ownership contributes to an increased sense of empowerment as it relates to the worker-owners' ability to control and influence the decision-making and knowledge acquisition processes that affect both their jobs as well as the overall health of the organization.

These last two points are particularly salient; time and again, in our experiences interviewing managers and worker-owners, we witnessed the power of ownership to create an "us together" mindset between the two groups. And there is no doubt that it empowers both management and worker-owners. Here's a representative account from a company in the construction industry. The worker-owners in this company feel very comfortable with the open-book philosophy, primarily because they truly realize that communication works best when it is a two-way street, not just top-down information dissemination. One employee stated that if they have a problem, they can usually talk to someone with relevant authority about it within 24 hours. Similarly, when walking on the factory floor, it is not uncommon to find managers from all levels of the firm interacting with the production worker-owners—answering questions or just chatting to see how things are going. Relatedly, a common observation by worker-owners is how much they appreciate upper level management's willingness to solicit their input on a wide variety of relevant issues. A welder related the following example,

> I got a lot of friends and family that are in different companies that aren't ESOP or an employee owned facility like this and you're not going to hear them say "Well my boss was asking my input on this or anything." I got to honestly say this facility is a little different than the rest of them out there. They do ask your input, they do come out and strive to find out what do you think.

Shared leadership and shared collaboration. Worker-owners tend to be much more hands-on in terms of their desires to be involved in decisions that affect them and the organization than non-worker-owners. Thus, for an empowerment effort to be successful, worker-owners need to have access to information necessary for them to make informed decisions. In other words, pushing the decision-making authority down the ladder is good only so far as the worker-owners also have freedom to access information relevant to the decision-making process. Consequently, shared decision-making is highly dependent on shared knowledge since failure to allow worker-owners access to the relevant information they need undermines their ability to make good decisions. Of course, the corollary exists, a point James Surowiecki captures nicely in his highly influential 2005 book, *The Wisdom of Crowds*.

> So what would the wider distribution of real decision-making power look like? To begin with, decisions about local problems should be made, as much as possible, by people close to the problem . . . Instead of assuming that all problems need to be filtered up the hierarchy and every solution filtered back down again, companies should start with the assumption that, just as in the marketplace, people with local knowledge are often best positioned to come up with a workable and efficient solution. The virtues of specialization and local knowledge often outweigh managerial expertise in decision-making.[23]

Before we move to the third component in figure 4.1, an important point about the relationship between the three empowerment elements should be made. When considered independently, each of these three empowerment characteristics has been shown to have positive organizational benefits, though the findings are decidedly mixed in terms of the magnitude and the certainty of the effects. However, a much clearer, much stronger relationship exists when all three are present within the same organization at the same time.[24] As Kruse et al. state,

> Why should employee ownership without participation [shared decision-making and shared knowledge] have a substantial effect on worker effort if workers have no way to respond to the incentives of ownership? Similarly, why should opportunities to participate without incentives—say through teams of quality circles, where there is no economic payoff to additional effort—generate the types of behavior that will substantially improve company outcomes? . . . both ownership without participation, and participation without ownership, can even decrease performance by frustrating worker expectations and increasing conflict. Firms need incentives and opportunities working together for employee ownership or any other form of organization to yield improved performance. There is evidence that employee ownership and participation are positively correlated (Freeman and Dube, 2000; Conyon and Freeman, 2001), so that employee-owned firms are more likely to have participative structures than other firms, and conversely.[25]

Element 3: Shared Entrepreneurship Dynamics and Employee Innovation

The third element in figure 4.1 suggests that a firm becomes an innovative, shared entrepreneurial organization when it recognizes the potential inherent in its workforce and commits to SO, SL, SC, and shared knowledge across different levels in the company. An important and common method of capturing this sharing is through the creation and implementation of an ESOP that is committed to all four forms of sharing. Thus, employee ownership is a logical outcome of an innovative, entrepreneurial HRM philosophy. And in terms of figure 4.1, we capture this aspect of the SE–innovation relationship with the dashed line labeled "Entrepreneurial management philosophy" that encompasses elements 1–3.

There is, however, something of more importance to discuss about element 3. As our figure indicates, in addition to being the last factor in the "Entrepreneurial management philosophy" theme, element 3 is also the first component in our second theme, "Innovation from shared entrepreneurship." A closer look at this variable reveals the critically important role it plays in this second theme as well.

Element 3 includes two forces that powerfully affect worker-owners when an organization implements SO: an increased sense of employee empowerment, and exposure to the powerful incentives of SO. We have included the ownership variable in two places: as one of the three empowerment elements, consistent with the element 2 discussion previously, and as its own independent characteristic, labeled in figure 4.1, element 3 as "2. Ownership incentives." We do this to highlight the role incentives associated with SO are expected to play in the development of the firm's worker-owners as a source of innovation. At the same time, noting its role in element 3 as a constituent variable in the empowerment strategy (i.e., "1. C. Shared ownership") reminds us that employee ownership itself is likely to be less effective in the absence of the other two critical empowerment processes. And since we've already examined the empowerment variables in element 2, we now turn our attention to the second item in element 3, ownership incentives.

Ownership incentives and innovation. Economists have identified at least four ways that property ownership can lead to economic progress. First, owners have a strong incentive to maintain the quality of their property; failing to do so results not only in a reduction of its effectiveness, but also leads to a decline in its financial worth. Second, private ownership tends to promote the conservation and thoughtful development of resources for future endeavors and opportunities.

The last two incentives associated with ownership are particularly relevant to our discussion on worker-owner driven organizational innovation. Economists have long noted that ownership is a powerful force for motivating people to use their property in creative and more productive ways. The benefits of doing so are at least twofold: the positive direct effects of increased productivity, and the concomitant increase in the value of the property itself. And finally, property owners have, in the words of economist James D. Gwartney, "a strong incentive to develop things they own in ways that are beneficial to others."[26] Doing so increases their value to others and, thus, to themselves.

To see more clearly how these last two ownership incentives tie-in with employee innovation, a brief discussion on an important concept from the organizational entrepreneurship literature is in order. Within this context, the term "proactiveness" refers to organizational efforts to "prepare for the future by 'seeking new opportunities which may or may not be related to the present line of operations, introduction of new products and brands ahead of competition, strategically eliminating operations which are in the mature or declining stages of the life cycle' (Venkatraman, 1989, p. 9490)."[27] The key point is that worker-owners in proactive firms are motivated to take a leadership role in creating innovative goods, services, processes, or solutions to problems as a means of securing a competitive edge in their business markets. And how can organizations create this level of employee initiative? By making them owners of the firm and tapping into the motivation stemming from the incentives inherent in ownership.

Element 4: Organizational Culture Supportive of Employee-Generated Innovation

Element 4 identifies the important role that organizational culture plays in the process of worker-owner driven innovation. Scholars studying the antecedents of innovation have noted the power and importance of an organizational culture that encourages, supports, and rewards employee innovation. In a recent study of small and medium-sized firms, for example, Cakar and Erturk found that "SMEs (Small and Medium Enterprises) that are involved in activities that create perceptions of empowerment develop a stronger ability to increase innovation."[28] After an analysis of the literature and in conjunction with their findings, the authors conclude, "taking into consideration that innovation is essential in converting ideas into something profitable, managers should encourage new ideas to channel the creative ability of employees into innovations. Therefore, organizations need to facilitate innovation by creating and maintaining a cultural environment that supports idea generation and creativity."[29]

In terms of prescriptive suggestions for workplace leaders, the innovation literature has several suggestions for creating an innovation-supportive culture that dovetails nicely with our emphasis on decentralization and employee empowerment. In the study noted previously, Cakar and Erturk suggest that organizations concentrate on sharing important and accurate information as well as increasing, and subsequently rewarding, worker-owner autonomy in decision-making and idea generation. Similarly, Staubus and Lynch point out the importance of encouraging worker-owners to "experiment, try out new approaches and pilot ideas on the work floor."[30] Management should, however, be careful to view unsuccessful efforts as "learning events" rather than failures. They also value the importance of sharing ideas and information, particularly among those worker-owners mostly likely to be a true source of innovation:

> Provide a continuous flow of business information to those whom you will rely on to innovate. People can't meet customer needs they don't know about, improve cost structures they have no metrics for or streamline processes they

don't understand. Organizations that limit information access to a chosen few are limiting the capacity of their employees to innovate...By sharing ideas, new evolutions of the idea build a momentum that ultimately creates competitive advantage, which in turn shows up as higher profitability.[31]

In terms of the scholarly literature, it's clear that for employee innovation to emerge and flourish, upper management must be committed to creating and maintaining a workplace environment that values employee empowerment and is willing and able to encourage, support, and reward innovative efforts from its worker-owners. And in terms of the "real world," at least as it's represented by our experiences with companies, managers seem to understand these prescriptions and are more than willing to implement them in their workplaces. Indeed, one of the most consistent, powerful themes that we have observed in SE companies involves the supportive attitudes and behaviors of corporate leaders toward the other worker-owners. These comments from Atul Jain, the CEO of the communications consulting firm TEOCO, are typical of the leaders we interviewed:

> As CEO of the company, I understand that I have no control over anybody. I can't get anybody to do anything...so I don't spend my time trying to control people...what I try to do is to conduct myself in a manner that may encourage people to work in a certain way. I can try to create an environment that is encouraging; an environment in which people wish to excel.

The secret to making it work, according to Atul, is that "you have to create a culture of sharing in the decision-making process." The core values of TEOCO are manifested in the degree of employee involvement within the organization, as well as the many significant ways employees contribute.

Our experiences strongly suggest that management in shared entrepreneurial, innovative firms such as those in this book, are highly motivated to create and maintain an environment that allows the benefits associated with decentralization and empowerment to emerge and flourish. Regardless of the degree of SO—be it in the form of an ESOP where the worker-owners own approximately 10 percent or less of the company but, as a group, are the largest shareholder (e.g., Herman Miller Inc.), or at the other extreme where ownership is in the form of a cooperative (e.g., Equal Exchange)—managers clearly perceive their relationship with worker-owners in terms of "we" rather than "us vs. them." The two quotes here, from our interviews at SRC Holdings, capture CEO Jack Stack's desire to turn his worker-owners into "business people," by which he means business owners and entrepreneurs such as himself. They would need a departure from the normal business model. Why? Because they wanted to build a business of business people. This cultural shift—from a company of employees who just show up and make a product to a company of worker-owners who are trained to become business people—did not happen overnight. As Stack notes, "It's a result of a pattern that we get the behavioral change that converts somebody into a business person and into a leader."

None of this is lost on SRC where emphasizing innovation contributes mightily to its tremendous track record of growth. Jack Stack captures this sentiment when he states that SRC is trying to "train people to build innovation. Build creativity. Build entrepreneurs." Not surprisingly, a great deal of research, development, and experimentation takes place at SRC. SRC enjoys a large degree of success with its innovation efforts, frequently more so than its competitors. These efforts are typically successful because the worker-owners at SRC have a strong understanding of the business aspects of their innovative ideas. And since employees realize that they will be accountable for their ideas—and have to convince others as to their merits—the likelihood that good ideas come to the table is increased.

Of course, it's not enough for only management to be aware of the importance of an employee-empowering cultural environment; worker-owners also must recognize and appreciate the efforts of the leaders in this regard. As an example, consider the following quote from an employee with Heavy Construction Systems Specialists, Inc. (HCSS), a service firm that provides software for the heavy construction and related industries. Note Chris's (regional manager for technical services and training and implementation manager) awareness of the important relationship between management's willingness to share information and employee ownership:

> As we were working on our annual end-users meeting during which 800 to 1,000 people come to Houston to visit with us, I saw an opportunity to refine our knowledge of the HCSS customer base. I said to Mark [his supervisor at the time], "How many of our top customers show up to the user group meeting?" Mark did not know the answer and he asked me to find this info and others. So, I went to our CEO and asked him. It seemed like real internal [confidential] information that you would not give a new employee...and he gave it to me...Mike (The CEO) always says he wants to give us the tools to do our job. So, it's very rare, very rare that you would ask for information on something that Mike wouldn't share with you...He tells us a lot of stuff that I can promise you you'd never hear in another company if you're not on the executive level. From the biggest deals we're working on to the money we'll make out of these deals...He will share this information with us, to make sure that we're all engaged...Because we're owners, we should know.

In the next section, we look at the end product of the employee-empowering, managerial supporting culture: employee innovation.

Element 5: Employee-Driven Innovation

In this final element, we discuss three different forms of employee-driven innovation: innovative improvements in the production process, innovation in physical goods, and innovation in the development and delivery of services. Also, we also provide illustrative examples and excerpts from our experiences with companies practicing SE.

Innovative improvements in processes. An important type of innovation involves improvements in the processes of the organization, particularly in terms of consistent technological improvement. Indeed, several SE companies are noted for their superior product production capabilities, short development time cycles, and strong emphasis on continuous innovation and technological improvements in their operational functions. For example, the philosophy of maximizing operational efficiency is very much a part of the corporate environment of a construction industry SE firm. The firm works very hard at keeping its processes as efficient as possible. It has a manager who travels to various facilities implementing processes. For instance, they have implemented the 5S Program (sort, set in order, shine, standardize, sustain), an initiative designed to emphasize and promote clean and organized work spaces. As another example, the firm has experimented with the arrangement of the elements in its production flow processes as a means to increasing efficiency. And although the customized nature of its products makes automation challenging, they do employ automated machinery, especially in the handling of sheet metal. These and other such practices help to keep its costs and production times down.

Importantly, a common observation made by upper management executives at these firms is that much of the innovation and implementation in processes comes from the ground up, from the nonmanagerial worker-owners. At HCSS managers and worker-owners joined together to develop a unique and innovative method of providing customer service that also allowed the firm to subtly market its products and gather important customer information at the same time. This "employee-to-employee relationship approach" focuses on people's needs and not simply on business needs. It is referred to as a "Help-inar." Tom (VP, technical services) developed it in 1997. This concept is based on the premise that to develop a genuine relationship with potential customers, the best person to market HCSS services is not always a salesman. Tom, with a background in psychology, believes that rather than being in the business of selling services, the company is there to solve customers' problems. Since most of the actual end users of the software are the client companies' "techies," the best people to interface with them are HCSS's "techies," without the interference of the sales department. Tom went on to describe it as follow:

> All a Help-inar is, [where] we take our technical people and travel them around the country and put them in a meeting room in a hotel. Customers can come in and ask them questions all day. They just get help. The end result of that is the customers love it. They're able to come in and get help, but then also hear about some of the other stuff that we're doing and a lot of our new products. So they become sales events, but there's no salesman there. It's only the technical people, which mean that customers hear what you're doing, but they don't hear it with a sales spin. They're hearing from an employee who's technical in nature, which they almost take that differently.

Worker-owners are often also the source of innovative ideas that lead to the improvement of existing goods and products or to the development of entirely new goods, as we discuss in the following section.

Innovation in goods and products. Virtually every company in this book reported numerous instances where nonmanagerial worker-owners played instrumental roles—often dominant ones—in the creation, design, and development of new goods and products. This is not really surprising given that, consistent with our discussions earlier, the organizational culture in these firms is intentionally designed to provide a fertile environment for such contributions. In fact, several managers included this element, employee-driven innovation, as a major source of their firm's competitive advantage. The firms go to considerable lengths in securing quality personnel as discussed in chapter 5 and also motivating the talent that they already have. More than one firm had a highly regarded and highly visible award given to any worker-owner who played an instrumental role in developing a new product. At one firm, in the lobby were golden eggs with patent numbers on them in a nest with the patents on the wall behind it. In another, the wall of the lobby was covered with pictures of new products and the individual or team that had developed them. Clearly, the purpose of such displays was to encourage all in the development of new product ideas. These firms are trying to take advantage of the wisdom of all the worker-owners, and not depend solely on formalized R&D efforts. As a result, it is not uncommon for worker-owners on the production floor or those out doing service in the field to generate valuable ideas in SE firms. The freedom to express and share their ideas and the very positive encouragement they receive for doing so tend to be self-perpetuating. As the director of finance at an employee-owned company explained, worker-owners are constantly looking for new ideas everywhere:

> Other companies that are in tangential industries might come to us and say, "How'd you like to partner with us?" Then that might start us thinking about different opportunities, for example, we got into fiberglass manufacturing to achieve vertical integration with the new industry we were getting into...Then we came up with a better way to build extruded fiberglass panels, and so on.

Employee-owned SRC Holdings Inc., a remanufacturing enterprise based in Springfield, Missouri, is well-known for both its innovative managerial philosophy (CEO and founder, Jack Stack, is credited with popularizing the "open book management" philosophy) and its innovative products and services. A good example of the reliance on worker-owners to develop innovative solutions can be found in how the worker-owners at SRC developed a way to convert a diesel engine for an irrigation system into a natural gas engine, potentially a very important innovation. At most firms, a technical innovation such as this would be the end point of the employee contribution. Not so at SRC. The worker-owners calculated that such an engine could provide up to 67 percent savings and pay for itself within six months. They also helped to come up with a marketing plan. They knew who to work with and how to go about making this specific innovation profitable. This brief account highlights an important benefit of worker-owners: they have both the knowledge and the incentives to propose, realize, and deliver innovative technical solutions as well as the financial and overall business savvy to understand the business implications of their ideas and solutions.

Worker-owners' contributions to firm innovation are not limited to process improvements or new product development. They are often instrumental in providing innovative services as well.

Innovation in services. Though most of the ethnographic studies referenced in this book involve companies whose primary output is goods and products, a few would more accurately be described as service-oriented firms. HSCC, referenced earlier, is one such firm; another is KCI, the Maryland-based civil engineering and planning firm. Consider the following example showing the strong initiative, creativity, and drive to solve a difficult engineering problem for their clients that characterize the worker-owners. At KCI, the worker-owners understand that they cannot simply rest on their laurels and continue to do business as it has always been done. Innovation is seen as key to continued growth and development and KCI has been involved in some innovative, forward-thinking projects. For instance, Harvey Floyd, a senior vice president and chief client services officer, recalls one innovation done to mitigate the impact of a bridge on the environment:

> There were just a number of things that were blocking fish passages, so the fish couldn't go back up the river to spawn, they hadn't for years. So as part of the mitigation effort, the State Highway Administration agreed to create these natural fish passages. They didn't want fish ladders. They didn't want pipes. They wanted natural. Well, this is something that we haven't necessarily done on the East coast, but they're doing it in the West. So some of our guys went out to the West and studied what was being done out there by literature searches, talking with people, and going out visiting. We saw what they were doing, but what they were doing they were doing in a rural area. We had to do this in an urban area, so our environmental scientists and our hydrologic people actually developed the design method to take that technology and apply it in an urban environment. What they did was they built these natural fish passages in the bottom of the streams, so depending on what type of fish you had, it would determine how strong the fish—what current the fish could swim up, how strong the current could be, and how long they could (swim against) it, their endurance. So what they had to do was they had to design these rock ladders, basically, these fish ladders so that the fish could make it up through the current, and then they had to space boulders to form these little resting areas for the fish so they could get up the stream...you would never know that it was a manmade thing. It just looks like it's natural, but in actuality, they were purposely built and constructed so the fish could get up over the natural blockages. We won a lot of awards for that because that was very innovative.

Caveats

Before we move to the concluding portion of this chapter, three important qualifications about the SE–innovation path in figure 4.1 are in order. First, we want to make clear that the existence of an ESOP is neither a sufficient nor a necessary condition for the presence of high levels of worker-driven innovation within the firm. As discussed in previous chapters of this book, the majority of corporations that have some form of ESOP/employee ownership plan implemented them primarily for tax and/or other financial accounting benefits rather than for their effects on employee-related innovative outcomes. No doubt, then, there are many corporations that are oblivious to the innovation-motivating aspects of their ESOPs. It's also easy to see that the presence of an ESOP is not necessary for employee-driven innovation to occur; there are many corporations with strong reputations for employee-generated innovation that do not allow employee-ownership as part of their organizational structure.

The second point is similar to the first in that it cautions the reader against drawing too many absolute conclusions on the basis of figure 4.1. Specifically, we warn against taking the diagrammed progression of steps in the SE–innovation path too literally. While our own experiences, as well as those of our colleagues, suggest that the path in figure 4.1 is representative of many, perhaps most SE companies (see, e.g., the SRC case study), we are by no means arguing that this progression should be understood as being necessarily exhaustive, linear, step-wise, or deterministic in nature. As a good example of an organization with a strong commitment to innovation that definitely did not move along the path in figure 4.1, let's briefly consider the following example.

The original founders of this leading firm in its industry had engineering backgrounds but, critically, were cognizant of the potential advantage their workforce represented, particularly as a source of innovation. After forming the firm, it met with strong, immediate success. This early success was the result of its strong commitment to R&D and its willingness to engage its worker-owners in the innovation process from the very beginning. As a means of rewarding their workforce and to secure future benefits derived from ownership, the owners decided to turn their workforce into worker-owners via the introduction of an ESOP. Thus, in terms of our figure, we might say that the firm started at stage 4 with a strong corporate culture supportive of worker-driven innovation and, over the next eight years, moved through stages 5, 1, and 2, ultimately reaching the ESOP adoption stage 3. This example could be drawn from a number of firms that we interviewed.

The final observation we want to make here is that it may prove fruitful to view the path as potentially cyclical for some firms. That is, as firms come to realize the power of shared entrepreneurial management to effect desired organizational outcomes such as employee-driven innovation, the tendency will be to further increase the leaders' commitment to these ideas. Thus, a self-reinforcing cycle may emerge where worker-ownership powers organizational innovation, which powers leadership commitment to shared entrepreneurial concepts, and so on. We offer a bit more analysis on this interesting possibility in the next section where we also wrap up this chapter with some concluding comments.

Concluding Comments

One could argue based on the work of Gary Hamel that organizational innovation leads to SE, which in turn leads to innovation in products, operational processes, or services.[32] In other words, by treating organizational innovation as a distinct form of innovation, we create a logical chain that implies that increasing organizational innovation increases SE, which in turn increases greater product, operational, or service innovation. This, of course, is the path illustrated in our figure 4.1 and represented by the first theme entitled "Entrepreneurial management philosophy." The chain can become a cycle as the firm continues to increase its organizational innovations over time as we have seen in the case of KCI and others in which continued organizational innovation leads to greater SE, which in turn leads to more innovation in products, operational processes, or services, and back to increasing organizational innovations. When an organization gets to this point, it has created a sustainable competitive advantage that, as stated earlier, it is the longest lasting that can come from the four types of innovations—product, process, market, and organizational. The reason for this is clear—SE, an organizational innovation, creates the environment for a stream of product, process, and market innovations.

To elaborate on this critical point, command and control organizations seek stability. In seeking this property, they become stifling and develop inertia. Even when they stumble across breakthroughs such as Xerox did at its Menlo Park facility by inventing both the mouse and the graphical interface that is the basis of the personal computer/tablet, and more recently, Kodak did by developing the key patents for the digital camera, they fail to turn them into successful business opportunities. Organizations practicing SE tolerate living on the edge of chaos. By doing so, they develop dynamic homeostasis. They develop and exploit one business opportunity after another. When Bill Gore was asked by a puzzled interviewer about how such an approach worked, he replied with a grin, "So am I. You ask me how it works? Every which way."[33] It is like the difference between watching a spinning plate balancing act on the Ed Sullivan Show and Cirque du Soleil. In one the only real action is when things go wrong and with the other, there is an awe-inspiring constant change. In organizations such as Gore, Herman Miller, Mondragon, HCSS, and others that practice SE there is a constant stream of innovation.

As stated previously, many scholars and business experts believe that for at least the foreseeable future, continued innovation and technological advancement are likely to be major drivers in the spread of economic globalization and the growth of economies around the world. Clearly, identifying the various organizational variables that drive innovation is of great value to both academic and corporate interests. Herein lay the purpose of this chapter: specifically, we looked at the relationship between the concepts "shared entrepreneurship" and "innovation." Throughout this book, SE is viewed as consisting of four central ideas, each of which represents a movement of organizational power down the hierarchy and shared with the nonmanagerial worker-owners. Consequently, the SE components—shared ownership, shared leadership, shared collaboration, and freedom—played a critical role.

As a means of looking at the SE–innovation relationship, we presented a formulation consisting of five components grouped into two thematic relationships. Our methodology involved a combination of scholarly work and applied observations taken from ethnographic studies done in work settings. We utilized general findings from the scholarly literature as the basis for the five elements in figure 4.1, and then provided excerpts drawn from ethnographic studies as supporting material.

Finally, a word about prescriptive suggestions based on our formulation and case study experiences. Although it was not the purpose of this chapter to provide a set of normative recommendations for current or potential leaders of employee-owned companies, we would like to share three observations that we feel are particularly powerful and relevant to a successful SE endeavor in terms of innovation. First, and probably the most important, is to fully recognize the power of ownership to alter employee behavior in ways beneficial to the firm and, ultimately, the worker-owners themselves. Worker-owners view the firm as a collaborative effort, rather than as an enterprise that consists of a confrontational "us vs. them" employment environment. Consequently, they are much more incentivized to create new, innovative ideas and pursue them through to completion knowing that they and their colleagues stand to benefit alongside the company. Second, the organizational philosophy must include a commitment to empowering worker-owners, and doing so by decentralizing decision-making authority and allowing worker-owners access to any information and knowledge necessary to make decisions. Recalling from our earlier discussion, to capture the maximum benefits of worker ownership the presence of the other three empowerment components of SE must be secured. Third, leaders at all levels must work hard to create and maintain a culture that encourages, supports, assists, and rewards worker-driven innovation efforts. This requires corporate leaders to recognize that a systematic, structural, and active collaborative culture supporting employee empowerment and ownership must be a top organizational priority.

Notes

1. For example, see Christensen, C. M. 1997. *The innovator's dilemma: When new technologies cause great firms to fail.* Cambridge: Harvard Business University Press.
2. Hill, C. W. L., & Jones, G. R. 2007. *Strategic management* (7th edn). Boston: Houghton Mifflin.
3. Erturk, A. 2012. Linking psychological empowerment to innovation capability: Investigating the moderating effect of supervisory trust. *International Journal of Business and Social Science*, *3*: 153–165.
4. Gordon, R. J. 2012. Is US economic growth over? Faltering innovation confronts six headwinds. *Policy Insight No. 63*, Center for Economic Policy Research, September.

5. Blasi, J. R., Freeman, R. B., & Kruse, D. L. 2013. *The citizen's share: Putting ownership back into democracy.* New Haven, CT: Yale University Press.
6. See Noe, R. A., Hollenbeck, J. R., Gerhart, B., & Wright, P. M. 2013. *Human resource management* (8th edn). New York: McGraw-Hill Irwin; and Blasi et al., *The citizen's share.*
7. Pfeffer, J. 1995. Producing sustainable competitive advantage through the effective management of people. *Academy of Management Executive, 9*: 55–72.
8. Wichitchanya, W., & Durongwatana, S. 2012. Human resource management and organizational innovation. *The Business Review, 20*: 221.
9. Staubus, M., & Lynch, R. P. 2010. Unlock creative genius through employee ownership. *The Beyster Institute Newsletter,* UC-San Diego, Spring.
10. Avermaete, T., Viaene, J., Morgan, J., & Crawford, N. 2003. Determinants of innovation in small food firms. *European Journal of Innovation Management, 6*: 8–17.
11. Hamel, G. 2007. *The future of management.* Boston: Harvard Business School Press.
12. Welborne, T. M., & Cyr, L. A. 1999. Using ownership as an incentive: Does the "too many chiefs" rule apply in entrepreneurial firms? *Group and Organization Management, 24*: 438–460.
13. Pfeffer, Producing sustainable competitive advantage.
14. Knyght, P. R., Kouzmin, A., Kakabadse, N. K., & Kakabadse, A. P. 2010. Auditing employee ownership in a neo-liberal world. *Management Decision, 48*: 1304–1323.
15. Hill & Jones, *Strategic management.*
16. Bryson, A., & Freeman, R. B. 2010. How does shared capitalism affect economic performance in the United Kingdom? In Kruse, D. L., Freeman, R. B., & Blasi, J. R. *Shared capitalism at work* (pp. 221–224). Chicago: University of Chicago Press.
17. Hamel, *The future of management.*
18. Lawler, E. E., Mohrman, S. A., & Ledford, G. E. 1996. *Creating high performance organizations: Practices and results of employee involvement and Total Quality Management in Fortune 1000 companies.* San Francisco: Jossey-Bass.
19. Surowiecki, J. 2005. *The wisdom of crowds.* First Anchor Books.
20. Kruse, D., Freeman, R., Blasi, J., Buchele, R., Scharf, A., Rodgers, L., & Mackin, C. 2003. Motivating employee-owners in ESOP firms: Human resource policies and company performance. *National Bureau of Economic Research,* NBER Working Paper 10177. http://www.nber.org/papers/w10177.
21. Pfeffer, Producing sustainable competitive advantage.
22. Bannister, D. 1995, August. Making employee ownership a competitive advantage. *Management Review, 84*: 46.
23. Surowiecki, *The wisdom of crowds.*
24. Kruse et al., Motivating employee-owners in ESOP firms.
25. Ibid.
26. Gwartney, J. D., Stroup, R. L., Lee, D. R., & Ferrarini, T. H. 2010. *Common sense economics: What everyone should know about wealth and prosperity.* New York: St. Martin's Press.
27. Vora, D., Vora, J., & Polley, D. 2012. Applying entrepreneurial orientation to a medium sized firm. *International Journal of Entrepreneurial Behavior and Research, 18*: 352–379.

28. Cakar, N. D., & Erturk, A. 2010. Comparing innovation capability of small and medium-sized enterprises: Examining the effects of organizational culture and empowerment. *Journal of Small Business Management, 48*: 325–359.
29. Ibid.
30. Staubus & Lynch, Unlock creative genius. http://rady.ucsd.edu/beyster/media/newsletter/2010/spring/unlock.html. Accessed: January 20, 2014.
31. Ibid.
32. Hamel, *The future of management.*
33. Shipper, F., & Manz, C. C. 1999. W.L. Gore & Associates, Inc.: A case study—1998. In Arthur A., Thompson, Jr., & Strickland, A. J. *Strategic management: Concepts and cases* (11th edn), (p. C-499). Homewood, IL: Irwin.

CHAPTER 5

Culture in Shared Entrepreneurship Firms

*Thomas J. Calo, Wayne H. Decker,
and Christy H. Weer*

"Organizational culture" has been defined as a system of shared, taken-for-granted assumptions that holds a group together and that determines how it reacts to its environment.[1] More succinctly, it has been described as "the way we do things around here."[2] Organizations with healthy cultures are said to have enhanced employee morale and team cohesiveness, enhanced employee performance, and strengthened alignment toward goal achievement. The purpose of this chapter is to describe the cultural components most typically found in shared entrepreneurship (SE) firms, and to provide support for the benefits to be derived from such cultures in terms of organizational performance.

While an elusive concept, organizational culture has often been illustrated with the help of an iceberg metaphor. Although we see elements of an organization's culture on the surface, just as we see "the tip of the iceberg," it's what is hidden from obvious view that is most important. Much like the saying "We are unable to see the forest for the trees," when it comes to understanding organizational culture, we tend to fail to see the trees for the forest. The forest that we see is the overall culture, yet we often cannot recognize that the forest (culture) is indeed comprised of many different trees (e.g., symbols, individual organizational policies and practices), each with its own unique influence on the make-up of the forest. While each tree may be insignificant on its own, when aggregated together, each contributes to the overall environment in which it resides. Similarly, while we see the overall culture and its impact on the organization, to understand it fully requires an awareness and appreciation of every organizational policy, practice, value, and tradition.

In essence, an organization's culture defines what is important to the organization. It is the shared values and beliefs embedded in the culture that provide the guidance that shapes the expectations of behavior, directs how decisions are made, and gives rise to its policies and practices. Consequently, it can be said that everything that occurs in an organization "makes sense" within the context of that particular culture. Ken Iverson, the chief executive officer (CEO) of NUCOR, one of the largest shared ownership organizations in the United States, illustrated the critical importance of a successful organizational culture when he said the following to explain NUCOR's success, "I'm certain that our culture accounts for more than half of our success as a business."[3]

Although significant research has explored antecedents and outcomes of organizational culture within traditional organizations, the purpose of this chapter is to explore organizational culture within SE firms. Our goal is to provide an overview of the common characteristics of organizational cultures associated with such organizations. While customers such as those who buy Gore-Tex® clothing, for example, may be unaware of such differences, fundamental differences do indeed exist more deeply in SE firms.

The Human Case for Shared Entrepreneurship

Early management thinkers believed that employees were motivated primarily through monetary means. Frederick Taylor, the father of scientific management, espoused a purely economic model that reduced all decisions, actions, and human motivation to financial considerations, including time and money. This type of management belief system, which assumes that employees are motivated primarily or exclusively by money, operates under the assumption that the interests of the worker are in fundamental conflict with the interests of the organization. The inevitable outcomes are counterproductive practices leading to compliance and reporting requirements designed to control worker behavior, large corporate staffs, and unnecessary overhead. This gives rise to the "muscle administrator," who "presides over an organization that is directed from the top, pyramidal, and authoritarian."[4] Not surprisingly, worker response tends to be reflected through reduced motivation and the notion of "work just hard enough to not be fired."

The vicious cycle is continued by management's attempts to increase motivation and performance through either various forms of threats of negative consequences for lack of performance or monetary incentives in an attempt to motivate employees. While much has been written about the potential perverse effects of such practices, the most significant negative outcome is that workers will focus only on behaviors that avoid punishment or are in their self-interests. Such an environment focuses almost solely on extrinsic motivation. While there is limited consensus on the relative role of extrinsic versus intrinsic motivation, our research demonstrates that SE at least mitigates the more negative aspects of behaviors that can disrupt collaboration and cooperation.

Traditional organizations exist primarily to maximize the financial return for shareholders. Decisions, therefore, are based largely on external forces, and they are often made with a short-term focus. By contrast, in a shared entrepreneurial organization the workers benefit directly from the value they create, resulting in a longer-term focus as well as a focus on maximizing benefits for the organization as a whole, including all stakeholders (customers, suppliers, community). Cultures are more effective when the focus is on the entire organization, rather than on individuals' self-interests.

Various efforts to enhance organizational performance occurred throughout the twentieth century, such as gain sharing, piece rates compensations, and different forms of profit sharing. At their core, these plans attempt to increase worker motivation on a purely economic basis by rewarding demonstrated increases in individual or organizational profitability. On the other hand, SE firms create a cultural check on leaders. Management control alone can take an organization in the wrong direction, as was seen during the financial crisis with the collapse of various organizations such as Enron. SE mitigates the risks of complete management control by making such control mechanisms unnecessary for maintaining appropriate order and control in the organization. Morningstar, a leading food processor, has illustrated this principle quite well. Featured in a *Harvard Business Review* article titled "First, let's fire all the managers," Morningstar created the needed organizational discipline and high performance without traditional bosses, titles, or promotions.[5]

This discussion of SE introduces the issue of the paradox of control in organizations. Organizations are integrated systems, and like every system, there must be elements of order and control. Vastly different models exist for achieving the requisite discipline, focus, and harmony needed for an organization to succeed. Though organizations will vary along a continuum, there are two contrasting paradigms. The dominant paradigm in modern organizations has been achieved by the bureaucratic structure with its well-known elements of hierarchical control and power derived by organizational position. The diametrically opposed paradigm is self-organizing spontaneous order. This concept, as applied to organizations, derives largely from the work of Stuart Kauffman, who contends that order exists within any complex system, including organizations.[6] Economist Friedrich Hayek argued that at the macro-economic level, the market mechanism was superior to hierarchical control.[7] Adam Smith's concept of the invisible hand is used as an example of how this works at the macro level.[8] Another more recent example of how self-organizing spontaneous order can be effective at the macro level is a study that found that no country having both a democratic government and a free market has had a major famine.[9] Kauffman asserts that self-organization is a principle of nature in which complexity and chaos give rise to workable and spontaneous order in the system. When applied to organizations with SE, workers use their knowledge, skills, and self-motivation to develop workable solutions to problems to create order out of potential chaos.

The glue that holds a bureaucratic organization together is the hierarchical structure. In contrast, the glue that holds a shared entrepreneurial organization together is its culture. SE organizations feature a noticeable shift from the management paradigm of hierarchical control to various forms and degrees of worker self-management. The command and control business model, which saw tremendous success throughout most of the twentieth century, seems increasingly under pressure. Much of that pressure arises from the deteriorating relationship between workers and management. Until the period beginning in the mid-1980s to early 1990s, employees were often seen as explicit stakeholders whose interests were of high importance to management, as well as to shareholders. Certainly after World War II, the relationship of employees to management was based on the principle of mutuality. This relationship was often described as a "psychological contract," which was understood to be a relationship based on mutual expectations between organizations and workers in which, in exchange for hard work and loyalty to the organization, the employee could be reasonably assured of job and financial security.[10] In the 1956 classic book *The Organization Man*, the relationship between employees and the organization was governed by the standard described as "be loyal to the company and the company will be loyal to you."[11] The simple premise at the time was that the goals of the individual and the goals of the organization were one and the same. This unspoken assumption of mutual loyalty had a profound effect on the relationship between the employee and the organization. When employees believed that their long-term interests were being served by the organization, a reciprocal and trusting relationship evolved. Employees became heavily invested psychologically in the organization and responded with high levels of engagement. Companies such as IBM and Kodak were typical of this model. Lifetime employment was assumed for workers in these companies.

Today, however, this "psychological contract" paradigm is largely extinct. For many reasons, among them corporate mergers, restructuring and downsizing, outsourcing, the shift to part-time workers, and especially the short-term profit pressures from Wall Street, this relationship has eroded. Add to this the ethical and financial scandals of the 1990s, and the financial meltdown of the early 2000s, and it is easy to see how the importance of the employee as an organizational stakeholder has rapidly deteriorated. Both IBM and Kodak ultimately had massive layoffs. Even Herman Miller, a shared entrepreneurial organization, had to lay off a large number of employees to save the company during the dot-com bust, but the company developed a new social contract with its employees and did not have to lay off any employees in the Great Recession of 2008. This will be discussed further in chapter 8. Yet once the relationship of mutual trust and interdependence began to erode in their organizations, employees began to feel increasingly insecure and disconnected. There will inevitably be negative consequences when trust and security are absent from the workplace. Organizations and researchers have struggled to find an effective alternative paradigm to the psychological contract.

Perhaps the most fundamental reality is that traditional organizations rest on a foundation that is ultimately unstable. Social science and organizational behavior literature describe traditional organizations as operating on the basis of the principal-agent dilemma. The agency relationship has been defined as a contract in which principals engage agents to provide service on their behalf by delegating decision-making authority to agents.[12] The dilemma arises from the reality that shareholders/owners are the principals, and the managers/employees are the agents of the owners. The managers of the organization (the agents) are expected to act in the best interests of the principals (shareholders/owners), and not in their own best interests or in that of the employee.

A duality of human behavior is that our human nature leads us to an inevitable focus on our own self-interest and self-directed behavior. Trying to balance the often conflicting motives of self-interest and responsibility to the owners is a challenge to us as individuals, but especially for organizations. Principals, therefore, develop multiple mechanisms and protections to attempt to align the interests of the agents with those of the principals. The underlying challenge is that the goals of both parties are ultimately in conflict with each other. SE firms by their very nature can mitigate many of these conflicting goals, because they are less impacted by the agency dilemma. At the macro level there are many similarities between traditional organizations and SE firms, because they both struggle to compete, survive, and prosper. However, it is at the micro level that the distinctions between these different models of organization become evident, and help to explain why SE firms may be an antidote to the traditionally structured and managed organization.

The Distinctiveness of Shared Entrepreneurship Firms

So what is so distinctive about SE firms? To follow a popularized method for describing a phenomenon—*it's the culture, stupid!* Our research suggests that the cultures of SE firms incorporate essential differences from traditional organizations in two broad areas—*core values* and *human resource management practices*—which explain the fundamental differences in structure, operation, and performance outcomes. We will provide specific examples of the patterns we have observed in the firms profiled in this book, as well as in other SE firms.

Common Values in Shared Entrepreneurship Firms

Our research and that of others leads us to propose that six core values are among the most commonly proclaimed and internalized in SE firms. These are *freedom, community, transparency, egalitarianism, merit,* and *fairness.* While the organizations profiled in this book, as well as other SE firms, vary as to the extent and methods for incorporating these values into the culture, these core values seem to be characteristically found in SE firms. We shall briefly describe the core values we have observed in these organizations. After doing so, we shall proceed to a more in-depth presentation of human resource (HR) practices, which support these values, along with numerous specific examples from the companies studied.

Freedom
While it is increasingly common for organizations to proclaim that they practice employee empowerment, the value of freedom takes the notion of empowerment to a very different level. Employees in SE firms not only have the power to provide input for decisions, but they can make important decisions themselves. Giving lower-level employees the authority to make on-the-spot decisions in order to serve customers is a common example. Freedom goes beyond

the ability to make short-term decisions. Such freedoms remove dissatisfiers and demotivators. As stated in chapter 1, there are other forms of freedoms that motivate people and help them to reach their full potential such as:

- Freedom to develop
- Freedom to make mistakes and to fail
- Freedom to question and to investigate
- Freedom of access to information
- Freedom to decide and to act
- Freedom from boundaries
- Freedom from arbitrary limitations such as work hours, location, dress, and so on[13]

Freedom for individuals to develop and act is critical if worker-owners are going to develop the skills and talents needed to optimize the benefits of SE.

Community

Worker-owners in SE firms tend to have a strong sense of community. They recognize that they will spend more of their waking hours with their work colleagues than their family members. The organization substitutes for the extended family of earlier times. They often take great pride in being members of the organization. It can be their primary reference group.

In addition, the worker-owners recognize that their success is impacted by their peers. Hiring processes in these firms often stress obtaining a "cultural fit" and, for this reason, hiring is often a slow process that involves the seeking of input from many employees. Atul Jain, founder, chairman, and CEO of TEOCO, advises explicitly to "hire slow." The concern for "cultural fit" is further illustrated by the preference to "promote from within." The frequent practice of holding meetings to discuss important issues and involving all employees or large groups of them contributes to the feeling of "we're all in this together."

Transparency

The leaders of SE firms typically keep few, if any, secrets. These leaders practice "open book management." This includes full financial disclosure. Typically, financial education is provided to maximize the likelihood that employees understand the information they are provided. Two-way communication is frequent in these firms. The previously mentioned, large-scale meetings facilitate transparency. Transparency builds trust. When tough times hit, trust built through transparency pays off. For example, the worker-owners at Mondragon voted themselves a pay reduction in the Great Recession of 2008. The worker-owners at Herman Miller took a one-day furlough every two weeks during the same recession. Of course, no one likes having to take a pay cut, but when the worker-owners understand that it is needed for the good of the company, it is accepted. Without transparency such understanding could not be developed.

Egalitarianism

While SE firms vary with respect to the degree to which they are democratic, there is a strong egalitarian nature to these organizations. They are characterized by equality of opportunity and fair treatment. There is generally less physical and psychological separation between those at the top and those at the bottom compared to that in most traditional organizations. Some of these companies even include employee representatives on the board of directors. In these firms, it is more common to find employees "pitching in where needed" without concern for job titles. An additional outcome of the participatory meetings held in these companies is reinforcement of egalitarian values.

Merit

Although community and egalitarianism are major values of SE firms, individual merit is also valued. Rewards for performance are typically part of compensation packages. Meritorious employees are often given recognition, as well as cash awards or stock. These rewards reinforce feelings of ownership and foster a sense of being appreciated, which, in turn, contribute to a minimization of turnover. Merit pay is also given frequently at the group and organizational level. Recognition of merit at the group and organizational level helps to reinforce the importance of collaboration.

Fairness

It goes without saying that merit awards should be distributed fairly, but the importance of fairness goes beyond rewarding exceptional performance. SE firms tend to champion fair treatment of employees across all endeavors. Fairness in job promotions and the handling of grievances are prominent features of these companies. Also, the range in pay across job levels tends to be less than that found in typical corporations. Top executives, while making more money than lower level employees, are typically paid less than their counterparts in firms that are not employee owned. In the latter organizations, the pay of the top executives is considered by many to be unfair as it is perceived as exceeding the value of the executives' contributions.

Treating each other fairly is also championed. For example, in rare cases at W. L. Gore & Associates an associate "is trying to be unfair," in Bill Gore's own words. In one case the problem was chronic absenteeism, and in another an individual was caught stealing. "When that happens, all hell breaks loose," said Bill. "We can get damned authoritarian when we have to."[14] However, due to peer monitoring and pressure, worker-owners tend to treat each other fairly without intervention by organizational leaders.

Human Resource Management as a Strategy

Proclaiming common values that are designed to shape and reinforce the culture is an essential role for leaders of organizations. While the stated values for establishing the foundation of an organization's culture reflect the desired state of the organization, such a culture that lives by its values is realized only through the means by which it is implemented. An organization's culture is most evidently reflected in its HR policies and practices. Organizations can achieve very little by excellent technology and other resources alone. At the organizational level, the goal of HRM is to achieve a competent, motivated, and loyal workforce. Both researchers and practitioners alike have increasingly recognized how the study of organizational culture is the bridge between the individual and the organization, as it creates the distinction between one organization and another by establishing its sense of identity. Managing HR effectively requires shaping the internal work environment to create the organization's unique culture. It is in its HR practices that an organization demonstrates its perception of the role and importance of its employees, and ultimately its culture. As Peter Drucker once famously proclaimed, "All organizations now say routinely, 'people are our greatest asset,' yet few practice what they preach, let alone believe it."[15] Yet, there is clear and growing evidence that links HR practices to organizational effectiveness. HR has taken on an increasingly important role in shaping as well as implementing corporate strategy.

Despite the common proclamations that employees are important and relevant, it is important to determine if a specific focus on employees through an organization's HR practices makes a difference in terms of individual and organizational effectiveness. More specifically, if HR practices do make a difference, what are the distinct HR practices that typify and distinguish SE firms that explain their uniqueness and high levels of performance? Human resource management practices are a tangible manifestation of an organization's and its leaders' underlying workforce mindset. It is their inherent belief systems that take shape in the HR practices. From our collective research we have observed common patterns with regard to HR practice. It is the unique mindset of these organizations that leads to practices that are not typically found in more traditional organizations.

There is much anecdotal evidence that employee-focused HR practices have a positive impact on employee attitudes and behavior, and subsequently on organizational performance. Conventional wisdom would also assume such a positive relationship. But tangible evidence is crucial. While there is empirical organizational research that demonstrates this relationship, we sought and found insight from the cases profiled later in this book. Not surprisingly, though, we also found support in the research literature. While the practices that develop in any organization are unique to and appropriate for that organization, we have observed a commonality of practices that inform our understanding of what distinguishes SE firms from traditional organizations. We believe that it is these distinctions that in large measure contribute to the success of these organizations. It is important to note that these summary conclusions were reached through an *inductive* process. By observing, analyzing, and then reflecting upon our observations, common practices emerged. This open-ended and exploratory approach allowed us to examine these observations and consistent patterns without the bias of "expecting" to find certain practices, and then to place these observations into a broader perspective. Moreover, traditional organizational theory provides us with little guidance, since most organizational research studies are focused on studying organizations that operate under variants of the traditional bureaucratic and shareholder models. Described here are the areas of HR practices that we observed in our research and how these practices operate in SE firms. Specific examples from the cases are referenced to provide a vivid illustration of the purpose and effect of these HR practices.

Recruitment and Selection
The hiring processes at SE firms tend to be thorough and lengthy. These organizations tend to adhere to the philosophy of Atul Jain, CEO of TEOCO, who claims that the secret to building and maintaining a strong culture is to "hire slow" as stated earlier and to also "fire fast." His message is to carefully ensure that all new hires are not only competent, but will adapt to the organization's culture. At Google also, the hiring process is arduous. Its leaders believe that B-level people, informally known as bozos, will hire other B-level and maybe even C-level people. Their motivation to do so is to hire people that will not challenge their point of view. Google's leaders believe that this will make it harder to attract and retain A-level, exceptional people and will initiate an irreversible downward organizational spiral.[16]

From our observations and interviews, the importance of cultural fit for SE firms cannot be overstated. At Equal Exchange, the probationary period for new employees is one year, while at Mondragon it is five years. The processes also tend to differ from those of traditional organizations in terms of who is involved in the ultimate hiring decision, the number of steps in the process, and the selection criteria used. For example, at MBC Ventures, groups of peers interview job candidates and employees at Equal Exchange also have significant input into hiring decisions. At TEOCO, technical competence is essential, but cultural fit is considered so important that the CEO interviews and approves the hiring of every new employee because the hiring process is considered vital to the maintenance of the company culture. Similarly, top executives at HCSS interview candidates for positions at all levels to help ensure the maintenance of a strong culture, but other employees, including the potential colleagues of the candidates, also participate in an active manner.

Staffing higher-level positions is also an important consideration at these organizations. At Herman Miller, W. L. Gore & Associates, SRC Holdings, and consistently in most SE firms, promoting employees within the organization is preferable to hiring outsiders, as it is feared that outsiders hired into senior positions may not fit into the culture as well. This belief extends especially to the selection of executives. Herman Miller has hired an outsider as president only once since its incorporation as Herman Miller in 1923, and that was not a success. Before and after then all presidents have been selected internally. W. L. Gore & Associates, founded in 1958, has selected all of its presidents internally. KCI Technologies fosters promotion from within by posting job openings internally five days before advertising them externally. A further reason these organizations champion promotion from within is that they see advancement as a prime employee motivator. Hiring from the outside rather than promoting from within would not only be potentially demotivating to employees, it could also be considered an obvious sign of failure of the leadership and the employee development process.

Socialization and Orientation

Recruitment and selection is considered only a first step. Once an employee is hired, the socialization process is taken as seriously as the hiring process. SE firms typically make extensive efforts to orient the new hire to the organizational culture and to ensure the employee is prepared to do the job. A major portion of the HCSS orientation program is spent discussing the history of the company, the characteristics of the industry, the interpersonal relationships within and outside the company, and why these are so important for the success of HCSS. The socialization process for employees is also typically repeatedly reinforced in SE firms. At TEOCO socialization begins at new employee orientation and continues through continuous reinforcement by references and updates to HR policies and practices. Equal Exchange has an extensive socialization process. Every Thursday morning "Equal Exchange Time" is held for one and a half hours. During Exchange Time, lectures and discussions cover topics such as fair trade, co-op history, or issues affecting their farmer partners. New employees are practically required to participate, while all other employees are encouraged to attend. The discussions are recorded and shared via Equal Exchange's intranet with remote employees and regional offices. Cody Squire, who joined Equal Exchange right out of college a few years ago, described Exchange Time thus: "It's one structured thing you can depend on having every week just to learn about something new, to look deeper into something you already knew about, or to hear from somebody who just returned from working with farmer co-ops in Peru." Socialization also occurs informally in these organizations. The policies and practices, the vocabulary used, the daily activities, and the company rituals are all constant reminders of the cultural values.

Socialization occurs as well through various forms of mentoring relationships. SE firms recognize that culture is also transmitted through leaders and culturally established members who serve in one-on-one relationships with newly hired employees to ensure their successful transition to the culture. Mentors are assigned to new employees at Equal Exchange, HCSS, and KCI technologies. At W. L. Gore the approach is similar, but the term "sponsor" is used instead of mentor. At another SE firm new employees are assigned a mentor with knowledge with respect to the new hire's job duties. The relationship is somewhat like an apprenticeship. On the other hand, in the orientation program at HCSS, employees and mentors work in different departments. This approach is assumed to facilitate the employee feeling free to discuss work and personal issues with the mentor. At KCI Technologies the year-long, formal mentoring program has been found to reduce turnover significantly.

Training and Development

Continuous development of skills is championed at SE firms. As Jack Stack at SRC Holdings says, "Our real business is education. We teach people about business. We give them knowledge that allows them to go out and play 'The Great Game of Business.'"[17] At HCSS it is believed that "everybody is constantly learning new things." Multiple opportunities for continuous learning are provided constantly because the expansion of intellectual capital is seen as crucial to the quality of the intellectual engagement. Training and education opportunities can be roughly divided into the following categories: technical, interpersonal, governance, and financial.

Technical training is essential and indeed common in most organizations regardless of whether they are SE firms. Without continuous technical and job-specific training in every aspect of the business, organizations cannot compete in this age of continuous change and competition. Employees at such organizations are even seen to some extent as creating their own jobs as their skills improve, and as the company and its environment change. At SRC Holdings, cross-training is prevalent. Broadening skills is seen as not only making work more interesting, but also reducing the likelihood the company will ever need to lay off employees. With the goal of increasing intellectual capital, Equal Exchange maintains its own library. The value placed on learning at SE firms is exemplified by the prominence of educational assistance among the employee benefits described later.

Interpersonal training is important for day-to-day operations, interactions, and maintenance of the culture. Such training is effective in developing community-oriented skills for working in and leading teams, asking nonintimidating and nonjudgmental questions, and learning how to engage in corrective, developmental, and laudatory feedback. The employee development programs at KCI Technologies emphasize interpersonal skills and teambuilding. As mentioned in chapter 2, WorldBlu stresses the importance of both communicating openly and listening actively in its list of principles for democratic organizations.[18] At TEOCO, employees are encouraged to pose questions to senior leadership in public meetings about any aspect of the business. However, to avoid any possible misinterpretation of intentions, all such questions are required to begin with "I wish I knew."

Governance training is seldom, if ever, provided in hierarchical command and control organizations. It is critical to move worker-owners from legal to psychological ownership. For example, Equal Exchange, with approximately 100 worker-owners, has an extensive training manual on how it is governed, which is covered with first-year employees during Exchange Time. At Mondragon with over 80,000 worker-owners, governing bodies including members of governing councils, managers including directors and members, especially new members, all took part in cooperative education programs at Mondragon's Management and Co-operative Centre in 2012.

Last but not least, financial education is important so that worker-owners think like entrepreneurs. They need to know how their contributions both routine and innovative impact the bottom line. Opening the books to the worker-owners provides them with the information and financial education that is necessary for understanding it. When employees have free access to the financial statements and the financial acumen to understand them, it is difficult, if not impossible, for financial fraud to go undetected if worker-owners are engaged. Companies that practice SE provide multiple opportunities for their employees to be financially engaged. SRC Holdings has built it into business practices and into the Great Game of Business. Every week the relevant figures are reviewed openly in each unit on company time from the top level to the local operational level. Worker-owners are asked to contribute, and at the floor level are asked for specific numbers. Management does not simply issue a prepared statement to employees. Rather, these meetings are an active dialogue. At Atlas Container the same is true. Paul Centenari will ask employees piercing questions when reviewing the financial statements in what is called an all-hands meeting. At HCSS, the worker-owners are asked to estimate the stock price each year. The person with the closest estimate to the price determined by an outside consulting firm is recognized at a companywide meeting. Companies practicing SE find a multitude of ways to engage their employees financially, to have them access and understand the numbers, and understand how what they and others do affects the numbers. Financial education that leads to financial literacy is essential in SE firms to make financial transparency meaningful. Access to numbers is not enough. Without understanding, numbers alone are meaningless. By creating a financially literate workforce SE firms live up to their value of transparency.

Employee Engagement
SE firms vary to the extent that they practice democracy, but as a group, these organizations demonstrate with actions, not just words, that each employee is valued and respected. This highly positive view of employees is aptly stated by Herman Miller in describing its "quest to tap the diversity of gifts held by all." TEOCO describes its environment as one of "collegiality and mutual respect." Similarly Equal Exchange strives to have an environment that is "safe, respectful, and constructive." Along with those ideals, Equal Exchange has implemented a culture of internal participation and democracy. At W. L. Gore there is a strong belief that consensus decisions tend to be of high quality and can be implemented quickly. Similarly, at Namaste Solar it is believed that people who participate in a decision are more committed to it and that it is appropriate that decentralized decision-making accompany the shared risk and reward that is inherent in its structure.

Employees are trusted and permitted freedom of action in SE firms to a greater extent than in traditional organizations. MBC Ventures does not supervise employees closely. At more than one of the SE firms a philosophy exists empowering employees to "take care of the customer first" in time-sensitive situations. Any required documentation can be handled later. HCSS is tolerant of honest mistakes. They are seen as facilitating growth and spawning the realization that something needs to be changed. In SE firms treating people well is seen not only as humanitarian, but also as a fruitful business tactic. Generally, employees becoming owners has virtually no effect on organizational performance unless those employees also participate in decision-making.[19]

Even when some hierarchy exists, SE firms usually provide the freedom for all employees to be heard. This freedom for input is viewed as minimizing any resistance employees might have to a decision. MBC Ventures exhibits significant employee involvement in decisions, including having union employees on its board of directors. KCI Technologies includes an employee representative on its board of directors. In addition, there are many avenues for employee input at KCI. These include a companywide committee, anonymous survey boxes, a blog, and town hall meetings.

Meaningful participation by employees requires that they are able to acquire the necessary information to make effective decisions and provide wise counsel to others. This may be accomplished through "open book management" and through communication channels. These approaches are prominent in SE firms. For example, SRC Holdings is one of the early adopters of open book management. HCSS considers access to information to be a cornerstone of its culture. Likewise, Herman Miller lists "transparency" as one of its core values. TEOCO and Namaste[20] utilize "all hands meetings" to communicate with employees. MBC Ventures strives for open communication across all levels of the company. Not only do numerous formal opportunities exist for communication in meetings at SE firms, but it is not unusual for managers at all levels to be conversing informally with other worker-owners. Jody Hoffer Gittell in her study of Southwest Airlines found such communications to be so important to effective and harmonious running of the organization that she referred to it as "relational coordination."[21]

A culture of high employee engagement also tends to foster high levels of motivation. As described at TEOCO, "You work for yourself, not an employer." At HCSS it is believed that the employees' "ownership mentality" means doing whatever it takes to take care of issues. This mindset fosters creativity and pride in one's accomplishments and helps employees feel they can make an impact. Similarly, SRC Holdings sees employees taking responsibility and being innovative as stemming from a strong ownership mentality. The key is not merely that SRC employees are owners, but that they think like business partners. It has been demonstrated that such feelings of ownership are more important in influencing employee performance than is the actual share of ownership.[22]

It is common in SE firms for work to be viewed as somewhat like a game or to be fun. SRC Holdings has a culture based on what it calls the "Great Game of Business." The organization stimulates the competitive nature of worker-owners using goals, scorekeeping, and team-based rewards to make work seem like a game. This approach is seen as making them think and act like entrepreneurs. At W. L. Gore a core value is "to make money and have fun doing so." Likewise, TEOCO seeks to create joy through work, especially as a result of shared decision-making. These efforts increase the likelihood that employees will experience intrinsic rewards from their work as well as obtain extrinsic rewards such as financial gain. This can help organizations retain employees in times when profit sharing or bonuses are minimal or nonexistent.

Although teamwork is by no means unique to SE firms, it tends to be prevalent in them. At SRC Holdings it has been observed that employees realize it is in their best interest to work as a team. The performance visibility of teamwork created by programs such as the Great Game of Business at SRC Holdings generates peer pressure for the worker-owners to perform well.[23] MBC Ventures has a team structure throughout the organization. To some extent there are overlapping memberships. Employees typically fulfill multiple job roles, helping each other out as needed. Employees have commented that the freedom to learn different jobs makes work more interesting. Similarly, at HCSS a good employee is seen as versatile and willing to pitch in when and where needed. Skills determine task assignments more than do job titles. Herman Miller also relies heavily on employee interactions, as its structure is based on teams (typically cross-functional), caucuses, and councils.

Rewards and Recognition
Employee ownership has limited impact upon employee behaviors if there is little connection between performance and rewards.[24] Furthermore, achieving a meaningful connection between performance and rewards requires that performance be accurately measured. Multiple perspectives are better than one, as is the case with most organizational processes. SE firms tend to utilize multiple inputs in evaluating employees. Most of the awards given at TEOCO are peer-to-peer awards. Employee involvement is especially widespread at Equal Exchange and HCSS where true 360-degree feedback processes for employee evaluation are utilized. At W. L. Gore & Associates a committee approach is used to evaluate each associate to create a community of purpose.

SE firms typically reward employee merit with a wide array of compensation plans and noncash benefits, as well as performance awards and recognition. Employees often cite these rewards as reasons for which they feel appreciated. Rewards go far beyond serving as a consequence of individual effort. They are intended to reinforce the cultural values. The peer-to peer awards at TEOCO are given for those employees who best exemplify the company's core values. At HCSS it is believed that its profit sharing plan serves to reduce conflicts between departments as employees realize that while different departments have different priorities, they also have mutual interests. It is assumed at HCSS that to be effective their profit sharing plan must be easy to understand, pay a significant amount, and be fairly allocated.

Very significantly, leaders in these organizations live by the values they espouse. Go to Herman Miller and ask to see the CEO's office. It will be like everyone else's open office. There is also no executive retreat. At Herman Miller there is a 34-room Marigold Lodge, which is open to all employees and their families. It is on the National Register of Historical Places. If a production level employee makes a reservation, the CEO cannot pull rank and bump the employee out. The leaders of even the largest of these companies are not furnished club memberships, limos, or other perks typically associated with being the CEO of a large organization. Offices are not palatial, but are functional and sometimes messy. No express elevators to the executive suites exist because the leaders of these organizations typically work on the same floor as other employees. The executives at Herman Miller share an atrium-like two-story open-office area with other employees in a building called The Design Yard. The building is shared with the Design & Development Center. Egalitarianism is a fundamental value in SE firms, and it shows in many ways including office arrangements and architecture.

An egalitarian organization is not possible without practicing fairness, especially regarding grievances and rewards. It is typical for the CEOs of these organizations to have an open-door policy, and to also "manage by walking around." It is important to note, however, that fairness and egalitarianism is not to be equated with equality of outcomes. SE firms strive for equality of opportunity, not of outcomes. These are not communal organizations. Pay levels or raises are not equal in these organizations, but they are fair based on external equity and internal performance. Raises are based most typically on merit, which is an extension of the value of fairness. This approach to pay could be characterized by Bill Gore's statement, "No contribution, there is no paycheck."[25] In these organizations, equity theory is the foundation of compensation practice. Workers' outcomes are expected to match their inputs, and vice versa. It is commonly predicted that when command and control structures are removed, the problem described in the social science literature as social loafing, or in economics as the free rider, will become more evident. However, the reality is that in SE firms this problem rarely exists, as everyone has a stake in organizational outcomes. Peer monitoring, peer pressure, and peer reinforcement tend to mitigate this phenomenon.

While individual merit is highly rewarded, so, too, is collective merit. Since these organizations strive for collaboration, teamwork, and interdependence, the collective performance of the organization is rewarded through various profit sharing arrangements. These programs include bonuses based on company profitability at HCSS, Herman Miller, KCI, MBC, and TEOCO. Herman Miller and SRC are among the companies at which profit sharing occurs via the awarding of shares of stock.

The value of fairness is further exhibited through the pay practices for executives. While the founders and executives may have a larger share of the actual ownership of the organization, the compensation practices provide evidence of the value of fairness in action. This is a further way in which SE firms live out their values in practice. For example, at both Equal Exchange and Mondragon, there are explicit guidelines for the ratio between the highest and lowest paid employee-owner. At Equal Exchange it is 4 to 1, and at Mondragon it is approximately 10 to 1. At Equal Exchange this ratio was adopted to reflect the fair trade ethic inside the organization. At Mondragon, the ratio has increased over the years as the size of the organization and the responsibility of the top executives has grown. Even when there is no explicit ratio, executive pay is not grossly disproportionate to the pay of lower level employees. For example, in 2010 the pay of the CEO at Herman Miller was the lowest in the industry while it was the best performer in the industry.[26]

Generous benefits are also typically an important element of reward and recognition at SE firms. TEOCO employees receive a "splash vacation" every five years in addition to their regular vacation. This unique benefit provides a company fully paid vacation for the employee and a guest to go wherever they want, and all expenses are reimbursed up to pre-set limits. HCSS places a strong emphasis on health and wellness, and has a comprehensive health plan along with modern workout facilities. The company sponsors and even pays employees' registration fees for competitive athletic events. At KCI Technologies and SRC Holdings, tuition assistance is a benefit found to be particularly beneficial by employees. Nucor Steel not only reimburses employee education expenses, but does so also for employees' spouses and children.[27] An extensive range of benefits is offered to employees at Herman Miller. In addition to tuition assistance and benefit-related health and wellness, employees are offered concierge services, on-site banking, and product purchase discounts. W. L. Gore has supported numerous wellness programs and has offered on-site child-care. Equal Exchange is especially generous with vacation time and sick days, which may be used for oneself or to care for a relative. These organizations are truly concerned with the "whole person." They recognize the extent to which employee performance is impacted by mental and physical well-being.

As might be expected, layoffs are uncommon at SE firms. SRC Holdings has a commitment against layoffs. One purpose of its prevalent cross-training is to help protect jobs in difficult times by enabling employees to transfer to other positions. At SRC it is believed that having laid off good people would make it more difficult for the company to recover when times get better. Nucor Steel has also resisted laying off employees despite hard economic times to enhance employee loyalty. Herman Miller has had to drop its long-held tradition of no layoffs, but it has responded by redesigning its benefit plans to be more portable. Its version of the "psychological contract" has shifted from guaranteeing long-term employment to assisting employees in advancing their careers regardless of their eventual length of service at Herman Miller.

Conclusion

Ownership exists as both objective and psychological states.[28] The latter is more difficult to achieve. It is what separates the employee-owned organizations that outperform their competitors from those that don't. Successful SE firms have cultures that are characterized by inclusiveness, engagement, and collaboration. Employees are highly involved in all major decisions impacting the organization, since they are trusted. This engagement begins with the giving of input when employees are hired and continues with the orientation and development of coworkers. These organizations embrace open book management and open communication. Organizations in which teamwork dominates facilitate communications, motivate their employees, and generally produce better results than those in which employees work alone for the most part. When the leaders of a firm empathize the values and human resources strategies covered within this chapter, a collaborative culture will be built. Such a culture will provide the human infrastructure for developing the product, process, market, and organizational innovations discussed in chapter 4. In addition, employees are more likely to experience the growth needed to sustain such creativity and the joy from doing so as compared to those in a traditional organization. Furthermore, they are more likely to feel truly appreciated than those in a traditional organization.

Moreover, SE firms almost invariably reward employees through recognition programs and a wide assortment of compensation and benefit plans. In such organizations extrinsic rewards are typically tied to performance. Often, rewards are earned through both individual performance and performance of the organization as a whole. The latter approach is seen as key to promoting collaboration among employees. Regardless of whether or not the organizations can provide employees with long-term employment, they care about their employees' professional growth and personal well-being. These cultural characteristics generally lead to healthy bottom lines for SE firms.

It is important to emphasize, however, that such positive results are most likely achieved when there is an overall organizational culture focused on the principles of SE. Even traditional organizational research has demonstrated that HR practices can have a demonstrated effect on productivity. However, the evidence suggests that the greatest gains in productivity occur when organizations adopt groups or clusters of complementary HR practices.[29] Making small or individual changes has little to no effect on productivity. Our research clearly illustrates the prevalence of a collective set of values and HR practices that, in combination, result in uniquely collaborative organizational cultures. So it is indeed the overall culture, the collective system of shared beliefs, values, and consequent HR practices, that distinguishes SE firms from more traditional organizations.

Notes

1. Schein, E. H. 1992. *Organizational culture and leadership* (2nd edn). San Francisco: Jossey-Bass.
2. Deal, T. E., & Kennedy, A. A. 1982. *Corporate cultures*. Reading, MA: Addison-Wesley.
3. Iverson, K. 1998. *Plain talk: Lessons from a business maverick* (p. 75). New York: John Wiley & Sons.
4. Walker, D. E. 1976. When the tough gets going, the going gets tough: The myth of the muscle administration. *Public Administration in Review, 36*: 439–445 (guide p. 440).
5. Hamel, G. 2011, December. First, let's fire all the managers. *Harvard Business Review, 89*: 48–60.
6. Kauffman, S. A. 1993. *The origins of order: Self-organization and selection in evaluation*. New York: Oxford University Press, Inc.
7. Hayek, F. A. 1964. Kinds of order in society. Formerly published in *New Individualist Review, 3*: 3–12. http://oll.libertyfund.org/index.php?option=com_content&task=view&id=1269&Itemid=280. Accessed: November 12, 2013.
8. Smith, A. 1776. *An inquiry into the nature and causes of the wealth of nations*. London: W. Strahan and T. Cadell.
9. Hamel, G. 2007. *The future of management*. Cambridge: Harvard Business School Press.

10. Levinson, H., Price, C., Munden, K., & Solley, C. 1962. *Men, management, and mental health.* Cambridge, MA: Harvard University Press.
11. Whyte, W. H., Jr. 1956. *The organization man.* New York: Simon & Shuster.
12. Jensen, M. C., & Meckling, W. H. 1976. Theory of the firm: Managerial behavior, agency costs, and ownership structure. *Journal of Financial Economics, 3:* 305–360.
13. Nobles, B., & Staley, P. 2010. *Freedom-based management: Building a culture that enables and encourages fully empowered employees to produce awesome business success.* http://www.42projects.org/docs/FreedomBasedManagement.pdf. Accessed: December 21, 2011.
14. Shipper, F., & Manz, C. C. 1996. W. L. Gore & Associates, Inc.: A case study— 1993. In Thompson, Jr., A. A., & Strickland, A. J. *Strategic management: Concepts and cases* (9th edn) (pp. 917–931). Homewood, IL: Irwin.
15. Drucker, P. F. 1991. The new society of organizations. *Harvard Business Review, 70*(5): 95–105.
16. Hamel, *The future of management.*
17. http://www.greatgame.com/about/jack-stack-src/. Retrieved: November 13, 2013.
18. http://www.worldblu.com/democratic-design/principles.php. Accessed: November 13, 2013.
19. Quarrey, M., & Rosen, C. 1997. *Employee ownership and corporate performance: The National Center for Employee Ownership Technical Report.* Oakland, CA: National Center for Employee Ownership.
20. Lawrence, A. T., & Mathews, A. I. 2010. *Namaste Solar.* London, Ontario: Ivey Publishing.
21. Gittell, J. H. 2003. *The Southwest Airlines way: Using the power of relationships to achieve high performance.* New York: McGraw-Hill.
22. McHugh, P. P., Cutcher-Gershenfeld, J., & Bridge, D. L. 2005. Examining structure and process in ESOP firms. *Personnel Review, 34:* 277–293.
23. Burzawa, S. 1998. Corporate management in an employee-owned company: There's more than one way to be participatory. *Employee Benefit Plan Review, 53:* 56–60.
24. McCarthy, D., Reeves, E., & Turner, T. 2010. Can employee share-ownership improve employee attitudes and behaviour? *Employee Relations, 32:* 382–395.
25. Shipper, & Manz, W. L. Gore & Associates, Inc.
26. Shipper, F., Manz, K. P., Adams, S. B., & Manz, C. C. 2012. Herman Miller: A case of reinvention and renewal. In Thompson, Jr., A. A., Strickland, A. J., & Gamble, J. E. *Crafting & executing strategy: The quest for competitive advantage: concepts and cases* (18th edn) (pp. C319–C332). New York: McGraw-Hill.
27. Boyd, B. K., & Gove, S. 2000. Nucor Corporation and the U.S. steel industry. In Hitt, M. A., Ireland, R. D., & Hoskisson, R. E. *Strategic management: Competitiveness and globalization* (4th edn). Cincinnati: South-Western Publishing.
28. Pierce, J. L., & Rodgers, L. 2004. The psychology of ownership and worker-owner productivity. *Group & Organization Management, 29*(5): 588–613.
29. Ichniowski, C., Shaw, K., & Prennushi, G. 1997. The effects of human resource management practices on productivity: A study of steel finishing lines. *American Economic Review, 87:* 291–313.

CHAPTER 6

Shared Entrepreneurship: A Path Forward

Frank Shipper

There can be little doubt both from the prior research cited and the companies highlighted in this book that the business case can be made for a paradigm shift from the conventional hierarchical command and control business model to shared entrepreneurship (SE). By one estimate based on research, companies that practice SE have the potential to be 50 percent more profitable and have a market capitalization value 50 percent greater than those that do not.[1] In addition, the preponderance of evidence suggests that such firms are more profitable, and do not drop as far in a recession and recover faster and stronger than their competitors. For example, Herman Miller increased its market value 115 percent between 2008 and 2012 and its percentage of industry capitalization from 8.88 percent to 18.87 percent, a 106 percent increase. In other words, not only did Herman Miller's market value increase over 100 percent, but its relative strength in the industry increased over 100 percent too.

The worker-owners of SE firms enjoy incredible opportunities to grow and be financially successful. It is hard to measure individual growth opportunities, but there are some indicators of how attractive these companies are to employees. Many of the firms such as W. L. Gore, Herman Miller, and HCSS have been recognized nationally as best places to work. Others have received similar local recognition. All of them have low employee turnover rates. In addition, the number of applicants per open position often exceeds 100 and that was true before the Great Recession. At MBC Ventures former employees who had to be laid off when one product line was discontinued returned as soon as a position opened.

Financially, the typical employee at SE firms gets a piece of the pie. For example, the average employee in our case studies has $63,000 in his or her ESOP account. This amount will vary across the companies by the age of the plan and the success of the company and within a plan by the length of service, participation level selected by the employee, and the level of the employee. The average really underestimates the potential of an ESOP given that all employees with one year to their last year of service are included in the calculation.

Furthermore, the leaders and other worker-owners of these companies are conscious stewards of the planet. Some of the older companies were well ahead of green consciousness. As previously cited, Herman Miller discontinued the use of rosewood, a tropical hardwood, years before the green revolution. SRC Holdings has always been and is still a major recycler. Every engine core that it recycles represents iron ore, coal, limestone, and sand that do not have to be mined, and carbon dioxide and other pollutants that are not expelled in the smelting and conversion processes. In short, the companies featured in this book succeed in all three critical areas of profits, people, and the planet needed for sustainability. They achieve triple bottom-line success.

There is, however, more to why SE should be adopted. Across the world and within countries, we are seeing a great schism occurring between the "haves" and the "have-nots," with the middle class disappearing. We believe that when SE is practiced, the schism would be decreased and the middle class would be strengthened. This does not occur because of some kind of wealth redistribution, but because people are given the freedom to intelligently pursue liberty and happiness within their places of work. As Jack Stack, president of SRC Holdings, said, closing the gap is "going to come from showing the have-nots how the haves did it."[2] Thus, SE represents a path forward for worker-owners, the companies that practice it, and for the betterment of society.

For example, the impact that engaged SE can have on society can be seen in the Basque region of Spain. Much has been written about the success of Mondragon Corporation and its cooperatives. Collectively, they are the largest employer in the Basque region, the seventh largest in Spain, and the largest cooperative in the world. Mondragon Corporation sponsors Mondragon University with five campuses and a number of vocational training centers. It grew from a local technical college founded by a Catholic priest, José María Arizmendiarrieta, who is also recognized as the founder of the Mondragon Corporation. The benefits of the company extend throughout the Basque region. For example, the gross domestic product (GDP) per capita for this region in 2010 was $43,385 with an unemployment rate of 7.99 percent. In comparison, the GDP per capita and unemployment rate in Spain was $30,020 and 20 percent, respectively. In other words, in 2010 the Basque region was more comparable on key economic indicators to the Netherlands or the United States than the rest of Spain during the Great Recession. According to Eurostat, more than 35 percent of the adults in the age range of 25 to 64 have attained a tertiary education level in the region. This is the highest educational attainment level recognized by Eurostat. In addition, the violence due to the Basque Separationist Movement has practically disappeared. These outcomes echo the former chief executive officer (CEO) of ADT, Inc., Ray Carey's proposition that the practice of SE can contribute to peace *and* prosperity.[3]

What is going on in Mondragon and the other companies that practice SE are many Hawthorne experiments. The Hawthorne experimenter of the

1920s did not set out to improve worker's attitudes, but to increase productivity. Along the way they discovered that increasing productivity and making workers happy were compatible goals, but only if you gave them the freedom to meaningfully participate in shaping their work environment and to benefit from so doing. We have come far enough in our knowledge of management to know that increased competitiveness and improved quality of work life are compatible. Frederick Herzberg's final book was entitled *The Managerial Choice: To be Efficient and to be Human*.[4] He also recognized that it was possible to have a successful business and to positively stimulate employees. Kenneth E. Clark, former president of the Center for Creative Leadership, in his final book *Choosing to Lead*, echoed Herzberg's other point in that it is the leader's responsibility to create better organizations.[5] They cannot do it alone, but they will find that the great mass of employees will be willing to help them if given the freedom to share in the leadership, the creativity, and the economic gains of the organization. Leaders should not lament as did Henry Ford, founder of the Ford Motor Company, "Why is it every time I ask for a pair of hands, they come with a brain attached?" Company leaders should celebrate and recognize the opportunity for competitive advantages that is created when worker-owners have the freedom to meaningfully contribute.

Freedom to act is a recurring theme in organizations that practice SE. The employee-owners have the freedom to make a purchase, to take a trip, or to be responsive to a customer without checking with others. At W. L. Gore, the associates have the freedom to make decisions as long as they are not making one that could be catastrophic to the organization. This is called the "waterline" principle because if someone pokes a hole below the waterline, the boat is in immediate danger of sinking. In such a case, other associates are expected to be brought into the decision-making process. Gore from its beginning incorporated all four elements of SE as parts of its business model. Associates at Gore are encouraged to pursue innovations. Bill Gore claimed that "the number of patent applications and innovative products is triple" that of DuPont, a much larger company.[6] He also claimed that he did not know the number of experiments going on within Gore. His strategy was to provide the associates with the freedom, knowledge, materials, and other resources to pursue innovations.

The same freedom to innovate can be found from their inception in some of the Silicon Valley start-ups such as Google. In contrast, in companies such as SRC Holdings, an abrupt transformation occurred. Jack Stack and some of the other former International Harvester (IH) employees bought the plant that IH was going to shut down. When leaders of companies decide to change from hierarchical control to SE, the change often occurs over an extended period of time. Even when the change was triggered by a crisis, firms do not typically maximize all four components of SE from the start. For example, although SRC Holdings was an ESOP company from its inception in 1983, it did not become a 100 percent ESOP until 2011. KCI became a minority employee-owned company in 1988 and 100 percent employee-owned in 1998. In the past five years, it has adopted a more flexible structure, which creates more opportunities for shared leadership. SE companies often evolve in their approach.

We have seen in these organizations that there is no substitute for good leadership in developing SE. There has been much written about substitutes for leadership, but there are none.[7] Good leadership can overcome obstacles such as abysmal organizational structure, but the best structure cannot overcome poor leadership. In SE start-ups, the leaders may never have to confront the restricted boundaries of hierarchical structures. In other cases, the leaders have to overcome poor structure, such as Jack Stack did at SRC Holdings and Paul Centenari at Atlas Container. At Atlas, the poor structure was not only on the organizational charts, practices, and mindset, but was also reinforced in the building. Office employees and factory workers were segregated by bathrooms and walls. One of Paul Centenari's first actions was to knock a hole in the wall separating the office from the factory and install doors from the factory floor to the bathrooms that formerly had been designated for white-collar employees only. The power to turn around failing organizations has been demonstrated a number of times. SRC Holdings is just one of the better-known examples.

Leadership is shared in these organizations; it is not an attribute that is assigned to a few. Everyone is provided with the freedom to emerge as a leader. You emerge as a leader by demonstrating that you can make things happen, develop others and constructively resolve conflict, and that others will work with you to make things happen. By doing so, you build your credibility as a leader. As Margaret Hance, first female mayor of Phoenix, Arizona, would frequently say, there is no leadership without followership. She was first elected to office in 1976 and then won three additional consecutive two-year terms as mayor, which was unprecedented. She was an emergent leader herself. She broke the "good old boys" hold on the mayor's office and retained that position because of her ability to get things done through the support of others. She was offered a position in the Reagan administration, but turned it down saying "the job was heavy on administration and light on dealing with people."[8] Although no one would mistake the city of Phoenix or the government of most, if not all, cities for an environment of SE, leaders who practice shared leadership can make remarkable things happen in such environments.

An attribute of the leaders who practice shared leadership is the ability to establish mutual trust between themselves and their followers whether peers or subordinates. In addition to the normal Theory Y assumptions that these leaders have of their followers, they believe in the goodness of many. Initially, they assume that people are trustworthy. If someone proves not to be trustworthy, leaders of SE companies can deal justly with the individual, including firing him or her. Several such cases were discussed earlier in the book. Mutual trust is critical to the success of an organization that empowers people because freedom comes with responsible empowerment and both are unlikely without a high level of mutual trust.[9] The converse, distrust, could potentially make command and control leadership a self-fulfilling prophecy.[10] Distrust would likely lead to a lack of feelings of freedom needed to try new things, to be innovative. Employees could have a fear that making a mistake would be treated by the leader as an opportunity to punish, not as a learning opportunity. Thus, mistrust and SE are unlikely to coexist.

Another key observation is that once a leader chooses to develop an SE organization then over time the organization will move toward greater freedom and openness. For example, Equal Exchange had a matrix to suggest who makes which decisions up until 2007. They experimented with another model until 2011. Then, the worker-owners by vote adopted the Glass Model, which has elements that are similar to the Governance Matrix, but slightly less specific providing greater freedom and flexibility in the decision-making process. At KCI, the organizational structure moved from a geographic to a discipline-based structure to improve sharing of resources, especially in recessionary periods. Lines of authority in the organization might not have been as clear after the reorganization, but overall the organization was more permeable. Information and resources could now flow more freely to where they could be best used than before. It was expected that there will be more shared and collaborative leadership, and according to Terry Neimeyer, CEO, this proved true and beneficial during the 2008 Great Recession. At Herman Miller, cross-functional task forces have supplanted departments as a primary operating mechanism. Once the genie, freedom, is let out of the bottle there is no going back without dire consequences.

From the changes that we have observed, development of SE is a process and not an end. As people move toward SE, they find that their old mental models are limiting and that they must develop new mental models. As stated in chapter 1, traditional organizational theory does not even have the language to describe SE. Yes, it is organic, but that is a broad generalization that is about as useful as describing leadership as consideration and initiating, which were also too broad to be informative. Thus, we have introduced a number of new terms to describe organizations such as permeable, self-organizing, autocatalytic, plasticity, and chaining. These terms all describe processes needed for SE to be effective. Again, it is not that an organization has these processes or not, but to what degree these processes are present. In addition, as the organization and the individuals coevolve, so does the degree of permeability, self-organization, autocatalysis, plasticity, and chaining increase. Just as there is no final state of organizational success there is no final state of shared organizational governance. There is always room for improvement. Instead of the old saying "If it ain't broke, don't fix it," leaders and all worker-owners need to adopt the mindset of "If it ain't broke, improve it."

The founders of the companies that practice SE often do not come into leadership positions without prior experience in a hierarchical command and control organizations. Some of what they experienced would be classified as "autocratic exploitive" in Rensis Likert's terms.[11] At TEOCO, Atul Jain related how frustrated he was working in an organization where employees, including himself, were treated unfairly. He vowed that would not happen to the worker-owners at TEOCO. At SRC Holdings, Jack Stack described how at International Harvester employees were laid off by the thousands. He vowed that it would not happen at SRC Holdings. At W. L. Gore & Associates, Bill Gore described how hierarchical control stifled innovation. He vowed that it would not happen at Gore.

Another attribute that is common across the organizations that practice SE is that strategic human resource management begins with the leaders. In relatively small companies such as HCSS and TEOCO, the leaders of these companies are intimately involved in the hiring process. In addition, the employee-owners are intimately involved in the hiring process including interviewing candidates for employment. The current worker-owners have a larger role in the hiring process than just interviewing. At W. L. Gore & Associates, no one is hired unless there is an associate willing to serve as the sponsor for the new hire. Equal Exchange follows a ten-step process before someone is made an offer including interviews with current employee-owners. After the one-year probationary period all employee-owners at Equal Exchange can vote on whether the new hire will become an employee-owner or not. Obviously, considerable attention must be paid to human resource management, beginning with selection because of the need for a good fit of worker-owners with the ownership culture that exists on a daily basis. The importance of extending human resource management extends through the development of technical, financial, and teaming skills.

All of these attributes are essential to some degree, and they must be institutionalized. Leaders will come and go just as assuredly as taxes and death. It takes time for these attributes to become institutionalized. Usually, having a founding leader or a leader who transforms a traditional command and control to an SE organization and who stays as an active leader for 20 or more years helps to institutionalize the necessary attributes because, as mentioned in chapter 1, the first rule of good leadership is to be a good role model. When you have a good role model at the top, good leadership will spread through the organization due to spontaneous learning, that is, imitation. It is the way people most commonly learn complex behaviors such as leadership. In other words, having a good role model for a score of years or more helps to institutionalize shared leadership; this is essential to having an SE environment.

In the end, companies that practice SE create a free-flowing market for ideas, talent, and performance within the company. Harvard economist and former Harvard University president Lawrence Summers wrote, "The invisible hand is more powerful than the [un]hidden hand. Things will happen in well-organized efforts without direction, controls, plans. That's the consensus among economists."[12] Within an organization practicing SE, the leaders are trying to create a micro-economy where well-organized efforts occur without command and control hierarchies.

They do this without the negative consequences of hierarchical command and control organizations where a few have the power to control the paths to success. Some hierarchical organizations resort to a rank and yank system to retain talent where a forced ranking system is used to determine who is to be fired each year. The rankings are sometimes done by a single manager.[13] Such systems ignore the wisdom of the crowd within the organization and allow one person to determine the value of employees. At Gore, cohorts of associates who know each other's work are asked to rank everyone in the cohort on "contribution" to Gore in the past year. An associate may be in several cohorts.

Committees are set up to take these data and synthesize multiple rankings to arrive at an evaluation for each associate. Separate compensation committees then determine the compensation for that associate. Thus, the bias or wisdom of one is replaced by the wisdom of many.

Another way that SE organizations avoid the negative consequences of hierarchical command and control organizations is by practicing open-book management. They go beyond lip-service to the concept. They hold weekly or monthly meetings to review the ongoing results. Employees know what is happening and what is likely to happen. As an old Holiday Inn tag line said, "The best surprise is no surprise." By keeping everyone informed and engaged the employee-owners are not surprised with unpleasant news.

When unavoidable setbacks do occur, such as the 2008 Great Recession, the companies that practice SE have precrisis practices that soften the blow. For example, each cooperative at Mondragon Corporation uses democratic practices to make decisions. At some of the hardest hit cooperatives the employee-owners were asked to vote on taking a pay cut during the recession and did so. At Herman-Miller, the executives took a 20 percent pay cut while the other employee-owners took a 10 percent pay and hourly cut in spring 2009. On June 1, 2010, the time-and-pay cuts were discontinued due to Herman Miller's quick turnaround.

The emphasis that SE companies put on training also softens the blow. Herman Miller has what it calls a "social contract" with its workers. Mike Volkema, chairman of the board, explains it as follows:

> We are a commercial enterprise, and the customer has to be on center stage, so we have to first figure out whether your gifts and talents have a match with the needs and wants of this commercial enterprise. If they don't, then we want to wish you the best, but we do need to tell you that I don't have a job for you right now.

As part of the implementation of the social contract, benefits such as educational reimbursement and 401K plans were redesigned to be more portable. This was done to decrease the cost of changing jobs for employees whose gifts and talents no longer matched customer needs. Through the internal training programs and educational reimbursement for external development, Herman Miller tries to provide the worker-owners with the freedom to match their skills with the needs of the customers. Layoffs are not needed as often by companies that practice SE as among traditional organizations. This benefits the company as well as society.

The emphasis on training and education helps with precrisis cross-training and the repositioning of employee-owners during a crisis to where there are growth opportunities. Gore purposefully clusters its plants so that repositioning associates can happen in both good and bad times with minimal disruption of the lives of associates and expense to the company. NUCOR during a recession reallocates production employee-owners to maintenance and sometimes to construction tasks to prevent having to lay them off.

As will be seen in the cases following this chapter, the prerecession practices help SE firms soften the blow and not sink as low as their competitors in a recession. Their emphasis on developing innovative products, processes, or services means that a higher percentage of their products are in the growth stage of the product/market life cycle curve, which helps them to withstand the economic slowdown better than their competitors with a higher percentage of their products in the mature and declining stages. Their emphasis on no layoffs except when the survival of the company is at stake means that they can ramp up production quicker because they do not have to hire and train new employees as the worker-owners on furloughs/reduced hours are available and eager for full-time employment.

Challenges Ahead

This future will not happen without facing and resolving multiple challenges. First, there are the organizational challenges. To begin, leaders need to acknowledge that hierarchical command and control is not what will be needed in a globally competitive economy. They must also acknowledge that there is no one thing, no silver bullet, that will provide a sustainable organizational competitive advantage. To develop an SE organization from its start-up—a "greenfield" site—requires leadership with the right values and the right mindset such as that of Bill Gore or Atul Jain. The personal values of leaders such as courage and integrity are critical for stepping into the space of a new SE venture. Many will need to have the courage of someone like Rene McPherson who, when he was turning around Dana Corporation, replaced the corporate policy manual with a one-page statement of values. He believed "that all employees were entitled to control their own work and to share in the company's profits."[14] He radically changed Dana Corporation even when he had board opposition. The desired hope is that, as in an organization studied with a history of over 30 years of SE, anyone can question whether a proposed action fits the organizational values. Anyone in a meeting can say, "I don't think that fits our values."

To make the change in a company with a tradition of hierarchical command and control requires a systematic analysis of the organization, including the leadership, the governance structure and processes, the organizational culture, and the human resource management strategy and processes. How each can be changed to move the organization forward needs to examined.

As a first concrete step, SE leaders usually institute some form of broad-based employee ownership. This concrete step signals that things are not as they have always been. From what has been observed it appears that a combination of a short-term form, such as profit sharing, and a long-term form, such as an ESOP, is better than either one alone. Actually, corporate America seems to be doing fairly well in this area, as almost 36 percent of the workers in the private sector are now included in some form of broad-based employee ownership plan.[15] Second, financial ownership must move to psychological ownership. In interviews with new employees many of them did not understand the broad-based employee ownership program in which they were included. One executive estimated that it took five years before the typical employee got it and another estimated that it did not happen until the value of a worker-owner's account equaled one year's pay. Whatever the case, this is too slow. Companies such as Equal Exchange with Exchange Time every week and SRC Holdings with its weekly meetings and their Great Game of Business approach to keeping everyone's focus, and keeping it fresh and interesting appears to shorten the time between when someone joins the firm and when they understand how what they do impacts their own personal bottom line whether it be through profit sharing, an ESOP, or both.

The second step is for the organization to increase the freedom of workers to make contributions. As stated in chapter 5, *only 10 percent* of employees are given the freedom to make decisions and extensive training and information on the business performance, especially relative to competitors.[16] This is the area in which the greatest improvement is needed. All employees must be given the freedom, training, and information to become entrepreneurs, to go for the brass ring.

There are societal challenges, too. The largest one is to contribute to improving the educational system. This improvement is imperative as intellectual capital has become the critical capital in the age of innovation. It is estimated that the American education system hit its zenith in 1963 and has been on a downward slope since; the evidence is overwhelming that the US education system is in trouble. By one estimate it ranks seventeenth in the world in reading, thirty-first in mathematics, and twenty-third in science.[17] The SAT scores have been readjusted upward for both English and Math, but especially for Math. In 2009–2010, only 78.2 percent of that student cohort graduated with high school diplomas. According to the Organization for Economic Co-operation and Development, this ranks the United States twenty-first from the top. In addition, other countries' graduation rates are increasing while the United States' is stagnating.[18] In other words, 21.8 percent of the 2009–2010 cohort will have only the skills needed to do the most menial of minimum wage jobs.[19] By one estimate, 2,000,000 STEM (science, technology, engineering, and mathematic) related jobs were unfilled in the depth of the 2008 Great Recession because of a lack of qualified graduates. Such outcomes are unacceptable.

The numbers do not tell the whole story. The core issue is that the education system in the United States does not provide its students with the skills needed to allow them the freedom to participate fully in the twenty-first-century economy. Father José María Arizmendiarrieta realized a similar problem in the Basque region of Spain in the 1940s. In 1943, he founded a Polytechnic School. Today it has grown into multiple polytechnic centers and Mondragon University, a democratically administered educational center open to all young people in the region. Mondragon Corporation was not founded until 1956. The resulting improvements in the quality of life for the region were cited in the beginning of this chapter. A skilled workforce is a necessary condition to having a vibrant economy.

The positive impact of high-quality education is evident in other countries, too. In India, the Indian Institute of Technology (IIT) has led to an economic miracle. The same can be found in China. Within the United States, economic miracles can be found around Stanford University and the Massachusetts Institute of Technology (MIT). High-quality education has the ability to lift people out of poverty. It has the ability to strengthen the middle class. Businesses must demand more and assist the educational system. Another public challenge is to realign public policy with broad-based ownership of economic capital. Before the industrial revolution, the critical economic capital was land. Public policies were established to prohibit primogeniture (the inheritance of all by the oldest son) and to sell as much public land to as many citizens as possible. As the critical economic capital has changed to business ownership in the twentieth century, public policies were established to encourage small business ownership and various forms of profit sharing and employee ownership.[20]

During the Clinton and Bush administrations in the United States, laws were enacted that had the opposite effect. For example, Section 162(M) of the Internal Revenue Code limited the deductions for fixed pay to the top five executives to $1,000,000, but left unlimited other forms of compensation such as stock grants, profit sharing, and gain-sharing packages for them. In contrast, ESOPs are restricted to a modest amount, 25 percent of covered payroll (this limit also includes employer contributions to other defined contribution plans) for corporate tax deductions.[21] In other words, the tax code favors the top five executives over the typical employee.[22] This unequal treatment is antithetical to creating a favorable environment for shared ownership, a key cornerstone for SE.

Some argue that government policies that are supportive of broad-based employee ownership are needed.[23] Obviously, they would be helpful to expedite the growth of SE. SE when effectively implemented can be, however, such a competitive advantage that as long as adverse policies are not implemented, SE companies will succeed. Both aggregated statistics and case studies cited in this book support this assertion. A growing number of SE companies are becoming industry leaders. The challenge is for leaders in other companies to take the initiative to make the change.

A Final Word

The organization that can succeed in the highly competitive global marketplace will have to be one where everyone has the freedom to contribute and the freedom to share in their contributions. It will have to be a place where work is not just a technical or professional activity, but an engaging activity, an avocation. As Jack Stack points out, not everyone will try to grab the brass ring, but everyone should have the freedom to try to grab it. What a multitude of studies of such organizations have demonstrated is that by being part of an organization that practices SE, a significant number of people do grab the brass ring. As a result, they and their fellow employee-owners receive higher pay and benefits than those working in comparable traditional command and control organizations. They are also less likely to be laid off and when they choose to retire, they have a higher nest egg. In addition, society benefits because worker-owners place a lower burden on government for services than employees of traditional companies.[24] By creating an SE organization, the leaders have a quintessential win-win, an organization that can be innovative and profitable and an environment where people can grow and prosper.

Notes

1. http://www.menke.com/blog/why-should-you-consider-an-esop/. Accessed: December 27, 2013.
2. Helm, B. 2013. 5 unexpected benefits of opening your books. http://www.inc.com/burt- helm/five-benefits-of-opening-your-books.html. Accessed: November 8, 2013.
3. Carey, R. 2004. *Democratic capitalism: The way to a world of peace and plenty.* Bloomington, IN: AuthorHouse.
4. Herzberg, F. 1976. *The managerial choice: To be efficient and to be human.* Homewood, IL: Dow Jones-Irwin.
5. Clark, K. E., & Clark, M. E. 1993. *Choosing to lead.* Greensboro, NC: Center for Creative Leadership.
6. Shipper, F., & Manz, C. C. 1996. W.L. Gore & Associates, Inc.: A case study— 1993. In Thompson, Jr., A. A., & Strickland, A. J. *Strategic management: Concepts and cases* (9th edn) (pp. 917–931). Homewood, IL: Irwin.
7. Dionne, S. D., Yammarino, F. J., Atwater, L. E., & James, L. R. 2001. Neutralizing substitutes for leadership theory: Leadership effects and common-source bias. *Journal of Applied Psychology, 87*(3): 454–464.
8. http://www.azlibrary.gov/azwhf/women/hance.aspx. Accessed: October 7, 2013.
9. Yukl, G. 2002. *Leadership in organizations.* Upper Saddle River, NJ: Prentice-Hall.
10. Argyris, C. 1964. *Integrating the individual and the organization.* New York: John Wiley.
11. Likert, R. 1961. *New patterns of management.* New York: McGraw-Hill.
12. Summers, L., quoted in *The commanding heights: The battle between government and the marketplace that is remaking the modern world* (pp. 150–151), by Yergin, D., & Stanislaw, J. New York: Simon & Schuster, 1998.
13. Kwoh, L. 2012. "Rank and yank" retains vocal fans. http://online.wsj.com/news/articles/SB10001424052970203363504577186970064375222#printMode. Accessed: November 5, 2013.
14. http://www.automotivehalloffame.org/inductee/rene-mcpherson/97/. Accessed: December 27, 2013.
15. http://www.nceo.org/articles/widespread-employee-ownership-us. Accessed: May 5, 2014.
16. Lawler, E. E., Mohrman, S. A., & Ledford, G. E. 1996. *Creating high performance organizations: Practices and results of employee involvement and Total Quality Management in Fortune 1000 companies.* San Francisco: Jossey-Bass.
17. http://ourtimes.wordpress.com/2008/04/10/oecd-education-rankings/. Accessed: December 22, 2013.
18. http://wamu.org/news/morning_edition/12/02/21/graduation_rates_increase_around_the_globe_as_us_plateaus. Accessed: December 28, 2013.
19. http://www.ed.gov/blog/2013/01/high-school-graduation-rate-at-highest-level-in-three-decades/. Accessed: December 28, 2013.

20. Blasi et al., *The citizen's share.*
21. http://www.nceo.org/articles/esop-tax-incentives-contribution-limits. Accessed: May 15, 2014.
22. Ibid.
23. Alperovitz, G. 2013. *What then must we do? Straight talk about the next American revolution.* White River Junction, VT: Chelsea Green Publishing; Blasi et al., *The citizen's share.*
24. Rosen, C. The impact of employee ownership and ESOPs on layoffs and the costs of unemployment to the federal government. http://www.nceo.org/assets/pdf/articles /EO_Costs_of_Unemployment.pdf. Accessed: February 15, 2013

PART II

Shared Entrepreneurship in Action

This section focuses on examples of shared entrepreneurial enterprises in action. All the firms were tracked through the Great Recession. All of them, for which financial data were available, came across as being in good financial health and were outperforming their industry competitors. The firms profiled in this section represent a cross-section of industry—manufacturing to service, high to low tech, small to large, and local to international. They engage in cutting-edge practices covered in the first section of the book—shared ownership, shared leadership, shared collaboration, and others that foster freedom of employee action. Thus, the worker-owners are engaged and rewarded for their contributions, and everyone has the opportunity to act with an entrepreneurial spirit. Innovation bubbles up from everywhere resulting in high organizational success and individual growth. Yet, none of them do it the same as the others. What could work for you?

CHAPTER 7

SRC Holdings: Winning the Game while Sharing the Prize

*Vera L. Street, Marc D. Street, Christy H. Weer,
and Frank Shipper*

Introduction

In 1981 Jack Stack, SRC's current chief executive officer (CEO), was sent to Springfield, Missouri, by his employer, International Harvester (IH), to see if there was any hope of saving the small remanufacturing plant located there. Increased global competition, particularly from Japan, and the poor performance of the US economy had wreaked havoc on many US manufacturing firms across a wide range of industries. IH had been particularly hard-hit, laying off thousands of employees and closing plants all over the United States. As Stack recalls "We [IH] closed 17 factories in a two-year period of time. We laid off 1000 people a week for two years... we went from 115,000 people down to 11,000 people in 1981–82."

In short order, Stack was instructed to sell the Springfield plant. But here the story takes a fateful turn: rather than scuttle the plant and resort to employee layoffs, Stack and 12 other of his fellow managerial colleagues decided that they would buy the plant from IH and, along with their employees, run the business themselves. This was no easy task, however. The group did not have a lot of cash to put down toward the purchase and, consequently, had a difficult time procuring financing. Finally, after two years of offers, counteroffers, and loan rejections, they successfully secured financing and purchased the plant from IH for $9 million in 1983. But the new firm, Springfield Remanufacturing Corp. (SRC), was born via precarious financial arrangements: Stack's purchasing group put up only $100,000 of the $9 million, and borrowed the other $8.9 million at an 18 percent interest rate! Nevertheless, they were optimistic that they could make the firm successful. The following year they instituted an employee stock ownership plan (ESOP) and turned SRC into an employee-owned organization. And with that important move, the firm was about to achieve remarkable success that continues to this very day. Consider that in 1983 the stock of SRC was worth $.10 per share but by 2001 it was valued at more than $81 per share. Revenues had grown from $16 million in 1983 to $160 million during this time and the number of employees had increased dramatically, from about 120 in 1983 to 900 in 2001. And SRC has continued the successful run over the past decade. Currently, it has over 1,200 employees, generates over $450 million in annual revenues, and as of 2012, its stock was valued at $361 per share.

The remarkable growth of the firm since 1983 has, not surprisingly, led to changes in its areas of business activity as well as to its corporate structure. Currently, the parent company is SRC Holdings, an umbrella entity that consists of numerous companies spread across 12 business units engaged in activities ranging from manufacturing to packaging to management consulting and training. But despite this diversity of business interests, their primary business expertise and core competency is remanufacturing. In the case of SRC, remanufacturing is the process of taking used transportation parts and returning them to their OEM (original equipment manufacturer) specifications. Typically this involves dissembling, cleaning, machining, repairing/replacing, and reassembling the unit, the result being a product that is as good or better than the original and is warranted as such. Their remanufacturing-focused divisions serve a wide range of businesses including those in the agriculture, automotive, defense, construction, mining, commercial trucking, and locomotive industries. And their clients are among the largest manufacturing firms in the world: General Motors, Komatsu, Navistar, John Deere, and CNH Global to name a few.[1]

SRC also has interests outside remanufacturing. For example, NewStream Enterprises (NSE) was created in 1990 to help clients in the transportation industries manage their supply chain functions more effectively and efficiently. NSE engages in a wide variety of activities including warehousing, inventory control, and facility management. And the success of NSE has allowed it to recently expand its functions to include government packaging and kitting.[2] Another SRC subsidiary, SRC Logistics, specializes in third-party logistics to manufacturers, distributors, and retailers in a wide range of industries. SRC Logistics uses its location in southwestern Missouri as a strategic advantage that it can provide its clients in terms of shipping and warehousing activities.[3]

Perhaps the most interesting—and definitely the most unique—unit of SRC Holdings is the Great Game of Business (GGOB) division. This unit takes its name from the best-selling business book Jack Stack published in 1992 as a response to the tremendous amount of interest in SRC that accompanied its meteoric rise from near oblivion just nine years earlier. In this text, and in his 2002 follow-up book *A Stake in the Outcome*, Stack describes the elements and ideas comprising the GGOB philosophy and shows how they contribute to SRC's success. This philosophy is summarized in the following ownership rules:

1. The company is the product.
2. A company isn't worth anything if nobody else wants to own it.
3. The bigger the pie, the bigger the individual slices.
4. Stock is not a magic pill.
5. It takes a team to build equity.
6. Failures are fine as long as they strengthen the company.
7. Ownership needs to be taught.
8. You build ownership culture by breaking down walls.
9. Getting out is harder than getting in.
10. To maximize equity value, you have to think strategically.
11. A company is only as good as its people.
12. Ownership is all about the future.
13. You Gotta Wanna.

Importantly, Stack argues that these ideas can be adopted and successfully implemented by other firms across a wide range of industries as well. Indeed, it was this belief, buoyed by the success of both the firm and the books, that led to the creation of the Great Game of Business division. Thus, from a broad perspective, the purpose of the GGOB division is twofold: first, to promote and monitor the GGOB philosophy within and across the various SRC business units, and second, to make the GGOB philosophy available to the general business public via its managerial coaching, training, and consulting activities, publications, and products.

Culture and Employee-Owners

SRC takes great care to hire the right people to fit with their unique culture. The 1,200 employee-owners are very experienced and, for the most part, reasonably well educated with the majority holding a high school diploma or more advanced degrees. SRC employees have been characterized as warm and open, of high quality, and having a lot of common sense. In general, employees are engaged, and they feel like they make a difference (and judging by SRC's tremendous success, they do make a difference!). As Keith Boatright, director of human resources stated, "This company is set up for a monstrously prosperous run." They don't want to just come in, put in their time, and go home. Boatright, for example, reflecting on the cultural effects at a personal level, says, "I will be better for having been a part of this company in probably five years than at other companies. And I can't say [that] about many companies. Even though you might be productive and do good things, you will not necessarily be a better person." He continues on to describe how the work-life balance at SRC will most likely allow him to be healthier, better trained, and have the time and opportunity to engage in volunteer work in the community.

The combination of quality employees and the organizational and owner-ship structure of the firm helps to create a culture at SRC that is an advantage in and of itself. As Boatright puts it, "There is definitely a cultural advantage as much as there's a competitive advantage with SRC." At the core of this cultural advantage is the idea that having a great company is not just about building a good product or service, it's about building the company itself. When Jack Stack and his colleagues bought SRC from International Harvester, they decided that in order to put the focus on building a company, they would need a departure from the normal business model. Why? Because they wanted to build a busi-ness of business people. This cultural shift—from a company of employees who just show up and make a product to a company of employees that are trained to become business people—did not happen overnight. As Stack notes, "It's a result of a pattern that we get the behavioral change that converts somebody into a business person and into a leader." The basis of these patterns is an "open book" environment that strongly emphasizes sharing, explaining, and educating employees, particularly in the area of financial literacy. The goal is to encourage employees to own and understand the "numbers" driving their respective business units as well as the various SRC businesses as a whole. Consequently, this open book environment helps to bring the employees into the cultural fold, so to speak.

Because of these patterns and the fact that the employees have equity in the company, there is a strong ownership mentality among the employees at SRC. They tend to be driven and exhibit a strong desire to succeed. One may fear that such a mentality might lead to people stepping all over one another in order to get ahead. In fact, the truth is just the opposite. The employee-owners realize it is in their own best interests to work as a team to get the best outcomes for everyone. In effect, the incentives deriving from ownership are powerful forces for coordinating employee efforts. And when one considers the large financial benefits SRC employee-owners have enjoyed over the last couple of decades, it's not surprising to learn that most of its employees are commit-ted to working there for the long haul. And in an era of low organizational dedication and high employee mobility, SRC's culture of long-term employee commitment is all the more impressive.

Many characteristics of SRC lead to the potential for long-tenured employ-ees, but there are three that particularly stick out. First, SRC is strongly com-mitted to protecting and helping its employees, especially in difficult economic times. Second, employees have both the opportunity and the encouragement to explore career moves across the company, even to the point of changing job disciplines if they so desire. And third, SRC places a strong emphasis on suc-cession planning.

Employees are the priority in the organization and job stability is a main goal of SRC. A critical reason for its success in this area is the firm's philoso-phy of protecting and supporting its employees. In tough times, rather than responding to reduced work demand and laying people off as a result, the com-pany's focus on long-term growth helps to justify keeping everyone employed. For example, when recession hit in 2008, the company chose to reduce working hours rather than lay off employees, so they could keep everyone employed. There is even a hierarchy of actions SRC is willing to provide employees, designed to provide buffer and reduce the likelihood of layoffs. In addition to these stabilizing, "work community" facilitating approaches, SRC also encourages employees to recommend qualified family members for employment. At SRC, there is no nepotism policy, so not only can you stay, you can even bring in your family to work for SRC if there are appropriate positions. (Jack Stack has two sons that work for SRC.) Indeed, Jack Stack says he and others want to make the world better and pass a better life on to future generations. In short, SRC really works to keep its employee-ownership community intact and committed to staying with the firm.

A second important factor in SRC's efforts to develop and retain long-tenured employees involves the organizations' emphasis on employee exploration and movement within the company. Younger employees often don't know exactly what they do for a career, and for other more experienced employees, a change of pace in terms of functions and responsibility can be beneficial. SRC recognizes and actively addresses this. If, for example, an employee is willing to put in the effort and learn new skills, the company will help them out. Allowing employees to move to different functions can help them better understand the business as a whole, which is especially critical in a company like SRC where they strive to turn their workers into business partners. Consider, for instance, that SRC has employees that have moved to and from accounting, logistics, operations, and even marketing. There are also opportunities for international travel, tapping into SRCs business activities in Europe, China, and India. As Dennis Sheppard, general counsel and CFO, put it, "I would say you're limited only by your own creativity and your own desire and willingness to work for what you want. You also have opportunities that—at least in this community—you wouldn't find many places." This is not to say that employees are pressured to change jobs or to travel. Employees are respected regardless of their career choices.

SRC also has a good understanding of the importance and value of institutionalizing succession planning as a component of their personnel philosophy. Such plans are highly supported throughout the organization and signal to employees—particularly those higher up in the corporate structure—that SRC values commitment and productivity and is willing to provide a long-term career mechanism that benefits both the employee and the firm. Promoting from within is an excellent way of signaling commitment to employees. And since the employees own the firm, all benefit from a well-executed succession plan, not just management and the employee in question.

Shifting gears a bit, an important question to consider is: Does the fact that SRC has an ESOP positively affect the company's culture? In the case of SRC, the answer is mostly "Yes," but this is not to say that everyone buys into the ESOP concept. It is important to keep in mind that the presence of an ESOP alone is not sufficient to guarantee a cohesive corporate culture nor is it sufficient to assure corporate success. As noted earlier, at SRC the employees aren't just owners, they are owners who think like business partners. They understand what being an owner means and how and why the company is performing as it is. And perhaps most importantly, they understand how to affect that performance. This is the direct result of their open book philosophy that requires financial literacy of the employees—that is, the employees "own the numbers" aspect. This is not to say that every single employee "gets it" or buys-in to the same level. Indeed, the business literacy that is required does not come easy for everyone. It can be very intimidating to someone who has not gone to college or taken business courses. Indeed, those that don't "get it" likely won't get far in the organization. As Boatright describes:

> Again, if you're punching the clock—and I worked in those kinds of environments where people they just want to come in, do their job and walk out. You are expected to do more here. So it's not a, hey I don't wanna do it. No, you've got to understand it. If you're gonna think and act like an owner, you've gotta understand the financials. And some people, that's just not there. And so yeah, I think some of our associates, they ride 'em and they ride each other. They are hard on each other. So if you've got somebody that's not stepping up, you've got a temp that's not fitting in culturally, yeah, they'll make it known and they won't go any further.

Though SRC has had tremendous success with its ESOP, there are potential cultural pitfalls it tries to guard against. One is that it can be easy for the ESOP to be viewed by the employees as an entitlement. This is particularly a threat at SRC because of its success in the marketplace and the resulting very comfortable financial environment for its employees. Although an entitlement attitude is something to be ever vigilant about, such an attitude is not currently a problem at SRC. One big aid for avoiding an entitlement attitude is accountability. Employees at SRC are clearly held accountable for the line item(s) to which they contribute and are expected to accept that responsibility. They also realize that an error by one employee can negatively impact many fellow employees.

Another potential threat specific to SRC's culture is the possibility of a substantial increase in turnover (from retirements) in the top ranks of the firm in the not too distant future. Most companies worry considerably about the effects of a new CEO, for example. In terms of the culture at SRC, this is particularly true given the dominant influence of Jack Stack. But SRC has two important characteristics that, it is hoped, help to mitigate this risk. First, as previously mentioned, SRC has strong succession plans in place. This means that at least some of these potentially top-level vacant positions will be filled with insiders that already know, understand, and buy-in to the SRC culture. Even when it comes to outside hires, SRC has recently been very successful at bringing people into the fold—of course trying to take care that there is a cultural fit before they are brought on. And, in the case of Mr. Stack, it is likely that even if he does step down from his position as CEO, he will continue to have involvement with the organization (unless it seems he is stepping on the new CEO's toes).

Despite the potential pitfalls, SRC's culture appears to be resilient—even through tough times. Unless there is a breach of trust between upper management and the other employee-owners, the culture is likely to remain a cornerstone of competitive advantage for SRC into the foreseeable future.

Shared Leadership

Jack Stack once lamented, "Well, I came to the conclusion that in the years that I had been in business, I never, ever read a guru that said, 'Maybe people don't like working for somebody else.'" But rather than fight this seldom acknowledged fact, Stack decided to turn it to SRC's advantage. The result? SRC's extensive, proactive implementation of "shared leadership." At SRC, it really is the case that employees are not just employees; they're actually *employee-owners*. And this distinction is very important since the shared leadership philosophy empowers employee-owners with decision-making discretion and authority. Consequently, employees are responsible for completing their daily activities and, in the course of so doing, empowered to make many decisions for themselves. Of course, productivity would suffer if employees were completely unaccountable for their behaviors and actions; SRC realizes this and addresses it through policies and procedures. Finding and maintaining the right balance between empowerment and formal policy is not always easy, but SRC expends great effort to maintain the appropriate balance.

The challenge of shared leadership involves continually building leaders throughout the organization. And although not all employees want the pressure or have the commitment requisite for leadership, at SRC an unexpectedly large number do. Indeed, as Stack notes, about three-quarters of employees embrace the chance to be leaders. Not surprisingly, then, decision-making authority and leadership permeate all levels of the organization. As Rich Armstrong, president of the Great Game of Business, puts it, it is critical that upper management earnestly believes "that the people in the organization can actually contribute to the success and it's not just the top guys that make all the strategic decisions and that's all that matters."

But shared leadership at SRC isn't based solely on a decentralized decision-making philosophy. Trust and accountability are two additional values that contribute to SRC's widespread shared leadership foundation. In order for employees to bring their thoughts and ideas into the open, they have to believe that upper management will respect them, appreciate them, and, when deemed advantageous, act on them. SRC's management absolutely understands this and responds by turning employee belief into organizational reality. Not surprisingly, this two-way communication of trust can lead to great outcomes for SRC. Consider that some of the best ideas for changing SRC's remanufacturing processes have come from those who do the remanufacturing. In fact, ideas come from all parts of the organization. Jack Stack likes to recount the story of how a janitor at SRC gave him critical financial advice, which he willingly listened too (only later finding out that the man was a former stock broker), and the company ended up benefiting from this exchange.

On the other hand, employees recognize that shared leadership means that they will be held responsible and accountable for their actions and decisions. For instance, employees who grind crank shafts at SRC don't just have the important technical skills to do the job—they also know how their actions affect other elements of the organization. And perhaps most importantly, as employee-owners, they understand how it affects the bottom-line and why it is in their own best interest to take charge and be accountable for better outcomes. Because of this, there's not a lot of finger-pointing at SRC if something does go wrong.

Another important way SRC promotes shared leadership throughout the organization includes the use of committees, giving employees the opportunity to take leadership roles. For example, each of SRC's business units has an Ownership Culture Committee. This committee largely consists of a group of employees tasked with helping to spread an attitude of ownership throughout their unit, particularly among their new employees. A second example is the ESOP Steering Committee, another entity comprised entirely of employees. This committee is designed to help facilitate a widespread understanding and acceptance of the ESOP among employees. If past performance is any indicator, it appears that this committee has been very effective.

In one sense, a culture of shared leadership is not surprising in a company such as SRC. As we described briefly, much of the leadership mindset is due to the nature of the internal environment at SRC. Essentially, SRC's employees are also owners who think like business people, understand their financial impact on the company, and are empowered to do something about it. In return for the substantial degree of responsibility that accompanies this shared leadership, employees are given the opportunity, support, and encouragement to "rise to the top and bring their ideas to the top." And, of course, there are also the financial benefits of being a part owner of SRC.

Human Resources

In many organizations, the human resource function plays little or no role in the strategic plans of the firm, instead often laboring under second-class status. At SRC, this is emphatically not the case. Thus, in this section, we look at the important role of HR at SRC from the perspective of the various HR functions.

Job Analysis Functions

As is the case with most large companies, the HR department at SRC is responsible for the creation and monitoring of the numerous job descriptions. In a firm like SRC that provides employees input and leeway in their job behaviors, this is a considerable challenge for HR personnel. Although clearly not practical from a policy standpoint, Boatright says that Jack Stack would prefer that all job descriptions say "business person." This is understandable given that SRC explicitly treats employees as individual business persons. The need for strong HR job description-related actions has increased in recent years. Indeed, delineating responsibilities and skills has become more of a focus given SRC's extensive succession planning.

An important area of HR focus in SRC involves policies concerned with employee conduct in the organization. As Boatright indicates, incidents involving harassment, discrimination, and conflicts of interest are rare at SRC. This may well be due to the HR department's efforts at detailing and communicating expected employee conduct. SRC has a code of conduct as well as an employee handbook that, among other things, contains the firm's ethics policy. SRC also conducts harassment training.

Recruiting

Currently, SRC uses web services like Career Builder and Monster for recruiting. SRC also taps into talent from nearby universities through the use of careers fairs. In fact, the organization wants to become more involved in this area, particularly via building relationships with institutions that have specific programs geared toward its needs. However, much of the recruiting is by word of mouth. Since the employees tend to be strong proponents of the firm, current SRC employees represent an excellent recruiting tool. In a similar vein, family members of employees are commonly recruited as well.

One area that can be troublesome for SRC when recruiting new employees is that they do not pay top wages. This liability is strongly offset by the tremendous success of the ESOP: prospective employees can reasonably believe that if they make a career for themselves at SRC, they can have substantial financial assets when they cash out their ESOP shares. It should also be noted that SRC has a strong benefits package and, according to many employees, there are important intangibles (such as career stability) that go along with working at SRC. Also of relevance is the fact that Springfield, Missouri, has a low cost of living.

Selection

The selection process varies throughout the organization, but it is fair to say that it is an extensive process. Many of the current employees at SRC are empowered to make decisions regarding new hires. And because of the strong ownership mentality that permeates the firm, these employees are motivated to identify those prospects most likely to succeed at SRC. The following quotes from Keith Boatright and Ron Guinn embody this idea:

> It's an investment and at the end of the day, one, you need to make darn sure that you need the position and two, whoever you get, you basically write 'em a check, giving them your equity. So, if you're gonna go and do that, you better make darn sure that that investment is understood by everybody.
> And there's a subliminal thing that happens there because once you get in the door, your panel of peers to get you in here, feel some level of responsibility because they brought you here and they told the rest of their partners that this is the person that we want so. I've definitely have seen people that served on panels' kind of take someone under their wing and make sure they get started well. They got a vested interest in seeing that person succeed.

An additional method that SRC sometimes employs is through the use of temporary positions and internships as a sort or proving ground, before individuals are hired permanently. This allows both the firm and the prospective employee a chance to try each other out, so to speak.

Training

Rich Armstrong describes the importance of training to SRC by noting that SRC has "doubled-down" on training. Indeed, the organization engages in many different types and modes of training, working diligently toward achieving the right mix of training and identifying the most efficient schedule for the various training programs. Examples of types of training at SRC include: financial literacy training, technical training, and entrepreneurship training. Among the different forms these training may take are classroom training, simulations, experiential activities, and informal training.

One of the most important aspects of training at SRC is training for the Great Game of Business. This area of training helps SRC's employee-owners to think and act like business people. By becoming financially literate and developing a deeper understanding of how SRC conducts its business activities, employees are capable of much more than merely focusing on the basic task requirements of their job. Because they are able to see the big picture, they are in a position to make contributions that can better the organization. Such contributions frequently have the potential to positively affect both the employee's and the firm's bottom line. For instance, they may suggest a process improvement that will save money or they may foresee and help the company avoid a potential safety issue. Training the employee-owners at SRC to be business people rather than just task masters really provides SRC with a competitive advantage and sets it apart from its competition.

At SRC, employees are also trained on the specifics of their employee stock ownership plan. Employees are typically given information about the ESOP via their employee handbook when they are first hired. Their ESOP knowledge increases over time as they come to experience the ownership culture, and when they are closer to being able to see the financial rewards of the ESOP.

Cross-training is another important aspect of SRC's training approach. Cross-training employees not only allows them to broaden their horizons and keeps them interested, but also serves to help protect jobs in difficult times. That is, if a cross-trained employee is currently working in an area that is seeing a downturn (and having consequent overstaffing), the employee could be transferred to another area in which they are needed more, rather than being laid off.

All employees are given the freedom to cross-train by completing modules referred to as "Initiatives" at SRC. Some typical modules in financial literacy at SRC Electrical are "Yo-Yo" Training, the GGOB Two-Day Experience, GGOB Profitability, Small Staff Huddle, Read Jack Stack's Books, Financial Literacy Exam I: Income Statement, Financial Literacy Exam II: Balance Sheet, GGOB Committee Member, and "Cash 2 Cash." This training is displayed on a large wall chart so everyone can see who has completed what.

In addition to these formal training mechanisms, a great deal of informal, hands-on training happens at SRC. Often an informal mentor of sorts will help instruct the employees on the proper way to do the tasks and processes required by their job. These employees are paired together until the trainee can perform the job on his/her own, which frequently requires some form of certification. This type of informal training can involve a new employee or an existing employee who is learning a new skill. Also, it's not uncommon for an experienced employee to try to help a new employee settle in and get up to speed, especially if the experienced employee was involved in the hiring decision of that employee in the first place. Many SRC employees feel a responsibility not just to the new employee whom they advocated, but also to other existing employees. This is so because their support of the new employee says, in effect, that they view the new employee as a potentially good partner, one with whom they're comfortable sharing the equity in the firm.

Also of note is the fact that SRC also offers tuition reimbursement. This is offered for technical and managerial development. Local institutions offer not only degrees, but also certificates in areas ranging from particular engineering expertise, to purchasing, to managerial disciplines. And along these lines, SRC has a partnership for a specialized technical program with a local college. Various divisions of SRC have also been considering a formal mentor program, and a leadership program is another training idea that may materialize in the future.

Many benefits can be seen from the training that goes on at SRC, and as such it is viewed as a valuable investment rather than a required expense. Training is viewed as part of the growth engine at SRC. As Jack Stack puts it, "And so what we began to see is the more we taught, the more people taught us." Well-trained employees are needed in place to facilitate growth within a current SRC business, and they are needed to manage the spinoff/creation of new business. The employees are also winners since they gain skills, advance in the organization, and generally make themselves more valuable.

Evaluation and Retention

Currently, SRC is experimenting with a performance evaluation system that allows attractive opportunities for personal growth. This system involves the development of "profiles" that has the potential to really help employees understand where their interests lie. Traditional performance evaluations are also conducted at SRC and vary by division and position. Some are done by supervisor rating, and some are done collaboratively. Interestingly, for most divisions, performance evaluations are not tied to base compensation. However, there is a lot of performance recognition done within the organization. For example, luncheons, outings, and awards are used to highlight exceptional achievements. Importantly, SRC employees generally understand the business, and thus they know on their own when they are failing or succeeding and are typically motivated to act accordingly.

Such investments in finding the right people to work at SRC are consistent with SRC's commitment to protect and keep those employees once they are found. Another way to try to keep employees is through offering valued benefits. Some of the benefits include generous holidays, bereavement leave, wellness programs, tuition reimbursement, and retirement planning sessions. Training is also valued by employees. At SRC numerous training opportunities are available for employees to better themselves.

Thus, SRC has many HR activities aimed at successfully recruiting and retaining the very best employees. Of course, this does not mean that nobody ever leaves. Recent combined voluntary and involuntary turnover has run about 13 percent annually. From an involuntary side, SRC tries to hire the right people in the first place, but there are cases where employees just don't work out. Such terminations are primarily decided at the division level. The corporate level usually has little involvement other that of legal and procedural oversight. As far as voluntary turnover is concerned, it should be pointed out SRC has had a lot of retirements recently, particularly in their more mature businesses, and they hire quite a few current college students (in more entry level positions) that SRC knows eventually move on. However, they have to guard against their talent being hired away, given that they work for a well-respected company.

Operations

The introduction to this case study noted the wide variety of businesses and industries SRC is involved in, ranging from logistics support to employee and management business training. But its bread and butter, so to speak, involves the field of remanufacturing. The various companies within SRC Holdings remanufacture products such entire engines, fuel systems, and electric components for a wide variety of markets including agriculture, trucking, mining, and various construction-related fields. Remanufacturing is a very complex process, much more so than repairing or rebuilding. In remanufacturing the product is completely disassembled and cleaned; all parts are inspected and, if necessary, replaced. The endpoint of this process is to return the entity involved to its OEM specifications. SRC's expertise in the remanufacturing process is so high that the remanufactured product is as good as or, in many cases, better than new. Indeed, the warranty will meet or exceed that of a new product.[4]

Given here are a few of the policies, in this instance from SRC Electrical, that are instrumental in driving SRC's remanufacturing activities and doing so with surprisingly efficient asset utilization:

- Closely monitoring and working with vendors (shipments are checked and vendors can go on probation if there are issues)
- Using ideas from lean techniques like the "5 S's" (sort, set in order, shine, standardize, and sustain)[5]
- Updating testing equipment
- Giving incentives for employees to cross-train and/or gain additional skills

As previously described SRC Holdings considers its employees to be a source of competitive advantage. Thus it is not surprising that, in terms of operations and productions, the organization places a high priority on employee safety. From updating equipment to using more people-friendly solvents for cleaning, SRC is constantly working to keep its employees safe. Employees watch out for themselves and for others where safety is concerned. Importantly, safety is not taken as a given—it is constantly monitored and reinforced. Recognizing achievements, as well as concerns, regarding safety are commonplace at meetings. In sum, then, SRC Holdings' operations can be characterized as quality, efficient, and safe.

Marketing and Sales

SRC's marketing and sales teams have two major roles. The first involves developing and maintaining strong relationships with the existing customer base. Many of SRC's products are sold to vehicle OEMs such as John Deere and CNH Global. Inasmuch as SRC strives to establish and build long-term relationships with these OEMs, they typically view and treat them as valued partners rather than just customers. A very important element in this area is that, unlike some of their competitors, SRC usually doesn't compete with the OEMs by selling to the aftermarket. Instead, they help the OEMs and their dealers to sell SRC's products, a policy that is very much appreciated by their partners.

Not surprisingly, much of the marketing done is by word of mouth, frequently via the relationship building with the OEMs. Building strong, solid relationships motivates the OEMs to portray SRCs as a credible supplier to end consumers. From SRC's perspective, confidence in the quality of its products, services, and customer service is the foundation on which these relationships are built, a confidence that ultimately carries through to the OEMs. Consider, for example, that it is not uncommon for customers to come to the plants and talk to the people actually doing work on their products and work orders. Indeed, oftentimes SRC's customers will cultivate relationships with specific SRC employees, to the point that they know they can call on them specifically if they have a question or concern about their orders.

The second major role marketing at SRC focuses on involves developing forecasts and communicating this information to everyone in the organization. The basis for these forecasts is their strong knowledge of both their existing client base and of those firms that are not yet customers. Twice a year the sales and marketing personnel compile and analyze information about their customers, potential customers, and competitors and present this information to everyone in the company so that firm-wide forecasts and projections can be made. These reports are relied on heavily for workforce planning, product planning, and determining strategies on how to best rise above the competition. Clearly, the marketing and sales teams at SRC play a pivotal role in the firm's strategies and tactics.

Finance and Financial Sharing

As noted in the introduction to this case, SRC started out on a very precarious financial footing. But through the hard work of its employees and the insight of top management, SRC not only survived, but established a financial track record of envious proportions. Indeed, recently Jack Stack indicated he would not be surprised to see SRC's stock price more than double over the next couple of years.

Currently, SRC's revenues are approaching the $437 million mark and it expects to generate earnings of about $24 million in 2013. Furthermore, in order to save on interest costs, it intends to eliminate long-term debt (while maintaining a reasonable level of operating debt) in the next few years. Finally, its current ratio tends to be fairly high, and its capital intensity tends to be relatively low for its type of business, both positive signs. Thus, even in these currently troubled economic times, SRC is a financially sound organization.

In one sense, given that most employee-owners at SRC actually understand the financials and how their personal actions play a role in the financial health of the organization, it's not overly surprising that the firm is financially solid. Of course, it's also not surprising that these employee-owners want to share in the company's financial rewards. What may be a bit surprising, however, is that, for the most part, the basic compensation at SRC is neither explicitly tied to the financial health of the company nor to the employee's specific contribution to the bottom line (i.e., it is not based on employee performance evaluations).

There are however, several ways that the financial gains of the company are shared with employees, the most obvious being through the shared ownership in the employee stock ownership plan. Consider, for example, that if an employee participated in the ESOP when it started in 1983 and continued through until this current year, they would have at least $400,000 in the ESOP. And although SRC has had opportunities to sell the corporation outright to external buyers—thus making a lot of money for many SRC executives—the firm has remained loyal to its original employee-centered principles. In fact, SRC has recently moved from being partly owned by management to being 100 percent owned by employees via the ESOP. This was done for a number of reasons, with the main one being to pass the company on to the next generation. Currently, the plan is functioning such that each year after the company valuation, the employees receive shares proportional to their eligible compensation.

In addition to the ESOP, SRC provides several other financial benefits to its employees. Three of these are options, bonuses, and the 401K program. The option program, which is currently being redesigned, gives greater incentives for performance to some department managers as well as to various executives. Bonuses are tied to specific goals across the various SRC units and serve to incentivize desired behaviors on the part of the employees. The 401K program involves a 5 percent match of employee contributions by the firm. Beyond simply monetary considerations, the 401K program is beneficial in two other ways: first, it gives the employees the ability to diversify their portfolio beyond their ESOP stock holdings; and second, the assets in the employee's 401K can be used to help secure a loan if so desired. In sum, the strong financial position of SRC provides numerous financial benefits for the employees as well.

Innovation

In today's globally competitive environment, organizational growth through innovation and development is absolutely imperative. A commitment to innovation drives product enhancement, the creation of new product lines, and occasionally even the development of an SRC company. Innovative developments affecting internal processes can lower costs, which, in turn, typically lead to more sales, higher revenues, more profit, and overall organizational growth.

None of this is lost on SRC where emphasizing innovation contributes mightily to its tremendous track record of growth. Jack Stack captures this sentiment when he states that SRC is trying to "train people to build innovation. Build creativity. Build entrepreneurs." Not surprisingly, a great deal of research, development, and experimentation takes place at SRC. SRC enjoys a large degree of success with its innovation efforts, frequently more so than its competitors. These efforts are typically successful because the employee-owners at SRC have a strong understanding of the business aspects of their innovative ideas. And since employees realize that they will be accountable for their ideas—and have to convince others as to their merits—the likelihood that good ideas come to the table is increased. In terms of innovation and growth, SRC is able to leverage the knowledge and incentives for success that drive their employee-owners.

By way of illustration, consider the following account involving irrigation systems. Employees at SRC worked out how to convert a diesel engine for an irrigation system into a natural gas engine, potentially a very important innovation. At most firms, a technical innovation such as this would be the end point of the employee contribution. Not so at SRC. Employees calculated that such an engine could provide up to 67 percent savings and pay for itself within six months. They also helped to come up with a marketing plan. They knew who to work with and how to go about making this specific innovation profitable. This brief account highlights an important benefit of employee-owners: they have both the knowledge and the incentives to propose, realize, and deliver innovative technical solutions as well as the financial and overall business savvy to understand the business implications of their ideas and solutions.

As a result of such fruitful innovation, growth has been a common occurrence at SRC and, despite the projected weakness of the overall US economy, is expected to continue into the near term as well. It should be noted, however, that growth frequently poses challenges for an organization. At SRC, two such challenges involve hiring new employees. Often, a large influx of employees can make integration into the organizational culture a substantial difficulty. Because SRC has such a strong and unique culture, it is not uncommon for new hires to struggle in truly understanding and buying into the overall corporate philosophy. A second concern involves finding enough people with the requisite qualifications and experience. Keith Boatright believes this is the biggest obstacle to growth at SRC. Consequently, SRC is trying to recognize that although they definitely want to foster innovation and expansion, it's probably wise if the firm's growth is carefully managed and controlled.

External Environment

There are many forces in the external environment that play important roles in how SRC makes its business decisions and executes its various strategies. At the business environment level, these forces include key constituents such as customers, suppliers, and competitors. At the larger, more general environmental level, trends in the economic and political-legal aspects of our society can have significant impact on SRC's activities.

In terms of the business environment, an important factor involves those businesses with which SRC has established and maintained relationships. As noted previously, SRC typically has developed strong relationships with many of the OEMs to which it sells parts. Recall that whereas most other remanufactures and manufacturers fiercely compete with the OEMs by selling parts to retailers, SRC has generally chosen to not take this route. Developing and maintaining relationships with suppliers is also emphasized strongly at SRC. The increased degree of coordination that frequently results from these strong relationships is particularly valuable in addressing the challenges stemming from the global nature of SRC's supply chain.

An interesting strategy employed by SRC involves the development of joint ventures. SRC leverages its unique cultural and managerial expertise by establishing partnerships with companies often with the intent of selling its stake in the joint venture once the new entity is up and running. An important benefit to SRC from successful joint ventures is the resultant liquidity from the buyouts. And apparently SRC has become pretty efficient and successful with these efforts. As Rhonda Alexander, Great Game of Business coach development and trainer at SRC, puts it, "Nobody gets a joint venture from zero to sixty faster than SRC." And the 60 she is referring to is $60 million.

The competitive element is also another important variable in SRC's business environment. Competitive pressures keep prices low and margins tight for most of the industries in which SRC operates. As such it is critical that SRC keeps a close watch on its competition and, more broadly, on the industries in which they operate. Consequently SRC expends much time and energy monitoring and collecting information on their competition. For example, they have scoreboards where they keep score of the strengths and weakness of their main competitors as they relate to those of SRC. They gather information from company websites, from customers, from banks that follow particular industries, and from the competition itself through relationships they have established over time.

The overall labor market currently poses substantial challenges to SRC as well. As mentioned earlier, because of its record of growth and its unique employee-ownership culture, it can be challenging for SRC to find the right talent to staff its various companies. Consider, also, that the United States currently has a relative shortage of engineering talent in the labor pool. For firms with heavy engineering needs like SRC, this poses a particular challenge. Jack Stack also points out that the decline in standing of science, technology, engineering, and math in the American educational system is particularly harmful to the business models and ideas championed by SRC. And as a final observation, consider that SRC's employees are often highly sought after by other firms, thus forcing SRC to be very vigilant with their employee retention efforts.

Moving from the business level to the general environment, as Stack sees it, one of the biggest external threats to SRC is the decreasing economic freedom in the United States. In particular, the increasing influence of government entities via business regulations is a serious challenge for SRC. SRC has traditionally been very successful at creating new businesses: amazingly, in less than 30 years, they created over 60 businesses. In the current climate, however, creating a new business has become increasingly difficult because there are more regulations and greater costs required to start the business in the first place. Existing SRC businesses feel the regulatory burden also—the Environmental Protection Agency (EPA) and other governmental agencies have been increasingly tough on products like the engines that SRC remanufactures. Also, a benefit that SRC has enjoyed in the past was the flexibility from employees being able to fill in where needed across the different companies in SRC's portfolio. This too has become more difficult because of increased regulation. Current trends in regulation have not been favorable to the ESOP business structure as well. And the administrative costs associated with simply following and understanding new rules and regulations are considerable and are likely to keep growing in the future.

Finally, the most recent economic downturn needs mention. SRC was fully expecting the economic downturn, and they felt they were mostly ready for it. SRC management is constantly examining possible business contingencies and developing potential plans for when tough times do occur. In fact, SRC intentionally developed their portfolio of businesses and products to include those that fare better in a fast growing economy and others that perform relatively better in a downturn. For example, early on the truck market was huge for SRC, but they soon realized that that particular market faces a recession every six years or so. They also realized that car parts went up during these recessions and acting on these two pieces of knowledge, diversified their business portfolio accordingly. All of this is not to say that SRC has been unscathed in the current economic slowdown. Various divisions at SRC have needed to invoke less than desirable measures such as temporary cuts in employee hours and/or pay. Nevertheless, SRC works hard to live up to its cultural values by making every effort to keep jobs first and foremost, even if that means other benefits have to be cut to do so. It's important to point out that such measures are perhaps better accepted at SRC than at other firms since their employee-owners understand why the measures are necessary in the first place and how they affect the overall health of the organization.

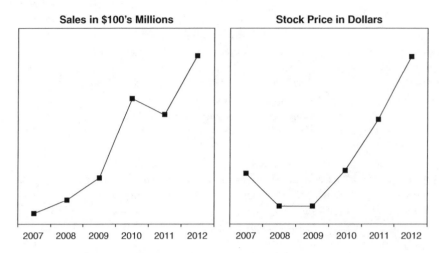

Figure 7.1 SRC Holdings' sales and stock evaluation, 2007–2012.
Data for graphs provided by SRC Holdings, Inc.

The impact of the Great Recession of 2008 on SRC Holdings' sales and stock evaluation can be seen in figure 7.1. Its sales grew through the recession. This is counterintuitive for a company that produces capital goods.

In figure 7.1, the valuation of the stock dropped during the recession. This occurred because stock valuation models for privately held corporations take into account both the general economic conditions as well as corporate performance. In this case corporate performance improved during 2008 and 2009, but the decrease in economic conditions dropped the estimated value of the stock. By 2011 and 2012, due to continued strong performance of SRC Holdings and improved economic conditions, the stock set records in both years as to estimated value.

The Great Game of Business

SRC's Great Game of Business initiative incorporates many of the previously discussed business elements including employee financial literacy, shared leadership, employee equity ownership, and incentive-type pay plans. But it also emphasizes two additional elements that are critical to SRC's success: transparency and the spirit of competition. Although the GGOB is practiced across the numerous business units of SRC, its specific implementation varies from division to division. This flexibility allows each division to determine what works best for them. And if a division tries something new or unique and is very successful, the knowledge of this new best practice is shared with other divisions.

A very important GGOB element involves tapping into the tremendous productive potential of competition. As the name "Great Game of Business" implies, business is viewed as a game in which SRC employees are competing in a variety of settings as a team against competitors. According to Jack Stack, there are three components to a game. First, there are rules that, in business, are set by the marketplace. Second, there is a scorecard. In the business environment, the scorecard consists typically of financial metrics. Generally speaking, the better the financials, the more successful the business. Third, there must be a prize for the winners—the "what's in it for me?" aspect that drives the individual employees. At SRC, this prize takes many forms including increased wages, better benefits, bonuses, and ownership equity in an organization that is succeeding.

The use and emphasis on games is ingrained at SRC. Although the ultimate game is to win in the marketplace, games are conducted at many different levels and across a variety of time frames. At the macro level, for example, games will be run at the corporate or division level and focus on a couple of key metrics for an entire year. This focus is called the Critical Number. On a smaller level, games may also involve a specific area of the production floor and focus on achieving a particular outcome across a time period as short as a week or a month. The point here is that games are used at all levels of the organization and can be very specifically targeted. And, as Stack notes, they serve multiple purposes in the organization: "We use games to incent or reward or to teach? And to have people have fun in their organization. And every time they see that goal, they throw that fist up in the air and they feel good about what they did."

In order for the use of games to be successful, the employees that comprise the various teams must know what is going on. Consequently, transparency is another important cornerstone of the Great Game and is prevalent throughout the SRC companies. Indeed, in "Open-Book Management: Its Promise and Pitfalls," author Tim Davis says that Jack Stack at SRC implemented the first complete system of open book management, a popular management technique with transparency as its core.[6] Consider that daily cash statements are available to any employee, and everybody sees weekly financials. About every two weeks there are meetings between the corporate staff and general management to look at their strategies and identify any potential issues that may be surfacing. Additionally, there are company-wide monthly meetings where reports from not only the corporate staff, but from various committees are shared with employees. And every six months, the sales and marketing teams make a presentation to everyone in the company. Also, information and education about the ESOP is consistently available to employees.

It's important to point out here that a lot of the information made readily available to the employees does not come from the top to be disseminated downward. Actually, much of the financial information originates at the bottom, is consolidated at the top, and then is redistributed back out to the employees. Thus, financial numbers are tracked and conveyed upward from the department that is actually responsible for them in the first place. Jack Stack explains why this is so important: "And there's no ands, ifs, or buts and no grey areas when you're talking about numbers. And numbers are nothing more than stories about people. That's all numbers really are, all right? So if you can get people to own the numbers, you know, then you can begin the process of knowing where to make a difference."

A prime illustration of this transparency-driven, bottom-up ownership of the numbers at SRC involves something known as the "weekly huddle." At SRC Electrical, for example, the weekly huddle is intense, informative, competitive, and fun. Employees file into a room and sit in teams of ten or so with their binders of relevant information. Some general announcements and discussion occur regarding safety and quality issues. Then attention turns to the giant income statement template on the wall. Employees responsible for particular line items are called upon to report those numbers. When calculations are necessary, the teams plunge in to find the answer. As the income statement is generated, the leader of the huddle calls attention to any areas of concern or interest that need to be discussed. After the income statement is complete and discussion subsides, the huddle concludes with a game of "SRCopoly," a fun, though competitive, way of facilitating better understanding of their balance sheet. Witnessing a huddle in action definitely allows for an understanding of how and why employees at SRC so readily buy in to the ideas and behaviors needed for the continued success of the organization.

It is important to point out here that consistency, repetition, and the development of predictable behavioral patterns are also important keys to the success of the Great Game of Business. These aspects allow employees to know what to expect when, help to reinforce accountability for everyone, and assist employees in better understanding the business side of issues via repetition and application of key concepts.

Underlying the effectiveness of GGOB elements such as the huddle is the training employees receive early in their employment. In the first few weeks at SRC an employee is typically trained on the more traditional aspects of their job, as might be expected. However, they also sit in on the huddles and, as a result, begin to develop an understanding that there is much more to their job than the standard expectations. At that point they start more formal training, beginning with the basics of financial literacy, the basics of the Great Game, and on to employee ownership and SRC's ESOP.

The corporate-wide advocacy of transparency, consistency, and employee education was present at the genesis of the Great Game of Business. Looking back, Jack Stack recalls:

> And so I promised—I said very, very simply, "We will teach you everything that we learn." We told them that the objective is the company. That the responsibility will be to create a great company. We knew that they could create great products. We knew that they could create great services. We spent *115 years* [Manufacturing in America] teaching people how to do their job. I would contend, it's probably the 1 percent we talk about all the time that really understands the metrics of the company, all right?
>
> And so I promised them. I said "Look, we will, we will build programs. We will accelerate the learning process. We will get you to the point of getting it where you can interpret the metrics and then you can make the decisions based on the facts and figures that you have in front of you."

And this approach has worked. The GGOB has been so successful that there is now a Great Game of Business division at SRC, as previously mentioned. Not only do they handle much of the formal internal training across the various SRC companies, but they also offer their expertise to other unrelated companies by teaching them how they would benefit from implementing the ideas and concepts comprising the GGOB. And there is plenty of external praise from the business media suggesting that it's doing a good job spreading the GGOB philosophy to the American business community at large. *BusinessWeek*, noting that representatives from more than 4,000 companies across the globe have visited the GGOB unit in Springfield, called SRC a "Management Mecca." GGOB has recently been featured on *MSNBC* and in the *New York Times* and the *Wall Street Journal*. The book *Great Game of Business* was selected as one of the "100 Best Business Books of All-Time." In July of 2013, it was reissued as an expanded twentieth-anniversary edition. It debuted as the number one best-selling business paperback according to the Neilson Book Scan. In addition, the GGOB philosophy was chosen as the *Number 1 Most Innovative Business Practice* by *INC* magazine.[7]

Looking Forward

The worker-owners at SRC recognize that they face many challenges and obstacles about which they have spoken candidly. They believe that the GGOB philosophy that they practice every day throughout SRC Holdings will allow them to overcome whatever challenges and obstacles may come their way. Apparently, over 4,000 companies and multiple media outlets at least partially agree with the worker-owners. The GGOB philosophy and it associated practices represent a departure from business as usual. Will the unusual become the usual?

Notes

1. www.srcreman.com. Retrieved: July 8, 2012.
2. newstreaming.com. Retrieved: July 8, 2012.
3. www.srclogisticsinc.com/homepage.php. Retrieved: July 8, 2012.
4. www.srcreman.com. Retrieved: August 2, 2012.
5. www.epa.gov/lean/environment/methods/fives.htm. Retrieved: August 6, 2012.
6. Davis, T. R. V. 1997. Open-book management: Its promises and pitfalls. *Organizational Dynamics,* Winter: 7–20.
7. http://greatgame.com/about/. Retrieved: July 9, 2012.

CHAPTER 8

Herman Miller: Unrelenting Pursuit of Reinvention and Renewal

Frank Shipper, Karen P. Manz, Stephen B. Adams, and Charles C. Manz

Herman Miller is widely recognized as the leader in the office furniture industry and has built a reputation for innovation in products and processes since D. J. De Pree became president over 90 years ago. Herman Miller is one of only four companies and the only non-high-technology enterprise named to *Fortune*'s "Most Admired Companies" and "The 100 Best Companies to Work For" lists and also to *FastCompany*'s "Most Innovative Companies" list in both 2008 and 2010. The three high-technology organizations selected for these lists were Microsoft, Cisco, and Google. Unlike most firms, especially those in mature industries and most of its office furniture rivals, Herman Miller has pursued a path distinctively marked by reinvention and renewal.

Will its propensity for using innovation to reinvent and renew its business once again allow the company to flourish and grow? How far and how fast might the company be able to push its annual revenues above the 2013 level of $1.78 billion?

Background

Herman Miller's roots go back to 1905 and the Star Furniture Company, a manufacturer of traditional-style bedroom suites in Zeeland, Michigan. In 1909, it was renamed Michigan Star Furniture Company and hired Dirk Jan (D. J.) De Pree as a clerk. D. J. De Pree became president in 1919. Four year later D. J. convinced his father-in-law, Herman Miller, to purchase the majority of shares and renamed the company Herman Miller Furniture Company in recognition of his support.[1]

In 1927, D. J. De Pree committed to treating "all workers as individuals with special talents and potential." This occurred after he visited the family of a millwright who had died unexpectedly. At the visit, the widow read some poetry. D. J. De Pree asked the widow who the poet was and was surprised to learn it was the millwright. This led him to wonder whether the millwright was a person who wrote poetry or if he was a poet who was also a millwright. This story is part of the cultural folklore at Herman Miller that continues to generate respect for all employees and fuels the quest to tap the diversity of gifts and skills held by all.

In 1930, the country was in the Great Depression and Herman Miller was in financial trouble. D. J. De Pree was looking for a way to save the company. At the same time, Gilbert Rhode, a designer from New York, approached D. J. De Pree and told him about his design philosophy. He then asked for an opportunity to create a design of a bedroom suite at a fee of $1,000. When D. J. De Pree reacted negatively to such a fee, Gilbert Rhode suggested an alternative payment plan, 3 percent royalty on the furniture sold. D. J. agreed figuring that there was nothing to lose.

A few weeks later, D. J. received the first designs from Rhode. Again, he reacted negatively. He "thought that they looked as if they had been done for a manual training school and told him so." Gilbert Rhode explained in a letter his design philosophy—first, "utter simplicity: no surface enrichment, no carvings, no moldings," and second, "furniture should be anonymous. People are important, not furniture. Furniture should be useful." Rhode's designs were antithetical to traditional designs, but D. J. saw merit in them and this set Herman Miller on a course of designing and selling furniture that reflected a way of life.

In 1942, Herman Miller produced its first office furniture—a Gilbert Rhode design referred to as the Executive Office Group. He died two years later and De Pree began a search for a new design leader. Based largely on an article in *Life* magazine, he hired George Nelson as Herman Miller's first design director.

In 1946, Charles and Ray Eames, designers based in Los Angeles, were hired to design furniture. In the same year, Charles Eames designs were featured in the first one-man furniture exhibit at New York's Museum of Modern Art. Some of his designs are now part of the museum's permanent collection.

In 1950, Herman Miller under the guidance of Dr. Carl Frost, professor at Michigan State University, was the first company in the state of Michigan to implement a Scanlon Plan. Underlying the Scanlon Plan are the "principles of equity and justice for everyone in the company." Two major functional elements of Scanlon Plans are the use of committees for sharing ideas on improvements and a structure for sharing increased profitability. The relationship between Dr. Frost and Herman Miller continued for more than four decades.

During the 1950s, Herman Miller introduced a number of new furniture designs including those by Alexander Girard, Charles and Ray Eames, and George Nelson. Specifically, the first molded plastic (fiberglass) chairs were introduced and the Eames lounge chair and ottoman were unveiled on NBC's

Figure 8.1   Eames lounge chair and ottoman.
Courtesy of Herman Miller.

Home Show with Arlene Francis, a precursor to the *Today Show* (figure 8.1). Also in the 1950s, Herman Miller began its first overseas foray selling its products in the European and Latin American markets.

In 1962, D. J. became chairman of the board and his son, Hugh De Pree, became president and chief executive officer (CEO). D. J. had served for over 40 years as the president.

During the 1960s, many new designs were introduced both for home and the workplace. The most notable design was the Action Office System, the world's first open-plan modular office system of movable panels and integrated desk and storage components. By the end of the 1960s, Herman Miller had formed a subsidiary in England with sales and marketing responsibility throughout England and the Scandinavian countries. Also, it had established dealers in South and Central America, Australia, Canada, Europe, Africa, the Near East, and Japan.

In 1970, Herman Miller went public and made its first stock offering. The stock certificate was designed by the Eames Office staff. In 1971, it entered the health/science market, and in 1976, the Ergon chair, its first chair design based on scientific observation and ergonomic principles, was introduced. In 1979, in conjunction with the University of Michigan, it created the Facility Management Institute that helped established the profession of facility management. Also, in the 1970s, Herman Miller continued to expand overseas and introduce new designs.

By 1977, over half of Herman Miller's 2,500 employees worked outside of the production area. Thus, the Scanlon Plan needed to be overhauled since it had been designed originally for a production workforce. In addition, employees worked at multiple US and overseas locations. Thus, in 1978, an ad hoc committee of 54 people from nearly every segment of the company was elected to examine the need for changes and to make recommendations. By January 1979, the committee had developed a final draft. The plan established a new organization structure based on work teams, caucuses, and councils. All employees were given an opportunity to discuss it in small group settings. On January 26, 1979, 96 percent of the employees voted to accept the new plan.

After 18 years Hugh De Pree stepped down, and Max De Pree, Hugh's younger brother, became chairman and chief executive officer in 1980. In 1981, Herman Miller took a major initiative to become more efficient and environmentally friendly. Its Energy Center generated both electrical and steam power to run its million square foot facility by burning waste.

In 1983, Herman Miller established a plan whereby all employees became shareholders. This initiative appeared to be a natural outgrowth from the adoption of the Scanlon Plan in 1950. Employees from 1983 forward shared in both the ownership and the profits of the firm.

In 1984, the Equa chair, a second chair based on ergonomic principles, was introduced along with many other designs in the 1980s. In 1987, the first non-family member, Dick Ruch, became chief executive officer.

By the end of the decade, the Equa chair was recognized as a "Design of the Decade" by *Time* magazine. Also, in 1989, Herman Miller established its Environmental Quality Action Team to "coordinate environmental programs worldwide and involve as many employees as possible."

In 1990, Herman Miller was a founding member of the Tropical Forest Foundation and was the only furniture manufacturer to belong. That same year, it discontinued using endangered rosewood in its award-winning Eames lounge chair and ottoman, and substituted cherry and walnut from sustainable sources. It also became a founding member of the US Green Building Council in 1994. Some of the buildings at Herman Miller have been used to establish Leadership in Energy & Environmental Design (LEED) standards. Because of its environmental efforts, Herman Miller received awards from *Fortune* magazine and the National Wildlife Federation in the 1990s.

In the 1990s, Herman Miller again introduced some groundbreaking designs. In 1994, it introduced the Aeron chair, which had been added to the New York Museum of Modern Art's permanent Design Collection (figure 8.2) even prior to its public launch. In 1999, it won the "Design of the Decade" from *Business Week* and the Industrial Designers Society of America.

In 1992, J. Kermit Campbell became Herman Miller's fifth CEO and president. He was the first person from outside the company to hold either position. In 1995, Campbell resigned and Mike Volkema was promoted to CEO. At the time the industry was in a slump and Herman Miller was being restructured. Sales were approximately $1 billion. Mike Volkema had been with Meridian, a company Herman Miller acquired in 1990, for seven years. So with approximately 12 years of experience with either Herman Miller or its subsidiary and at the age of 39 Mike Volkema became CEO.

In 1994, Herman Miller for the Home was launched to focus on the consumer market. It reintroduced some of its modern classic designs from the 1940s, 1950s, and 1960s as well as new designs. In 1998, hmhome.com was set up to tap this market.

Figure 8.2   Aeron chair.
Courtesy of Herman Miller.

Additional marketing initiatives were taken to focus on small and mid-size businesses. A network of 180 retailers was established to focus on both consumers and small businesses and a 3-D design computer program was made available to mid-size customers. In addition, order entry was digitally linked among Herman Miller, suppliers, distributors, and customers to expedite orders and improve their accuracy.

The First Decade of the Twenty-First Century

The first decade of the twenty-first century started off spectacularly with record profits and sales in 2000 and 2001. The board of directors approved a special one-time option grant of 100 shares to each nonexecutive, North American-based employee in June of 2000, and the Eames molded plywood chair was selected as a "Design of the Century" by *Time* magazine. Sales had more than doubled in the six years that Mike Volkema had been CEO.

Then the dot.com bubble burst and the events of September 11, 2001, occurred in the United States. Sales dropped 34 percent from $2,236,200,000 in 2001 to $1,468,700,000 in 2002. In the same years profits dropped from $144,100,000 to losses of $56,000,000. In an interview for *FastCompany* magazine in 2007, Volkema said, "One night I went to bed a genius and woke up the town idiot."

Although sales continued to drop in 2003, Herman Miller returned to profitability in that year. To do so, Herman Miller had to drop its long-held tradition of lifelong employment. Approximately 38 percent of the workforce was laid off. One entire plant in Georgia was closed. Mike Volkema and Brian Walker, then president of Herman Miller North America, met with all the workers to tell them what was happening and why it had to be done. One of the workers being laid off was so moved by their presentation that she told them she felt sorry for them having to personally lay off workers.

To replace the tradition of lifelong employment, Mike Volkema, with input from many, developed what is referred to as "the new social contract." He explains it as follows:

> We are a commercial enterprise, and the customer has to be on center stage, so we have to first figure out whether your gifts and talents have a match with the needs and wants of this commercial enterprise. If they don't, then we want to wish you the best, but we do need to tell you that I don't have a job for you right now.

As part of the implementation of the social contract, benefits such as educational reimbursement and 401K plans were redesigned to be more portable. This was done to decrease the cost of changing jobs for employees whose gifts and talents no longer matched customer needs.

Sales and profits began to climb from 2003 to 2008. In 2008, even though sales were not at an all-time high, profits were. During this period, Brian Walker became president in 2003 and chief executive officer in 2004. Mike Volkema became chairman of the board in 2004. They continue in these positions in 2014.

Then Herman Miller was hit by the Great Recession of 2008. Sales dropped 19 percent from $2,012 billion in 2008 to $1,630 billion in 2009. In the same years profits dropped from $152 million to $68 million. In March 2012, Mark Schurman, director of External Communications at Herman Miller, predicted that the changes made to recover from the 2001–2003 recession would help it better weather the 2007–2009 recession.

In 2010, Herman Miller introduced the SAYL line of chairs. The big selling point for the line was its affordability while offering a full-featured, ergonomically sound chair for which Herman Miller was famous. Although it was approximately half as expensive as the Aeron chair, it continued Herman Miller's tradition of design excellence. It won the "Product Design of the Year" from the 2010 International Design Awards (IDA) jury, a Silver 2011 International Design Excellence Award (IDEA) award in the category of "Office & Productivity," and a 2011 Core77 Design Award in the "Furniture and Lighting—Professional Designer" category.

In 2012, Herman Miller codified its long practiced organizational values and published them on its website under a page entitled "What We Believe." These beliefs are intended as a basis for uniting all employees, building relationships, and contributing to communities. Those beliefs as first articulated in 2005 are as follows:

- *Curiosity and exploration*: These are two of our greatest strengths. They lie behind our heritage of research-driven design. How do we keep our curiosity? By respecting and encouraging risk, and by practicing forgiveness. You can't be curious and infallible. In one sense, if you never make a mistake, you're not exploring new ideas often enough. Everybody makes mistakes: we ought to celebrate honest mistakes, learn from them, and move on.

- *Engagement*: For us, it is about being owners—actively committed to the life of this community called Herman Miller, sharing in its success and risk. Stock ownership is an important ingredient, but it's not enough. The strength and the payoff really come when engaged people own problems, solutions, and behavior. Acknowledge responsibility, choose to step forward and be counted. Care about this community and make a difference in it.

- *Performance*: Performance is required for leadership. We want to be leaders, so we are committed to performing at the highest level possible. Performance isn't a choice. It's up to everybody at Herman Miller to perform at his or her best. Our own high performance—however we measure it—enriches our lives as employees, delights our customers, and creates real value for our shareholders

- *Inclusiveness*: To succeed as a company, we must include all the expressions of human talent and potential that society offers. We value the whole person and everything each of us has to offer, obvious or not so obvious. We believe that every person should have the chance to realize his or her potential regardless of color, gender, age, sexual orientation, educational background, weight, height, family status, skill level—the list goes on and on. When we are truly inclusive, we go beyond toleration to understanding all the qualities that make people who they are, that make us unique, and most important, that unite us.

- *Design*: Design for us is a way of looking at the world and how it works—or doesn't. It is a method for getting something done, for solving a problem. To design a solution, rather than simply devising one, requires research, thought, sometimes starting over, listening, and humility. Sometimes design results in memorable occasions, timeless chairs, or really fun parties. Design isn't just the way something looks; it isn't just the way something works, either.

- *Foundations*: The past can be a tricky thing—an anchor or a sail, a tether or a launching pad. We value and respect our past without being ruled by it. The stories, people, and experiences in Herman Miller's past form a unique foundation. Our past teaches us about design, human compassion, leadership, risk taking, seeking out change, and working together. From that foundation, we can move forward together with a common language, a set of owned beliefs and understandings. We value our rich legacy more for what it shows us we might become than as a picture of what we've been.

- *A better world*: This is at the heart of Herman Miller and the real reason why many of us come to work every day. We contribute to a better world by pursuing sustainability and environmental wisdom. Environmental advocacy is part of our heritage and a responsibility we gladly bear for future generations. We reach for a better world by giving time and money to our communities and causes outside the company; through becoming a good corporate citizen worldwide; and even in the (not so) simple act of adding beauty to the world. By participating in the effort, we lift our spirits and the spirits of those around us.

- *Transparency*: Transparency begins with letting people see how decisions are made and owning the decisions we make. So when you make a decision, own it. Confidentiality has a place at Herman Miller, but if you can't tell anybody about a decision you've made, you've probably made a poor choice. Without transparency, it's impossible to have trust and integrity. Without trust and integrity, it's impossible to be transparent.

All employees are expected to live these values. In a description of the current processes that follow, numerous examples of these values in action can be found.

Herman Miller Entering 2013

As 2013 began, Herman Miller introduced Living Office (figure 8.3). The Living Office is not a singular product, or even a collection of designs, but rather a research-based, contemporary understanding and philosophy toward the open office, specifically identifying the universal work modes and interior settings that enable the highest performance and greatest satisfaction among both individual users and their organizations. But unlike prior open offices, it could also be viewed as the antithesis of the cubicle office about which Scott Adams, the creator of Dilbert, lampoons frequently in his comic strip. The Living Office was featured on CBS Sunday Morning on May 19, 2013. It was described as having design elements akin to a living room or Starbucks. Robert Propst, the designer of the Action Office in the 1960s for Herman Miller, was quoted on the show saying, "Not all organizations are as intelligent and progressive, they make little bitty cubicles and stuff people in them, barren rat hole places." In contrast, the Living Office is designed to foster—camaraderie, connection, spontaneous interaction, and group expression—attributes that Herman Miller believes are essential

> to attract, nurture, enable, and retain the talent that will drive innovation and execution, and bring an organization's strategy to life. In turn, they must give individuals something that can be had nowhere else: a personal, even spiritual connection to work and colleagues; a platform for increased productivity and effectiveness; and a more naturally human experience of interaction and creation.[2]

Also, featured on the CBS show was Brian Walker's new wall-less Living Office workstation. The Living Office concepts, and multiple new office landscape systems, were introduced to the industry at the NeoCon tradeshow in June 2013 to critical acclaim.

Management

Mike Volkema is currently the chairman of the board, and Brian Walker is the president and chief executive officer. Walker's compensation was listed by *Bloomberg Businessweek* as $693,969 in 2011. Compensation for CEOs of five competitors was listed by *Bloomberg Businessweek* to range from $777,923 to $973,154. Walker and four other top executives at Herman Miller took a 10 percent pay cut in January 2009, and they took another 10 percent pay cut along with all salaried workers in March 2009. The production workers were placed on a nine days in two weeks work schedule effectively cutting their pay by 10 percent as well. A little over one year later in June 2010 most employees' pay cuts and furloughs were rescinded. That the executives would take a pay cut before all others and twice as much is just one way human compassion is practiced at Herman Miller.

According to the Securities and Exchange Commission (SEC) regulations a publicly traded company must have a board of directors. By corporate policy,

Figure 8.3   Scenes from a Living Office.
Courtesy of Herman Miller.

the majority of the 14 members of the board must be independent. To be judged an independent, the individual as a minimum must meet the NASDAQ National Market requirements for independent directors (NASDAQ Stock Market Rule 4200). In addition, the individual must not have any "other material relationship with the company or its affiliates or with any executive officer of the company or his or her affiliates." Moreover, any

> transaction between the Company and any executive officer or director of the Company (including that person's spouse, children, stepchildren, parents, stepparents, siblings, parents-in-law, children-in-law, siblings-in-law and persons sharing the same residence) must be disclosed to the Board of Directors and is subject to the approval of the Board of Directors or the Nominating and Governance Committee unless the proposed transaction is part of a general program available to all directors or employees equally under an existing policy or is a purchase of Company products consistent with the price and terms of other transactions of similar size with other purchasers.

Furthermore,

> It is the policy of the Board that all directors, consistent with their responsibilities to the stockholders of the company as a whole, hold an equity interest in the company. Toward this end, the Board requires that each director will have an equity interest after one year on the Board, and within five years the Board encourages the directors to have shares of common stock of the company with a value of at least three times the amount of the annual retainer paid to each director.

In other words, board members are held to standards consistent with the corporate beliefs and its employee stock ownership plan (ESOP) program.

Although Herman Miller has departments, the most frequently referenced work unit is a team. Paul Murray, then director of Environmental Health and Safety, explained their relationship as follows: "At Herman Miller, team has just been the term that has been used since the Scanlon Plan and the De Prees brought that into Herman Miller. And so I think that's why we use that almost exclusively. The department—as a department, we help facilitate the other teams. And so they aren't just department driven." Teams are often cross-functional. Membership on a team is based on the ability to contribute to that team. As Gabe Wing, then Design for the Environment lead chemical engineer and more recently Murray's successor, described it, "You grab the appropriate representative who can best help your team achieve its goal. It doesn't seem to be driven based on title. It's based on who has the ability to help us drive our initiatives towards our goal."

Teams are often based in product development. When that product has been developed, the members of that team are redistributed to new projects. New projects can come from any level in the organization. At Herman Miller leadership is shared. One way in which this is done is through Herman Miller's concept of "talking up and down the ladder." Workers at all levels are encouraged to put forth new ideas. As Rudy Bartels, environmental specialist said, "If they try something that they have folks there that will help them and be there for them. And by doing that, either—whether that requires a presence of one of us or an email or just to say, 'Yeah, I think that's a great idea.' That's how a lot...in the organization works." Because the workers feel empowered, a new manager can run into some behavior that can startle them. As Paul Murray recalled,

> I can remember my first day on the job. I took my safety glasses off...and an employee stepped forward and said, "Get your safety glasses back on." At *Company X, Company Y,*[3] there was no way would they have ever talked to a supervisor like that, much less their supervisor's manager. It's been a fun journey when the work force is that empowered.

The beliefs are also reinforced through Herman Miller Cares, a philanthropic arm of the company that manages gifts from the company's foundation and encourages employee participation through community service. True to its practice of shared leadership, Herman Miller Cares distributes funds and other resources based in part on employee involvement. As explained by Jay Link, then manager of Corporate Giving, the program works as follows:

> Our first priority is to honor organizations where our employees are involved. We believe that it's important that we engender kind of a giving spirit in our employees, so if we know they're involved in organizations, which is going to be where we have a manufacturing presence, then our giving kind of comes alongside organizations that they're involved with. So that's our first priority.

In addition, all employees can work 16 paid hours a year with the charitable organization of their choice. Herman Miller sets goals for the number of employee volunteer hours contributed annually to its communities. Progress toward meeting those goals is reported to the CEO.

The Environmental Affairs Team has responsibility for such areas as solid waste recycling and designing products from sustainable resources. It was formed in 1988 with the authorization of Max De Pree. One success that it has is in the reduction of solid waste taken to the landfill. In 1991, Herman Miller was sending 41 million pounds to the landfill. By 1994 it was down to 24 million pounds and by 2008 it was reduced to 3.6. Such improvements are both environmentally friendly and cost-effective.

These beliefs are carried over to the family and community. Gabe Wing related how: "I've got the worst lawn in my neighborhood. That's because I don't spread pesticides on it, and I don't put fertilizer down." He went on to say how his wife and he had to make a difficult decision the summer of 2009 because Herman Miller has a policy "to avoid PVC (polyvinyl chloride) wherever possible." In restoring their home, they chose fiber cement board over PVC siding even though it was considerably more costly. Gabe went on say, "Seven years ago, I didn't really think about it."

Rudy Bartels is involved in a youth soccer association. As is typical, it needs to raise money to buy uniforms. Among other fund-raisers that it has done is collecting newspapers and aluminum cans. As he tells it, "When I'll speak they'll say, 'Yeah, that's Rudy. He's Herman Miller. You should—you know we're gonna have to do this.'"

These beliefs carry over to all functional areas of the business. Some of them are obviously beneficial, and some of them are simply the way Herman Miller has chosen to conduct its business.

Marketing

Herman Miller products are sold internationally through wholly owned subsidiaries in various countries including Canada, France, Germany, Italy, Japan, Mexico, Australia, Singapore, China, India, and the Netherlands. Its products are offered through independent dealerships. The customer base is spread over more than 100 countries.

Herman Miller uses so-called green marketing to sell its products. For example, the Mirra chair introduced in 2003 with PostureFit Technology was developed from its inception to be environmentally friendly (cradle-to-cradle principles). These chairs are made of 45 percent recycled materials, and 96 percent of their materials are recyclable. In addition, they are assembled using 100 percent renewable energy. In 2003, *Architectural Record* magazine and *Environmental Building News* named the Mirra chair as one of the "Top 10 Green Products." Builders that use Herman Miller products in their buildings can earn points toward LEED certification. In 2014 the next generation Mirra

Figure 8.4   Herman Miller Mirra chairs in a case room at the Franklin P. Perdue School of Business.

Kathy D. Pusey.

Figure 8.5 Herman Miller Mirra chairs in a conference room at the Franklin P. Perdue School of Business.

Kathy D. Pusey.

2 chair has set a new reference point, further reducing the chair's total mass by 20 percent while enhancing comfort and performance, and increasing the weight-bearing capacity to accommodate users up to 350 pounds.

Herman Miller segments its markets into work, specialty and consumer, healthcare, education, and international. Many products are marketed across segments. Some examples of how its chairs are used in the educational market are contained in figures 8.4 and 8.5.

To enhance its marketing analysis and promotions, Herman Miller also segments it markets geographically. The North American, Asian, EMEA, and Latin American markets are all tracked independently.

Production/Operations

Herman Miller is globally positioned in terms of manufacturing operations. In the United States, its manufacturing operations are located in Michigan, Wisconsin, Georgia, and North Carolina. In Europe, it has considerable manufacturing presence in the United Kingdom, its largest single national market outside of the United States. In Asia, it has manufacturing operations in DongGuan and Ningbo, China.

Herman Miller manufactures products using a system of lean manufacturing techniques collectively referred to as the Herman Miller Performance System (HMPS; figure 8.6). It strives to maintain efficiencies and cost savings by minimizing the amount of inventory on hand through a JIT (just-in-time) process. Some suppliers deliver parts to Herman Miller production facilities five or six times per day.

Production is order-driven with direct materials and components purchased as needed to meet demand. The standard lead time for the majority of its products is 10 to 20 days. As a result, the rate of inventory turnover is high. These combined factors could cause inventory levels to appear relatively low in relation to sales volume. A key element of its manufacturing strategy is to limit fixed production costs by outsourcing component parts from strategic suppliers. This strategy has allowed it to increase the variable nature of its cost structure while retaining proprietary control over those production processes that Herman Miller believes provide a competitive advantage. Because of this strategy, manufacturing operations are largely assembly-based.

The success of the Herman Miller Performance System was the result of much hard work. For example, in 1996, the Integrated Metals Technology (IMT) subsidiary was not doing well. IMT supplied pedestals to its parent company, Herman Miller. Its prices were high, lead time long, and quality was in the 70 percent range. The leadership of the subsidiary decided to hire the consulting arm of Toyota, and thus Toyota Supplier Support Center (TSSC)

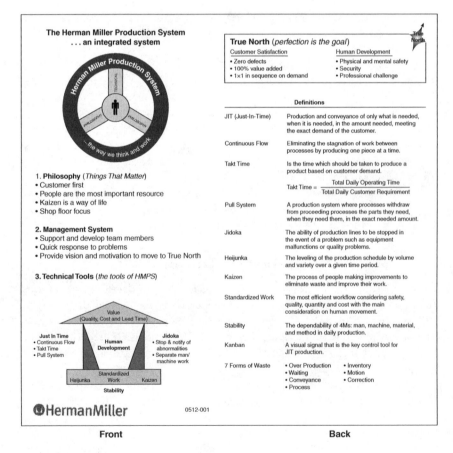

Front   Back

Figure 8.6   The Herman Miller production system.
Courtesy of Herman Miller.

was hired. Significant improvements were made by inquiring, analyzing, and "enlisting help and ideas of everyone." For example, quality defects in parts per million decreased from approximately 9,000 in 2000 to 1,500 in 2006. Concurrently, on-time shipments improved from 80 percent to 100 percent and safety incidents per 100 employees dropped from ten to three per year.

The organizational values mentioned earlier were incorporated into the design of The Greenhouse, Herman Miller's main production facility in Michigan. The building was designed to be environmentally friendly. For example, it takes advantage of natural light and landscaping. Native plants are grown without the use of fertilizers, pesticides, or irrigation. After the facility was opened, aggressive paper wasps found the design to their liking. Employees and guests were frequently stung. In keeping with Herman Miller beliefs a solution was sought. Through research it was learned that honey bees and paper wasps are incompatible. Therefore, 600,000 honey bees and their 12 hives were co-located on the property. The wasps soon left. Two additional consequences were that due to pollination by the bees the area around the facility blooms with wild flowers and a large amount of honey is produced. Guests to the home office are given a four-ounce bottle of the honey symbolizing its corporate beliefs.

Human Resource Management

Human resource management is considered a strength for Herman Miller. It has frequently been listed on *Fortune*'s "100 Best Companies to Work For," including in the year 2010. It had approximately 278 applicants for every job opening. In the 2009 downturn, Herman Miller cut its workforce by more than 15 percent, reduced pay of the remaining workforce by at least 10 percent, and suspended 401K contributions. Employees praised management for "handling the downturn with class and doing what is best for the collective whole" according to *Fortune* magazine's February 8, 2010, issue. *Fortune* also estimated voluntary turnover to be less than 2 percent. On June 1, 2010, the time-and-pay cuts of 10 percent begun in the spring of 2009 were discontinued due to Herman Miller's quick turnaround.

Herman Miller practices "business as unusual," as pointed out many years ago by Hugh De Pree, former president, and it appears to pay off in both good and tough times. Herman Miller shares the gains as well as the pains with its employees, especially in regards to compensation.

Pay is geared to firm performance and it takes many forms at Herman Miller. As in other companies all employees receive a base pay. In addition, all employees participate in a profit sharing program whereby employees receive stock based on the company's annual financial performance. Employees are immediately enrolled in this plan upon joining Herman Miller and are vested after one year. Profit sharing is based on corporate performance because as one employee explained:

> The problem we see is you get to situations where project X corporately had a greater opportunity for the entirety of the business, but it was difficult to tell these folks that they needed to sacrifice in order to support the entirety of the

business when they were being compensated specifically on their portion of the business. So you would get into some turf situations. So we ended up moving to a broader corporate EVA (Economic Value Added) compensation to prevent those types of turf battles.

The company offers an employee stock purchase plan (ESPP) through payroll deductions at a 15 percent discount from the market price. Also, all employees are offered a 401K where each employee receives a 100 percent match for the first 3 percent of salary that he or she contributes. Again, employees are immediately eligible to participate in this plan upon joining Herman Miller and immediately vested. The company match was suspended in 2009 due to the recession. Through the profit sharing and the ESPP, the employees own approximately 8 percent of the outstanding stock.

Furthermore, all employees receive a retirement savings plan whereby the company deposits into individual 401K accounts an additional 4 percent of compensation. Employees are immediately eligible to participate in this plan upon joining Herman Miller, but are required to participate for five years before being vested. Additionally, a length of service bonus is paid after five years of employment. Finally, the company pays a universal quarterly bonus to all nonexecutive employees based on the company's performance against EBITDA objectives. Executive bonuses are paid annually. This is in addition to the other compensation programs, including profit sharing, with the same calculation used to determine both employee and executive bonus potential.

Thus, pay takes a number of forms at Herman Miller, but most all forms are at least partially, if not wholly, contingent on corporate performance. One employee summed up pay as follows, "You can dip into Herman Miller's pocket several times based on the performance of the company."

Brightscope, a financial information company that focuses primarily on retirement plans and wealth management, rates Herman Miller's profit sharing and 401K plan as having the lowest fees in the industry while being above average in company generosity, participation rate, and account balances. According to Form 5500, a report that all companies with more than 100 employees in a retirement plan have to file with the federal government under ERISA (Employee Retirement Income Security Act), the average employee balance was approximately $79,000 as of December 31, 2012. The amount in an individual's account can vary significantly depending on tenure with the company and level of compensation.

Other benefits also take many forms at Herman Miller. Employees are given a range of benefits as they are in many organizations. Some are, however, quite different from those found in other organizations such as a $100 rebate on a bike purchase. It is justified as "part of our comprehensive program designed for a better world around you." Other benefits that Herman Miller provides that are identified by the company as "unique" are:

- 100 percent tuition reimbursement
- Flexible schedules: job sharing, compressed workweek, and telecommuting options

- Concierge services—from directions, dry cleaning, greeting cards, or a meal to take home, these services make it easier for you to balance work and home life
- Employee product purchase discounts
- On-site services including massage therapy, cafeterias, banking, health services, fitness center, fitness classes, and personal trainers

Herman Miller, in keeping with its beliefs, offers extensive wellness benefits including fitness facilities or subsidized gym memberships, health services, employee assistance programs, wellness programs/classes, and health risk assessments. The other benefits that are offered that most large organization also offer include health insurance, dental insurance, vision care plan, prescription plan, flexible spending accounts, short- and long-term disability, life insurance, accidental death and disability insurance, and critical illness/personal accident/long-term care. All benefits are available also to domestic partners.

Herman Miller has changed its pension plans to a defined contribution retirement program from a defined benefits program. It stated in its 2013 letter to shareholders that such a change will "strengthen its balance sheet while returning greater cash to shareholders." The changeover is expected to be completed in 2014.

When appropriate, Herman Miller promotes people within the organization. Education and training are seen as key to preparing employees to take on new responsibilities. For example, Rudy Bartels, environmental specialist, as well as multiple vice presidents began their careers at Herman Miller on the production floor.

Three other benefits are unique to Herman Miller. First, every family that has or adopts a child receives a Herman Miller rocking chair. Second, every employee that retires after 25 years with the company and is 55 years or older receives an Eames lounge chair. Third, Herman Miller has no executive retreat, but it does have an employee retreat, The Marigold Lodge, on Lake Michigan. This retreat is available to employees for corporate related events, such as retirement parties and other celebrations, and in some instances includes invited family and guests.

Finance

During normal economic times, financial management at Herman Miller would be considered conservative. Through 2006, its leverage ratio was below the industry average and its times interested earned ratio was over twice the industry average. Due to the drop-off in business the debt-to-equity ratio rose precipitously from 1.18 in 2006 to 47.66 in 2008. To improve this ratio, over 3 million shares were sold in fiscal year 2009.[4] In the four previous fiscal years, Herman Miller had been repurchasing shares. The debt-to-equity ratio was reduced to 3.81 by the end of 2009. To improve short-term assets, dividends per share were cut by approximately 70 percent and capital expenditures were reduced to zero in 2009 (financial statements for years 2006–2010 can be found in tables 8.1 and 8.2).

Table 8.1 Consolidated balance sheets

Consolidated Balance Sheets (In Millions, Except Share and Per Share Data)	June 1, 2013	June 2, 2012	May 28, 2011	May 29, 2010	May 30, 2009	May 31, 2008
Assets						
Current Assets:						
Cash and cash equivalents	$82.7	$172.2	$142.2	$ 134.8	$ 192.9	$ 155.4
Short-term investments	—	—	—	—	—	15.7
Marketable securities	10.6	9.6	11.0	12.1	11.3	—
Accounts receivable	178.4	159.7	193.1	144.7	148.9	209.0
Less allowances in each year	—	—	—	4.4	7.3	5.6
Inventories, net	76.2	59.3	66.2	57.9	37.3	55.1
Deferred income taxes	22.1	20.4	21.2			
Prepaid expenses and other taxes	8.1	17.6	25.4	45.2	60.5	58.0
Other	21	16.5	12.6	—	—	—
Total current assets	**399.3**	**455.3**	**478.1**	**394.7**	**450.9**	**493.2**
Property and equipment:						
Land and improvements	26.7	19.2	19.9	19.4	18.8	19.0
Buildings and improvements	160.0	146.0	149.5	147.6	137.4	139.4
Machinery and equipment	558.3	533.7	531.0	546.4	552.0	547.4
Construction in progress	20.3	12.6	13.0	10.7	9.8	17.4
Gross property and equipment	**765.3**	**711.5**	**713.4**	**724.1**	**718.0**	**723.2**
Less: accumulated depreciation	(581.2)	(555.5)	(544.3)	(548.9)	(538.8)	(526.9)
Net property and equipment	**184.1**	**156.0**	**169.1**	**175.2**	**179.2**	**196.3**
Goodwill and indefinite-lived intangibles	227.0	144.7	110.4	132.6	72.7	40.2
Indefinite-lived intangibles	62.3	39.3	23.2	25.0	11.3	—
Other amortizable intangibles, net	48.0	31.1	24.3	43.1	53.2	—
Other assets	25.8	11.0	9.3			53.5
Total assets (in $)	**946.5**	**837.4**	**808.0**	**770.6**	**767.3**	**783.2**

Liabilities and shareholders' equity

Current liabilities:

Unfunded checks$	—	—	6.4	4.3	3.9	8.5
Current maturities of long-term debt	—	—	—	100.0	75.0	—
Accounts payable	130.1	115.8	112.7	96.3	79.1	117.9
Accrued liabilities	159.9	136.2	153.1	112.4	124.2	184.1
Total current liabilities	290.0	252.0	272.2	313.0	282.2	310.5
Long-term debt, less current maturities	250.0	250.0	250.0	201.2	302.4	375.5
Pension and post-retirement benefits	39.6	37.9	51.6	—	—	—
Deferred compensation	—	12.1	11.0	—	—	—
Other liabilities	47.4	37.1	24.6	176.3	174.7	73.8
Total liabilities	**627.0**	**589.1**	**603.0**	**690.5**	**759.3**	**759.8**
Shareholders' equity:						
Preferred stock, no par value (10,000,000 shares authorized, none issued)	—	—	—	—	—	—
Common stock, $0.20 par value (240,000,000 shares authorized, 58,375,931, 55,048,858, 57,002,733 and 53,826,061 shares issued and outstanding in 2012, 2011, 2010 and 2009, respectively	11.7	11.7	11.6	11.4	10.8	11.1
Additional paid-in capital	102.9	90.9	82.0	55.9	5.9	—
Retained earnings	331.1	288.2	218.2	152.4	129.2	**76.7**
Accumulated other comprehensive loss	(124.3)	(140.6)	(104.2)	(136.2)	(134.1)	**(60.1)**
Key executive deferred compensation	(1.9)	(1.9)	(2.6)	(3.4)	(3.8)	**(4.3)**
Total shareholders' equity	**319.5**	**248.3**	**205.0**	**80.1**	**8.0**	**23.4**
Total liabilities and shareholders' equity (in $)	**946.5**	**837.4**	**808.0**	**770.6**	**767.3**	**783.2**

Table 8.2 Consolidated statements of operations

Consolidated Statements of Operations (In Millions, Except Per Share Data)	June 1, 2013	June 2, 2012	May 28, 2011	May 29, 2010	May 30, 2009	May 31, 2008
Net sales (in $)	1,774.9	1,724.1	1,649.2	1,318.8	1,630.0	2,012.1
Cost of sales	1,169.7	1,133.5	1,111.1	890.3	1102.3	1,313.4
Gross margin	605.2	590.6	538.1	428.5	527.7	698.7
Operating expenses:						
Selling, general, and administrative	429.2	394.9	366.0	317.7	330.8	395.8
Restructuring expenses	1.2	5.4	3.0	16.7	28.4	5.1
Design and research	59.9	52.7	45.8	40.5	45.7	51.2
Total operating expenses	490.3	453.0	414.8	374.9	404.9	452.1
Operating earnings	114.9	137.6	123.3	53.6	122.8	246.6
Other expenses (income):						
Interest expense	17.2	17.5	19.9	21.7	25.6	18.8
Interest and other investment income	(0.4)	(1.0)	(1.5)	(4.6)	(2.6)	(3.8)
Other, net	0.9	1.6	2.4	1.7	.9	1.2
Net other expenses	17.7	18.1	20.8	18.8	23.9	16.2
Earnings before income taxes and minority interest	97.2	119.5	102.5	34.8	98.9	230.4
Income tax expense	28.9	44.3	31.7	6.5	31.0	78.2
Equity loss from nonconsolidated affiliates, net of taxes	(0.1)					
Minority interest, net of income tax					(.1)	(0.1)
Net earnings (in $)	**68.2**	**75.2**	**70.8**	**28.3**	**68.0**	**152.3**
Earnings per share—basic	1.17	$1.29	$1.24	$.51	$1.26	$2.58
Earnings per share—diluted	1.16	$1.29	$1.06	$.43	$1.25	$2.56

Source: Herman Miller's 10_K's.

152

For fiscal year 2008, 15 percent of Herman Miller's revenues and 10 percent of its profits were from non-North American countries. In 2007, non-North American countries accounted for 16.5 percent of revenues and approximately 20 percent of Herman Miller's profits.

Financially, Herman Miller holds true to its beliefs. Even in downturns, it invests in research and development. In the dot.com downturn it invested tens of millions of dollars in R&D. Inside Herman Miller this investment project was code named "Purple."

In the December 19, 2007, issue of *FastCompany* magazine commenting on this project, Clayton Christensen, Harvard Business School professor and author of *The Innovator's Dilemma,*[5] is quoted as saying, "Barely one out of 1000 companies would do what they did. It was a daring bet in terms of increasing spending for the sake of tomorrow while cutting back to survive today."

Herman Miller continues to receive awards both for the design of its product and for its treatment of its employees. For example, in 2011, it was designated as one of ten design icons in *FastCompany*'s "Thirty Companies That Get It," and in 2012, Herman Miller was recognized with the Huntington Pillar Award, given by the Women's Resource Center to companies that demonstrate outstanding dedication to empowering women in the workplace.

Accessories Team: An Example of HM's Strategy, Leadership, and Beliefs in Action

Herman Miller's Accessories Team was an outgrowth of project "Purple." One of the goals of this project was to stretch beyond the normal business boundaries. Office accessories is one area in which Herman Miller has not been historically involved even though it is a big part of what the independent dealers sell. Once identified, "Robyn (Hofmeyer) was tapped to put together a team to really explore this as a product segment that we could get more involved with," according to Mark Schurman, director of External Communications at Herman Miller.

In 2006, Robyn established the team by recruiting Larry Kallio to be the head engineer and Wayne Baxter to lead sales and marketing. Together, they assembled a flexible team to launch a new product in sixteen months. They recruited people with different disciplines needed to support that goal. Over the next two years, they remained a group of six. Some people started with the team and then as it got through that piece of work, they went on to different roles within the company. The team during its first eight months met twice a week for half a day. Twenty months out it met only once a week.

The group acted with a fair amount of autonomy, but it did not want complete autonomy because "we don't want to be out there completely on our own because we have such awesome resources here at Herman Miller," Robyn explained. The group reached out to other areas in the company when different disciplines were needed for a particular product, and tapped people that could allocate some of their time to support it.

Wayne described what happened on the team as follows: "We all seem to have a very strong voice regarding almost any topic; it's actually quite fun and quite dynamic. We all have kind of our roles on the team, but I think other than maybe true engineering, we've all kind of tapped into other roles and still filled in to help each other as much as we could." Another member of the accessories team described decision-making as follows:

> If we wanted to debate and research and get vary scientific, we would not be sitting here talking about the things that we've done, we'd still researching them. In a sense, we rely upon our gut a lot, which I think is, at the end of the day just fine because we have enough experience. We're not experts, but we're also willing to take risks and we're also willing to evolve,

Thus, leadership and decision-making was shared both within the team and across the organization. Ideas and other contributions to the success of the team were accepted from all sources.

Out of this process has grown what is known as the "Thrive Collection." The name was chosen to indicate the focus on the individual and the idea of personal comfort, control, and ergonomic health. Products included in the collection are the Ardea® Personal Light, the Leaf® Personal Light, Flo® Monitor Arm, and C2® Climate Control. All of these are designed for improving the individual's working environment. Continuing Herman Miller's tradition of innovative design the Ardea light earned both Gold and Silver honors from the International Design Excellence Awards (IDEA) in June 2010.

The Industry

Office equipment (classified by Standard & Poor's Research Insight as "Office Services & Supplies") is an economically volatile industry. The office furniture segment of the industry was hit hard by the recession. The AKTRIN Research Institute stated in a 2003 industry report, "Corporate profitability is one of the most forthright determinations for business office furniture acquisition." Neither the industry nor Herman Miller has returned to their sales peaks of 2007. Herman Miller's stock market value of $1,647,752,000 at the end of 2012 represented 18.26 percent of the total stock market value of the industry identified by Standard & Poor's Research Insight as" Office Services & Supplies." Both figures represented increases over 2011, 2010, 2009, and 2008 of $1,077,920,000, $1,437,979,000, $1,095,322,000, and $765,389,000, respectively, for stock market value, and 11.68 percent, 12.78 percent, 11.14 percent, and 8.88 percent of total stock market value of the industry, respectively. According to Hoover's, Herman Miller's top three competitors are HNI Corporation, Haworth, Inc., and Steelcase, Inc. All three of these are different than what Hoover's listed as the top three competitors for Herman Miller in 2012. The Great Recession of 2008 created significant turmoil for the industry. Herman Miller, however, appears to have strengthened its position as the industry leader.

The industry has been impacted by a couple of trends. First, telecommuting has decreased the need of large companies to have office equipment for all employees. Some companies such as Oracle have a substantial percentage of their employees telecommuting. The majority of Jet Blue reservation clerks telecommute. Second, more and more employees are spending increasing hours in front of computer screens than ever before. Due to this trend, the need for ergonomically correct office furniture has increased. Such furniture helps to decrease fatigue, injuries, and medical conditions such as carpel tunnel syndrome.

As with most industries, the cost of raw materials and competition from overseas has had an impact. These trends tend to impact the low-cost producers more than the high quality producers.

The Future

In a June 24, 2010, press release Brian Walker, chief executive officer, stated,

> One of the hallmarks of our company's history has been the ability to emerge from challenging periods with transformational products and processes. I believe our commitment to new products and market development over the past two years has put us in a position to do this once again. Throughout this period, we remained focused on maintaining near-term profitability while at the same time investing for the future. The award-winning new products we introduced last week at the NeoCon tradeshow are a testament to that focus, and I am incredibly proud of the collective spirit it has taken at Herman Miller to make this happen.

Three years later, at the 2013 NeoCon tradeshow, Herman Miller continued to be recognized for its design excellence as the newly introduced Living Office swept the Best of NeoCon showroom design awards, and five of its new designs received Best of NeoCon recognition.

The financial results in 2013 (tables 8.1 and 8.2) and first quarter 2014 (tables 8.3–8.5) suggest that this strategy is working. In the 2013 Proxy

Table 8.3 Herman Miller, Inc. condensed consolidated statements of operations (unaudited; dollars in millions, except per share data)

	Nine Months Ended			
	August 31, 2013		September 1, 2012	
Net sales	$468.1	100.0%	$449.7	100.0%
Cost of sales	298.1	63.7%	300.0	66.7%
Gross margin	170.0	36.3%	149.7	33.3%
Operating expenses	130.9	28.0%	114.9	25.6%
Restructuring expenses	—	0.0%	0.5	0.1%
Operating earnings	39.1	8.4%	34.3	7.6%
Other expense, net	4.6	1.0%	4.3	1.0%
Earnings before income taxes	34.5	7.4%	30.0	6.7%
Income tax expense	12.0	2.6%	10.0	2.2%
Net earnings	—	0.0%	—	0.0%
Earnings per share—basic	$0.38		$0.34	
Weighted average basic common shares	58,727,106		58,318,702	
Earnings per share—diluted	$0.38		$0.34	
Weighted average diluted common shares	59,336,842		58,615,662	

Source: Herman Miller Reports Significant Operating Margin Expansion in the First Quarter of Fiscal 2014, Press Release, September 18, 2013.

Table 8.4 Herman Miller, Inc. condensed consolidated statements of cash flows (unaudited; dollars in millions)

	Three Months Ended	
	August 31, 2013	September 1, 2012
Net earnings	$22.5	$20.0
Cash flows provided by operating activities	38.2	28.7
Cash flows used for investing activities	(6.2)	(15.1)
Cash flows used for financing activities	(4.3)	(1.3)
Effect of exchange rates	(0.3)	(0.2)
Net increase in cash	27.4	12.1
Cash, beginning of period	$82.7	$172.2
Cash, end of period	$110.1	$184.3

Source: Herman Miller Reports Significant Operating Margin Expansion in the First Quarter of Fiscal 2014, Press Release, September 18, 2013.

Table 8.5 Herman Miller, Inc. condensed consolidated balance sheets (unaudited; dollars in millions)

	August 31, 2013	June 1, 2013	Percentage Change
Assets			
Current assets			
Cash and cash equivalents	$110.1	$82.7	15
Marketable securities	11.0	10.8	6
Accounts receivable, net	172.4	178.4	−3
Inventories, net	77.4	76.2	12
Prepaid expenses and other	55.6	51.2	−10
Total current assets	426.5	399.3	5
Net property and equipment	182.8	184.1	8
Other assets	363.7	363.1	1
Total assets	$973.0	$946.5	4
Liabilities and shareholders' equity			
Current liabilities			
Accounts payable	$130.2	$130.1	−10
Accrued liabilities	166.6	159.9	6
Total current liabilities	296.8	290.0	−1
Long-term debt	250.0	250.0	0
Other liabilities	85.2	87.0	−4
Total liabilities	632.0	627.0	−1
Shareholders' equity totals	341.0	319.5	18
Total liabilities and shareholders' equity	$973.0	$946.5	4

Source: Herman Miller Reports Significant Operating Margin Expansion in the First Quarter of Fiscal 2014, Press Release, September 18, 2013.

Statement, CEO Brian Walker's letter that began "Dear Fellow Herman Miller Shareholder," read in part as follow:

> With great contributions across the entire organization, we made significant progress in 2013 toward our long-term vision and financial objectives: delivering on our strategy for diversified growth, expanding into higher margin segments and categories, and continuing to enhance the Herman Miller global brand.

We have also strengthened our balance sheet and followed through on our commitment to enhance your returns with increased dividends. Of course we have more work in front of us—we don't have an off-season at Herman Miller—but we are all energized by last year's results and believe we have built a foundation for continued growth and prosperity.

We have begun a new era at Herman Miller driven by our mission-"Inspiring designs to help people do great things"-and our insights into how society and our customers' needs are changing. To be frank, the mission of Herman Miller has always been grounded in the consistent belief that "design is a response to social change." Our former CEO Hugh De Pree wrote in 1968, "Our principle objective at Herman Miller is problem-solving in the various areas of living." While many organizations feel threatened by change, we thrive on it and believe it creates opportunity.

A year ago at this time we declared that 2013 would be a year of significant investment with the aim of strengthening and accelerating our diversified growth, while continuing to enhance our balance sheet. We also pledged to increase the cash we return to shareholders. While we still have work to do, our financial performance in fiscal 2013 is proof that we're making good on those promises.

Throughout the fiscal year, our North American business segment faced the headwind of sluggish demand from U.S. federal government and healthcare buyers. This was offset by robust business activity across the remainder of our core non-government office furniture business, which helped drive growth for the segment as a whole relative to fiscal 2012.

Our international business segment also experienced a mixed demand picture, with lagging sales in the U.K. and other European economies being more than offset by increases in China and the Middle East. We are improving our existing production capabilities and preparing for new growth in emerging markets. The integration of POSH manufacturing in China continues steadily, and we will begin the construction of a new facility next spring to consolidate our U.K. operations serving EMEA. We also have plans in development for India and Latin America that hold further promise for growth in those markets.

Our Specialty and Consumer segment posted solid sales growth this fiscal year, driven by the investments we've made in developing our offering across both commercial and retail markets. The Herman Miller Collection continues to grow in reach and quality, with a number of reissued iconic designs and innovative new material options. Our alliances with Italian companies Magis and Mattiazzi are another source for new products and enhance our brand with consumers and specifiers. We have been developing our channels to market, with new shop-in-shop merchandising initiatives in the retail channel, as well as continued investment in our online marketing and fulfillment capabilities.

In April we reached a major milestone with our acquisition of Maharam Fabric Corporation, a premier design brand in commercial interiors and recognized internationally for the highest quality textiles and wall coverings. The addition of Maharam to our Specialty and Consumer segment is a powerful strategic accelerator for our entire business on multiple levels. We instantly became a North American market leader in their core product areas, with the ability to leverage our resources to further Maharam's reach into new markets.

In a press release accompanying the first quarter results for 2014, Mr. Walker explained,

> This quarter's performance reflects continued progress in the execution of our strategy, with a strong contribution from the higher margin growth categories and related channels where we have been steadily expanding our presence. It also reflects operating improvements we have implemented in some of our operations that have been underperforming. These results demonstrate that our strategy of innovation, diversification, and operational excellence is working.

While the company's performance has steadily improved through first quarter 2014, executives at Herman Miller faced two particular questions: (1) Will the strategies that have made Herman Miller an outstanding and award-winning company continue to provide it with the ability to reinvent and renew itself? (2) Will disruptive global, economic, and competitive forces compel it to change its business model?

Notes

1. At Herman Miller, people including the president are referred to by their first or nick names or in combination with their surnames, but hardly ever by their titles or surnames alone.
2. Herman Miller Press Release of June 10, 2013, entitled, "Herman Miller Introduces Living Office™: the Holistic Solution for the New Landscapes of Work."
3. The names of the two Fortune 500 companies were deleted by the authors.
4. Herman Miller's fiscal year ends on May 30.
5. Christensen, C. M. 1997. *The innovator's dilemma: When new technologies cause great firms to fail.* Boston: Harvard Business School Press.

CHAPTER 9

Equal Exchange: Doing Well by Doing Good

Benita W. Harris, Frank Shipper,
Karen P. Manz, and Charles C. Manz

Introduction

In 1983, Rink Dickinson, Jonathan Rosenthal, and Michael Rozyne were all recent college graduates and working for a food co-op warehouse in the Boston area. They began to question the system: What if food could be traded in a way that is honest and fair, a way that empowers both farmers and consumers? What if trade supported family farms use of organic methods rather than methods that harm the environment? Almost simultaneously they started to hear about groups in Europe who were doing *fair trade*. The advocates of fair trade wanted to ensure that the producers of products such as coffee, teas, and chocolate would get a better price for their crops while supporting improvement in their environmental, social, and political conditions. Rink, Jonathan, and Michael liked the idea. According to Rink, they "were basically food co-op people, interested in connecting small, local farmers with consumers to change the marketplace." It was not their intention to found a company at that time. They took the idea to the board of directors of the co-op warehouse. Half of the board supported the idea and half voted against it. It became apparent to them that if they were going to pursue their vision, they were going to have to develop an organization.

Over the next three years they met once a month to develop the plans and raise the capital for founding their own organization. During that time Rink said they used their jobs to learn about cooperatives, small farmers, entrepreneurship, marketing, and "making mistakes, right and left." The food co-op gave them "a great environment to learn some skills." In 1986, they decided to launch Equal Exchange (EE). By that time, their ambition was "to change the way food is grown, bought, and sold around the world."

Before the company could be launched, capital had to be raised. The three young entrepreneurs quickly learned that no institution, including organizations that specialize in high-impact social justice ventures, would lend them money. Thus, their fund-raising focused on family, friends, and their contacts. According to Rink, the general pitch was, "We want you to invest in this project and it is almost guaranteed to lose all of your money." On those terms they were able to raise $100,000.

Thereafter, no additional money was raised for several years. To stretch out the initial investment Rink described the founders as "living very low on the food chain."

EE embarked on its pioneering efforts to sell fair trade products in the United States with coffee from Nicaragua. From the beginning, EE paid the producers an above market price for their products out of a desire to help provide a better, more stable income and to more equitably distribute the proceeds of the final sales. The producers are typically small farmers indigenous to their region. On each product the company slogan—"Small Farmers, Big Change"—was prominently displayed.

Not content to just "change the way food is grown, bought, and sold around the world," the founders of EE formally adopted a hybrid worker-owner co-op structure in 1990. They believed that such an ownership structure would make the employees feel valued and that they would in turn be willing to invest their whole being in the organization. Key to this new structure was shared employee ownership. Each worker-owner buys one share of Class A voting stock. No one did or can even today own more than one share of voting stock. Worker-owners can also buy unlimited shares of Class B, nonvoting stock. Thus, power, and potentially leadership, is distributed equally across all worker-owners on a democratic one-person/one-share/one-vote basis.

The Year 2013

Twenty-seven years later not only is EE doing good—it is doing well. Sales of EE have grown from zero in 1986 to $1,000,000 in 1991 to $51,046,384 in 2012. Sales increased each year during the Great Recession. In 2012, sales increased by 9 percent over 2011. Sales and profits are projected to set company records in 2013. All EE products (coffee, tea, chocolate bars, cocoa, sugar, bananas, almonds, and olive oil) are fair trade and most products are organic.

Co-executive directors Rink Dickinson and Rob Everts, and the worker-owners of EE are still interested in changing the world through socially responsible business. Its mission statement reveals the heart of EE: "To build long-term trade partnerships that are economically just and environmentally sound, to foster mutually beneficial relationships between farmers and consumers and to demonstrate, through our success, the contribution of worker co-operatives and Fair Trade to a more equitable, democratic and sustainable world." In 2006, EE announced, "Our Vision in 20 Years... [To build] a vibrant, mutually cooperative community of two million committed participants trading fairly one billion dollars a year in a way that transforms the world."

Functional Areas at Equal Exchange

To fulfill its vision and mission, the founders, for philosophical reasons, developed a hybrid model that combined worker-ownership with a cooperative model to coordinate the functions. EE is a relatively small company, approximately 100 worker-owners, with geographically dispersed operations; worker-owners may fulfill multiple functions.

Equal Exchange Governance Model

As portrayed in figure 9.1, EE has a board of directors that is elected by the worker-owners, who in turn hire the executive director/s. Currently, the position is called "the office of executive directors" as it is shared by Rink and Rob. They are responsible for hiring the employees, who later may become worker-owners, but that does not happen without significant input from the other worker-owners. The worker-owners nominate candidates for the six *inside* board members and a joint, three-person worker-owner/board/management committee nominates candidates for the three *outside* seats. The worker-owners elect all nine seats, three each year. In turn, the board of directors hires the executive directors.

The executive directors are not board members. According to Lynsey Miller, market development leader and a former board member, "They're at the board table, but they don't have votes. They are very active in that discussion and agenda setting." Thus, the worker-owners who elect the board and hold two-thirds of the seats are also responsible for hiring the executive directors.

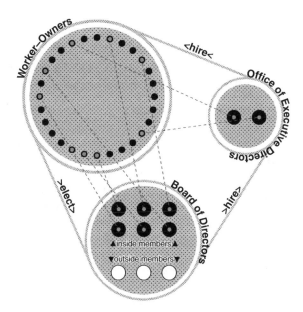

Figure 9.1   Governance model for Equal Exchange.
Courtesy of Equal Exchange.

All members of the board serve three-year terms. Instead of electing a new board every year, two inside directors and one outside director are elected to the board each year to promote continuity on the board.

This circular structure reinforces the following four concepts that are at the heart of the EE governance model:

1. The right to vote (one vote per worker-owner, not per share)
2. The right to serve as leader (e.g., board director, or other elected office)
3. The right to information
4. The right to speak your mind

EE provides the following elaboration on this model on its website: www. equalexchange.coop.

> A worker cooperative is an alternative for-profit structure based upon standard democratic principles. It is not designed to maximize profits, nor returns to investors, but rather to bring to the workplace many of the rights and responsibilities that we hold as citizens in our communities. These principles include one-person/one-vote equality; open access to information (i.e., open-book management); free speech; and the equitable distribution of resources (such as income.) . . . The delegation of responsibilities is very much like that of conventional firms—which allows for efficiency—except that at EE those at the "bottom" of the organizational chart are, as owners, also at the "top" of the same chart.[1]

Rob describes the genesis of this governance model as follows:

> From the beginning, it has been a culture in a context of participation and shared ownership of strong management. The founders were quite clear that ownership would be shared and that ultimately accountability for the highest level decisions would be shared and that we would attempt to build a strong cultural of internal participation and democracy. There was no interest in having it be a collective.

One important position in this governance model not shown in figure 9.1 is that of the worker-owner coordinator. This individual is elected by the worker-owners, but is not a board member. The worker-owner coordinator has many duties, the most public and demanding of which is facilitating the meetings of the cooperative that are held at least quarterly. Overall the coordinator is often akin to a police officer directing traffic. He or she does not make the rules of the cooperative, but is empowered by the cooperative to keep their portion of the system moving smoothly, so that the necessary work may be completed. To do this the coordinator directs the jostling interests, opinions, and emotions of the members as best he or she can. One goal is to strike a balance between members' rights to ask questions, be heard, and press for changes with maintaining an environment that is safe, respectful, and constructive.

The coordinator is automatically the representative of the worker-owners on certain "tripartite" committees and will serve next to representatives of the board and management. One example is the committee that nominates outside board members. The coordinator also leads the ten-member worker-owner cabinet. The cabinet is a group of volunteers, accountable to the coordinator. They carry out essential cooperative functions such as maintaining the internal education program and conducting the complex, multiballot, multi-site elections.

A secondary function for the coordinator is to give the "state of the cooperative" presentation at the annual meeting in May. It is an assessment of how well EE is functioning *as a cooperative*, not as a business per se. The worker-owners can call a meeting of the cooperative by presenting signatures of 10 percent of the worker-owners to the worker-owner coordinator. If a worker-owner wants to bring something to an upcoming meeting, and has either the coordinator's consent or the required number of signatures, the coordinator would be responsible for putting the individual on the agenda and working with that person so that the idea is thought out and well presented.

As can be seen by this description of the governance model, the need for communication and coordination is complex for it to operate successfully. Initially EE used a matrix to communicate the decision-making process. The matrix was used from approximately 1998 to 2007, but no longer. The matrix was developed "to identity decision-makers and illuminate the decision making process for key governance decisions at EE."[2] In 2007 the board of directors adopted the Policy Governance model designed by John Carver (see http://www.carvergovernance.com/model.htm). That model supplanted use of the Governance Matrix. Later, in 2011, the cooperative explored new governing models proposed by various worker-owners. The co-op voted to adopt one dubbed "the Glass Model." The board was obliged to utilize this in place of Policy Governance. The Glass Model has elements that are similar to the Governance Matrix, but slightly less specific providing greater freedom and flexibility in the decision-making process. Recruiting, selecting, hiring, developing, and retaining employees who can operate within this governance model and flex with the needs of the organization are critical. Thus, in the next section human resource management (HRM) will be discussed.

Human Resource Management

The worker-owners focus considerable attention on human resource management because of the need for a good fit of worker-owners with the ownership culture that exists on a daily basis. Recruitment is probably EE's HRM area of least worry. Whenever it does advertise an open position, it has multiple applicants. Because of its reputation, primarily spread by word of mouth, EE has no problem with obtaining a significant and qualified applicant pool. The hiring process is quite extensive and is considered critical to the success of EE. Two unusual aspects of the hiring process are that every potential new worker-owner goes through a three-stage interview process and the hiring process is not considered complete until after the review process and the new hire has been on the job for three months.

Once hired the employee is matched with a mentor and is on probation for one year. There is approximately a 5 to 10 percent new employee turnover during the first year. After the first year, all worker-owners vote on whether to offer the employee worker-ownership status (i.e., the chance to join the cooperative). Before the vote, the mentor and the employee's supervisor circulate written statements on behalf of the candidate. With rare exceptions only those new employees who have fared well reach this point. New hires that have been poor employees, or seem ill-suited for the co-op, are generally weeded out by this time. Almost all worker-owner candidacy votes are taken online, but current worker-owners may also request an in-person meeting for a discussion and vote. In such a case all worker-owners are free to discuss the individual's fit for EE before the vote is taken. Worker-owners can vote "yes," "no," or abstain. Unless 20 percent or more worker-owners vote "no" the candidate is welcomed into the co-op. Over 95 percent of employees who make it to the one-year point are accepted as worker-owners. When one is not accepted it can be a traumatic event for all.

During the probation period the employee is expected to participate in a curriculum to learn about the mission of EE, how it works, and to be prepared for the responsibilities of worker-ownership and governance. The worker-owners feel that it is very important to develop and strengthen a worker-ownership culture. To support the development of the culture, EE has developed an *Owners' Manual* that is over two hundred pages in length. To both support this effort for new employees and to reinforce the worker-ownership culture for all, every Thursday morning is "Exchange Time" for one and a half hours. Exchange Time lectures and discussions cover topics such as fair trade, co-op history, or issues affecting its farmer partners. New employees are practically required while all other employees are encouraged to participate. The discussions are recorded and shared via EE's intranet with remote employees and regional offices. Cody Squire, who joined EE right out of college a few years ago, enthusiastically described "Exchange Time" as: "It's one structured thing that you can depend on having every week just to learn about something new, to look deeper into something you already know about, or to hear from somebody who has just returned from working with farmer co-ops in Peru." In addition to Exchange Time, EE has "10 percent time." Employees can use 10 percent of their work time for purposes unrelated to their core functions. This time can be used to cross-train, work on governance committees, or learn more about the product. For example, Lynsey used her 10 percent time to serve on the board of directors, where she helped create the 20-year vision for EE. Mike and his colleague Danielle, in Quality Control, led a program called "The Brew Crew." It is a year-long curriculum on coffee. People from other departments participate in coffee quality trainings every two weeks for a year.

To develop future leaders, EE uses an unusual 360-degree peer evaluation process. As is normal, peer, subordinate, superior, and self-evaluations are performed. The unusual aspect of EE's process is that all those who provide feedback must sign their forms. In other words, the feedback is not anonymous. Alison Booth, manager of EE's Espresso Bar in Seattle, Washington, described how it worked for her:

> If I'm being evaluated, my supervisor and I will have access to them ... Sometimes they are just nice to hear, but not terribly helpful; sometimes they're a little hard to hear. Most of the time, people are really careful to give constructive criticism, to give specific examples of things we could do better or things we did well.
>
> Then I do a self-evaluation, and my boss does a supervisor's evaluation. He combines his thoughts with my evaluation and the peer evaluations and pulls them all together. We talk about what's working, areas for improvement and what to focus on in the next year.

To further increase intellectual capital, EE maintains a library to which all employees have access. Mike described the library as "awesome ... it's full of DVD's and books on anything from economics to feminism to Fair Trade to." The worker-owners also have responsibility for the education committee, originally, a board committee. At EE, education was identified as a "vital function. In shifting accountability for this committee, Worker-Owners became more accountable for their own education and the orientation of new employees to our co-operative."[3]

The worker-owners staff many roles in this model, and share in both profits and losses. Because EE operates as a worker cooperative, profit sharing is referred to as "patronage." "Patronage" is a common term used in cooperatives where co-op members receive a share of the profits, or bear a portion of losses, based on the extent they have participated in the co-op. At EE all worker-owners who worked a full year receive the same amount without regard to rank or seniority as all contributed the same amount of labor time. The total potential patronage distribution consists of 40 percent of net income after state taxes and preferred dividends are paid. Half of this distribution is reinvested in EE, and half is paid in cash. In years of losses the patronage rebates are charges against the retained distributions.

In area of benefits, EE "is generous" according to Brian Albert, chief financial officer, who had approximately 30 years with some well-known international firms before joining EE. For example, it offers all employees 12 sick days. A worker-owner can use them for him/herself, to take care of a sick child, to attend a doctor appointment, or to spend time with a sick parent. All worker-owners receive two weeks of vacation for the first two years. After that, they receive four weeks. After their eighth year they receive five weeks. In addition, employees receive the standard holidays plus the Friday after Thanksgiving.

EE is also generous in the area of pay, whereby it pays above average at the novice level jobs, but pays below average for senior level management positions. It maintains a top-to-bottom pay ratio of four-to-one. It clearly states on the website that this ratio was adopted to reflect the fair trade ethic inside the corporation.

Production

EE has not been content to be a single-product company. Its four major products and their percentage of sales are coffee (80.1 percent), chocolate (16.1 percent), tea (2.7 percent), and snacks (1.1 percent). Snacks include products such as organic tamari roasted almonds. In 2010, EE increased its stake in Oke USA, an importer and seller of organic bananas, to 90 percent. Oke USA sales were $4,400,000 in 2010. In 2011, EE introduced organic olive oil. In 2010, EE sold $38,487,000 of its products other than bananas. Ninety percent of its coffees are certified organic whereas 100 percent of its tea, cocoa, chocolate, sugar, and bananas are certified organic.

To produce organic coffee, chocolate, tea, and its other products for sale to others, EE must first secure the raw materials. The producers of these products are spread around the world. EE buys raw product from four continents— North and South America, Africa, and Asia—and almost exclusively from developing countries.

For example, coffee is grown largely in developing countries and is often the second most valuable commodity after oil exported by them, according to John M. Talbot, a sociology professor at the University of the West Indies in Jamaica. Cacao, the key ingredient for chocolate, is also exported only by developing countries. The large multinationals typically buy their raw materials from either large plantations or large sellers of coffee. The large sellers depend on middlemen, often referred to as "coyotes," to buy the coffee from small growers. According to an article in the April 25, 2011, issue of *Time* magazine, Ugandan coffee farmers get 0.66 percent of the retail value of their product. In contrast, the US Department of Agriculture estimated that US farmers receive 12 percent of the retail value.

EE buys directly from cooperatives that represent small producers and thereby helps these co-ops to internalize the activity, and profits, formerly captured by the middlemen. It buys raw materials from over 40 small farmer cooperatives in 25 countries at higher prices than typical. In its 2009 annual report, EE defined its sourcing standards as:

- *Quality*: Find the best beans.
- *Flavor*: Select sweet beans with unique flavor characteristics.
- *Farmer partners*: Trade with small farmer cooperatives that share our vision of community empowerment.
- *Direct relationships*: Import directly from farmer cooperatives.
- *Fair price*: Pay above the market price, often above fair trade prices.
- *Environment*: Support sustainable agriculture, the preservation of sensitive areas, and reforestation of degraded land.
- *Commitment*: Source all our coffee according to the quality of the beans and the quality of the source.

EE supports the cooperatives with both financial and technical assistance. In its 2008 Disclosure Document to Sell Class B Preferred Stock, the relationship with small farmers was described as follows, "Our Commitment: we pay a fair price to the farmer, trade directly with democratic co-ops; supply advanced credit and support sustainable agriculture." In other words, EE goes beyond just paying a fair price; it prepays on its contracts with the cooperatives. It also provides assistance to the cooperatives to ensure that they can provide a high quality product.

Mike Mowry, a quality control specialist, described what he did on a trip to Nicaragua as follows: "We do a lot of work going down and actually training about quality. Even with their quality departments, we do extensive training on how to roast samples and how to cup coffee.[4] The whole idea is collaborating with their tasters and our tasters." EE maintains that "great" coffee can be obtained from many sources. What sets it apart is that it buys "great" coffee from "great" sources.

Based on its initiatives, EE also provides assistance to the small farmer co-ops beyond food products. For example, it has provided assistance for training programs for women in Guatemala, an ecotourism project in Nicaragua, and new classrooms in El Salvador.

When all of the sourcing standards work well, quality product is shipped to EE for further processing. However, sometimes EE has to break off a relationship with a co-op for either quality-control reasons or compromised governance of the cooperative, such as not living up to expectations of accountability, transparency, and democratic governance.

Another difficulty with attempting to reach EE's production standards is illustrated with its history of bringing tea to market. In the 1980s, when EE consisted of a small staff of five or six, tea was typically grown on large plantations; obtaining the product from small farmers was difficult. When EE first imported tea during the late 1980s, the tea came from Sri Lanka and was a generic tea that may not have been from small farmers or fair trade. At that time there were no "fair trade" standards for tea. That would only come later. However, EE did know the exporter, an exemplary grassroots nonprofit/self-help organization called the "Sarvodaya movement." It still operates today. In fact, it was one of the key players in relief and reconstruction after the 2004 Indian Ocean tsunami. At that time, working in solidarity with a locally rooted, progressive, self-empowerment organization—who would also receive a sizable portion of the tea profits—was the moral equivalent of "fair trade." That trade link was lost after approximately three years due to interruptions caused by the bloody Sri Lankan civil war.

Around 1997, EE made a second attempt at procuring tea from a region of India famous for tea, Darjeeling. By then the formal fair trade standards had been created for tea. To EE's dismay, it was focused on plantations, and yet EE plowed ahead. A hurdle was that there was no tea available that was fair trade certified *and* organic *and* high enough quality for EE's market *and* from small farmers. The market demanded the first three criteria, but not the fourth (which was most important to EE). EE with the help of key, even ironic, allies in Darjeeling and Germany began to create a path that it thought gave it the best chance to eventually deliver a tea with all four characteristics. Rodney North, spokesperson for EE, characterized its most important ally as "ironic" because it was a big tea plantation called TPI. In fact, it had been one of the model plantations for fair trade tea certification. The owners of TPI, the Mohan family, shared EE's aspirations to bring small farmers into the fair trade system. Thus, in the early years, 50 percent or more of the tea EE imported was from the TPI estates, and TPI gathered tea leaf from co-ops of small farmers around them for the rest. TPI also assisted these co-ops with organic certification, fair trade certification, rehabilitating their tea bushes, and improving quality. Over time it shifted the tea blends to become more and more sourced from small farmers.

There were many more evolutionary steps thereafter so that today EE has a line of twelve teas. Ten are 100 percent small-farmer tea leaf. And two are "other" (neither small-farmer sourced nor traditional estate); that is because one, the mint, is sourced from a US farm, and the other, chamomile, is from an exemplary philanthropic Egyptian NGO (nongovernmental organization) farm entity called SEKEM. "But it is only a temporary source until we locate a suitable Fair Trade certified co-op of organic, small-scale chamomile growers," asserts Rodney.

When EE quality products are received in the United States, additional processing may have to be performed. Coffee has to be roasted, tea packaged, bananas ripened, and chocolate processed. Then the product has to be marketed and distributed.

Marketing and Distribution

EE markets and distributes its products through multichannels: (1) retail outlets, (2) an interfaith network, (3) schools, (4) the Internet, and (5) EE cafes. Approximately 72 percent of its products are sold through retail outlets, including health food stores, food co-ops, by-the-cup shops (i.e., cafes and restaurants), universities, and chain stores. The consumer-owned food co-ops were EE's first sales channel and remain the largest sales segment. In contrast, selling to the larger grocery store chains is particularly difficult because as the former director of marketing explained: "It is tougher to succeed in that channel, because we don't have the marketing dollars that major food companies have, and that's been something that's been a struggle to try to figure out how to succeed because you need to have a national brand awareness, which is really tough to do on a small budget." Thus, EE has developed some unconventional promotional strategies. In fact, Lynsey referred to them as "guerilla marketing." In the early days, she described some of the marketing: "We would go out on the streets of Boston handing out coffee samples and when the police would come over to ask if we had a permit, we'd try to get them to have a coffee sample because we didn't get permits; kind of have to think on your feet and talk your way through challenges." Another guerilla marketing tactic it uses is grassroots events. Beside traditional in-store product demonstrations, EE staffs do many public speaking events, organize consumer letter-writing campaigns to ask supermarkets to carry its products, and even go door to door to get its message across.

The interfaith channel is EE's second largest distribution channel with approximately 20 percent of sales. It includes a dozen formal partners: American Friends Service Committee, American Jewish World Service, Catholic Relief Services, Baptist Peace Fellowship of North America, Church of the Brethren, Disciples of Christ, Lutheran World Relief, Mennonite Central Committee US, Presbyterian Church USA, United Church of Christ, United Methodist Committee on Relief, and Unitarian Universalist Service Committee. The fair trade products distributed through these interfaith partnerships affords faith-based organizations another opportunity to live in accord with their values and to discuss their connections and fellowship with those who grow and harvest food around the world. EE also provides materials to educate consumers on issues of economic justice, sustainable farming, and the effects of an increasingly industrialized food industry dominated by a small number of firms.

The development of the interfaith channel is a great example of entrepreneurship in action among the worker-owners at EE. Prior to the mid-1990s, EE worked with congregations on an ad hoc one-by-one basis. Then Timothy Bernard, a Lutheran minister, and Erbin Crowell, an EE salesperson, hit upon the idea of establishing formal relationships with faith-based communities. As related by Rodney, "Erbin had to sell this idea internally to Rink and others, and Timothy had to do likewise within the Lutheran community's leadership. Eventually, they created a pilot project which grew to be very successful."

Another example of entrepreneurship within EE was led by Virginia Berman. She began with focusing fund-raising opportunities with elementary, middle, and high schools. Instead of selling items such as magazine subscriptions and popcorn, the schools would sell fair trade products from EE. Then she heard from the teachers who wanted to help the students to grasp the significance of fair trade. In response she requested and received funding to create educational materials. Currently, there is a flexible and engaging free-to-download curriculum targeted for grades four to nine at http://www.equalexchange.coop/educationaltools.

To reach the technologically savvy, EE has embraced social media such as Twitter, YouTube, and Facebook to communicate its message to current and potential consumers. Additionally, EE takes advantage of the electronic media to offer an unusually active, in-depth, and outspoken blog and to provide e-newsletters to which anyone can subscribe. All of these efforts are, as Lynsey said, "to try to connect with the public and consumers." The use of social media also reinforces its marketing efforts through retail stores and the interfaith network. Moreover, it leads to its fourth marketing channel, the Internet. In 2011, Internet sales to individual shoppers accounted for approximately 2 percent of sales. EE expects these Internet sales to hit one million in 2012. Currently, EE is looking at how to expand its Internet sales. Over half of interfaith sales previously discussed are also executed via online stores. Thus, in total approximately 12 percent of EE's sales come through the Internet.

EE's two cafes are its fifth form of marketing and distribution. It started selling its products through cafes prior to the 2008 recession. One of them is in Boston and the other in Seattle. Due to high capital costs and the challenge of winning new customers it takes even popular cafes like these two 18 to 24 months to reach the breakeven point. For now EE has placed on hold the further addition of cafes. Instead, it is trying a different approach to reach customers.

In keeping with the EE tradition of thinking outside the box, it has developed cafes on wheels. They are described by Brian as follows:

> We have two custom built tricycles very close to completion. They'll be in the Boston market probably within the next 30 to 60 days. They are stand alone. They have marine batteries and they carry all the supplies they need. They can brew coffee right there onsite. If you park it here in the morning and not much action, you can park it over there in the afternoon, yeah, that seems to be a better spot. It's kind of a brand building, and they have kind of a wow factor.[5]

In addition, some of the independent cafes have also adopted mobile approaches to reach the customers. For example, Common Grounds: A Fair Trade Café in Salisbury, Maryland, uses a converted trailer to reach customers at community events such as West Wicomico Heritage Bike Tour and Salisbury University's Freshman Move-In Day.

As with all fair trade products, which tend to occupy the premium or gourmet segment of their categories, the pricing is above that charged by mass-marketers such as Maxwell and Kraft. This reflects the higher quality, the higher unit costs of a small firm, but it also supports the higher prices paid to the producers. Yet, the prices for EE products are still on par with much larger competitors, such as Starbucks, Peet's, and Green Mountain, who offer comparable quality coffee. To persuade customers to buy its product, without the aid of expensive marketing campaigns, EE uses a significant amount of informational marketing. For example, as stated earlier, on the packaging of every chocolate bar, tea bag or box, and bag of coffee is the slogan "Small Farmers, Big Change." In addition, information on how the product is grown, who grows it, where it was grown, and why it is different often appears on the packaging material. Sometimes pictures of growers also appear. To further differentiate the products, fair trade and USDA Organic seals are on the packaging materials, as well. EE tries to use every opportunity to get its message across and connect with the public and consumers.

Finance

EE issues two forms of stock—Class A Common Stock and Class B Preferred Stock. Every worker-owner must own one share of Class A stock, and no more. No one else may purchase it. This ensures equal voting rights, one-person/one-vote, and to a larger degree, equal power among all worker-owners. Worker-owners purchase a share when they are elected into the company after completing their probationary first year. When originally issued in 1990, each share was worth $2,000. In January 2011, each Class A share was worth $3,170. To prevent the cost of stock ownership from being an obstacle to joining the cooperative, new worker-owners, once elected, are provided with an interest-free loan to purchase their share. They have four years to repay the loan and it can be repaid with the cash portion of the patronage distribution.

Both worker-owners and outsiders can own Class B Preferred Stock. Shares sell for $27.50. Dividends are declared annually by the board usually in January and are targeted at 5 percent. Originally, individual shares could be purchased. As Rob related, "Someone could buy a share for their grandchild for $27. We loved that type of thing, but we are operating under limits of 500 maximum outside shareholders. If you exceed that limit, then it is considered to be publicly traded." In 2011, preferred shares had to be purchased in lots equal to or greater than $10,000. When EE offers its preferred shares, it does so in the following manner according to Rob:

> We do have to be diligent and deliberate about talking to people and sharing. We have a very extensive disclosure document that everyone has to look at before they invest in us. There's got to be some connection to EE to get them here in the first place, whether it's a personal connection or whether they represent an account of ours; maybe they actually are a worker-owner and they want to be an investor, too. It has to be people who fundamentally know us and have direct access to the books and can see quite closely.

To assure direct access to financial information, EE practices an extreme form of open book management. Privately or closely held firms such as EE are not required to make available to the public an annual report, but the company publishes each year's annual report on the web. The financial statements for 2007–2012 (tables 9.1 and 9.2) were extracted from those reports. EE goes further in its practice of open book management by putting all of its annual reports dating back to 1986 online including a Spanish language version for its many suppliers in Latin America that represent 90 percent of EE's imports.[6]

Preferred shares are sold as a long-term investment. Preferred stockholders can redeem them for their full price only after five years. Shares cannot be redeemed until after two years and then for only 70 percent of their value, 80 percent after three, and 90 percent after four. In addition, there is provision in the disclosure statement that the board of directors "may postpone or delay a request for redemption" if the total debt-to-total equity ratio exceeds 2:1 or the redemption would cause it to exceed that ratio.

Class A Common Stock and Class B Preferred Stock have the following unusual restriction and explanation for that restriction on them in the disclosure document:

> On the sale of all the assets, liquidation or dissolution of the corporation, any residual assets left after the payment of all debts shall be distributed first to the Class B shareholders in the amount equal to the balances in their internal accounts and then to the current members or, if said residual assets are insufficient, then on a pro rata basis in proportion to the relative balances in their internal accounts. Any assets remaining after said distribution shall be distributed to an alternative trading organization as so determined by the Board of Directors of the corporation.

Table 9.1 Equal Exchange, Inc.: statements of operations and retained earnings (all values in dollars)

	2007	2008	2009	2010	2011	2012
SALES	29,370,480	34,440,241	35,832,510	36,525,856	46,819,829	51,046,384
COST OF SALES	18,866,940	22,446,593	23,075,260	23,659,316	33,617,786	37,343,411
GROSS PROFIT	10,503,540	11,993,648	12,757,250	12,866,540	13,202,043	13,702,973
OPERATING EXPENSES	8,646,241	9,535,120	10,771,023	11,234,758	11,350,116	11,799,883
INCOME FROM OPERATIONS	1,857,299	2,458,528	1,986,227	1,631,782	1,851,927	1,903,090
OTHER (EXPENSE) INCOME:						
Interest expense	(737,131)	(720,437)	(622,848)	(323,662)	(387,182)	(479,668)
Reduction of investment to market value		(80,000)				
Bad debt expense—loans	(38,759)	(80,000)				
Charitable contributions expense	(5,296)	(105,000)				
Interest income	22,118	9,314	3,754	14,832	7,346	4,420
Bad debt (expense) recovery, net—trade		(14,265)				
	(759,068)	(990,388)				
INCOME BEFORE INCOME TAXES	1,098,231	1,468,140	1,367,133	1,322,952	1,472,091	1,428,422
PROVISIONS FOR INCOME TAXES:						
Current	325,000	435,000	430,000	484,000	689,000	502,000
Deferred	110,000	165,000	163,000	94,000	(40,000)	146,275
	435,000	600,000	593,000	578,000	649,000	648,275
NET INCOME	663,231	868,140	774,133	744,952	821,042	780,706
RETAINED EARNINGS, Beginning of year	1,619,725	2,069,068	2,654,249	3,174,783	3,595,014	3,987,139
Less: preferred stock dividends paid	(213,888)	(282,959)	(253,599)	(324,721)	(428,917)	(510,893)
RETAINED EARNINGS, end of year	2,069,068	2,654,249	3,174,783	3,595,014	3,987,139	4,256,952

Note: Table compiled from annual reports available on Equal Exchange's website.

Table 9.2 Equal Exchange, Inc.: balance sheet (all values in dollars)

	2007	2008	2009	2010	2011	2012
ASSETS						
CURRENT ASSETS:						
Cash and equivalents	381,497	212,717	376,667	823,699	757,429	489,817
Accounts receivable—trade, net of reserve for possible uncollectible accounts of $50,000 in 2009 and 2008	1,973,098	2,227,843	2,185,768	2,655,707	2,849,063	3,123,181
Notes receivable—other	34,174	88,628	324,996	17,538	34,800	131,836
Inventories	8,193,630	10,839,429	8,293,729	8,290,646	15,117,041	14,698,437
Prepaid expenses, advances in inventory, and other current assets	766,611	928,227	415,139	535,330	800,338	855,604
Deferred income tax asset	77,000	145,000	115,000	377,496	367,496	361,221
TOTAL CURRENT ASSETS	11,426,010	14,441,844	11,711,299	12,700,386	19,926,167	19,709,896
PROPERTY AND EQUIPMENT, NET	7,311,901	7,473,243	7,017,564	6,653,683	5,979,771	5,968,678
OTHER ASSETS:						
Intangible assets, net	49,794	35,434	28,994	211,153	182,212	99,140
Investments	151,326	190,870	381,861	68,513	43,360	83,360
Notes receivable, net of current portion	281,188	234,473	6,039	38,501	39,249	3,230
TOTAL ASSETS	19,220,219	22,375,864	19,145,457	19,672,236	26,170,759	25,864,304
LIABILITIES AND STOCKHOLDERS' EQUITY						
CURRENT LIABILITIES:						
Notes payable—lines-of-credit	4,022,153	5,164,438	624,928	567,952	3,463,192	1,746,266
Capitalized lease obligations, current portion	420,470	447,679	432,124			
Mortgages and other notes payable, current portion	319,677	1,639,829	550,639	121,793	1,253,534	1,536,277
Accounts payable and accrued expenses	1,079,240	940,158	1,089,703	1,539,374	2,198,802	3,269,931
Accrued expenses and other current liabilities	660,063	769,526				
Corporate income taxes payable					271,632	
Patronage rebates payable	418,205	255,255	421,875	147,000	376,382	329,745
TOTAL CURRENT LIABILITIES	6,919,808	9,216,885	3,119,269	2,376,119	7,563,542	6,882,219

Continued

Table 9.2 Continued

	2007	2008	2009	2010	2011	2012
TOTAL CURRENT LIABILITIES	6,919,808	9,216,885	3,119,269	2,376,119	7,563,542	6,882,219
LONG-TERM LIABILITIES						
Capitalized lease obligations, noncurrent portion	1,572,897	1,125,216	693,092	—		
Mortgages and other notes payable, noncurrent portion	3,259,969	2,875,097	3,190,008	3,228,784	2,616,521	2,301,539
Deferred income taxes	404,000	637,000	770,000	900,000	850,000	990,000
COMMITMENTS AND CONTINGENCIES						
TOTAL LIABILITIES	12,156,674	13,854,198	7,772,369	4,128,784	3,466,521	3,291,539
STOCKHOLDERS' EQUITY:						
Preferred stock; authorized 9,999,500 shares; issued and outstanding, 399,948 shares in 2012, 390,116 shares in 2011, 333,262 shares in 2010, 290,429 shares in 2009, and 201,864 shares in 2008	4,829,986	5,680,390	7,978,429	9,156,382	10,728,960	10,999,389
Common stock; authorized 500 shares; issued and outstanding, 106 in 2012, 108 shares in 2011, 107 shares in 2010, 99 shares in 2009, and 93 shares in 2008, 85 shares in 2007	232,555	260,903	282,683	313,343	318,753	314,233
Less: common stock subscriptions receivable	(68,064)	(73,876)	(62,807)	(60,682)	(59,480)	(40,191)
Retained earnings	2,069,068	2,654,249	3,174,783	3,595,014	3,987,139	4,256,952
TOTAL STOCKHOLDERS' EQUITY	7,063,545	8,521,666	11,373,088	13,004,057	14,975,372	15,530,383
TOTAL LIABILITIES AND STOCKHOLDERS' EQUITY	19,220,219	22,375,864	19,145,457	19,355,278	26,170,759	25,864,304

Note: Table compiled from annual reports available on Equal Exchange's website.

Basically the capital gain due to the company's growth, if it is ever realized through a sale, stays within the fair trade community, rather than being distributed to stockholders. According to Rodney:

> The mission purpose of this treatment is to remove the temptation that the Company would ever be sold for personal financial gain, and reflects that EE was created to do something quite specific, to carry out Fair Trade and to model a new approach to business, and not as vehicle to generate wealth for any one stakeholder. Therefore, the likelihood is that the company will remain independent, despite a steady stream of buy-out offers, and its mission remains intact. As the mission and the dividends, not the capital gain, are the basis for investment, this protects the stockholder's interest.

This version of a "poison pill" to prevent takeover by outsiders is not commonly encountered. Some at EE call it the "No Exit Strategy." Brian related the following regarding this provision: "Anecdotally, I bumped into an attorney, she specializes in ESOP's and employee owned accounts...she said that our by-laws are maybe a little over the top, but in the next breath said she's used them more than once as the model for others."

To raise additional working capital EE uses an unusual method for debt financing. Anyone can buy an EE Certificate of Deposit (CD) through Eastern Bank of Massachusetts. The minimum for these CDs is at $500. By 2012, EE had raised over $1 million via CDs. It also has received loans from the Calvert Foundation, Everance, religious institutions, and individual supporters. These organizations and individuals are referred to as mission lenders. Although atypical, the financial policies collectively support EE's unusual governance model for a for-profit corporation.

The Industry

The industry consists of large multinationals that sell coffee, chocolate (i.e., Hershey, Nestle, and M&M/Mars), tea (i.e., Lipton), and other competitive products and small competitors. With the addition of bananas, Dole and Chiquita became competitors. Rob says that EE is a victim of its own success. Since 1986, a number of fair trade firms have sprung up. Rob estimates that 700 or 800 other coffee roasters—large and small—are doing some amount of fair trade. For example, Starbucks now sells more fair trade coffee than EE, but it is a small percentage of Starbucks's total sales. The same is true of Dunkin' Donuts. In contrast, the US companies deeply engaged in fair trade tend to be small. According to a 2009 study by Fair Trade Federation (FTF), the average number of full-time employees in a fair trade company is fewer than ten.

In addition to other companies getting into fair trade, there are competing organizations to certify a fair trade product. In 2012, Fair Trade USA (aka Transfair) began to certify coffee, cocoa, and sugar grown on large-scale plantations and private estates as fair trade. Other terms such as "shade grown" applied in the industry to products sold by EE and others do not have a common definition.

Fair trade is growing rapidly. According to a 2012 report published by Fair Trade International global sales of fair trade certified goods were $6.6 billion in 2011, a 12 percent increase from 2010 and 44 percent over 2009 sales.[7] Fair Trade Federation estimated in 2008 the total market for fair trade products bought in the United States was $1.18 billion. Rodney estimates that at retail, fair trade in the United States in 2011 was over $2 billion. In the same FTF report, increases in sales by product varied even for the same country. For example, fair trade coffee, the largest fair trade product, grew approximately 32 percent between 2010 and 2011 in the United States. In contrast, tea grew by 21 percent and cocoa by 67 percent in the same time period in the United States. Obviously, fair trade is growing more rapidly than non-fair-traded products. This growth is occurring in part because natural and fair trade products have gone mainstream.

In 2006 the Hartman Group reported, "Almost three-quarters (73 percent) of the U.S. population consume organic foods or beverages at least occasionally. Clearly, the conventional belief that all organic users are highly educated, high-income, Caucasian females should be put to rest." "LOHAS" is an industry term standing for "Lifestyles of Health and Sustainability" and may better serve as a moniker for those consumers who frequent outlets such as Whole Foods and food co-ops. According to Rodney, "They are interested enough in being healthier, and supporting environmental sustainability that they spend more time researching their purchases, they'll go out of their way, and they'll pay more (but not just any price). Some of them are also interested in matters of fairness and social justice—and will shape their purchases accordingly."

In a 2008 study by Alter Eco USA, 71.4 percent of US consumers reported that they had heard the term "fair trade." However, less than 10 percent surveyed reported that they had recently purchased a fair trade item. This pattern may be changing. Researchers from the Massachusetts Institute of Technology, Harvard University, and the London School of Economics found "substantial consumer support for Fair Trade, although a segment of price-sensitive shoppers will not pay a large premium for the Fair Trade label."[8] The consumers who were already purchasing premium coffee were willing to pay an additional 8 percent for fair trade labeled premium coffee. The Fair Trade Federation expects the market to continue to grow if distribution widens and consumers can more easily identify fair trade products.

Challenges

Although EE is the largest company in the United States that sells fair trade products exclusively and has continued to grow, Rob sees challenges ahead. One is the trend toward locally grown or prepared food. Obviously, coffee cannot be locally grown in the continental United States, but it is increasingly locally *roasted*, a very popular selling point.

The significant challenge that Rob sees is "how does EE remain entrepreneurial?" As he said:

One challenge ahead is being prepared to take more risks, being prepared to reinvest in ourselves structurally, or whether it's to spin off cooperatives. We're contemplating this with the retail cafe sector. Being prepared to take risks and also how do we look at this thing, a big company succeeding in many local markets where we aren't necessarily based there, that's a challenge.

Given EE's leadership, worker-owners, culture, and history, changes do seem inevitable. The question is "what changes will they make?"

Notes

1. http://www.equalexchange.coop/worker-owned/. Accessed: July 25, 2012.
2. Internal document entitled "Background to the Governance Matrix—October 2005 Version."
3. Internal document entitled "Evolution of EE Governance: Worker-Owner Oversight of Education Committee."
4. "Cup coffee" is an expression used to describe the industry standard process to test the quality of coffee.
5. The trikes were introduced after this interview was conducted. To see a *Boston Globe* article about them, see http://www.boston.com/ae/food/restaurants/articles /2010/09/22/thanks_to_equal_exchange_trikes_its_one_whole_cafe_with_cream _and_sugar_to_go/.
6. http://www.equalexchange.coop/annual-reports/index.php. Accessed: July 25, 2013.
7. See http://www.fairtrade.net/single_view1+M528a593be0f.html. Accessed: July 26, 2012.
8. Hainmueller, J., Hiscox, M., & Sequeira, S. 2009. Consumer demand for the fair trade label: Evidence from a field experiment, Working paper.

CHAPTER 10

TEOCO (The Employee Owned Company): Principled Entrepreneurship and Shared Leadership

Thomas J. Calo, Olivier P. Roche, and Frank Shipper

Introduction

Fairfax, VA, October 6, 2009. Atul Jain, founder of TEOCO, a provider of specialized software for the telecommunications industry, had been meeting all day to finalize a partnership agreement with TA Associates, a private equity firm. For Atul, the pace of activities had been relentless on this special day.[1] By all accounts, the last 12 hours had been hectic but the closing of the transaction was a success. The event had started with back-to-back meetings between TEOCO's senior management and their new partner's representatives and had culminated with the usual press conference to mark the occasion. The senior management teams of both organizations announced to the business community that TA Associates (TA hereafter) had made a minority equity investment of $60 million in TEOCO. It was indeed a memorable day, the culmination of intense and uneven negotiations between two organizations that did not have much in common except for deep industry knowledge and a shared interest in seeing TEOCO succeed.

This new partnership marked the end of a marathon, but Atul did not feel the excitement that usually comes with crossing the finish line. It was late and he was tired. Back in the quiet of his office, he reviewed, once again, the draft of the press release relating the day's event. As he read the various statements captured from the meetings, he still had the uneasy feeling that comes with making life-changing decisions when one does not have all the required information. There were so many unknowns. Partnering with the right investor, like many other entrepreneurial endeavors, was not a decision made in a vacuum. It was all about good timing, cold analysis, gut feeling, and luck; the latter was last but by no means least. Despite all the uncertainty, Atul felt that this was a worthy endeavor.

Atul had come a long way since his humble beginnings in India and a lot was at stake, not only for him but also for the 300 employees of the company. The TEOCO enterprise had been a successful business endeavor and at the same times a very personal journey. What had begun as a result of frustration with his old job in Silicon Valley 15 years ago had become one of the fastest growing businesses in the telecom software industry; and the fast pace of the company's development had not gone unnoticed. For quite some time now, TEOCO had been on the "radar screen" of investors looking for high-growth opportunities. However, Atul had never cultivated a relationship with potential external investors; he had remained congruous with his long-held business belief that an alliance with external financiers was rarely in the best interest of a company and its employees.

> I am often asked why we didn't approach an investor for money or seek venture capital. I have two answers to this question. My first answer is: that's not our way of doing business. I believe that every entrepreneur must aspire to be debt-free and profitable from the very first day. My second answer is: nobody would have given me the money even if I had asked! I also had a fear—that external investment might impact the culture and values that I wanted TEOCO to promote and cherish. I wanted to steer the TEOCO ship along a very different course. My dream was to set up an enterprise based on a model of shared success. TEOCO's success wouldn't just be my success; it would be our success. TEOCO wouldn't just have one owner; it would be owned by each of its employees—who would therefore be called employee owners.

But several months earlier, events had taken an unexpected turn; unsolicited financiers approached TEOCO once again, this time offering to invest a substantial amount of capital. Still, Atul was reluctant to engage in negotiations with a party that, as far as he knew, did not share TEOCO's values.

> [In the early days] we took a conscious decision not to accept venture capital. I have always had a healthy disdain for venture capital because it numbs the entrepreneur's competitive edge and enfeebles him. I still remember TEOCO's early battles with [competitors] Vibrant and Broadmargin and how difficult it was for us to compete with all that extra money flowing into the rival's coffers. But we took the hard road—and survived... What, then, went wrong with Broadmargin or Vibrant? If I have to over-simplify, I'd say that both were done in by venture capital. VC is an impatient master; it forces you to always go for the home run, and always push hard on the gas. With certain kinds of businesses this works; indeed, it might be the only way. Think of Google: their business space is so vast that only continuous and unbridled growth can sustain the venture. But TEOCO's space is very different; there is no exponential growth here that everyone can go chasing... I would guess that the size of the telecom Cost Management business is no larger than $100 million per year; so to survive you have to be patient and play your cards carefully. This isn't the place to be if you

are in a tearing hurry to grow . . . While this strategy of focusing on niche markets significantly limits our market potential, it does keep the sharks away. The big companies are not bothered by niche products for telecom carriers; they don't want to swim in small ponds.

Atul's comment reflected the situation a few years ago; TA's recent partnership offer was made in a new context. In this rapidly changing industry, there are constantly new directions in technology and the landscape continually shifts. The industry, consolidating quickly, required that in order to remain a viable player, TEOCO would have to change gears—sooner rather than later.

Until now, the primary focus of the company had been on the North American telecom carriers. However, with the anticipated consolidation of the telecom industry in North America, TEOCO needed to focus on international expansion. In addition, to leverage TEOCO's deep expertise in cost, revenue and routing, the company would soon need to swim "outside the pond" and enter the global business support system/operations support system (BSS/OSS) market. Here, TEOCO could find itself in competition with much larger players and it would be valuable to have a strong financial partner.

Indeed, the company had reached an important threshold in its organizational development. But if TEOCO was at a crossroads, so was its founder. Atul was in his late forties and he was not getting any younger. In this industry Atul had known many entrepreneurs who, like himself, had rapidly grown their businesses only to find out that "you are only as good as your last call." For a few of these entrepreneurs, one or two poor decisions had triggered a descent that had been as swift as their earlier ascent and they ended up with very little to show for their efforts. These were the intangibles. During rare moments of quiet reflection, Atul realized that his "risk return profile" had changed imperceptibly over time. Having all his eggs in the same basket and going for all or nothing had been fun in his mid-thirties when everything was possible, but it would be much less so in his early fifties when starting from scratch would be a very unappealing scenario for Atul and his family. Furthermore, he felt an obligation to create liquidity for the employees who had supported him on this 15-year journey and had their own dreams and goals. At the end of the day, any business has only three exit options: it could get listed, be sold, or go bankrupt! And the latter option is not particularly appealing.

It was in this context and mindset that he had agreed to listen to what TA had to offer. Founded in 1968, TA had become one of the largest private equity firms in the country. The company was managing more than $16 billion in capital by 2009 and it had an extensive knowledge of the industry. Atul was impressed by TA's approach, its willingness to take a minority position, and Kevin Landry, chairman and the "spirit" of TA. This private equity firm not only managed capital; it also had an impressive network of relationships. In addition, TA executives had been adamant that Atul remain in charge, and he was keen on continuing as the controlling shareholder. The fund would

Table 10.1 Board of directors

In addition to John Devolites, Philip M. Giuntini, and Atul Jain, TEOCO's board is composed of a majority of outside board members with deep telecom industry expertise:

Gabriel Battista, former chairman, Talk America: Gabe Battista formerly served as chairman of the board of directors of Talk America, where he previously served as CEO. Prior to joining Talk America in January of 1999, Mr. Battista served as CEO of Network Solutions, Inc. Before joining Network Solutions, Mr. Battista served as CEO, president, and COO of Cable & Wireless, Inc. He also held management positions at US Sprint, GTE Telenet, and The General Electric Company. He serves as a director of Capitol College, and Systems & Computer Technology Corporation (SCTC).

Brian J. Conway, managing director, TA Associates: Mr. Conway heads TA Associates' Boston office Technology Group, focused on recapitalizations, buyouts, and minority growth investments of technology-based growth companies. He is also a member of TA Associates' executive committee. Prior to joining TA Associates, Mr. Conway worked with Merrill Lynch in Mergers and Acquisitions and Corporate Finance. He serves on the board of directors for Epic Advertising, IntraLinks, and Numara Software.

Hythem T. El-Nazer, senior vice president, TA Associates: Mr. El-Nazer's focus at TA Associates is on recapitalizations, management-led buyouts, and growth capital investments in telecommunications, media, and other technology-based services companies. Prior to joining TA Associates, Mr. El-Nazer worked with McKinsey & Company and Donaldson, Lufkin & Jenrette—Investment Banking. He serves on the board of directors for eSecLending, Radialpoint, and is board observer at Orascom Telecom Holding SAE and Weather Investments SpA.

Robert J. Korzeniewski, former executive vice president, VeriSign: As VeriSign's executive vice president, Corporate Development and Strategy, Mr. Robert Korzeniewski is responsible for providing a consistent strategy and focus for investments and merger-and-acquisition activity. Mr. Korzeniewski served from 1996 to 2000 as CFO of Network Solutions, Inc., which was acquired by VeriSign in June 2000. Mr. Korzeniewski came to Network Solutions from SAIC, where from 1987 to 1996, he held a variety of senior financial positions.

Source: TEOCO's website.

appoint two board members (see table 10.1) but TEOCO's current management team would still lead the company as they had in the past.

Reviewing the details, Atul could not spot any flaws in the logic of the transaction. It was neither a marriage of love nor a "shotgun wedding," just a pragmatic alliance between two companies with complementary skills and resources at a time when such alliance was valuable to both parties: TA looking for a good investment and TEOCO shareholders looking for partial liquidity. As Atul reread the press release and a few of his quotes, he reflected that he meant every word.

> We are pleased to welcome TA as our first institutional investor. As a company that has avoided external capital for 15 years, we are delighted to find a partner that will strengthen TEOCO without changing the culture of our organization. We see this as the beginning of a new phase in TEOCO's history where we look to add even greater value to communications service providers worldwide.

This was definitively a new era and there would be no turning back. For better or for worse, this partnership had to work. Atul made minor corrections to the wording of the document and authorized its release.

Company Background and Activities

TEOCO's predecessor, Strategic Technology Group (STG), was founded as an S corporation in 1994. The company's initial focus was to provide high quality consultancy for IT projects. STG's first clients included Mobil, Siemens, Cable & Wireless, SRA, TRW, and Freddie Mac. The company started operations in April 1995 and three years later, in March 1998, the company name was changed to TEOCO (The Employee Owned Company). At the same time, TEOCO made the strategic decision to shift its business from consultancy to product development and to focus on the telecommunications industry. This was achieved through the acquisition of a fledgling software product that processed invoices of telecom payables. BillTrak Pro would ultimately become TEOCO's best-selling network cost management software.

Subsequently, the company grew rapidly. As the number of employees exceeded 75, the maximum numbers of shareholders an S corporation can have, the company changed its status to a C corporation to enable a broad-based employee ownership. Over the years preceding the burst of the "dot.com" bubble, TEOCO not only expanded its client base for its basic products but also invested substantial amounts of capital in three startups. These entities were: *netgenShopper.com* for online auctions; *Eventrix*, an event planning portal; and *AppreciateYou.com* to support employee retention. These Internet startups functioned as separate entities, each at their own location, with their own business goals and core values, managed by different entrepreneurs/managers; at the same time, they each relied on TEOCO's cash flow for their development.

Ultimately, none of these ventures emerged as viable businesses and this left TEOCO in a difficult financial situation. As a result, TEOCO registered its first year of losses in 2000. Atul recounted:

> This failure was devastating, but also a humbling experience. I learned the hard way that no entrepreneur can survive inside a technology incubator. We had to pay a price for all these transgressions... Our revenues were still impressive, but the money in the bank was dwindling rapidly... We were truly caught in deep and dangerous waters. I have often wondered what went wrong. It wasn't as if we made one big mistake... I guess we just took our eyes off the ball. Somewhere along the way, we lost our focus; we tried to do too many things at the same time and ended up getting nothing right. We had to quickly get back to our knitting. The question was: how?

Under Atul's leadership, TEOCO made the judicious decision to refocus its activities on its core industry expertise and its largest clients. To achieve this, the organization solidified its position in the telecom sector by improving its services and developing new products. In 2004, research and development efforts resulted in the patented XTrak technology, which today represents the core of the company's invoice automation solution. In addition, TEOCO was able to migrate from software licensing to the far more lucrative software-as-a-service model. Instead of a fixed licensing fee, the company charged a recurring monthly fee based on the volume of data processed for each client. As the recurring revenue model took hold, it became much easier to grow revenues from year to year and improve company's profitability.

In 2006, TEOCO acquired Vibrant Solutions, bringing in cost management and business intelligence assets with its 24 employees. Ultimately this resulted in the important development of TEOCO's SONAR solution for cost, revenue, and customer analytics. Finally, in 2008, Vero Systems was acquired, adding routing management and its 36 employees to the repertoire of communication service provider solutions.

This stream of acquisitions and internal development left TEOCO with a staff of about 300 employees and a portfolio of three major activities: cost management, least cost routing, and revenue assurance.

Cost Management

Cost management solutions include invoice automation and payable processing. Powered by XTrak, TEOCO's invoice automation solution processes over 1,000,000 invoices annually. This facilitates the audit and analysis of billions of dollars in current billings due to each telecom company. While the usual scanning of paper bills relies on optical character recognition technologies that routinely require hands-on intervention to correct misrepresented characters on complex invoices, the XTrak technology mines the original formats that produced the paper to create files for loading into cost management solutions. By eliminating the tedious, costly, and error-prone task of manual invoice data entry, telecom companies increase productivity and reduce costs by increasing the number of disputes filed and resolved and by reducing late-payment charges. In addition, TEOCO also processes "payables" on behalf of clients by managing the full life-cycle of invoice payment, including account coding, management review, and payment reconciliation. TEOCO's employees audit client invoices, comparing rates, inventory, and usage with other source data to identify and recover additional savings. Finally, the company manages disputed claims on behalf of its clients from creation through resolution. TEOCO has the technical capability to capture all correspondence between parties and can review and track every claim to resolution.

With regard to cost management, it is worth noting that the Sarbanes-Oxley Act of 2002 requires every listed company to implement a reliable reporting system. TEOCO's services support this compliance by improving the details and timeliness of the reports generated by/for telecom companies. TEOCO's rapid development in this area coincided with a market need that was augmented by the legal requirements imposed by the act.

Least Cost Routing

TEOCO's routing solutions help telecom companies determine the optimal route between two customers with regard to cost, quality of service, and margin targets. Capable of supporting multiple services and various networks, the company is able to monitor CDRs (call detail records) in near real time to identify bottlenecks, reroute traffic, and improve the quality of services for greater satisfaction of its clients' customers.

Revenue Assurance

Communications service providers can lose 5 to 15 percent of gross revenue due to revenue leakage. TEOCO's SONAR solution is an industry first in supporting switch-to-bill reconciliation. TEOCO combines its specialized industry expertise with high-capacity data warehouse appliances to create a unified CDR and makes a high volume of current and historical CDR data available on a single platform for in-depth analysis. This helps telecom companies uncover billing discrepancies, detect fraudulent behavior, reveal usage patterns, understand customer profitability, conduct margin analysis, and determine the financial viability of reciprocal compensation agreements.

Industry Landscape: Continuous Change

Competitors

TEOCO operates in a fragmented and highly competitive industry. Table 10.2 lists its competitors in each of the three major business segments. TEOCO operates mostly in North America; therefore, the main competitors in the cost management segment are Razorsight, Connectiv, and Subex. These same companies compete for revenue assurance, as well as others such as cVidya and Wedo. Finally, in the least cost routing segment, TEOCO faces a different set of competitors: Pulse Networks, Global Convergence Solutions, and Telarix. As Brian (Marketing & Communications Department) sees it: "So [from the customer's point of view] what we bring to the table is just end-to-end solutions that reach all of these different categories. While we still compete with certain people, it's on a specific product; not across the board."

Indeed, with the possible exception of Subex, none of these competitors operate in the same three business segments as TEOCO; and Subex does not provide a domestic least cost routing in North America. Since TEOCO derives 50 percent of its revenue from cost management and 25 percent from revenue assurance, Razorsight and Subex could be considered TEOCO's main business competitors. Faye, general manager/Account Management, summarizes TEOCO's current market position. "In North America, we dominate the cost management space. We've got a decent lock on least cost routing, which is a very operational and technical function that bridges between network and finance."

One of the ways TEOCO differs from most of its VC backed competitors is its focus on internal cost management. This manifests itself in two different ways. The management begins the year by making a conservative revenue plan for the year. The company then manages its expenses to be a fixed percentage of the projected revenues. Investments in sales, marketing, and R&D are adjusted throughout the year to ensure that expenses stay within the predefined limits. The second way cost management manifests itself is how the

Table 10.2 Industry landscape/major competitors

	Regions					Market Segments	
Vendors	NA	CALA	EMEA	APAC	OVERALL	Mobile	PSTN
1. Least cost routing							
Ascade	P	—	NP	NP	NP	NP	NP
Connective-Sol	NP	—	—	P	P	NP	P
GCS	NP	—	—	NP	NP	NP	NP
OrcaWave	NP	—	P	P	P	P	NP
Prime Carrier	P	—	P	P	P	P	P
Pulse Networks	NP	—	—	NP	NP	NP	NP
Subex	—	NP	—	—	—	—	—
Telarix	ML	P	ML	ML	ML	ML	ML
2. Revenue assurance							
Connectiva	P	P	NP	NP	NP	NP	NP
Connectiv	NP	—	—	—	P	NP	P
cVidya	NP	—	—	NP	—	—	NP
Razorsight	P	—	—	—	P	P	P
Subex	NP	P	ML	ML	ML	ML	ML
Qosmos	P	—	P	P	P	P	P
Wedo	NP	—	ML	NP	ML	ML	ML
3. Cost management							
Connectiv	P	—	—	—	P	P	P
Martin Dawes	—	—	NP	—	P	NP	P
Razorsight	ML	—	—	—	NP	NP	NP
Subex	P	NP	ML	ML	ML	ML	ML

Source: TEOCO Marketing Department.

Notes: NA = North America; CALA = Central America & Latin America; EMEA = Europe, Middle East, and Africa; APAC = Asia & Pacific; PSTN = Public Switched Telephone Network.

P = Has a presence in the market.

NP = Has a notable presence in the market.

ML = Is a market leader.

cost of each individual transaction is closely managed and monitored, whether it be purchasing hardware, leasing office space, renewing supplier contracts, recruiting new employees, or planning business travel.

One of the consequences of this strong discipline of cost management is that TEOCO is consistently profitable, something most of its competitors struggle to accomplish. This enables the company to focus its energy on clients and innovation.

Clients

TEOCO operates in an industry where clients are known and clearly identifiable. One of the key reasons clients buy from TEOCO is because its solutions have a strong ROI (return on investment). In other words, TEOCO's products quickly pay for themselves and then begin to generate profits for the companies that subscribe to them. As Faye described TEOCO's market:

The telecommunication space is who we sell to exclusively, and within that space, we have a relatively known and discreet customer list or target list, if you will. We don't sell cookies. Not everybody's going to buy what we're selling...I know who those customers are and I can identify groups within that addressable market that fall into natural tiers. So either because of their size or because of the market that they cater to, themselves, whether they're wireless or wire line or whether they're cable companies, I can identify who they are and then try to focus products and services that I think will best meet their needs.

There are four telecom companies that drive about 65 percent of TEOCO's domestic revenue: Verizon, Sprint, AT&T, and Qwest; these are the "platinum" accounts. For obvious reasons, they get a lot of attention from both the engineering and product delivery standpoints. Thirty-five other companies, including Cricket, Global Crossing, Metro PCS, Level 3, and Bell Canada, account for the remaining balance of revenues.

TEOCO, like most of its competitors, is client-centered. Smooth customer interactions are not only critical to increase sales and garner new relationships but also to develop new products. Over the years, most of the ideas for new products or improvements to existing products have come out of discussions with customers. Hillary of the Marketing & Communications Department described how TEOCO remains client-centered as follows: "Our number one avenue for receiving customer feedback is our TEOCO summit, our annual user meeting...where customers are able to talk one-on-one with not only TEOCO representatives but also with other customers to learn what they are doing...and then circling back with TEOCO."

Initially, TEOCO used its generic products, either developed in-house or brought in via acquisitions, to start relationships with new clients. More recently, however, the company has innovated solutions driven by specific clients. These, in turn, are adjusted to suit the needs of other clients. Dave, software architect, provided this example of an "evolutionary loop."

> With our first product [BillTrak Pro], we sold it to a number of different carriers resulting in a broad footprint of wireline and wireless carriers. Then we had account managers engage with our customers, and it's through conversations with our existing customers, generally, that the ideas for the next set of products come out... More recently, I'd say that most of our products are customer-driven, so what will happen is we'll have someone in the company that will identify a need at a specific customer. Then, we'll enter into some kind of partnership with them, whether we'll develop the application specifically to their needs and then work to resell that and make it useful to other customers as well.

Growth Strategies

TEOCO's Product Strategy: "Spidering" through Clients' Organizations

Since the number of clients is limited, two other ways to grow the business are cultivated. A company like TEOCO can either "productize" its current services or acquire a competitor with a different client base and cross-sell its products. Faye described this process.

> For the products we're selling, if we have two new sales a year, that's signifi-
> cant...maybe you could squeak out a third in a good year. So the majority of the
> sales growth really comes from existing accounts...most of the growth though is
> coming from those large platinum accounts. Those are the ones that have money
> to spend and where we're driving products, driving solutions, trying to help them
> tell us or help them identify where they have needs. The other way to grow the
> business is to acquire companies that have a different business and then cross-
> sell services. For instance, with the Vero acquisition, we added another 'vertical'
> line of business [least cost routing]...And then Vero had a relatively separate
> client base...so we were able to cross-sell products into each other's companies'
> portfolio of clients [i.e., TEOCO's clients buying least cost routing services and
> Vero's clients buying cost management products].

Faye joined the company in March 2010, a few months after the TA's investment in TEOCO with a charter to grow TEOCO's revenues with its smaller
customers. With Faye in position, the company became more market-driven
and far more aggressive in cross-selling its services and products among the
three main lines of business. As well, it adopted a more cohesive approach to
expand the client base, including leveraging its reputation for excellence and
for having the technical ability to solve problems across various business segments. Faye described how this worked.

> We're "spidering" through [our clients'] organizations. With each additional
> organization that we enter into, the stickier we become. Our software products
> run the gamut from mission critical to nice-to-have. And the more mission criti-
> cals and nice-to-haves we get, the stickier we are in that organization, in all the
> organizations...[For instance]...I'm not going outside AT&T, but I have—
> instead of two customers at AT&T, I now have ten. And they're distinctly dif-
> ferent sales each time.

TEOCO's Acquisition Strategy

For the first ten years of TEOCO's existence, Atul had built the business based
on the premise that growth had to be organic and financed through internal cash flow. To some extent, his views on acquisition were consistent with
his opinions about external financing from VCs and private funds. For Atul,
acquisition and growth financed by external funds represented a risky development strategy that could dilute a company's culture.

However, as noted earlier, internal growth through innovation had been
slow and limited in scope. Cross-selling products between vertical lines of business coming from acquired companies with a different client base offered far
more potential for the organization's growth. Therefore, it was just a matter of

time before TEOCO would decide to "experiment" with acquisitions as Atul recalled:

> When we started building TEOCO, I was very focused on organic growth. I felt that acquisitions tend to dilute culture and values. But then we happened to acquire a company called Vibrant Solutions (in 2006) and that acquisition went so phenomenally well, it gave us a lot of encouragement. The people were great, the product was solid and the client relationships were very valuable. They integrated well into our company and into our culture. We felt it made TEOCO a much stronger company. We had just broadened from cost management into revenue management before we acquired Vibrant, but I don't believe we would have been as successful in delivering on that without the expertise of the people that came from that acquisition.[2]

The subsequent acquisition of Vero in 2008 brought TEOCO closer to the network and strengthened its position in the marketplace, particularly with the larger customers. This reinforced TEOCO's belief that acquisition of carefully selected targets should be a key component of its overall growth strategy. Atul described his own transformation: "So at the end of that I said to myself maybe my narrow-minded thinking about acquisition diluting the culture was wrong, that in fact, if you do it right, you have an opportunity to strengthen the culture."[3]

From these two positive experiences, Atul established guidelines for the kinds of companies to target when scanning the market for future acquisitions. TEOCO would look for companies that:

- had people with deep industry expertise;
- offered solutions/products that the marketplace valued;
- had a solid customer base that had been established over time;
- offered potential synergies with current products/services offered by TEOCO;
- had not been able to develop their full potential due to poor management; and
- had a manageable size to facilitate their integration into TEOCO's current businesses.

Atul elaborated on these last two points:

> One thing you will see in the companies we acquire is that before the acquisition those companies were not running that smoothly. If they were, perhaps they wouldn't be up for sale or be affordable. We tend to acquire companies that present a challenge but also an opportunity for us to improve the business and make it much stronger and more valuable.[4]

What enabled TEOCO to successfully integrate Vibrant and Vero into its business? TEOCO brought to the table: (1) a solid core business that generated a positive and stable cash flow; (2) a well-established strength in cost management (not only for its clients but also for itself); and (3) a disciplined approach to the management of human resources. Indeed, TEOCO is conservatively managed and Atul is recognized by employees for his ability to select and retain the best while optimizing the use of the organization's human resources. TEOCO core strengths, when applied to the business of Vibrant and Vero, resulted in a bigger and better company.

TTI Acquisition Rationale: Going Global and Getting "Closer to the Network"

In December 2009, TEOCO began to consider the acquisition of the company that would become in 2010 its biggest acquisition ever—TTI Telecom. TTI was an Israel-based global supplier of service assurance solutions to communications service providers. The company had 300 employees and was listed on NASDAQ (TTIL). Through this acquisition, TEOCO would gain access to a wide array of intellectual property including a Mediation Platform, Fault Management, and Performance Management Systems, and valuable expertise in 4-G and data-centric networks. Service assurance is important in a data environment because it reduces jitter and packet loss during the delivery of high value data transfer. To some extent, TEOCO's existing portfolio of services and products would expand on TTI's well-recognized expertise in the next generation network (i.e., 4-G). In addition, TTI had an international client base that offered the potential to cross-sell TEOCO's existing product lines. On August 2010, TEOCO completed the acquisition, thus taking a big step in a new direction, which, as of this writing, has yet to show conclusive results, but is considered a positive move. Atul commented at the time of the TTI acquisition:

> Our last acquisition was Vero Systems (in October, 2008) and that brought us one step closer to the network. We were doing least cost routing and in that world you are trying to help determine how to terminate calls in the most cost-effective manner. The Vero solution got us working with network players and got us into the switches. It became clear that the closer we got to the network, the better business value we could create. So we started looking for companies that have intellectual property and an international client base that would bring us even closer to the network. TTI [Telecom] really fit that bill for us. TEOCO has traditionally been focused on North America so we thought acquiring a company with an international client base was of value to us. Their solutions in fault management, performance management and service management all bring us closer to network and assuring Quality of Service. We are good at handling large volumes of data and deriving intelligence out of that data. And we convert that intelligence into business value. A lot of people can derive intelligence from data but they aren't able to create actionable intelligence that creates bottom line value. We think we will be able to improve the economics of the data TTI collects for our customers. It may be a little into the future, but we believe this acquisition positions us to get to that future.[5]

TTI Acquisition Challenges

From a technical and marketing point of view, the acquisition of TTI represented a very logical move that would allow TEOCO to expand its business while remaining focused on telecom carriers. It fit many of the acquisition criteria that Atul had laid out (see prior section), but it also represented a substantial departure from previous acquisitions in three critical aspects: its size, its location and culture, and the means of its acquisition.

1. *The size of the target company:* In terms of revenues, TTI was four to five times larger than the last acquisition made by TEOCO and this purchase effectively doubled the size of the organization. On that point, Atul was the first to recognize that TEOCO was entering uncharted territories. He described the uncertainty as follows:

   All the other acquisitions were small. We bought a company with 24 employees, we bought a company with 36 employees, and this time we bought a company with 300 plus employees. So, this is going to present a completely different challenge and I don't know what that is going to be because I haven't dealt with it. So, it's yet to come.

From the outset, and unlike prior acquisitions, TTI remained an entity that was managed separately. Therefore, one of the key issues to be addressed in the short-to-medium term would be the degree of integration between the two companies.

2. *The location and culture of the target company:* TEOCO had essentially been operating in the United States, whereas TTI was located in Israel and was far more international in its operations. This created tremendous opportunities for marketing synergies and for cross-selling products to a different client base. As Faye saw it:

   I see leveraging a lot of the existing sales and marketing resources in Israel. I mean they have a strong presence in Israel, but they're really European. EMEA is big. But also CIS, they do a lot in Russia... MTS is one of their customers, which is just a huge, huge Russian company. Internationally, it's a brand new client base into which we can cross-sell the least cost routing and probably not the cost management products because they don't translate outside of North America as well. But certainly the least cost routing products. Taking their products into the North American base is definitely something we can do. And as far as clients' crossover versus new, they have about ten North American customers, only four of whom are existing customers of ours.

At the same time, however, it also exposed TEOCO's business to a pool of larger competitors that competed on a global basis. TTI was "swimming in a different pond" in which blue chip companies with well-recognized brands and deep pockets were aggressively marketing their services. Faye commented on the transition as follows:

We participate in a handful of shows, and again, that's expanding quite a bit this year because of the international presence and customer base... it's further complicated, though, by this acquisition of TTI because...they are a very sales and marketing-centric company, and it's going to be interesting to see how the cultures meld...I see a lot of Advil for me between now and then. We're going to have to get there. Traditionally, TTI has gone to a lot of shows and they like to build brand new booths and spend hundreds of thousands of dollars for each of these shows on their presence there, and [at TEOCO] we don't do that.

Indeed, TEOCO's management was cost conscious and not prepared to invest heavily in shows and other marketing activities where return on investment is difficult to measure. It was not evident how the two cultures would merge. TTI management might argue that substantial resources would be needed to compete in their market segment while TEOCO's management would probably take the position that overspending on marketing and poor cash-flow management were the reasons for TTI's financial problems prior to its acquisition.

3. *The means of acquisition:* One cannot understand the acquisition of TTI without first understanding how the alliance with TA changed the company's and CEO's ways of doing business, as well as their risk/return profile. To some extent TA gave TEOCO's management both the means and the incentives to take more risks. TA's involvement provided TEOCO with the credentials to approach financial institutions and increase the company's financial leverage to acquire a large target. It is one thing when a US$50 million company approaches a bank to finance the acquisition of another company of equivalent size. It is quite another when a US$16 billion equity firm with a substantial stake in the acquirer approves the transaction at the board level. Following TA's equity participation, no one ever asked TEOCO if they had the means to acquire TTI and complete the transaction. The legitimacy provided by TA's participation was essential for the financing of the acquisition of a listed company where time is of the essence. Avi Goldstein (CFO) described this transition as follows

> Before TA came on board, taking debt was something that was not on the table. And when TA came on board and they asked us, "Are you willing to take debt to finance acquisitions?" and we said, "Yes"...And maybe without TA we wouldn't go after TTI because of the debt, not so much because of the size of TTI.

While providing the means to be more aggressive in TEOCO's growth strategy, the partnership with TA also reduced Atul's aversion to risk. It was the TA "push-and-pull" strategy (i.e., providing the financial means while reducing the acceptable risk threshold) that allowed this transaction to materialize. Atul explained this further:

I haven't fully understood how the TA transaction has changed us. I think, over time, I will understand how it has changed us. All I can tell you is that I feel a degree of financial independence and I personally feel that it is more important for me to focus on making a greater difference for the world. I don't know that I could have supported this acquisition if I hadn't gotten liquidity because this acquisition had a much higher risk profile.

Company Culture and Philosophy

The background and evolution of TEOCO provide the context for exploring the unique way in which the organization functions, which in turn explains the basis for its success. Three different lenses provide the focus for this understanding: shared leadership; a culture of employee ownership; and human resources as a strategic function. These three characteristics have combined to contribute to TEOCO's success, as well as its competitive advantage.

Shared Leadership

The shared leadership team is comprised of three leaders of the organization with distinctly different, but complementary, skills and responsibilities. These leaders are Atul Jain (chairman and chief executive officer [CEO]), Philip M. Giuntini (vice chairman and president), and John Devolites (vice president and general manager) (see table 10.3).

Atul is the central figure in the story of TEOCO. By understanding Atul's background, philosophy of life, vision and style, the organization and its unique culture create a cohesive portrait.

Atul was born in India in the early 1960s. He has an older sister and an older brother. His father was a mid-level civil servant in India, now retired. Both of his parents live with him and his family, which is customary in Indian culture. Atul is married and has three children. His intellect and abilities were identified at an early age. When he was a teenager, he was invited to attend the prestigious Indian Statistical Institute, known as one of the best schools in India for the study of statistics, which required that the young Atul move away from home to live in another part of the country.

Atul was raised in the Indian religion of Jainism, an important aspect of his background that shaped his view of people and organizations. While he does not wear his religion "on his sleeve," it is evident that his religious beliefs and upbringing have had a significant impact on his leadership style and the culture he has shaped within TEOCO. Atul does not go to temple and does not even pray, so in that sense he does not consider himself to be a religious person. On the other hand, he expressed that he has internalized the culture and religion and that it manifests in his thinking about business. Jainism is an ancient but minority religion in India,[6] yet its influence far exceeds its size, as Jains represent some of the wealthiest Indians. Among its core beliefs are a philosophy of nonviolence toward all living things, vegetarianism, a strong belief in self-help and self-support, and a continual striving toward the liberation of the soul. These tenets can be seen in Atul as he believes that everyone is an "independent

Table 10.3 TEOCO/TTI leadership

Atul Jain, chairman and CEO: Atul Jain founded TEOCO Corporation in 1994. Prior to starting TEOCO Corporation, Mr. Jain was with a Silicon Valley firm called TIBCO for seven years. At TIBCO, Mr. Jain's focus was to work with Fortune 500 clients to design and build state-of-the-art software solutions leveraging the company's trademark TIB platform.

Philip M. Giuntini, vice chairman and president: Philip M. Giuntini joined TEOCO in February 2000 as vice chairman and president. Prior to joining TEOCO, Mr. Giuntini was president and on the board of directors of American Management Systems, Inc. (AMS), a $1B international business and information technology consulting firm headquartered in Fairfax, Virginia.

John Devolites, vice president and general manager: John Devolites is currently the vice president and general manager at TEOCO focusing on solutions for the communications service provider industry. Previously, Mr. Devolites served as president of professional services for Telcordia. His other work experiences include executive positions at PricewaterhouseCoopers, E-Commerce Industries, Andersen, American Management Systems (AMS), Alexander Proudfoot PLC, and Booz Allen Hamilton.

Avi Goldstein, chief financial officer (CFO): Avi Goldstein joined TEOCO in October 2008 and was nominated TEOCO's CFO in April 2009. Prior to joining TEOCO, Mr. Goldstein cofounded several startup companies as well provided consulting services in the telecom arena with a strong focus on mergers and acquisitions. Prior to that Mr. Goldstein served as an executive vice president and CFO of ECtel Ltd. (NASDAQ: ECTX) from its establishment until 2005. Mr. Goldstein led ECtel to a successful IPO as well as private placements and M&A activities.

Eitan Naor, general manager and CEO of TTI: Eitan Naor joined TEOCO in August 2010 and brings more than 25 years of leadership and experience in the global telecom and service assurance markets. Prior to joining TEOCO, Mr. Naor served as president and CEO of Magic Software (NASDAQ: MGIC), where he led a significant restructure of the business and regained focus in its worldwide network of partners, resulting in a significant increase in sales and a return to profitability in less than one year. Mr. Naor also had great success in his other professional roles, including president and CEO of ECTEL (NASDQ: ECTX), division president at AMDOCS, and vice president with ORACLE Israel.

Source: TEOCO's website.

soul," and that consequently he "can't make you do anything that you don't want to do." What stands out is that this type of thinking is very uncharacteristic for a leader. For example, he says:

> As a CEO of the company, I understand that I have no control over anybody. I can't get anybody to do anything...so I don't spend my time trying to control people...what I try to do is to conduct myself in a manner that may encourage people to work in a certain way. I can try to create an environment that is encouraging; an environment in which people wish to excel.

When he came to the United States it was not to be an entrepreneur but to study for a doctorate degree in probability and statistics. He describes himself as an "accidental entrepreneur." A disillusioning experience working for a Silicon Valley firm led him to reconsider his options. When commitments regarding future assignments and compensation were not honored, and he felt disrespected by the company's CFO, he became motivated to take the risk to establish his own company to prove that "you don't have to be an *&%$# in order to succeed in business." At the same time, this experience impressed upon him the importance of treating his future colleagues with fairness and respect.

Atul's personal leadership style, which is reflected by the organization, overall, is quite atypical, especially for an entrepreneur. Atul openly admits his shortcomings. While manifesting many of the traits of an entrepreneur, he sets himself apart by claiming that one of his greatest strengths is that he knows what he does not know. In fact, he even says, "I know that I don't know how to run a business." In conjunction with his perceived shortcomings, he also believed that you create joy at work by sharing the decision-making with others in the organization. The end result was his desire to establish a structure of shared leadership within TEOCO. He demonstrated this by establishing a "Steering Committee" of the senior employees within one year of the existence of the company, much prior to his association with Philip and John.

While there has been much discussion in the management literature on the potential value of shared leadership, few organizations have attempted it, and even fewer have utilized it successfully. In many respects, the notion of shared leadership is quite contrary to traditional beliefs about leadership in US organizations, which have strongly followed the military model of command and control. Atul's personal background and beliefs, coupled with a unique confluence of circumstances, have made shared leadership a major factor contributing to the success of TEOCO.

To understand why shared leadership at TEOCO was both possible and successful requires an understanding of the unique combination of personalities, leadership strengths, and styles, along with the career and life circumstances—not only of Atul, the founder and CEO, but also the other two members of the leadership team: Philip, president; and John, general manager.

Philip was a very successful, retired executive. Atul read an article in the *Washington Post* in September 1998 that profiled Philip's retirement from American Management Systems (AMS) after 28 years. He contacted Philip, established a relationship with him, and eventually persuaded him to become a member of TEOCO's board of advisors. Within a year, Philip agreed to come out of retirement to serve as the vice chairman and president.

John followed a path similar to Philip's. He served as president of professional services for Telecordia. His earlier career experiences included executive positions at PriceWaterhouseCoopers, American Management Systems (AMS), and Booz Allen Hamilton. He became a member of the board in 2000, and in February 2004 he joined the company as a senior executive. In January 2005, he assumed the role of general manager of its telecom business unit.

Personalities

In contrast with these two veteran executives, Atul was an entrepreneur with little or no experience in running a sizable business. However, he was a leader with a vision, strong intellect, and a passion to build a successful company. In explaining why shared leadership works at TEOCO when it has not worked at many other organizations, Atul says that "I recognize that Philip and John are far more seasoned business professionals than me...I go to them for guidance and advice and I will rarely do things that they do not agree with." That said, Atul acknowledged that there are many challenges to shared leadership.

> The single biggest thing it requires on my part is to give up a ton of decision-making authority, and most people in a CEO chair are not willing to do that. I have to be subservient to John and Philip, and I'm happy to be...I feel that it is not in my personality to be authoritative...being forced to conduct myself in an authoritative manner is offensive to my soul.

John underlined the importance of personality in ensuring the success of shared leadership. While working at consulting firms, he had studied this concept and he commented, "I will tell you that when you look at the situation, it comes back to the individuals and the egos that they have. And if they have large egos, this would not work." When first asked about describing shared leadership at TEOCO, he responded by suggesting, "How about shared fate?"

Complementary Management Skills
The skill sets of these leaders are very complementary, and together form a powerful combination for organizational success. This was described separately, and consistently, by each of them. Atul excels at cost management and judging people. He described his role as follows: "I really see my role as primarily focusing on culture and values and candidly I own all the decisions related to the ownership structure and internal management. However, I don't build anything and I don't sell anything."

Referring to Atul's strengths in cost management and people management, as opposed to direct customer interface, John noted that Atul rarely has customer interface, as Atul entrusts this responsibility to him. John's own skills and interests are focused on creativity and client relations. He sees his job as assembling people around clients and projects, and keeping customers happy. Finally, Philip is the one who makes it all happen. He is skilled at running a business that will endure, and has the organizational skills to free up Atul and John to do what they do best. As Philip describes, "We are all strong in a different place. Collectively, when we are together, we basically combine our strengths and eliminate our weaknesses...we do not compete with each other in our strong areas, and I think that is the key to it." John adds, "We would not be as successful if one of the other two of us weren't here." Atul shares the same view but from a different angle.

> I understand that I have certain strengths, and I tend to focus on playing to those strengths, and I have an understanding of what I'm not...I think incompetence can be valuable, if you know it. If you recognize that you don't know what to do, you're forced to ask others and the resulting collaborative environment has a power of its own.

Career and Life Circumstances
While personality and skills are important factors, it appears as well that life circumstances were a necessary precondition to the effectiveness of the

collaborative model at TEOCO. In their own way, each of these leaders acknowledged that at a different time and place, shared leadership would not necessarily have been a model they would have liked or one with which they would have been successful. As John described, "I think you have to be at a point in your life where you're pretty comfortable with who you are." All three of these men, as a result of their career circumstances, have done well in their professional life. All of them have "builder" personalities; they derive a great deal of satisfaction from growing a business. For these leaders, the journey of growing TEOCO into a successful enterprise is as important as the end result.

Culture of Employee Ownership

Atul has shaped the culture of TEOCO and ensures that it is continuously reinforced. This culture is founded on the core values of the company. As he expresses it, "I define success as 'living up to your values.'" Those values are rooted in a business philosophy he calls "principled entrepreneurship," which he defines as "a business where you have a set of values and you commit to living up to those values while trying to create business success." He further specifies, "They have to be a clear set of articulated values." In describing his success, he says that "what motivates me is to make as big a difference as I can for as many people as I can. And I was never in it solely for the money."

TEOCO has a clearly articulated set of core values (see table 10.4) and a very distinct culture. Atul explains that the former were established even before he knew what the words "core values" meant. The initial slogan for the company was: "We'll take care of our employees, they'll take care of our clients, and that will take care of the business." He says that the actual articulation of and focus on "core values" began after he read a 1999 *Inc. Magazine* article based on the book *Built to Last: Successful Habits of Visionary Companies,*[7] which caused him to ask, "*Who* are we?" rather than focusing primarily on "*What* do we want to be?"

A hallmark of TEOCO is the ownership culture that is embedded in the company. As an employee owned company, Atul wants all employees to buy and own TEOCO stock. Yet consistent with his overall philosophy of life, he does not believe he can make anybody buy the stock; he can only give them information and the opportunity to make that decision. He strongly believes that the environment created by employee ownership leads to better organizational performance and stronger employee commitment. He elaborated:

> I believe in the model of shared success. And I believe that if you share your success with the people that actually influence it and create it, then you create [something] extremely powerful. So, I'm fond of saying that TEOCO is a difficult company to beat—not because we are so good, but because it's tough beating a bunch of employee owners that feel so passionately about what they do.

He and the leadership team continuously seek to create and reinforce an "ownership culture" and have employees take an active part in ownership.

Table 10.4 TEOCO'S core values and value proposition

At TEOCO, The Employee-Owned Company, we are driven by our core values. These values are our guiding principles in all business initiatives:

Alignment with employees, clients, and community: We act in the best interest of our employees, clients, and community, consistently seeking partnership and mutual benefit.
Integrity, honesty, and respect: We value our reputation and conduct our business with integrity, honesty, and respect for each individual.
Acting with courage: We demonstrate a willingness to take risks, while conducting our business in a responsible manner.
Drive for progress through ownership: We are committed to a relentless pursuit of excellence, never being satisfied with the status quo. We are a team whose sum is greater than its parts and devoted to constant innovation.

TEOCO sets standards of excellence that others strive to emulate in our areas of focus—cost management, routing, and revenue management. TEOCO's value proposition is as follows:

Innovation: TEOCO's committed emphasis on one industry allows us unparalleled customer focus. We commit a significant share—up to 30 percent—of our annual revenues to research and development to address your precise needs.
Stability: TEOCO is the only firm in our industry segment that is financially sound, debt free, and employee owned. You can rest assured that we are responsive to your needs and will be there tomorrow.
Integrity: At TEOCO, acting with integrity is one of our essential core values. We focus intensely on developing mutually beneficial, trust-based relationships with customers and communicating honestly in every situation.
Deep industry expertise: Our team includes experienced professionals, many of whom have substantial telecommunications experience and/or have worked directly in service provider cost management organizations.

Source: TEOCO's website.

Carrie (director of human resources) has worked for TEOCO for seven years; previously she had worked for other organizations with stock programs that create an ownership stake in the company. She described her experience:

> I would say that TEOCO is the first company I've worked for where it is as big of a deal. And we make it such a large component of the culture and we spend a ton of time from an HR perspective making sure people understand all the different elements of ownership, why we feel it's important to us, what different programs and mechanisms are out there to provide ownership and allow them to have an ownership stake in the company.

Hillary is an employee who has worked for TEOCO for five years in various professional positions, but has not worked at any other company. She said she realized how much she appreciates the overall work environment at TEOCO when she compared her circumstances with that of friends. To describe the differences that may exist in working for an employee owned company as opposed to a traditional company, she said, "I think the employees here at TEOCO have a lot more knowledge about what's going on."

Dave, one of the earliest and longest-serving employees, when asked what employee ownership meant to him, said, "I've got a stake in the game. My kid's college education is riding on this whole thing. There are no two ways about it...I think a lot of the people in the company think that way." Additionally, John, general manager, explains further, "It's keeping people motivated. It's keeping them focused. I think employee ownership helps us with some of those things... [It's] a very powerful ally when you're in a market that's got a lot of competition in it."

In addition to the organization's core values and corporate culture, the sense of ownership is reinforced through three distinct types of mechanisms: (1) Employees' involvement in the decision-making process; (2) bonus and stock ownership; and (3) a philosophy of total compensation.

Employee Involvement in the Decision-Making Process

The secret to making it work, according to Atul, is that "you have to create a culture of sharing in the decision-making process." The core values of TEOCO are manifested in the degree of employee involvement within the organization, as well as in the many significant ways employees contribute.

"All-hands meeting"

At 11:00 a.m. on the first Thursday of every month, an "all-hands meeting" is held for all employees. This is a standing meeting, never moved or cancelled for any reason—one for US-based employees and one for employees in India. For those US-based employees who are geographically dispersed from corporate headquarters, a video feed goes out and an audio feed comes back so that questions can be posed from off-site locations. Each meeting lasts about 60 to 90 minutes and concludes with a pizza lunch.

These meetings have a structured format so that employees know what to expect. First, new employees are introduced; next, employee service anniversaries are acknowledged and celebrated (five, ten, and fifteen years' service awards are presented); and then there is a monthly drawing for the TeoStar Award. The second half of the meeting more formally introduces its principal objective: leadership providing a business update, as well as any news of particular interest to employees.

Once per quarter the meeting is devoted to detailed financial updates. This is described as an "open book" presentation; there is a review of the balance sheet and client revenues, an update from each line of business, and a discussion of new business prospects. Avi, CFO, elaborated that it is "not only one page of the P & L and one page of the balance sheet; it's pretty extensive." Based on his prior experiences as a CFO, he said this is "like having a shareholder's meeting every quarter." Further, he specified that the company practices "open book management" and that the employees can see the books at any time.

The February meeting each year is devoted to a presentation on the year-end financials, and employees are informed what percent of their target bonus they will receive. As of 2011, all employees with more than three years of service have received more than 100 percent of their target bonus for the last several years. Miscellaneous presentations are also made on topics of relevance, such as an update on the internal stock market.

Every meeting concludes with an open segment called "benefits and concerns." First, employees are encouraged to discuss any benefits received or positive experiences that have happened in the company. Mutual support and a form of company "cheerleading" is adopted. This is followed by a unique opportunity for any employee to raise any issue of concern. No question is considered out of bounds, and senior management is expected to respond openly and fully. The only ground rule is that every question must be phrased in the format of "I wish I knew." For example, "I wish I knew why our financials were not as good this quarter," or "I wish I knew why we do not have a benefit such as . . ." Atul said that this protocol ensures that concerns are presented in an impersonal and nonoffensive manner; rather than being a challenge, each question focuses on looking for an explanation. He said that this approach has been "a game changer," "has really changed the tone of the meetings," and reflects the way in which owners would treat each other.

The A-Team

In addition to the opportunity to raise issues at the "all-hands meeting," a standing group of employee representatives meets each month. TEOCO's advisory team, simply called the A-Team, serves as an interface between the employee owners and the leadership team. The team is comprised of twelve people: eight full-time members and four alternates. Any employee can bring any issue to the A-Team, and the A-Team can bring any issue they choose to the leadership of the company. Similarly, the leadership can bring any issue to the A-Team. This is considered a mechanism to involve employees in the governance of the business; its chief function is to provide a voice to the employee-owners. The membership rotates each year, and outgoing members choose the incoming team. By design it is not intended to be composed of management, and the majority of the members are lower level employees. As well, it intentionally includes a cross-section of members: single, married, from all geographic areas, and from different levels within the organization.

Bonus and Stock Ownership

All employees receive an annual cash bonus. The program seems to function more like a traditional profit sharing plan, as it is not individual performance-related. The bonus pool equals 15 percent of pretax and prebonus profit of the company for the calendar year. The plan is designed to be entirely transparent. Each employee has a target bonus of 8 percent of base salary. The eligibility for the bonus percentage increases as the employee rises to different organizational levels, as follows:

- 20 to 40 percent—executive leadership;
- 20 percent—vice president;
- 16 percent—senior principal;

- 12 percent—principal;
- 8 percent—all other employees.

Titles have no meaning at TEOCO in the traditional sense of their relationship to a level of job responsibility. Rather, titles are determined on the basis of the employee's value to the company. There is a vice president, for example, who does not manage anyone.

In addition to bonuses, employees can purchase stock or receive stock options. At the initial founding of TEOCO in 1994, the only ownership vehicle was for employees to purchase stock outright. At the beginning of the company, Atul offered employees a specific number of shares to purchase, and he claims that every employee took full advantage of this opportunity. However, by 1999–2000, the value of the stock had risen to a level that Atul explains made it difficult for employees to purchase outright, so traditional stock options were awarded, instead of requiring employees to fully purchase the shares at the time of the grant. While acknowledging that options are necessary, Atul strongly believes that "option holders are not the same as shareholders," because he believes that the mere granting of options does not create ownership.

With regard to purchasing stock, it should be noted that employees have the option of taking their annual bonus in stock up to a maximum of 60 percent. The remaining 40 percent is intended for use in paying taxes.

The stock plan also provides for repurchase rights. If an employee is terminated, the company has the right to repurchase the stock, with two exceptions. If an employee worked for the company for at least five years and owned the stock for a minimum of three years or if an employee worked for the company for ten years and owned the stock for at least a year, they may retain the stock, with the rationale that since they contributed many years of service to the success of the company, they should be able to continue to benefit. However, for others the stock is typically repurchased by the company.

Starting in January 2007, the company decided to replace its 401K match with an employee stock ownership plan (ESOP). When the ESOP was implemented, it was both a bold and a controversial decision. Atul came to the reluctant conclusion that if he wanted to create a broad-based ownership, an ESOP was needed as an involuntary mechanism. This was a difficult decision for him as it risked making existing employees unhappy, but he finally realized that it "was the only method to create broad-based ownership [because] educating and cajoling and encouraging was never going to work broadly enough."

His struggle with the ESOP was further complicated by the fact that Philip and John were not initially supportive. Their resistance delayed implementation for a year or two. This issue put the shared leadership model to a test; still, he said that even though he is the CEO, "there are times I know the right answer and they just don't see it, and I accept their decision." Only when these two had fully embraced it was the ESOP adopted. In the end, ESOP became very successful. While some employees were initially unhappy, they eventually saw how the TEOCO stock has outperformed the market since its inception in 2007.

Despite his belief in the need for the ESOP, Atul maintains that it does not create "ownership culture" in the same way that voluntarily investing one's own money to buy shares does. However, he wanted to achieve a broad-based ownership, which, in his opinion, would not have been possible otherwise. From his perspective, ownership means wealth and the real benefit would be realized if the company was sold or went public. A successful and attractive company, especially one in the high-tech field, can expect to sell at a high multiple of the price-to-earnings ratio, which would result in an impressive return for employees, rewarding them for their exemplary performance and company loyalty.

A Philosophy of Total Compensation

Atul's philosophy of compensation is that base salaries should be in the range of 0 to 10 percent below the going market rate. He believes that employees can accept this as a trade-off for a supportive and respectful work environment, a sizable bonus, along with the benefits of employee ownership. He even prefers it when a new employee takes a modest pay cut to join TEOCO, because he believes it is "a very resounding affirmation that they believe in our company and in our core values." He went on to say: "We work our hardest if we are happier, if we enjoy our work and if we feel that we belong. That's why TEOCO has chosen to be an employee owned company; you don't work for an employer here, you work for yourself."

Since every TEOCO employee owns some company stock and receives an annual bonus and generous benefits, he feels that they are not underpaid. This full range of benefits seems to be highly valued and appreciated by employees. Hillary, for example, said that these make it difficult for her to consider leaving to work at another company. In comparing TEOCO's benefits with those her friends receive at other organizations, she is especially appreciative; three weeks instead of two weeks of vacation, the casual work environment, and the flexible schedule were all cited.

Finally, TEOCO never misses an opportunity to recognize employees' commitment to the company, as well as their performance, by distributing awards. These awards reinforce the core values of the company: excellence, dedication, and team work. It should be noted that these are peer-to-peer awards in which fellow employees are recognized for actions that exemplify one of the core values (see table 10.5 for an exhaustive list of TEOCO benefits and awards).

Human Resources as a Strategic Function

In addition to shared leadership and employee ownership programs, the third component of TEOCO's competitive advantage is the way the senior executive team emphasizes the importance of managing TEOCO's main asset: its human resources. In many organizations, human resources is seen as a necessary cost of doing business; the HR function typically operates at a functional level or, at best in far fewer companies, at the executive level.[8] At TEOCO, however, Atul has elevated HR to the strategic level. While there is a dedicated human

Table 10.5   TEOCO's benefits and awards

Flexible schedule: Flexible working hours occur on an informal basis and vary from job to job and department to department. While there is no formal HR policy on flexible working hours or working from home, this approach is consistent with its performance-driven culture in that what ultimately matters is employee performance. Even though employees may be permitted flexibility with schedules and working from home, they are expected to be available nights, weekends, and even vacations when there are pressing deadlines or problems to troubleshoot.

Snacks and beverages: Company-provided snacks, coffee, and other beverages are made available throughout the day for all employees.

"Splash vacation": After completing five years of service (and on every subsequent fifth-year anniversary) employees are provided with an extra week of paid vacation. They are also provided with a reimbursement of up to $2,000 for expenses incurred (transportation, lodging, etc.) in taking a vacation for themselves and their family to any place of their choosing.

ACE Award: ACE stands for attitude, commitment, and excellence. This is TEOCO's version of an "Employee of the Year" award, and is given annually to the employee who best exemplifies these three qualities. The winner, who receives stock and a cash award, is chosen by a committee comprised of previous winners of the ACE Award.

MVP Award: The Most Versatile Player Award, similar in concept to the ACE Award, is given annually to an employee who may not rise to that level of excellence, but who contributes to the organization in multiple ways. The winner receives stock and a cash award. Like the ACE Award, the winner is chosen without any management involvement, and the selection committee is comprised of previous winners of the award.

TEOCO Star Award: This is a peer-to-peer award in which employees recognize fellow employees for doing something that exemplifies one of the core values. This award would be TEOCO's version of a "spot bonus," with the exception that it is peer-to-peer rather than given by a supervisor. For example, one employee being helpful to another on a project might garner them a recommendation for the award. At the monthly "all-hands meeting," there is a drawing among all those nominated that month, and the winner receives a $150 Amex gift card as well as official acknowledgment.

One-Year Service Award: All new employees, on their first anniversary of employment, are given a plant, a balloon, and a card signed by other employees to acknowledge their first anniversary.

resources director, Atul effectively serves as the organization's chief human resources officer.

For most organizations, the human resources policies and practices are transactional in nature. At TEOCO, the HR function has become the principal means of cultural transmission and reinforcement. In addition, Atul devotes strategic focus on HR because of his belief in the potential of an empowered workforce. To some extent, part of the company's overall strategy is working from the "bottom up." The company relies on the abilities of its employees to understand what the market needs and develop new products. An example of how the empowered workforce functions at TEOCO was related by Dave (software architect): "We are not structured in a way that we have a team for incubating products... it's through conversations with our existing customers, generally, that the ideas for the next set of products come out."

Meanwhile, it is the shared leadership model that provides the opportunity for Atul to be so strongly and strategically focused on HR while depending on John, Faye, and others to bring in the revenues. In an organization whose principal assets and competitive advantage are its human and intellectual capital,

Atul and the shared leadership team have recognized the strategic importance of HR to its success.

The culture at TEOCO revolves singularly around the principle of employee ownership; it is embedded in the language, the policies and practices, the daily activities, and even the rituals at TEOCO. There is a formal HR policy manual, which is kept continuously current. While the manual is comprehensive in its scope, it is somewhat limited in specific details. Atul's stated philosophy of a policy manual is that "less is more," and the existing manual is larger than he would prefer. His rationale for not wanting to embed detailed procedures into the policy manual is that he prefers to have as few rules as possible. He believes that every employee will always want to do what is in the best interest of the company, and to reinforce the culture at TEOCO he believes that doing the right thing might at times require violating a policy.

TEOCO's articulated core values, and the resulting organizational culture, are evident in the working environment as well as in the HR policies and practices. The overall environment could be described as one of collegiality and mutual respect. Atul's background and beliefs support his desire for peace at the office, wanting employees to respect one another, and not wanting them to feel insecure about their jobs. Hillary validated this perception when she said, "I think the environment is one of my favorite things about TEOCO." She claims that Atul comes by her office every week, and she thinks it is the same for many other employees as well. She described that "he walks around" and is very interactive. Brian independently said that "I get high-fives from Atul probably four days a week." He noted that many new employees, especially those who come from larger organizations, often comment on how surprised they are that the CEO recognizes them, let alone that they see him come down to their floor. Further, Brian mentioned that interpersonal relationships are very important at TEOCO. For many employees some of their best friends work there, and "that's a really big benefit that isn't on any paperwork or on any contract."

The socialization process at TEOCO begins at new employee orientation and is continuously reinforced through the HR policies and practices. Carrie (director of HR) believes that the principal mission of HR is to help shape employee perceptions, especially as it relates to employee ownership, and to impress upon every employee the core value of "driving for progress through ownership."

The HR policies and practices demonstrate their critical importance through the resulting work environment. Taken together, the culture of employee ownership, combined with the strategic focus on HR, serves to recruit, motivate, and retain the TEOCO workforce.

The importance of human assets to the company's success is highlighted by the active involvement of its CEO and chairman in the hiring process. He interviews every applicant before a hiring decision is made. As he says, "Nobody gets hired without meeting me, and nobody gets hired without getting my nod." The two areas in which he exercises tight-fisted control are hiring and cost management. He believes he has developed unique expertise to know "who to hire and what to look for." His focus is not only on technical competence, but on "cultural fit" as well. In many ways Atul could be described as the keeper of the culture. He gets so deeply involved in the hiring process that he says he is sometimes asked if he doesn't have anything better to do, and he responds by saying that there is nothing more important because the hiring process is so vital to the company's continued success.

TA, TTI, and the Future of TEOCO

How will the story of TEOCO unfold with the investment by TA and the acquisition of TTI? From a purely business perspective, these decisions were justifiably necessary and defensible. However, each of the three distinctive characteristics of TEOCO's model of success, the shared leadership model, the culture of employee ownership, and the resulting HR policies and practices, is being challenged in this postacquisition environment.

Impact on Shared Leadership

The scope of the combined enterprise presents challenges that may strain the shared leadership model. TA's investment already added two influential directors to TEOCO's board. While directors usually have a "nose in, hands out" approach to management, the representatives of investment funds appointed to a company's board tend to be far more proactive in their "dialogues" with the senior team managing their investment. The subsequent acquisition of TTI added a fourth executive, Eitan Naor, into the leadership mix and in the last two years, Avi (TEOCO's CFO) has also become a key member of the Executive Leadership Team. Considering the distance between TEOCO and TTI, as well as their respective nearly equal sizes, it remains to be seen how the strengths and weaknesses of each leader will play out in the management of this new entity. For instance, Atul's well-recognized skills in hiring and motivating employees on a daily basis may not prove as beneficial or essential for TTI.

Impact on the Culture of Employee Ownership

Avi claims that the cultures have nothing in common. Yet the senior management team seems adamant that the culture of TEOCO has not and will not change. Faye says, "I don't think there's been significant change." Still, she acknowledged the inevitability that an aggregated culture will arise in which each organization impacts the other. But she adds, "I can see [Atul] sitting in that chair right now saying, 'It's not going to happen.'"

These statements are not surprising, as it is nearly universal that in this situation company executives proclaim that their acquisition will not change the corporate culture. Yet some degree of change is inevitable, and change has already occurred. These events will inevitably impact business activities and decision-making. The TTI acquisition and the investment of TA enhance the likelihood that within the next three years TEOCO may be acquired by a larger corporation, go public, or require some other fundamental organizational realignment. Before agreeing to the TA investment, Atul says that he went to the employees for their consent. He believes the employees were comfortable with the transaction or he would not have done it; he says that the employees are aware of its positive impact as well as the potential outcome.

Atul is determined to continue on the same path as before these major events. He points out that a condition of TA's investment in TEOCO was that he retain the role of CEO because he is so essential to the culture of the company. The bank, as a condition of the loan for the purchase of TTI, had the same requirement. Meanwhile, Atul is intent on TA receiving a good return on their investment in TEOCO. He described his role: "I will no longer do that with a sense of obligation; I will do that with a sense of joy. You know, if you do something out of joy, you do it differently than when you do it out of a sense of obligation."

An immediate impact is that these two events place a strain on employee ownership. The ownership mix shifted significantly with the TA investment. Prior to this equity transaction, Atul controlled 75 percent of the shares, while employees owned 25 percent from all combined sources. Post-TA, the employee share was halved as they were offered approximately 60 percent liquidity on their previous ownership.. Given Atul's ownership, and his intention to maintain a controlling interest in the company, coupled with TA's sizable equity stake, an issue that arises is whether there is any meaningful future opportunity to expand employee ownership. This is further compounded by the near doubling of the total number of employees.

An interesting paradox, according to Atul, is that despite the lower total employee ownership, there is a perception that the TA liquidity has strengthened the culture of ownership. He said that he "predicted that post-TA our payroll deductions [to purchase stock] would go down. It has increased...because [the employees] see a success story," even though the stock purchase price has since increased. Atul attributes this pattern to the fact that employees witnessed other employees making significant sums of money from the TA transaction. He claims that now they truly understand and value ownership. As he says, "Once you've made money out of ownership, it changes you forever. And until you do, you don't believe it." Atul felt a very deep sense of gratitude to his long-term employees for their loyalty and sacrifice in creating value for TEOCO. The TA transaction allowed him to fulfill his commitment that one day they would get a return on their investment of time and money into TEOCO.

While these events will inevitably bring about changes in the way the company is managed, John believes that these will not dilute the culture. The TA investment "allowed TEOCO to preserve something that I think is pretty important to the way we operate, which is having employee ownership in the business, and that employees have a piece of it." A firm believer in employee ownership, he has "worked at the world's largest employee-owned company, for Telecordia, which was owned by SAIC." He claims that TEOCO is heavily modeled after SAIC in terms of employee ownership as a mechanism. He sees the role of employee ownership as:

> If you're just paying people to show up to work and they get an annual bonus—those are two factors. But if you introduced the third factor of employee ownership—why

wouldn't you treat that as a means to motivate the employees beyond just simply giving them a salary and giving them a bonus? . . . And that's what Dr. Beyster [the founder of SAIC] figured out before anybody else figured it out.

These perceptions by senior management were validated by Carrie, HR manager. When asked about the relatively small percentage of total stock owned by employees, she claims that the perception of employee ownership continues to be important, and that all employees still have opportunity to build additional equity. She cited, for example, that every new employee is granted a certain amount of ownership rights; they determine how much stock they want to purchase either through payroll deduction or the internal stock market. Brian validated this further when he said that once employees realize the benefits of being invested in the company, it changes their perspective. Like Atul, he underlined that this reality became clear for many employees when they witnessed others cashing out a portion of their equity with the TA investment. As he said, "Once that clicks in, it builds on it."

It remains to be determined if the employees of TTI will become owners, and whether they will embrace the culture of ownership. It is also uncertain how TEOCO's employee perceptions may change in terms of the growing price of ownership and the potential diminished opportunity for share availability.

Impact on Human Resources as a Strategic Function

The TTI acquisition will strain Atul's role as the organization's chief human resources officer and as someone who has been intimately and deeply involved in all HR-related decisions of the company. Dave describes Atul's current role in HR activities as follows: "Atul is very, very, very engaged at the staffing and who's working on what and the hiring process. Its personnel stuff. Personnel and costs are the two things he focuses on . . . it blows my mind the level of detail and recollection he has on individual people and what's going on in the company."

As the company continues to grow, and as the complexity of issues expands, it will become increasingly difficult to maintain this level of involvement in details. A further challenge will be the issue of the standardization and consistency of application of HR-related policies and practices. Atul has a strong aversion to formal policies, preferring instead to have maximum flexibility and discretion in deciding HR issues. He described his perspective thus: "Life is all about making decisions and the reason management exists is to use judgment. Too many people want to make too many rules and they don't want to use judgment and I feel that if judgment doesn't exist then management doesn't have a job."

Given the increasingly litigious and regulated work environment for organizations, such a philosophy can create challenges for HR. When asked about Atul's philosophy of a policy manual where "less is more," HR Director Carrie admitted that there are some policies "that do cause me a little heartburn just because it's a little tough to administer without having something solid." One example she cited is that the sick leave policy is administered on an honor system. The only way to monitor abuse, she says, is indirectly by the impact such abuse may have on employee performance. As the company gets larger, she believes it would be easier if there were specific guidelines to turn to in a dilemma, to be able to say, "Here's the policy." Yet despite the lack of specifications, she claims there appears to be a high degree of consistency in the administration of HR policies.

Whether HR will continue to be viewed as a strategic function and receive the executive focus that it has had will be tested as well in the new corporate environment.

Impact on TEOCO's Core Competencies

While Atul believes that corporate culture and philosophy have played "key roles in our success," he says "that without its distinctive core competencies the company could not have been successful." Whether the core competencies that TEOCO has built can carry over in the postacquisition environment is an unanswered question. That TTI is similar in size to TEOCO and that they are geographically separated are two factors that will pose challenges in transferring specialized expertise from the acquiring company to the acquired company and vice versa. Also, given that the two companies had different cultures at the time of acquisition, additional work will have to be done to ensure successful transference of core competencies.

Conclusion

The challenge for any organization with a strong culture and a loyal workforce is to sustain them and adapt them in the face of organizational change. Over a very short period of time, TEOCO has changed its capital structure and expanded its business. How and to what extent TEOCO manages these changes will determine whether it maintains its competitive advantage and, finally, what its overall fate will be.

Notes

1. All employees are referred to in this case by their first name, including the CEO because that is standard practice at TEOCO.
2. http://www.billingworld.com/articles/2010/09/teoco-ceo-reversal-on-acquisitions-complete.aspx.
3. Ibid.
4. Ibid.
5. Ibid.
6. Jainism is the least populous of the Indian religions; comprising approximately 0.5 percent of the population (Hindus represent approximately 80 percent, Muslims approximately 12 percent, and Christians approximately 3 percent).
7. Collins, J. C., & Porras, J. I. 1994. *Built to last: Successful habits of visionary companies*. New York: Harper Collins Publishers.
8. As Peter Drucker said, "All organizations now say routinely, 'people are our greatest asset.' Yet few practice what they preach, let alone believe it." *The New Society of Organizations, Harvard Business Review*, September/October 1992.

CHAPTER 11

HCSS: Employee Ownership and the Entrepreneurial Spirit

Olivier P. Roche and Frank Shipper

Never settle for being as good as you currently are.[1]

Introduction

HCSS (Heavy Construction Systems Specialists, Inc.) was founded in 1986. For the first few years, the company's office was in the home of its founder and president, Mike Rydin. Mike had previously worked in the estimating department of a large heavy construction company where he understood, firsthand, the importance of bidding and time crunches.[2] He decided to address this critical issue. Within a few years he hired his first employee, a programmer named Carl, and they created a software package, the DOS version of HeavyBid. This estimating software was made for infrastructure contractors who bid on projects ranging from $50,000 to over $1 billion. A key feature this young company offered was 24/7 product support; this was unusual at the time. Many times calls for help came in the middle of the night and were responded to by the president himself. Today HCSS still offers 24/7 instant support, now to over 3,500 companies.

In 1989, HCSS moved into its first office building and the company has continued to expand ever since. Starting as a single-product company, HCSS's product lines currently include a half dozen other software programs. HeavyJob, for example, gives foremen the kind of information they need to manage their work responsibly and efficiently. On a daily basis, this job tracking software transforms the information collected from the construction site so that it can be used at headquarters by management. This includes time card entry on both PC and handheld devices, instant production/cost analysis, and billing and forecasting, all of which interface with the contractor's accounting software. Another example of successful software developed by the company is Equipment360, an equipment maintenance program that gives a company/ customer the ability to track, identify, analyze, and resolve equipment maintenance issues before a major problem occurs. This delivers cost savings to the company through less downtime and fewer major equipment repairs, as well as lower fuel consumption. (A complete listing of the company's product lines is provided in table 11.1.)

In August 2009, the company moved into its own 45,000 square foot state-of-the-art facilities in Sugar Land, Texas, near Houston. Mike appreciates that HCSS has come a long way from its humble beginnings, yet he considers that much remains to be accomplished; there is always room for improvement. In the case of HCSS, this company growth has happened at the same time as adjusting to a more challenging economic environment with the downturn of 2008–2009. HCSS managed to keep its business profitable during this period, and did not see substantial growth again until 2012. The new facilities were built to accommodate twice as many employees as the company then had, so

Table 11.1   Product lines

HEAVYBID: HeavyBid is a powerful construction estimating software for infrastructure contractors bidding projects ranging from $50,000 to over $1 billion.

HEAVYJOB: HeavyJob is complete job tracking software that transforms job site information into valuable management information on a daily basis. It includes time card entry on both PCs and handheld devices, instant production/cost analysis, billing, forecasting, and interfaces to the customer's accounting software,

DISPATCHER: The Dispatcher is resource management software. It allows a company to track the usage of its equipment, tools, materials, and crews and to get the most out of them. It allows a company to plan, analyze, and improve usage of these resources.

EQUIPMENT360: An equipment maintenance program that delivers cost savings to customers through lower downtime, less major repairs, lower fuel consumption, and greater availability of its equipment. In essence, Equipment360 gives the customer the ability to track, identify, analyze, and resolve equipment maintenance issues before they become a problem.

BIDHISTORY.COM: This is a collection of historical bid pricing and bid tabs compiled from public DOT sites throughout the United States. The benefits of using Bidhistory.com include tracking and reviewing historical bid pricing tabulations and viewing historical average prices for specific bid items.

SAFETY: Safety management software along with consulting that helps a company capture daily safety activities, near misses, and incidents in the field, manage data in the office, and deliver reportables to the management team to move a company toward world-class safety practices. The software includes web-based management software and field entry software on laptops and mobile devices.

VECTR GPS: HCSS provides GPS units and web-based software that integrates the data from GPS units with other HCSS products such as The Dispatcher, Equipment360, and HeavyJob to give customers total control over their fleet of vehicles. It allows customers to make better decisions based on real information coming directly from the field. HCSS provides all-inclusive packages that include the GPS hardware units, data service coverage, and integration with other HCSS software products.

FUELERPLUS: This is fuel management software that allows a company to easily track the amount of fuel and other fluids being dispensed into equipment and fuel trucks. It captures all the activities of a fueler, automates the flow of this data to other systems such as other HCSS applications and other accounting systems. It also allows the company to generate reports to help managers realize the true cost of fuel as well as the fueler's activities.

Note: Information for table furnished by HCSS.

Table 11.2 HCSS financials (in thousands of dollars)

In US$	2007	2008	2009	2010	2011	2012	2013
Current assets	9,214	6,492	7,264	9,460	9,354	9,742	12,717
Current liabilities	4,216	5,650	6,147	6,625	6,476	6,996	7,462
Sales	17,495	19,289	17,868	19,344	20,271	22,342	28,706
Long-term liabilities	—	—	6,294	6,355	6,101	5,769	5,466
Net profit (loss)	2,987	2,459	1,734	2,336	2,3365	2,372	4,095

Source: Data provided by HCSS.

Note: The long-term debt of $6.3 million was incurred to finance the construction of the new building, which can accommodate 230 employees.

the building cost per employee was high during that period. Today the company has 140 employees and sales of over $28 million (see additional financial data in table 11.2). Mike is confident that HCSS has the financial resources to achieve its target growth, which is 15 percent per year. While adding additional human resources has always been a challenge in this industry, HCSS has so far been very successful in attracting and retaining motivated and highly capable employees while increasing its activities at a fast growth rate.

HCSS has codified its mission and values in the following statement:

HCSS Mission & Values

To help customers dramatically improve their business through our innovative, high quality software and exceptionally helpful service, while providing a great life for our employees.

- Create products of quality and real value.
- Be passionate in providing groundbreaking customer service.
- Admit mistakes and take steps to correct them.
- Exhibit genuine concern and respect for others.
- Help fellow employees be the best they can be.
- Accept responsibility for our shortcomings and improve upon them.
- Take the initiative without fear of failure.
- Never lie, steal, or engage in any deceitful practice.
- Spend responsibly without waste. Help the less fortunate.

How they have been implemented through a variety of strategies will be described in the subsequent sections.

Business Environment and Strategy

HCSS operates in a highly competitive environment. In addition to large companies offering standardized software with an established brand, such as the traditional Microsoft Excel software package, there are also a host of small companies, such as "BID2WIN" or "Hard Dollar," offering customized software.

For HCSS, a smooth interaction with its customers is not only critical to increase sales but also to develop new products. Over the years, most of the ideas for new products have come out of discussions with customers. As one of the company's software development managers Minh likes to repeat to the new recruits, "Our software is developed by our customers. The customers tell us what they need and we simply deliver what they want."

While this statement is true, it is deceptively simple. The most important part of the work actually takes place between the phase of listening to what the customers want and that of delivering the right product. The next critical piece is the reliable and personable after-sale support. The company's competitive edge lies in the implementation of this inventive phase where the employees translate a customer's needs into software that meets or exceeds their require-ments, at the same time maintaining high standards of work ethics and the motivation to solve customers' problems in an efficient and timely manner. No doubt, the skillful communication and good relationships between the mar-keting, sales, development, and support departments are major factors in this seamless service delivery. To achieve this level of coordination, employees have to be responsive, creative, and flexible. They must be able to address custom-ers' needs at the same time they are team players, looking beyond their own department's interests to look at those of the company as a whole. In other words, each employee has to behave like an entrepreneur developing his own business.

> Minh (manager, software development): I think it [i.e., the employee's ownership mentality] means that I need to do whatever it takes to take care of the issues that come up. Having pride in what you do and deliver. I think a reflection on the entire company is what we're delivering. How we connect with customers. How we talk to customers. Having that ownership of, "Whatever I do does make an impact." In my group, in particular, I really emphasize the importance of team chemistry, teamwork; getting people involved early beyond the scope of their regular duties. We endorse creativity and we want that from our employees. It's not, "Here's your job, go do it." It's, "Whatever you want to do. Come to me and let me know what your ideas are." We really foster the idea that you have and help you grow it.

At a more senior level, there is also an understanding that a corporation is a legal structure necessary to run operations and deal with other organizations. However, the company's real business and competitive advantage resides one level below. That is where the relationship between HCSS employees and the customer's employees develops and the problems of the latter are understood and resolved.

> Tom (vice president of technical services): So from an employer's standpoint, we wanted to make the kind of company that people wanted to stay at and be part of for the long term. And then from a software supplier standpoint, the thing that infuriated more customers than anything was the lack of ability to get somebody to go actually help them. The whole trend in software over the last 15 years has been to outsource your support and outsource your development. So all the parts of the software company got further and further away from

their customers. The programmers just became people who wrote code, and the quality assurance personnel just became somebody who didn't really know the product, but they knew how to press the buttons to break the code. Support just became somebody to look through a manual and answer questions over the phone. We wanted to do just the opposite of that. So we "reverse modeled" as an employer, but we also "reverse modeled" as a business. We wanted to be the kind of company that our customers and our employees would have relations with and know each other.

This "employee-to-employee relationship approach" focuses on people's needs and not simply on business needs (see table 11.3 for a description of the company's culture and its branding). It can be illustrated by two examples of special services provided by HCSS. The first is the "Help-inar," developed by Tom in 2007. This concept is based on the premise that to develop a genuine relationship with potential customers, the best person to market HCSS services is not always a sales representative. Tom, with a background in psychology, believes that rather than being in the business of selling services, the company is there to solve customers' problems. Since most of the actual end users of the software are the client companies' "techies," the best people to

Table 11.3 Lessons learned about building an employment brand

Don't waste time trying to fabricate an employer brand: You've already got a brand; your company's culture already defines your employer brand.

Use your culture to define your brand: You don't have to be a nationally known billion-dollar company in order to have a good employer brand. Build your brand around your culture and the people you hire will fit, excel, and stay.

Recruiters should become marketers: Recruiters must become expert marketers and champions of the company culture and brand.

Don't hide your culture: The culture of your company is already known to applicants from the moment they walk into your office or interact with the employees that work at your company. An authentic brand will build a better pipeline of applicants.

Hire people who fit your culture: The biggest mistake you can make is to hire someone who does not fit the culture.

Make your brand toxic for the wrong people: Showcase your culture to make it toxic for the wrong people and appealing to the right people. You will inevitably find the right people and the right people will find you.

Use multiple tools to promote your brand: Increase your brand recognition using social media, videos, dedicated websites, and job board branding.

Celebrate those who live the culture: Let your employees live up to their full potential and promote them to others as a great example.

Prove you have a great culture: Compete in "best companies to work for" contests to get feedback and gain credibility and recognition for your culture, which helps enhance your brand.

Executives must genuinely desire employees to have a great life: If the goals of helping employees live up to their full potential is solely driven by revenue/profit goals, your culture and brand will never flourish.

Source: Table provided by HCSS. Extract from keynote speech handout: "Your culture defines your brand," by Sebabi Leballo, organizational development manager.

interface with them are HCSS "techies," without the interference of the sales department.

> Tom: For "Help-inar", we take our technical people and travel them around the country and put them in a meeting room in a hotel. Customers can come in and ask them questions all day. They just get help. The end result of that is—-the customers love it. They're able to come in and get help, but then also hear about some of the other stuff that we're doing and a lot of our new products. So they become sales events, but there's no salesman there. It's only the technical people, which mean that customers hear what you're doing, but they don't hear it with a sales spin. They're hearing from an employee who's technical in nature, which they almost take that differently.

At that stage of interaction, removing the sales representative from the equation allows HCSS to establish a different relationship with its customers. Also, it allows the company to find ideas for its new products without the filtering of the sales department.

The second service provided by HCSS is instant support. Mike considers this to be fundamental. When clients encounter technical issues with the company's software, they contact the support department; with 24-hour live support, there is no waiting. During conferences and industry fairs, end users talk to each other and share their experiences with various software providers. HCSS's responsiveness to its customers' needs is now well-established in the industry and this has contributed to the firm's rapid development to become a leader in the construction and heavy highway market. As Tom says, "It always sounds kind of old and stale to say your people are your competitive advantage, but I think that it's not just the people here, it's the combination of the people without the restrictive rules that keep them from connecting with customers."

Human Resource Practices at HCSS

Hiring the Right Employees

HCSS uses several methods to recruit, like many other organizations in the industry. In addition to advertising on the web in many forms and using YouTube videos to highlight the company, the company also puts up a series of 3' x 8' banners along the property near the street two times a year for two weeks each (the maximum allowed by the sign ordinance), advertising the company and positions. Employees are also used heavily to recruit and the substantial employee referral fee of up to $4,000 has resulted in several dozen employees being hired from these referrals over the last several years. The recruitment process has evolved over time, but it has always been very thorough, to the point where it is sometimes perceived as lengthy to a fault, especially when there is pressure to fill a critical position. Indeed, recently Mike and the senior management team were seeking to hire a marketing director to fill a role that had been open for almost a year. The most recent candidate, after six interviews, was not hired. At the same time, there were eight other more junior positions open. Mike was optimistic that they would be quickly filled given the current high unemployment rate; nevertheless, with so many people involved in the selection process, staffing an empty slot is a time-consuming endeavor. Unlike the recruitment process in many other organizations, Mike and other senior executives are directly involved, not only for senior positions such as marketing director, but also for entry-level positions. At the mid-manager level, future team members participate in the process. Between human resources' criteria and that of the functional departments, Mike is aware that there are slight differences in the traits required for the best candidates, which lead to lengthy discussions. Mike supports this "collective wisdom"; the discussions are ultimately very healthy.

The result of this extensive process is a workforce well appreciated by HCSS clients for both its technical expertise and its diligence in solving problems. In addition, HCSS has a very low annual voluntary turnover, usually less than 3 percent of those that the company regards as an asset. Mike believes that time invested up-front is time saved later in several ways. It avoids a situation where employees who cannot adjust to HCSS corporate culture have to be terminated and replacements hired, and it saves the training that would be required for those replacements. But more importantly, it can save months or years of management involvement agonizing over how to handle a marginal employee and all of the negativity from those employees and those who inter-act with them.

Over the years, employees have joined the company for various reasons. The remuneration package is attractive, but it is not the principal factor. Indeed, in some cases, particularly at the lower levels, employees only realize how gener-ous it is once they have experienced the profit sharing program, which may be six months to one year after they have joined. Instead, most employees quickly learn to appreciate the "intangible" advantages associated with a position at HCSS. Through the open dialogue in the lengthy interview process, candi-dates learn about the atmosphere in the company and its casual environment. Both parties learn about the other; in the end, both must feel that there is a good match.

> Sebabi (organizational development manager): Before I accepted the position, I asked, "I'd like to talk to some of the employees just to find out what they really think about the company and the culture"... Sophie said, "Sure. You can come this afternoon. You can talk to anybody you want. Just walk around and pull anybody you'd like." I was going "What? You're not going to tell me, 'Talk to this person or only that person'?" And that impressed me. And that helped me to know that it was the right decision to come here, knowing that I could talk to anybody. And I came and talked to a few people, but just that freedom to talk to any employee stood out to me.

By talking to so many potential colleagues at different levels, both the employer and candidate are able to evaluate if they have work/family values and work ethics in common. If they do, the candidate is hired. As Melissa, a business analyst, says: "That goes back to the ownership mentality that your peers are the ones you're working with every day. They probably have a really good idea whether you're going to fit into their little group or not, and how you're going to react with the different personalities in their group."

HCSS treats its employees very well but performance is expected. Even after the extremely selective interview process, in some critical and customer oriented departments, such as support, the turnover is substantial during the first 90 days of employment. For a small company operating in this industry, there is very little room for slackers or people who don't share the same work ethics and "can do" attitude.

> Eric (major account manager): Some get weeded out in those 90 days. [During the interview] they may say all the right things like, "Oh, I'm loyal to customers. I have a good attitude. I'll go the extra mile." Until you get them over there and let those guys [other employees in the support department] determine that, you don't really know. If you ask our customers, "What's the biggest thing here?" it's the support, your attitude, your attitude towards support. And if someone comes in and they don't have that, they don't come close to making 90 days.

That said, past 90 days, the voluntary turnover is less than 3 percent and it is not uncommon to be 0 percent. This is very low for a company operating in the software industry. In 90 days, both parties will have assessed their compatibility. HCSS uses 90 days because that is when insurance starts. Once insurance starts, a terminated employee can remain on COBRA (Consolidated Omnibus Budget Reconciliation Act) for 18 months. As HCSS is self-insured, an employee terminated at 91 days can cost HCSS in medical bills for the next 18 months. Thus HCSS is making a huge commitment when keeping an employee past 90 days.

In terms of background, HCSS is quite open with regard to the profile of its employees. This reflects the diverse background of the senior management and the belief that during his/her career at HCSS, an employee will assume many responsibilities that were not anticipated when drafting the initial job description. In this way, the "can do" attitude, motivation, and aptitude to learn are as important as a degree or past experience. HCSS hires a person knowing that his/her job functions will continue to be adjusted, either because of changes in the challenges facing the company, or to adapt to the person's abilities and willingness to accept responsibilities and grow within the organization.

The recruitment process of Daniel, the receptionist and corporate ambassador, is a good example of the company's philosophy. Even the double title is illustrative. After completing a dual degree in international business and Spanish, Daniel was hired by a large US company. As he was about to finish his training program to become a manager, he decided to leave, unhappy with the corporate culture and the working conditions. Daniel decided to go back to school to get a master's degree in acupuncture, but at the same time he applied for the HCSS position as a receptionist. He was interviewed by human resources, his future manager and colleagues, and finally by Mike. He was obviously overqualified for the position, but during the interview process his interest in health and wellness was discussed. One thing led to another and his job evolved, based on the qualities he offered.

> Daniel (corporate ambassador): When I first started, I was asked if I would actually take on more responsibilities to help out some of the other managers [in the wellness area]. And they just thought I'd be a natural fit for it. I really enjoyed it. [After a couple of months] I realized that I needed more feedback from more people in the company, so I helped form a wellness committee, where one person from every single department is represented and they come to the meetings and we figure out where we want to go with the wellness program in the company... I'm the lowest rung of the company and yet I can go and talk to the CEO.

New Employee Orientation/Acculturation Process

At HCSS the support provided to employees during the first few months of their assignment is as important as the initial recruitment process. In a traditional orientation program, companies spend most of their time discussing matters such as benefits, health insurance, how to log into the network systems, and various company policies. These topics are also covered at HCSS, but most of the orientation program is spent discussing the history of the company, the characteristics of the industry, the interpersonal relationships within and outside the company, and why these are so important for the success of HCSS.

In addition, the company has developed a mentorship program in which a new employee is paired with an experienced one from another department. The mentor acts as a "confidante" to make sure that the integration process is progressing smoothly. The new employee can feel free to discuss any personal or family issues, as well, which is why it is important that the two work in different departments.

Finally, because of the rapid expansion, senior management decided that there was a need to organize additional opportunities for a direct interface among new employees, their families, and the senior management team.

> Tom: It's hard to connect with new employees now because there are usually multiple layers. So between them and myself, there are a couple different levels of supervision. They don't really work with me all the time. Between them and Mike, there's another level of supervision. So we try to do things with new employees where they get some one-on-one time with the executives at the company as a way for us to tell them what HCSS wants to be, and why we want to be that, and how we're going to get there. So we have dinners that we do when we hire a new employee. Or we'll take the new employee and the spouse to dinner with the executives, and so that the new employee and the spouse both get the opportunity to meet us. And we get to meet them and just kind of break down the barriers a little bit. And we do some stuff within their orientation where they get the chance to talk to the executives at the company.

Performance Review, Development, and Job Promotion

At HCSS, the collective hiring process described earlier is perceived as a logical preliminary step; the annual employee evaluations benefit from a similar

360-degree perspective. It is an anonymous review made up of two components. First, evaluators fill out a questionnaire in which each employee gets numeric grades (one to ten) for performance and ability to work as a team member, seven being considered the company average. Second, a group of peers is selected, usually including the colleagues with whom the employee interfaced the most during the preceding year. The members of this group make anonymous qualitative comments regarding the employee's performance. Then the direct supervisor discusses these comments with the employee to assess in which areas improvements are needed, as well as how to assist the employee in achieving his/her objectives. It is also a good opportunity for the employee to discuss any problem or challenges he or she faces in the organization.

At HCSS, formal titles do not mean a lot. Knowledge, people or technical skills, and the ability to solve problems are the reasons an employee is sought out by colleagues or customers. To some extent, job titles are a reflection of these recognized abilities. In this fast-paced environment, employees are problem solvers who do not always follow the chain of command. For instance, employee X may report to Y on the organization chart but he or she will not hesitate to talk directly to Y's supervisor or another colleague of Y's in another department, if this person has the information or the ability to solve the problem at hand.

> John (software developer): I do custom programming. I talk with customers about what they want, help work it up and prototype it for them, make sure this is what they want...I also help support when they have a problem, if they can't figure it out. "Is that a bug in the system?" Or a customer is making a suggestion that needs technical input. "Is this something that we can look at putting in?" We'll work with the product manager. "What's coming up?" And ways we can do it. It's a pretty flexible position really, and you can make of it what you want here. I mean, we're not structured in that, "Okay, in this role, you only do this, and in this role you only do that." It's really, "How much do you want to do and handle?" And so really, I think the main core ingredient at this company is problem solving.

There are several additional reasons why titles are not so important. First, employees, to some extent, "create their own job." They may have been initially hired for a specific task, but their job definition will change over time without any change in their title. As their skills improve, they may be able to spend more time solving other issues or they may discover some other tasks that they like to do or for which they have a natural talent. Second, the company and its environment change constantly. Some tasks disappear or, with experience and/or new software, take less time to complete; meanwhile, the organization faces new challenges. In this fast-changing environment, employees are task-oriented. That is why adaptability and aptitude to learn technical skills and develop people skills to be able to handle emerging challenges are so important within the organization.

> Melissa: So what I envision [in the near future] is a lot of the things I currently do now, that I've spent a lot of time on, would be made a lot more efficient, a lot

more automated. And then I will look for other avenues to use my skills in the company to make another area better. Or to learn more knowledge about the software we sell. That's one of the beautiful things here is if you do a good job and you have an interest in another area, as long as you do a good job, if you want to move that route, you're more than welcome to do that. Because here we concentrate on what your strengths are [and] how can we use them better.

A final reason is efficiency and cost-effectiveness. At HCSS, a good employee is one who is versatile and who understands the synergies that can be achieved when departments work together; someone willing to pitch in, whenever and wherever it's needed, for the good of the company as a whole. There is very little room for a "silo mentality" where an employee is only interested in the performance of his/her own department.

Genaro (regional manager for technical services): I've got a few roles. I help manage implementation support for our 1,200 to 1,300 companies in our West Coast region, which includes everything basically west of Texas. Recently, in the last seven or eight months, I've been assigned as the quality assurance manager for our flagship product as well, and took over that department to help kinda get some things in order. I help out with a lot of sales calls in our region and from some of the other regions, as well.

HCSS also encourages its employees to explore various interests outside the organization. For instance, expenses for employees attending ownership conferences are paid, as are those related to attending meetings of professional associations that present opportunities for development. For example, Chris (regional manager for technical services and training and implementation manager) participates at conferences as an active member of the National Utility Contractors Association where some of HCSS's existing and potential customers can be found.

HCSS grooms its own managers and rarely recruits them externally (an exception being the current search for a marketing director). However, while a promotion means facing new challenges, it does not necessarily guarantee an increase in salary or a larger office.

Chris: I went from technical services to training manager to implementation manager, regional manager, product manager. These are the things that I am going after. They'll give you the opportunity, especially if you vouch for one, and you knocked it out. Then you can really move to different areas in the company but none of those [moves] dictates my salary.

HCSS provides tuition assistance for work-related training programs at any university or college. The company also pays for off-premises seminars but primarily relies on peer-training and self-learning. Most employees are self-starters who learn new technologies and other things on their own. The organization has books they recommend, such as *First, Break All the Rules*.[3] About half of the staff has read it and participated in book studies. HCSS also offers courses in management and leadership to employees, some of which are taught by company executives. In an example of organizational development through peer interaction, the leadership team, composed of four or five senior managers, meets every month to discuss areas that need improvement. They start with basic information from the "Best Places to Work" surveys and they research what areas the employees would like to see improved in the company. This strategy has been paying off for HCSS in that it has been named one of the best places to work for in Texas for seven consecutive years. The local congressman referred to HCSS as the "Google of Sugar Land."

The attitude of each employee to never settle for what they already know creates a culture where everybody is constantly learning new things to ensure that they are up-to-date with their skills and their abilities to deliver high quality performance for the company. This dynamic self-perpetuates as employees recruit candidates with similar attitudes and abilities. At the same time, the organization supports new initiatives by paying for employees to go to conferences, training programs, and certifications. Once these outside programs are completed, employees teach what they have learned to colleagues. HCSS tries to encourage employees to think, "How can I enhance not just my own value but also that of everybody else?"

> Genaro: We like to self-learn. I would say that there is some technical training that we'll go through, and get everybody; but a lot of times, it's other people who took it upon themselves first to learn and then they're teaching the rest of us. That's how we keep current with a lot of things. Somebody will go—just the interest in it so much that they figure it out, and say "Hey. We might, as a support department, need to know about this" and then share that information with everybody else. So, it makes it—and we do send people over to do technical training. We've done that in the past, but a lot of our guys are better off just tinkering with stuff.

Overall, through the hiring, integration, and promotion processes of its employees, HCSS is continuously defining and refining its corporate culture. The end result is that employees tend to be versatile in terms of their abilities and willingness to complete various tasks. They are also "problem solvers," more interested in meeting new challenges than in getting a new title and a larger office. In addition, they tend to be self-starters willing to learn and share their knowledge with other employees. Finally, as noted earlier, there is very little room for the "silo mentality." Employees are networkers who know how to reach out to other communities/departments within or outside the company.

Fringe Benefits and Wellness

HCSS provides comprehensive health care and retirement benefits. The company does not provide day care per se, but it is very family oriented. In the case of an unexpected circumstance, employees are allowed to bring their children to the office. Often this benefits the company because employees facing emergencies do not have to call in sick; they can still work. This reduces the stress for the employee and at the same time it is another way to connect the employee's family to the workplace.

As for the health and wellness of employees, HCSS does not only "talk the talk"; the organization also "walks the walk." In addition to modern workout facilities, a soccer field, and a basketball court, there is also a running track on the company's premises. As Maria, a controller, says, "You'll see people running the track throughout the day, taking walks around the track, and take breaks. Maybe sales will go out and walk around. I don't know if they're talking business, but they're walking around the track. It brings people together. It's kind of a team-building issue, too." In addition, HCSS sponsors and pays registration fees for events such as: 5-K runs, marathons, and bike races. Some employees prefer indoor activities. Daniel,[4] along with his other numerous responsibilities, organizes Pilates sessions, teaches yoga, and is valued as a personal trainer. As well, he provides assistance and advice to employees during lunch breaks.

As for refreshments, company refrigerators are stocked with soft drinks, juices, and Gatorade. Each week a different department is in charge of kitchen duty, restocking on a daily basis with fresh fruits and vegetables—avocados, apples, oranges, grapes, carrots, strawberries, or whatever is in season and healthy.

Work and Family Life

HCSS organizes picnics and Christmas parties and invites the employees' families. Beyond these formal events, many employees continue their social interactions after office hours on and off the company premises. For instance, when some employees organize a movie night, the company picks up the tab for basic food and drinks. Other employees might go to a show with colleagues and their children. Finally, HCSS tolerates "underground" activities, such as online video games on company's computers, as long as it is after office hours.

Building Leadership and the Entrepreneurial Spirit

HCSS offers courses and training programs in management. It offers financial incentives to enhance employees' performance, but it does not stop there. Mike believes that perks and training opportunities would not fundamentally change the attitudes of the employees if it was not for the existence of three major characteristics of HCSS corporate culture: access to information, involvement in the decision-making process, and tolerance for honest mistakes.

Access to Information

In this fast-changing environment, it is essential for the senior management and decision-makers to keep an "open-door policy," not just in theory but also in practice. An open-door policy does not only mean that any employee can talk to the senior management and the chief executive officer (CEO) whenever they have ideas or problems. It also means that the senior management will provide them with the information they need to accomplish their objectives without having the manager "breathing down their neck" to make sure that the job is done. Very early in the company's development, Mike realized the limits of the hierarchical structure in which a CEO tells his manager what to do, who in turn tells the employee what to do. This strategy puts too much pressure on Mike to make the right decisions, make too many decisions, and not harness all of the brain power of the capable people that make it through their tough recruiting process. As a company grows, the temptation to add layers of management is difficult to resist, but a bureaucratic structure is not particularly cost-effective. Instead, Mike thinks it is better to invest time recruiting the right people, give them the adequate information, and let them run their business with little supervision. He decided that a flat structure in which employees assume ownership of their ideas and performance leads to a far more effective organization, particularly when these employees have been selected for their "can do" attitude and their ability to learn on their own.

> Melissa: I think that it's important for your employees to feel like they're a part of something bigger. That's a big basis for the ownership culture for me—communicating, open-book policy. It's more like you come here and you work more with family than you do, you don't just clock in and clock out. I mean you take ownership for the things you do, the things your coworkers do.

Chris, like the receptionist Daniel, was overqualified for the position that he initially accepted at HCSS. Although he had managed about 80 franchisees in his former job, Chris started as a support technician. Within one year, his managerial skills were recognized and he was promoted to the position of training manager. As a new technician, he had a firsthand experience of the company's open-door policy.

> Chris: As we were working on our annual end-users meeting during which 800 to 1,000 people come to Houston to visit with us, I saw an opportunity to refine our knowledge of HCSS customer base. I said to Mark [his supervisor at that time], "How many of our top customers show up to user group meeting?" Mark did not know the answer and he asked me to find this info and others. So, I went to our CEO and asked him. It seemed like real internal [confidential] information that you would not give a new employee...and he gave it to me...Mike always says he wants to give us the tools to do our job. So, it's very rare, very rare that you would ask for information on something that Mike wouldn't share with you...He tells us a lot of stuff that I can promise you you'd never hear in another company if you're not on the executive level. From the biggest deals we're working on to the money we'll make out of these deals...He will share this information with us, to make sure that we're all engaged...Because we're owners, we should know.

Trusting and Involving Employees in the Decision-Making Process

At HCSS, employees are involved in all major decisions, from hiring future colleagues to the deadline for a software release or the choice of the layout for their offices in the new building. One of the recent issues discussed with employees was the need to change the company's insurance provider, as well as the level of coverage that was needed. For these important deliberations, large meetings were held and everyone was invited to share their views and to help make the final decision.

> Chris: I remember this specifically. It was... "If we spend this much, this is the level of service we would get." And if we wanted to increase that, "We can spend more to get this higher level, but it's gonna come out of our bottom line." And at the end of the year, your share of the company's profits—and we all decided to self-insure some risks but to spend more on others because we wanted a higher level of insurance. It wasn't four or five people at the executive level saying "This is what we're doing." They let us decide. And that's just one example of a lot of things. So, yes, we do have a tremendous amount of trust with our executives.

Nevertheless, HCSS is a company, not a democracy. At the end of a discussion, Mike or a senior manager will make the final decision, notably when there is a stalemate or when an outcome is uncertain. Interestingly, there is less resistance from employees to implement a decision, even if they disagree with the final choice, when all options have been discussed and understood.

Tolerating Honest Mistakes

When an employee makes an honest error that is not repeated and the company tolerates it, there are benefits on two levels. First, it is very difficult for employees to take initiatives if there is zero tolerance for failure. Self-managed employees at HCSS, like managers in other companies, have to make decisions and take initiatives in a complex and fast-changing environment. A lack of tolerance stifles creativity and the entrepreneurial spirit of employees who fear negative consequences for their decisions. Second, a company's negative attitude toward failure inadvertently encourages employees to hide their mistakes as well as the consequences of their mistakes. Often, it is not the initial mistake that jeopardizes the viability of an organization but the long-term consequences of a cover-up when an employee fears sanctions.

> Melissa: I was in a test environment. I did a lot of testing to change some things. I accidentally sent out 2,000 alerts and faxes to customers telling them that they had not paid their maintenance fees. I don't know how accurate they were because we hadn't been using them in a long time. We immediately get these phones ringing off the wall; our in-boxes get filled with these replies to "What are you talking about?" So the first thing I did was I ran to Mike [CEO] and Tom [supervisor] and I said, "Look, I just sent out these emails by accident and dah, dah, dah," and I was upset. Rather than yell at me or whatever, Tom immediately sent out emails to all the same customers saying, "We were doing some testing. We apologize for the mistake"...At the end of the day, we did collect almost $10,000 from clients who had not actually paid their maintenance fees and we also installed a new password system to avoid repeating the same mistake. Here,

we accept mistakes. We expect you to learn from them and try not to make the same mistake again. But mistakes are a good way to grow and realize that something needs to be changed.

Corporate Governance and the Meaning of "Ownership"

Governance Structure

HCSS is an S Corporation and the company does not have to disclose any financial information to anyone. Still, they provide some data to Dun & Bradstreet and to large customers, in order to assure the latter that HCSS is a service provider in good financial health before they sign a long-term contract to design and roll out software. HCSS also provides information on financial performance and ongoing transactions to employees so they can assess the size and likelihood of their next "profit sharing" check. For obvious reasons, the company closely guards certain critical information, such as its ownership structures and margins on certain products and services.

With regard to ownership, a few stock options were provided to employees and outsiders who were associated with the start-up during the early years of operations. Otherwise, the company remains essentially owned and the finances controlled by Mike and his family. Only Mike, his wife, Sophie, and Tom, along with Mike's former partner and former accountant, both retired, attend board meetings. Mike votes the ESOP, the employee stock ownership plan, as an entity for most decisions and individual share participants only have an option to vote as individuals should a vote be required for a potential sale of the company. However, employees who have been in the plan a number of years see their ESOP accounts grow to significant values and even those that are new still seem to appreciate that they are receiving shares in the company. Indeed, the impact of the share ownership program on employees' behavior is leveraged through management practices that give employees access to information and actively involve them in the decision-making process whenever the company faces key issues. Here the practical meaning of ownership is that the employees "do business" the way an owner would, and the proportional sharing of the company's profit is an integral part of that.

Employee Stock Ownership Plans

Within the first few years, Mike had already decided to develop the entrepreneurial mentality of the employees and to encourage their involvement in the company's affairs. Nevertheless, the decision to implement an ESOP was not an easy one. There are pros and cons for employee-owned corporations. HCSS set up a trust and made tax-deductible contributions to it. These discretionary cash contributions were initially used to buy shares from selling owners and, subsequently, shares from employees leaving HCSS or selling their shares to diversify their portfolios. The stocks acquired by the trust are allocated to the individual account of each employee based on the level of their remuneration, which also serves as the basis to compute their end-of-the-year share of the company's profits. At HCSS, 25 percent of the profit sharing program is paid in shares that go to the ESOP account of each individual. All full-time employees with at least six months of service are included. The accounts vest overtime and, at HCSS, employees are fully vested after six years of service.

In addition to the tax breaks for both the owners and the employees, there are a few other advantages attached to ESOPs. First of all, participants are able to build their nest eggs for retirement while developing a sense of ownership in the company. Second, as employees build their stake in HCSS, there is an increased incentive to stay. This is particularly important in industries with high turnover rates such as the software development industry where employees typically stay an average of only 18 to 24 months with the same employer.

There are also a few disadvantages to ESOPs. First of all, employees have fewer options to diversify their portfolio. Indeed, most of the employees living in the Houston area, including HCSS employees, are painfully aware of the Enron bankruptcy. This bankruptcy ended up being particularly costly, especially for employees who had a lifetime commitment to and investment in this corporation; after the bankruptcy proceeding was closed, there was not much left for Enron retirees to live on. Second, as employees build their stake in the company and become majority shareholders, complex decisions can become difficult to make. Every shareholder has a different time frame. When long-term investments such as capital expenditures and research have a negative short-term effect on cash at hand and the profit sharing program, disagreements may emerge and, ultimately, the collective decision may not benefit the long-term interest of the company.

All the aforementioned scenarios were carefully considered before setting up the employees' stock ownership plans. Today, Mike still owns 34 percent of the shares, and employees about 30 percent in an ESOP trust. A majority of the remaining 34 percent is owned individually by employees and former business associates who received them in the company's early years. With the growth of the company, fewer shares were available to newcomers. As a result, over the last few years, these long-term employees were given the option to sell 10 percent of those shares every year. This allows the more senior employees to diversify their portfolio over time and for the company to have shares available to new employees. A few external investors mentioned earlier who provided technical advice or services, such as the accountant, lawyer, and programmer, own the remaining stock because they accepted shares in lieu of cash as payment for their services.

Stock Appreciation Rights

To complement the ESOPs, it was decided in 2007 to offer additional incentives and to increase the stake that each new employee had in the company. The main objective of stock appreciation rights (SARS) was to offer new employees, who had not benefitted from the company's fast growth as a start-up, the opportunity to benefit from future growth. This had to be achieved without offering shares, as they were not available, due to the limitations imposed on an S-Corp capital structure. Any employee who had worked more than 1,000 hours during that year was granted rights on 700 shares on the basis of the stock price at that time. At the end of the fourth year, that is, 2011, if the stock price has appreciated, each employee will exercise those rights and pocket the difference between the initial benchmark and the value of the stock. This stock appreciation will be considered and paid out as ordinary income.

End-of-Year Profit Sharing Program

At HCSS, the profit sharing program computation is straightforward. The first 10 percent of the company's net profits is booked as retained earnings for the company's use. The profit sharing pool for employees represents 60 percent of any profits above the 10 percent level. The profit sharing pool is then shared among employees. Individual profit share represents the same percentage of every employee's basic salary, from entry-level employees to senior executives. Profit sharing is given out and expensed in December. Profit is taken for 11 months, prorated for 12 months, and distributed to all employees prorated on their to-date compensation through November 30. Profit sharing was 18 percent and 22 percent of annual compensation for 2012 and 2013, respectively. During better years, it has sometimes reached or exceeded 35 percent. Seventy-five percent of the profit sharing program is paid in cash and 25 percent in stocks that go to the employee's ESOP account.

> Sebabi: And the thing that impresses me the most is that our CEO and our entire executive team do not sit there and make the assumption that, because they're at that level, they should get a disproportionately higher percentage of the profits of the company. It is still based on W-2 wages, of course, whatever your wages are. But everybody gets the same percentage. So if it's 25 percent for that year, then everybody gets 25 percent for that year. And I think that really, not only for me, personally, but for every employee, it makes them really buy into the whole concept that we're all in this together as a company, to help it to be more successful.

One advantage of the profit sharing program, particularly when the company has an established track record of treating its employees well and fairly, is that some employees accept a pay cut when they join HCSS. Others, particularly at entry level, accept salaries that would be considered low by industry standards. During the long interview process, nothing is more convincing for a candidate than to hear his or her future colleagues talking about their rewarding experience with such a system. By keeping starting salary at or slightly below-industry average, the company is in a better position in the case of an economic downturn. However, the company annual raises are far above industry averages and, over time, with or without profit sharing award, an employee's income rivals or exceeds industry norms.

Besides motivating employees, another major advantage of the HCSS profit sharing program is that it reduces difficulties in relationships between departments with different objectives. For instance, while the sales and support departments have different priorities, employees in one area know that what is good for the other department is also good for them.

> Eric: They [the support department] help me on my demos all the time and you'd think maybe there'd be some animosity because they spent all this time on a sale and they're helping the salesman and the salesman is the one that ends up getting the commission. But that support guy knows that it's going to the bottom line. It's going to profit sharing, too.

In retrospect, Mike reflects that while the initial plan to make employees feel and behave like owners was a good idea, ESOP was probably not the best way to achieve these objectives. Indeed, over the years, ESOP triggered a few unexpected issues in the areas of tax and succession planning. In addition, as ESOP reached a certain threshold, cash payments had to be made to employees selling their shares at times when the company needed the financial resources for its expansion. Finally, ESOP was too complex for most employees to see it as a motivator to join the company and to stay during the first years of their employment. As Tom says, "The ESOP is important, but it doesn't get people in the door. And it doesn't get them excited because a) people don't understand the ESOP, and b) it takes them a number of years to build enough value in the ESOP where the ESOP becomes attention-worthy."

Profit sharing programs are more palatable than other incentive mechanisms for the employees at any level and far easier to manage by the company during every phase of the business cycle. However, to make the profit sharing program even more meaningful to employees, Mike quickly understood that two additional conditions had to be met. First, the profit sharing program must be easy to understand and the allocation process transparent. Second, the amount paid must be significant and fairly allocated among employees. As noted earlier, transparency and fairness are essential to enhance teamwork within and between departments. Over the years, several employees have mentioned to Mike how many opportunities they had in their daily work to help colleagues. Any assistance provided to a colleague is a plus for the company as a whole and each employee knows that the added value generated will be fairly shared at the end of the year.

Each month a member of the senior management team leads the company lunch meeting to discuss financial performance and the ongoing transactions. However, not every employee has a financial background. Therefore, discussions about financials are usually limited to a basic review of the income statement. From the employee's point of view, the main interest is that he or she can estimate in real time the size that the profit sharing pool will attain by the end of the year. In addition, making employees aware of the financial situation by the company directly, as opposed to hearing through the rumor mill, is preferable, especially in times of financial difficulty. Finally, when efforts such as pay cuts and/or reduced hours are needed during an economic downturn, employees are able to put the request for sacrifice within the current business context. Financial pain is more bearable when it is understood and spread evenly.

> Maria: Every week we meet at the company lunch meetings with employees and we discuss various things going on in the company. It's very open. Everybody knows what's going on, what's going on with our products, what's new, what's different, et cetera. Some people go off, visit customers. They'll come back and tell us how that went, what they did, everything like that. But once a month, we will go over the financials... We look at sales. Sale figures, why they might have gone up or down. They'll ask, "Why is electricity so high this month?"... Pretty much anything. Then we look at our margins and see where they are.

Results

The results of HCSS's strategies can be found in its financial results (table 11.2) and its recognition as one of the best places to work for in Texas as discussed earlier. In addition, it can be found in its success as a competitor. Of the top 20 transportation contractors, 18 rely on HCSS software every day. The same is true of 22 of the top 25 heavy civil contractors.. Furthermore, it has been recognized as a leader in human resource management practices. In 2009, HCSS was named as one of the 15 winners of the *Wall Street Journal*'s "Top Small Workplaces" in America. By the end of 2012, HCSS had won the Gold Medal in the *Roads and Bridges* Contractor's Choice award for the seventh year in a row for its HeavyBid estimating software. In summary, HCSS is recognized as a leader by outside organizations for its many accomplishments.

Moving Forward: Expanding while Keeping a Competitive Edge

HCSS is conservatively managed, but well managed. The company has remained profitable even during the economic downturn and, except for the recent acquisition of their new headquarters, it has managed to finance its activities out of its own cash flow. Therefore, to finance future rapid growth, both internal and external financial resources are available.

One issue Mike has faced since the beginning is the pace of company growth. While subject to market conditions, an unlisted, family-controlled company has no real obligation to grow rapidly. To contrast HCSS with publicly listed companies, at HCSS there is no analyst's meeting at the end of every quarter during which so-called experts, who often do not know much about the industry, pressure for "growth," "upside potential," and "market momentum." Neither are there venture capitalists and institutional investors on the board of the company pushing for a strategy that would deliver a rapid growth in sales and profits in the medium term at the expense of the long-term viability of the company. Mike is not under these pressures. Therefore, one option is to simply maintain the same pace. Although it has taken Mike 27 years to grow to the current size, the company has quadrupled in size in the past 10 years.

But is it so simple? The company has come a long way since its humble beginnings and Mike did not spend half of his life growing HCSS to let it stagnate at its current level. Besides, the company always has new products in its pipeline and in this fast-changing environment, not taking advantage of market opportunities could be very costly in the long term. In this industry, competitors do not sit idle. In fact, HCSS is about to launch a new safety software product with applications not only for companies in the construction industry where most of HCSS's current customers operate, but also for other industries, especially the large manufacturing segment. This new software offers tremendous growth potential and the opportunity to create real value not only to clients but to employees and shareholders as well. However, introduction of this new software to a larger market requires the company to grow rapidly to get and keep the first mover advantage.

Could the company double in size over the next three years without destroying its culture and its competitive advantage? Mike recalls that even during the downturn, he still had six or seven entry-level positions open and unfilled. Quite a few applications were received but candidates rarely made it past the initial screening processes such that HCSS ends up hiring only about 1 percent of applicants. In addition to the lengthy recruiting process, for more senior positions, there are other issues.

For instance, considering its current corporate and governance structure, would it be possible for HCSS to attract and motivate the outside talent needed to complement the company's pool of internal managers? If so, what kind of incentive package would motivate these new senior executives to make the organization more efficient without destroying its unique corporate culture?

The company is currently headed by three senior managers: Mike with a background in philosophy, Tom with a background in psychology, and Steve with an MBA. It is this unusual mix of creativity and pragmatism, coupled with the fact that none of them are fundamentally money-driven, that made the company a success. Would a "hired gun" take the same pride in growing the business?

In recent years, leaders have been selected internally but Mike is aware of the limitations this creates. As the company grows rapidly, HCSS could find itself led by managers and directors who do not have prior leadership experience. And in fact, the grooming process is time consuming. Situations can also arise where the company does not have internal candidates available. Hiring outsiders is always possible, but it is not an easy process either. If anything, the ongoing search for a marketing director has proven frustrating and time consuming, considering the number of people involved in the process. Yet the collective wisdom attached to the current selection process has been key to hiring high quality employees who quickly adjust to the company's corporate culture.

In addition to the human resources issues, both at entry and more senior levels, there are also issues related to the communication flows between departments. Being close to the customer and being very responsive to their needs mean that the channels of communication have to remain highly effective. In this regard, is the current corporate structure adequate? Mike is aware of areas that need improvement. The support, implementation, and programming departments communicate well together, but the marketing, sales, and programming interface is not as effective. Can the company double its size while keeping the same structure?

Even at its current size, communication has become an issue, both horizontally and vertically. Mike often spots disconnects between the outcome of a discussion of the senior team members and the perception and understanding of this decision by the employees at more junior levels; sometimes the message becomes confused. Mike was adamant that the open-door policy was the best way to communicate directly with everyone but he wonders if this strategy will be sustainable with 280 employees when it is already difficult to succeed with over 140.

Mike knows that he must deal with these issues sooner rather than later. In a meeting with Chris, he noticed that employees in the customer support department were putting in long hours, even during the economic downturn. While there is nothing wrong with long hours over a short period of time, with business picking up, there is a risk that the situation would lead to the burnout of a few key employees. And in a business that relies heavily on employees' creativity and dedication to customers' needs, this situation cannot be left unattended for long without some unpleasant consequences that would be better avoided.

Notes

1. This statement was made by Melissa, a business analyst at HCSS. It reflects a value that is pervasive among her colleagues. HCSS employees are confident that they are "doing the job right." At the same time, they never stop looking for better ways to do it or opportunities to use their skills to solve new problems.
2. All employees are referred to in this case by their first name, including the president, because that is standard practice in HCSS.
3. Buckingham, M., and Coffman, C. 1999, May. *First, break all the rules: What the world's greatest managers do differently.* Simon & Schuster.
4. At HCSS, the corporate ambassador is more than a receptionist. This person greets visitors and helps them out. It is important for clients and visitors to have a first and lasting good impression of the company. The corporate ambassador knows and remembers the names of the visitors. He is also the person employees speak to when they have logistics issues to resolve, similar to a concierge at a luxury hotel.

CHAPTER 12

MBC Ventures, Inc.: An ESOP with a Union Partner

Richard C. Hoffman, Marvin O. Brown, and Frank Shipper

Introduction

MBC Ventures, Inc. (MBC), known as the Maryland Brush Company until a name change in 2011, is a 100 percent employee-owned United Steelworker employee stock ownership plan (ESOP) established in 1990. Throughout its recent history, the 161-year-old business has steadily increased its stock value. However, the future is less certain today as the firm's traditional brush business has matured, and its recent efforts at diversification have yet to be realized. The firm has proven to be quite resilient over the years having averted closure after being sold by PPG Industries in 1990. In an unusual partnership, the United Steelworkers of America union helped the firm's new owner-managers convert to an ESOP as part of a reorganization. This effort saved jobs and the company. Since that time, the firm's employees have proven to be its most valuable asset and a key source of its competitive advantage.

Company Background: The Genesis of an ESOP

MBC Ventures, Inc. began operations in 1851 as a supplier of paint applicators and maintenance brushes to the agricultural, industrial, and consumer markets in Baltimore, Maryland. In 1904, Pittsburgh Plate Glass (later known as PPG) acquired MBC as part of a diversification process that also included the acquisition of Patton Paint Company in Milwaukee, Wisconsin.[1]

MBC produced paint applicators that were sold to PPG's end user accounts, as well as maintenance and power brushes to its own industrial accounts. PPG announced its intention to sell MBC in October 1987. Several of PPG's competitors, as well as a group of MBC's management, expressed interest in purchasing the Baltimore operation. In addition, an official with the United Steelworkers of America, the union representing the Baltimore plant employees, decided to consider assisting a possible purchase of the operation by the employees. The union official then enlisted the services of an employee buyout specialist who conducted a study of the feasibility of an employee purchase of the operation. The consultant's conclusion was that the employee buyout was possible under the following conditions: (a) the union employees would have to make concessions in their compensation package, (b) the management employees would have to make a financial investment in the new operation, and (c) an interested commercial lender had to be secured. In addition, the specialist concluded that, not only could the employees buy the plant, but also it could be operated at a profit, and the loans used to finance the purchase could be repaid in about five years. Once this information was shared with the management of the Baltimore operations, who were also interested in purchasing the plant, management joined forces with the workers and submitted an offer to PPG. As stated by one of the employees, "What did we have to lose? We were going to be out of a job anyway," since the other potential buyers intended to move the operations out of state. In the end, only two bids were submitted for the purchase of the operation, and PPG accepted the offer from the employees. An additional part of the deal that helped secure financing for the employees was a long-term agreement by PPG to purchase brushes from MBC.

The issues that now faced MBC employees and management were how to structure the deal and how to raise the nearly $5 million necessary to fund the purchase. There are a number of methods by which an employee buyout of a company can be structured. These include, but are not limited to[2]: (1) An employee stock ownership plan (a trust fund that holds the stock allocated to the employees); (2) the employee cooperative; or (3) direct stock ownership of a regular corporation in which most or all employees directly own stock and few or no outsiders own stock. Moreover, federal tax laws permit substantial financial benefits to employee buyouts, including, but not limited to, possibly lower interest rates on borrowed funds and deductions for the payment of both principal and interest on the loans. The eventual deal accepted by the firm was the first option, whereby, a trust fund that holds the stock to be allocated to the employees individually was established. The money necessary to fund the purchase of the plant came from a variety of sources. First, union employees agreed to concessions in their compensation package. Specifically, the average hourly rate was reduced from $10.00 an hour to $9.40—a 6 percent decrease in hourly pay. In addition, there were reductions made to vacation time and changes made to the employee health plans. Second, funds were borrowed from both private and public sources. Specifically, the First National Bank of Maryland provided $3,035,000, the state of Maryland offered $1,500,000, the city of Baltimore issued $110,000 in debt financing, and the facility's management group provided $210,000. PPG accepted the employee offer, and the buyout was completed on February 1, 1990.[3] Under the agreement, the stock of the company was placed in a trust fund. As loans were repaid, the stock was distributed to the employee-owners. The agreement also called for the management group to sell back their stock in the company after five years. During that five-year period, there was no increase in the value of the company stock so each investing employee received back the same dollars they originally invested in the firm. At the time the company was formed in 1990, three loans were established between the company and the primary commercial lender. Three more loans, mirroring the mentioned commercial loans, were established between the company and the ESOP because no financial institution was willing to lend directly to the ESOP. The last of the commercial loans was satisfied in 2005. In 2010, MBC reorganized its debt. The State of Maryland loan was replaced with a commercial loan having more favorable terms, and two new loans were established. The first loan helped finance its initial 2009 investment in a new product line, and the second helped finance the 2010 acquisition of brush manufacturing equipment from Germany.

Business Environment and Strategy

Maryland Brush Company, the original company created as an ESOP in 1990, was reestablished as a division of the newly named MBC Ventures, Inc. in 2011 to address brush product customers. Maryland Brush began as a producer of brooms and brushes for industrial clients and consumers. Today, the Maryland Brush division focuses on brushes intended for industrial use (see examples at its online catalog at http://www.marylandbrush.com/brush_catalog.php).[4] The brushes are made of either metal or synthetic filaments for use on handheld or automated power driven machines to smooth, sand, or grind materials being processed by end user customers. Maryland Brush division brushes are sold primarily to the metalwork, millwork, tire retread, pipeline, and welding industries in North America and internationally.

MBC Ventures is a member of the American Brush Manufacturers Association that has represented manufacturers of brooms, brushes, mops, and rollers (SIC 3991) since 1917. The association has established standards for the industry, provided opportunities for members to learn about new products and processes, served as the industry's representative to government as well as provided a network for members.[5]

Currently, the brush industry is composed of about 80 brush manufacturers and another 80 supplier firms. It is a $200 million dollar a year industry. MBC ranks about fifth in the industry with less than 10 percent of the market. Unlike the other major competitors who carry other product lines such as abrasives and safety supplies, MBC focuses exclusively on brushes for industrial use.

The US brush manufacturing industry today is contracting in part because many brooms, brushes, and mops that were made by hand and sold to mass markets in the United States are now produced overseas in lower-wage countries. Furthermore, on the industrial side, many old line industrial firms have been consolidated and even closed their doors as the US economy shifted from a manufacturing to a service economy. Today's industrial brush market is truly a niche market.

Strategy for Changing Times

Faced with competing in a slow growth and even declining industry, MBC's management has taken a two-pronged approach to improve its firm's performance. In the traditional brush sector, it has consolidated its position and focused on the niches where it has a competitive advantage. In 2001, the firm discontinued its line of high quality, professional paint brushes that were mostly made by hand and sold to the mass market because it could no longer compete on price. The firm focused on the manufacture of engineered power brushes for industrial use, and the resale of commodity paint, maintenance and power brushes. As Steve Mullan, the firm's president and chief executive officer (CEO), noted, "We are investing in and developing niches where we can provide technical expertise for companies. In these areas we have a competitive advantage. We hope to leverage our niche brush market revenue as we seek to diversify the corporation, enabling us to grow." These niche market opportunities have taken the form of providing engineered solutions for its clients' production processes. By understanding the processes better, MBC can produce brush products that best suit the application for which it is to be used.

Diversification

Recognizing that its traditional brush market as a whole was stagnating or in decline, the firm has devoted considerable management time and effort in protecting its future revenue base by seeking a new avenue for diversifying the firm. In investigating new diversification alternatives, Steve noted the following as important considerations. First, "We think the brush business will not grow and likely will recede over the years." In selecting the right opportunity an important consideration was "to determine what we are good at and identify our strengths and weaknesses. We are good at manufacturing things made of metal." Additionally, "we wish to take a new product down different distribution channels from our brush business to increase our opportunity for success in our brush and our newly developed diversification endeavor." This would enable the firm to manage the product independently at some point in the future if it were deemed appropriate. In a process that took roughly five years, the firm narrowed its diversification product choices to two areas; either the alternative energy or environmental industries. With the help of consultants, MBC's management finally settled on an alternative energy technology. After the investigation and review of alternative energy opportunities, in 2009 the company selected to align itself with and invest in a Denver firm with its product known as Photensity.

In 2010, MBC purchased all intellectual property rights to the Photensity product and renamed it SkyLouver™. The SkyLouver system (for examples, see http://www.skylouversystems.com/)[6] is a unique rooftop solar energy system that harvests and distributes high quality daylight for use in the space beneath the installation, as well as large amounts of thermal energy. The thermal energy can be stored in insulated water tanks until needed to heat or cool room space or to satisfy the process heating or cooling needs of the facility. SkyLouver modules have articulating louvers that concentrate and direct natural daylight into a building, and convert the sun's energy into thermal energy through a heat transfer fluid. Compared to a photovoltaic solar panel that generates electricity, the SkyLouver technology is simpler to construct, is more efficient, and, as a result, it can be competitively priced. Additionally, all harvested energy is used by the facility, thus eliminating the transfer of energy to the grid where transmission losses occur. Buildings having a flat roof profile are candidates for this technology. According to Robert, the firm's manufacturing engineer, the product has a payback that is years faster than that of a traditional photovoltaic solar panel; this is expected to be appealing to a wide variety of customers.

Thus, MBC's strategy going into 2011 was that of a niche manufacturer of engineered brushes that was diversifying into the manufacture of SkyLouver solar modules and the accompanying storage and distribution systems. The first successful SkyLouver installation was completed in December 2011 on the roof of Building 9 at MBC's Baltimore facility. The 50 module system provides natural daylight to the brush making operation below. Approximately 90 percent of the day shift can be run with natural daylight provided by SkyLouver rather than from expensive artificial electric lighting. The thermal energy is collected on the second floor of Building 8 and heats and cools the SkyLouver assembly area. MBC received a $770,000 US Department of Energy CEEDI grant through the Maryland Energy Administration to help with expenses of setting up the SkyLouver manufacturing line and installing the product at its facility.

Management and Governance Structure

To say that MBC possesses a flat organization structure is truly an understatement. The firm's top management team consists of Steve and Tim Hartman, vice president. They are ably assisted in the task of managing the firm by a small office staff and a team structure that cuts across the entire organization. Management reports to and is greatly supported by an active board of directors (see table 12.1). Two things that are key to understanding the firm's governance are the structure and roles of teams and that of the board of directors.

Team Structure

Perhaps the second most revolutionary event in MBC's modern development after the ESOP was the installation of a team structure throughout the firm. In the early 1990s, with the change in management, the firm looked for a way to improve the organization, reduce expenses, and better utilize its biggest asset, its employees. "We decided to invest in teams, team development. We brought in consultants that provided extensive team training. All employees received training in group dynamics, problem solving, and various other team development areas. Classes in basic math and English training were provided to all individuals requesting assistance," according to Steve. In the beginning, many of the employees were not convinced of the team concept. As one team

Table 12.1   MBC Ventures, Inc. governance structure

Board of directors	
Mary Landry, chair 20 yrs. on board, external director, retired college librarian BA College of New Rochelle, MLS Columbia University, MA Management Notre Dame of Maryland University; board seat nominated by USWA District Director and affirmed by management	
Steve Mullan, president/CEO, 24 yrs., automatic appointment to the board	Tim Hartman, VP and corporate secretary, elected by salary group
Richard Benton, die setter and union president, 41 yrs with firm; union president automatic appointment to board	Gwen, team leader and shop steward, 40 years of service to the firm; elected by local union
Don Forcino, retired trainer and union organizer—external director appointed by USWA district director	Don Lamb-Minor, retired consultant, external director appointed by management

Top management	6 Teams	
Steve Mullan, president/CEO, 29 yrs. BSME Villanova University, MEME Carnegie-Mellon University, MBA Loyola of MD, PE, CMfgE	Customer Support Team	Brush Make Team
	Customer Sales Team	Brush Finish Team
	SkyLouver Team	Brush Support Team
Tim Hartman, vice president, 41 yrs. BS in Business Towson University		

leader noted, "A lot of the employees fought it . . . a lot of them had trouble taking direction from a peer worker." Today employees at all levels seemed to have embraced the team concept. As one team leader remarked, with the team concept, "you could be more involved. In the past, you went to a certain [work] station and stayed there. And now it's you go to this team, and you learn these different aspects of different jobs, and it's actually more interesting. You move around. You get to do more."

There are six teams in MBC's structure. Three of the teams are in the manufacturing area, and they are responsible for scheduling the work as well as keeping track of employee absences. The Brush Make Team, Brush Finish Team, and Brush Support Team mentioned in table 12.1 are comprised of unionized employees. The Brush Make Team headed by Colleen, a Cut and Bunch operator responsible for preparing all wire fill material for production use, is responsible for the initial steps of manufacturing brushes on traditional machines. The Brush Finish Team headed by Gwen, a Manual Section Machine operator, is responsible for the completion steps on another set of manufacturing machines. The Brush Support Team is the maintenance team headed by Harold, a machinist; his team members include a die setter, Richard (also president of the local union and a member of the MBC board), and a maintenance mechanic. The office team includes the president and vice president as well as the three other staff members who oversee the daily office operations. This team is headed by Ruth, the staff member in charge of Purchasing and Human Resources. As far as Steve's role on the team, it was noted that "he is sort of an independent observer of the team. But, yes, he sits in on our meetings and participates." The sales team is headed by Tim and is comprised of Baltimore-based and outside sales persons.

There are overlapping memberships on some teams. For example, a wage employee is on one of the manufacturing teams, but because he is also involved with shipping and receiving, he serves as part of the office team when working in that capacity. Having employees participate in more than one team reflects both lean staffing throughout the company and the need for extensive interaction among employees in a small organization. Most team members perform multiple roles over the course of a day or week. A major reason for this is that "a lot of people don't have 40 hours of actual work on their job,…so I might do a little die setting and, if they need me, I might go pack brushes. So you do other things" (Richard, die setter). Having multiple job roles is not without its problems as employees often felt that others were taking over their jobs and others felt that some employees tried to avoid more difficult work. In principle job flexibility worked in the following manner: "We all hold a certain title. But if you're finished in that area, and you go do somebody else's job, as long as that person is doing that job too, it's okay" (Gwen, team leader). As far as people gravitating to easier jobs, Gwen stated that "if I feel like somebody is treading on my toes, I just say something, or they'll do the same thing. And you just try and work it out."

Overall, MBC's employees are positive about the management style under Steve and the team concept from autonomy to the open communications it seems to afford the employees. The manufacturing engineer (Robert) expressed that "one of the benefits of the position that I'm in, my time is not necessarily regulated as I have tasks and things that need to be done. But I'm able to work at a self-pace with those items." Moreover, "the communication from all levels is open."

Board of Directors—Structure

MBC's board meets every month to assist in the governance of the firm given its lean management structure and high employee involvement. Seven people sit on the board: three appointed by the union, three appointed by management, and one neutral seat, appointed by the district union officer and approved by the company president. At this time the union members include the local union president, who is also a die maker for MBC, the leader of the Brush Finish Team elected by the union employees, and a retired union organizer appointed by the district director of the union. Management appointees are the company's president and vice president, and one external director approved by the president. The seventh seat is nominated by the local steelworkers' union and approved by MBC management (table 12.1). Mary Landry, the current board chair, has served in that capacity for 19 years. Her husband previously sat on the board. She replaced him upon his untimely death and was reelected to the position later once his term had expired. Directors who are not employees are paid a fee and cannot own shares of company stock unless those shares were earned as an employee. All board seats are subject to reelection at the company's annual stockholders meeting.

Board Processes

The board meets monthly to assist the management team in making strategic and financial decisions. A day or so after each of these board meetings, the union and employee representatives on the board hold a meeting with the union employees to disseminate information about the meeting to keep all informed.

Some key contributions of the board to the firm's management included its involvement in making the transition to an ESOP successful. In the first year, the management team at that time did not understand the power of an ESOP in harnessing the motivation of employee owners. The board took action in 1991, changing the management team to one more willing to work cooperatively with the employees.

More recently, the board played an important role in the firm's diversification decision. The process was initiated by Steve, who only too clearly realized that the brush business would not provide the growth the company sought. Steve had a challenge in convincing the board of the need to diversify. At some point there appeared to be a trust issue between Steve and the internal members of the board, "Why does he want to do that [diversify]?" Steve reasoned, "I don't want the board to rubber stamp anything. I want them to evaluate and understand where we are and what we face in the future. I want them to be convinced that diversification is the right thing to do." This discussion was protracted for almost three years. Once convinced of the need to diversify, the board turned to one of its members who had a marketing consulting practice and contracted his firm to help MBC identify diversification opportunities that matched the company's cultural, economic, and technical resources, and to come up with at least six ideas. The Photensity solar energy opportunity was about fifth on the list. The board sought input from employees as well. As one team leader noted, "We know the brush business is not going to go on forever...we wanted to grow. Do something, a new venture." Upon the ultimate selection of SkyLouver as its new diversified product line, Steve reflected that "we thought that this was a good fit given our assets, our people, our experience and our facility...all our strengths and capabilities." The total amount of funds devoted to investigating the solar opportunity was large, but a fraction of the firm's overall assets, so it seemed to be a reasonable risk for the company.

Formally, the board approves the officers of the company. The board also provides a list of nominees to function as board members for the following year, and this slate is presented at the annual meeting of the shareholders for their vote, along with approval of the auditing firm and any other business brought before the group. Any financial decision whose value is roughly half of the firm's assets is very significant and would be brought up for a shareholder vote. If the board decided to sell the company, this would have to be approved by a vote by all ESOP plan participants.

When asked how she felt about being a board member, Gwen, stated, "Very informational with regard to a lot of stuff that I would have never thought about before...how the company is run and who is controlling what. And it's very interesting...until you hear that stuff, you don't realize what's actually involved in running this place."

Other Forms of Employee Involvement

In addition to self-managed teams, MBC uses other specific programs to encourage employee involvement in the firm on a continuous basis. The two most prominent of these are the ESOP and gainsharing program that provide employees with a share in both the ownership and profits of the firm.

Employee Stock Ownership Program

Perhaps the most attractive benefit offered by MBC to its employees is the ESOP. To become fully vested in the ESOP, an employee must have worked at MBC for three years. The stock in MBC is distributed to MBC employees based on the number of hours actually worked in a year with a cap of 40 hours per week. Therefore, every employee, including management, must complete a daily timesheet containing the number of hours worked. Also, if an employee is sick and misses work, that employee will not be credited for hours worked and will not earn as much stock. As Steve stated, "It makes sense to count only those employees who are at work because those are the ones who have an opportunity to positively contribute to the organization." Because employees may work different amounts of time throughout the year, it is highly unlikely that any two employees would own the same number of shares of stock.

There are two types of distributions possible to employees under the ESOP. The first is called the retirement/separated employee distribution program. As explained by Steve, when someone separates, the year after their separation they are eligible for distribution. The distribution is made over five years with the employee receiving 20 percent of their shares in each of those years. Those shares can be put back to the company at the prevailing share value for that plan year. The separated employee has the option of when to begin the distribution. But, once the separated employee begins the distribution, it will continue for five years at which time the distribution concludes. The separated employee, in deciding when to begin the distribution, is taking a risk as to whether the value of the shares of stock will increase or decrease.

The second type of distribution is the diversification distribution. To qualify for this type of distribution, the employee must be fifty-five years of age or older and have ten years of service. An eligible employee may request a diversification distribution the year after the latter of these two events occur. This method of distribution lowers an employee's risk in that they can reduce their financial investment in MBC and instead develop or add to an independent individual retirement account (IRA). This distribution process occurs over five years, allowing an eligible employee to diversify up to 25 percent of their previously undiversified shares each year. During the sixth year of eligibility, an employee may diversify an additional 25 percent of the number of shares they earned since beginning employment for a total of 50 percent of all shares. The employee may roll over the funds into an IRA or put the cash in pocket, following the applicable state and federal taxes and regulations.

The ESOP represents an integral part of the compensation package at MBC. As stated by Steve, "The annual value of the shares has increased over recent years, and it provides employees with a greater sense of involvement in the company since the shares represent ownership of the business." As explained by Richard, "More so than the average person . . . you're really involved in things. You're involved in some of the decision-making on the floor where, before, with the supervisor, you were just told what to do without input."

Gainsharing

Another way in which MBC seeks to harness and increase employees' involvement in the company and positive contributions to performance is through gainsharing. Gainshare programs are generally designed to support team work and to reward employees when they meet predetermined standards. MBC managers and employees developed a gainshare matrix or model about 15 years ago after visiting a firm with a similar program.

A machine operator summed up MBC's program as follows: "You have to make a quota each hour, yes. That's how we get our . . . gainsharing. It goes by performance. It's a lot of elements. Its performance, its accidents, things like that all come into play. And if you go below the standard, you don't get gainsharing." MBC's gainshare model tracks and measures four broad performance areas and uses one or two measures for each area (weighted differently) that are tracked on a monthly basis using the matrix (table 12.2):

1. *Productivity*: measures performance to standard (35 percent of the total) of direct labor activity and indirect labor (10 percent of the total)
2. *Quality*: measures material consumed to standard (10 percent of the total) and customer credit memos—customer complaints or returns (10 percent of the total)
3. *Safety*: safety days-lost time due to accidents (5 percent of the total)
4. *Financial*: operating expense ratio—administration and selling costs versus manufacturing accomplishment (10 percent of the total) and operating income (20 percent of the total)

The firm used a number of years of historical data in developing the standard or the baseline for each of the seven elements of the matrix. Currently, the baseline reveals that performance to standard is 91.1, a goal achieved year after year. Likewise, the indirect labor ratio is fairly consistent at 115 percent or a ratio of 1.15 and so on across the baseline row on table 12.2. Consistent achievement above the standard may result in a quarterly payout to the employees. Consistent achievement below the standard would result in no payout.

The matrix is completed each month and distributed to all employees for performance feedback. At the end of the quarter, a potential payout is calculated with the first 900 points (equal to three baseline months) subtracted from the total points. Employees are rewarded only for exceeding the 900 point overall baseline standard. Once the total payout is calculated, half is retained

Table 12.2 MBC gainsharing matrix

MONTHLY	PRODUCTIVITY		QUALITY		SAFETY	FINANCIAL		
	Performance to Standard	Indirect Labor Ratio	Material Utilization	Credit Memos	Safety Days	Operating Expense Rati	Operating Income	
Mth – Yr _____	100.0	1.29	2,100	8	2	2.47	77,000	10
Direct % _____	98.0	1.27	2,300	11	3	2.53	72,000	9
Indirect _____	96.0	1.25	2,500	15	4	2.60	67,000	8
Material _____	94.0	1.23	2,700	18	5	2.67	62,000	7
Credit Memo _____	92.0	1.21	2,900	22	6	2.74	57,000	6
Safety Days _____	90.1	1.19	3,100	25	7	2.82	52,000	5
Oper Exp Ratio _____	88.1	1.17	3,300	29	8	2.90	47,000	4
Oper Profit _____ **Baseline**	86.1	1.15	3,500	32	9	2.98	42,000	3
	84.1	1.13	3,700	36	10	3.08	37,000	2
	82.1	1.11	3,900	39	11	3.18	32,000	1
	80.2	1.09	4,100	43	12	3.28	27,000	0
								Score
Weight	35	10	10	10	5	10	20	Weight

QUARTERLY

MONTH	POINTS	PAYOUT
_____	_____	_____ – 900 = _____ points
_____	_____	* 100 = $ _____
_____	_____	½ = $ _____ persons
_____ Total ==>	_____	= $ _____ /person max

by the company to help support the program. The other half is divided by the total number of employees (hourly and wage) on the payroll. A person's actual payout may be reduced due to absences (illnesses or unexcused reasons). Normal paid vacations count toward the payout. In recent years, the annual payout has been as high as 10 percent of an hourly worker's income. See box 12.1 for a complete example.

Box 12.1   Gainsharing measures and scoring

The gainsharing system used at MBC reviews four broad areas of company performance on a monthly basis: productivity, quality, safety, and financial. Each of these areas is assessed using one or two measures or standards with differential weights.

Measures: Performance to standard assesses direct labor involved in production only, not office or warehousing work. Management compares the value of what is produced to the value of the labor it took to produce it. Because performance is reported monthly but the work is not evenly distributed by month, the firm uses a two-month (current and prior month) weighted average for this measure. This carries the greatest weight in the matrix. Indirect labor or services and other nondirect manufacturing labor costs are taken into account here. In a similar fashion it is compared to the value of what has been produced and accounts for 10 percent of the model. The third measure used is the cost of materials used in production that month compared to standard; it is also weighted 10 percent. Next are credit memos that are developed from customer complaints and returns, also worth 10 percent in the matrix. The next element or measure is safety days or lost time accident days. For example, if today an employee is injured and leaves to get stitches, today is not a safety day. But the next day if the person is still out, then it is a safety day. On the financial performance side operating expense ratio takes all expenses (administrative and selling) except for direct and indirect labor and compares it to the value of what has been manufactured and it accounts for 10 percent of the score. Finally, operating income is 20 percent of the model. Operating versus net income is used because employees have more influence on the expenses associated with running the business and not the loans and tax decisions reflected in net income.

The actual performance numbers that appear in the matrix were developed from the company's own performance data over the years. The baseline represents the standard the company has consistently been able to meet.

Calculating GS points: The data are reviewed every month and a gainshare score is calculated the left-hand column entitled "Monthly." Each quarter the three monthly scores are totaled, and the potential payout is calculated according to the formula below the matrix entitled "Payout."

Perhaps an example is in order here:

Assume the following scores for each measure in the column labeled "standard":

Gainshare points are calculated by multiplying the score of the measure, which is the number from 0 to 10 listed in the column to the far right of the matrix itself, by the weight for the measure listed in the row at the bottom of the matrix itself. Thus, for a performance to standard of 100, it yields a score of 10 multiplied by the weight of 35 or 350 points for this single element. Remaining scores and calculation appear in the table that follows:

Sample March Monthly Gainshare Points

Measure	Standard	Score	Multiplied by Weight	GS Points
Performance to standard	101.4	10	35	350
Indirect labor	1.30	10	10	100
Material utilization	4,250	0	10	0
Credit memos	3	10	10	100
Safety days	0	10	5	50
Operating expense ratio	4.28	0	10	0
Operating income	29,500	0	20	0
			Total points for month	**600**

Determining the Payout

Quarterly		Payout		
Month	**Points**			
Jan	480	1610 minus 900*	710	
Feb	530	X's $100	$71,000	
March	600	X's .50	$35,500	
Total	1610	Divided by no. of	$1183.33/person	
		employees = 30	max (based on	
			hours worked)	

The monthly points are simply totaled up for the quarter. In the payout calculation, 900 points are deducted from the monthly total because that represents the points earned if the firm simply made the baseline each month. The gainshare program seeks to reward employees for exceeding baseline. Each person from the CEO to the shop floor can receive no more than the max amount. A person's share may be reduced due to absences (illness or unexcused); one is not penalized for paid vacation time.

MBC employees recognize the impact that the gainshare plan has on motivation and effort. In speaking about the monthly feedback, the tool and die maker noted that "It's got the gainshare matrix. You can follow that to determine how well you are doing, [and] if you need to pick it up a little bit... So if you do well, you get extra money in your pocket quarterly through gainshare."

A machine operator commented, "It's nice. I work hard to get [gainshare] and it's rewarding. We do good work. The brushes we put out are quality brushes, and there's pride in our work." The chair of MBC's board summed up the program and its impact by remarking, "Our employee owners are doing like 111 percent productivity because...if the whole plant does well in gainshare...they get a fair chunk of change if that gainshare averages out."

Business Operations

Manufacturing—Brushes

The order cycle for the company's brush products was described as follows:

> An order will come in. We have to determine if we have the materials to make or buy the product to satisfy the customer. If not, we create and manage all the work orders and the workflow. When it comes back, we get it into the system; we get the pick list out on the floor. And we bill the customer. We then receive the revenue, and we account for the revenue.

MBC's manufacturing operations are all located in a single plant in Baltimore. As a matter of fact, current production facilities took up only a quarter of the space available in the facility. In the past, the company had attempted unsuccessfully to lease some of the space. Given its entry into the alternative energy market with its SkyLouver product, the company has ample space to manufacture its new product line in the existing facility. Most of the brushes are made on machines that are operated by one person. The basic steps consist of cutting and sometimes twisting the filaments, which are then pressed between two metal stampings or plates to form the brush. Brushes vary in size by diameter, filament type, construction, and thickness. Different types of brushes can be made on different machines. Each machine can make multiple sizes of brushes, and the operators are responsible for their own changeovers when they are to start producing a different size brush for a customer. Both the wire and metal stampings are sourced from various suppliers, some of whom have done business with MBC for decades. Most of today's brushes are engineered to customers' specs. As one operator and team leader stated, "The most important thing is the customer. To make sure we get the work out in a timely fashion is what keeps us in business."

Operators had a targeted hourly quota; achieving or exceeding the quota provided points toward gainsharing numbers calculated each month. A couple of years ago MBC purchased a large $350,000 brush making machine from Germany to produce strip brushes. The machine operator who was to operate the machine and the company president traveled to Germany for one week to be trained on the use and care for the machine. This type of team work is an example of putting employee ownership to work.

MBC recycles cut wire and scrap metal that results from the manufacturing process. Bins are placed conveniently near the machines in the manufacturing area for that purpose. Employees are careful to separate metals. For example, brass wire goes in a bin separately from carbon steel or stainless steel. Paper and cardboard recycling is also practiced. As the manufacturing engineer remarked, "Everything is recycled here if it can be."

Team leaders and management also keep a close eye on safety measures making sure all who work in the production area have their safety glasses on, for example. As one machine operator put it, "There are so many areas for accidents."

Many of the production employees develop their skills on the job, although some have come from manufacturing backgrounds. For example, Joe had been a forklift operator prior to coming to MBC. He started working with basic equipment and gradually moved up to operating the brush making machines. Gwen started by making paint brushes by hand. When that operation was shut down, she moved to engineered brushes and learned how to run the machines on the job. She can now operate six different machines. Margie, a section machine operator, worked with Styrofoam products at other firms, as she stated, "That was light work. This is kind of physical. I came from that to this...It was a big change. I had a lot to learn...it took me awhile, but once you get it, you got it." More formal and external training occurs when new safety procedures or products are implemented, or when new machinery is acquired. Other than that the teamwork spirit seems to pervade the workplace and is apparent in how employees acquire new skills. Ruth, the Customer Service Team leader, describes training at MBC as follows: "It becomes a team function, and everybody participates...In the facility, we're always doing safety training, forklift operation, elevator things. There are union meetings on a regular basis that touch on safety. There's a lot of cross training of job functions that's done by the teams."

Manufacturing—Solar Panels

In January 2011, MBC hired Robert as the manufacturing engineer for the new SkyLouver solar project. Robert was formerly a tool and die maker for a supplier of stampings for MBC's brushes, so he was very familiar with the company and its products. He was attracted to the position for two reasons. First, the fact that the company was growing by diversifying, "bringing on the solar business which really excited [me]...as far as making things." Second, "It's an ESOP company, so that you have a stake in the profitability and the future." Robert's responsibility is to create the manufacturing processes within the facility, and to lead the fabrication of the production solar units. In learning about the new technology, the firm has relied on its newest technical employee and solar engineer John, who lives in Denver, Colorado. John was the lead engineer of the SkyLouver effort for a number of years before MBC purchased the technology in 2010. Steve and two team leaders traveled to Denver in 2010 to be trained on the assembly of SkyLouver. In developing the manufacturing process for SkyLouver, Robert and Steve relied on the following: (a) their new engineer (John) on the project, (b) their own limited knowledge of the SkyLouver product, (c) their experiences in various manufacturing environments, (d) suppliers' assistance with equipment and process techniques, and (e) their ability to search the Internet for additional ideas.

SkyLouver module solar panel production is being performed on two upper floors in Building 8 that had been unused since the cessation of paint applicator production a number of years ago. MBC installed a $90,000 elevator to handle movement of the large SkyLouver production equipment as well as the SkyLouver raw materials and finished components between floors. A sixth team was developed and comprised of SkyLouver technical, marketing, and manufacturing interests.

Quality Control

Teams perform their own quality control; each employee reviewing work performed in the previous operation as well as their own. Each brush finished goods' box is marked with the packer's name. The name of the production operator for each labor activity is recorded on the work order document. Each operator is responsible for the quality of products they produce. Through this documentation, any product complaints can be taken right to its manufactured source.

If raw materials used in brush manufacturing do not meet expected specifications, the matter is reviewed. After conferring with the supplier, the materials are returned to the supplier with a formal complaint according to MBC's ISO quality manual. To maintain supplier relations and increase employee understanding of the materials used in production, management occasionally takes production employees on visits of their suppliers' facilities.

The manufacturing engineer describes MBC's overall QC process as follows, "Well, here at Maryland Brush, everything that is made has a work process and checkpoints involved in that." These processes follow general guidelines of ISO 9001 standards.[7] MBC became ISO certified because the process helps the company understand and comply with the needs of the customer and because, according to Steve, customers were asking for products and services that conformed to ISO practices. The company's outside ISO registrar performs an annual audit of the operation, and employees perform self-audits annually as well. The audits, "make sure we're within standards, and we're doing things the way we're supposed to be doing them . . . And the larger customers out there now demand that their suppliers are ISO."

The process developed for producing the solar energy modules is based on the same quality principles the firm already adheres to based on its ISO quality management system. As Robert noted, "Quality is a mindset that was already here . . . if you bring on a different product, as much different as SkyLouver is . . . you still have the same quality mindset."

Customer Service/Marketing

MBC sells products all over the continental United States as well as internationally. Two of its larger foreign markets are Mexico and South Africa.

Customer relations and traditional order entry activities are managed by MBC's Customer Support Team. Team members include Susan, Ruth, Don, and Steve, all located in Baltimore, and Tim—located in New Jersey. The Customer Sales Team is made up of Tim, Jim, who lives in Illinois, and Bill, a new sales rep who joined MBC in 2012 to handle the SkyLouver sales and marketing effort. The team is supported by six geographic based sales representative firms who are commission only and represent other non-brush product lines in their territories. Tim covers a geographic region and manages the sales reps through promotion, education, and solicitation of orders for the brush effort. Jim is the member of the sales team who focuses on a specific industry—steel and nonferrous metal rolling mills for the brush effort. Tim indicated that sales personnel make essentially two types of calls: one type is at the distributor level usually with a sales rep, and the second is to end users who might be looking for help in designing a brush for a particular application. MBC has developed long-term customers for its brushes over the years. According to Susan, the firm's customers "are very dedicated... We have a great customer base. We're very close with a lot of our customers. We know their ordering habits and everybody's names."

MBC is similar to other industrial firms in the methods it uses to attract customers. The primary means is through its sales representatives. The firm also engages in cooperative advertising with distributors, having its products included in the distributors' catalogues and promotional literature. The firm also participates in multiple trade shows where it exhibits and demonstrates products and discusses its engineering services. The firm has two websites (www.marylandbrush.com and www.skylouversystems.com)[8] allowing customers to learn about the company and its abilities, and to look up products and request a quote. The marketing staff feels that MBC has picked up business from the Internet. The firm works to make it easy for the customer to buy products from them. Finally, the firm has joined buying groups where customers come together to increase their buying power from suppliers such as MBC.

SkyLouver marketing strategy is still being developed and implemented. It is a collection of efforts including displaying at trade shows and on the Internet, targeting of building owners/operators within specific industries, contacting building and energy consultants, architects, and service providers, and networking through available channels.

Human Resource Practices

In addition to the programs discussed under employee involvement, MBC employs other human resource management practices. MBC provides a generous compensation benefits package. Most of our employees have been hired by word of mouth. In the rare instance when an employee is laid off, they often do not seek employment with another company, but would rather wait until recalled by MBC. According to Margie, she was laid off in 2009 "for 6 months and for a period in 2002. I always come back," she said. In accordance with the union contract, an MBC employee who is laid off will maintain his or her seniority and benefits rights for up to one year after layoff. Interviews to hire potential employees are conducted by a group of the employees in the particular job category to be hired. For example, if the position that is being filled is an hourly position, then a group of hourly workers will interview the candidate. After the wage group completes its interviews, it will make a selection for the new hire, which is reviewed by the president.

A vacant salary position is filled in a similar manner with candidates being interviewed by a group of salaried employees. Once the salary group makes a final decision, it is reviewed by the president and the board of directors.

MBC offers its employees a number of other benefits. For example, the union workers also have a pension program partially paid for by MBC and partially paid for and administered by the union. As explained by Steve, "We have a traditional pension with our union group... We make a contribution every payroll. It's a small amount, and the Steelworkers fund most of it." MBC sponsors the pension plan for its union members, and a 401K plan for all employees. The 401K is a traditional program where employees invest pretax income into their accounts, and MBC matches the employee contribution up to a maximum of 6 percent. Employees are eligible to participate in the 401K program only after a 30-day waiting period. As with most 401K programs, the participation by the employee is voluntary, but as one employee stated, the vast majority of employees participate in the program. Caring for its employees and recognizing our ESOP roots, MBC also provides a very generous medical insurance program with minimal employee premium share requirements.

Recent Financial Performance

MBC Ventures like many small, closely held companies does not make its financial information public even though it practices open-book management internally. MBC has provided two graphs—one of sales and one of owners' equity—for the last six years (figure 12.1). As can be seen, overall sales decreased between 2006 and 2008. This decrease was due to MBC continuing to focus on the niches where it has a competitive advantage as addressed earlier. One can also see the positive effect on owners' equity as the firm's emphasis of high profit margin engineered brushes while decreasing the low margin commodity-priced ones. Between 2008 and 2009, the "Great Recession" hit sales hard because MBC products are used primarily in industries that manufacture capital goods. Stockholders' equity also decreased between 2008 and 2009, but not as steeply due to steps taken by management to reduce costs. That decrease continued between 2009 and 2010 as sales began to turn around in 2010. In 2011, as sales rose back to almost prerecession levels, the strategy to focus on high margin engineered brushes paid off as stockholders' equity soared.

Organizational Atmosphere and a Look to the Future

In general, MBC employees at all levels appear to be satisfied working for the company. The long tenure of many employees, the low turnover, and the fact

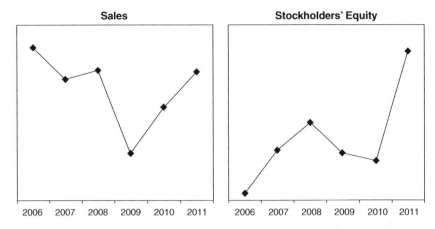

Figure 12.1   MBC Ventures, Inc.'s financial graphs.

that employees are willing to suffer through layoffs in hopes of being recalled are indications of their commitment. The positive work environment at MBC appears to be due to a number of factors. The employees describe what they best like about working at MBC:

> Ruth (office team leader): The first thing...It's a small company now, so I get to do a lot of different things. I'm always busy. Every day is new. So for me it's the work. The diversity of the work, and the fact that I can be involved in so many different things. [Second,] I would say that it is the flexible environment...The fact that you don't have a lot of supervision is good for self-directed people... [Third,] I would say the fact that we are employee owned...I think I have a big influence.
>
> Richard (tool and die maker and local union president): For me it's a great place to work because...you don't have that supervision standing over the top of your shoulder...You are involved in some of the decision making on the floor where, before, with the supervisor, you were just told, "You do this," and that's it.
>
> Robert (manufacturing engineer): Yeah, I get the feeling that this organization is one where you can go talk to whoever you need to talk to, and there's no standing on formality here...The communication from all levels is open.
>
> Colleen (team leader): Our union and our management get along well. And Steve respects us as workers. And...we respect him. I mean if we have a problem, we address it with him, and he treats us like human beings, which is important.
>
> Susan (accounting): The fact that it is an ESOP...Everyone gets along wonderfully. The office personnel, there's not many of us, but we work very closely together. The fact that we are employee owners...we control a lot of our future. And I have no intention of going anywhere else.
>
> Margie (machine operator): The best thing, I'd say, is our co-workers...You have to work together as a team and that's basically what we do. If we have a problem or something like that, we pitch in and help out, everybody works together as a team.

It appears that the positive aspects of the work environment at MBC are due not only to formal management practices employed such as the ESOP, gainsharing, and team structure, but also to its small size that facilitates communication and to the tone set by the management style of the president (Steve).

Despite its positive organizational environment, MBC faces some challenges over the next few years. In the short run, the firm will have to replace experienced employees in brush manufacturing who may decide to migrate to the new product group in SkyLouver once production picks up. There will be a number of retirements in the next few years; this will require recruitment of new employees who are bound to change the culture of the current work environment. Most important is the challenge posed by competing in a mature industry and the financial and emotional risk associated with the recent diversification effort of the SkyLouver alternative energy technology. In considering MBC's future, Steve pondered the challenge posed by the firm's new product line:

> It is hoped and expected that our solar business will be very successful and that it grows to be much larger than our brush business. If it does not grow to exceed our brush business, we will surely be disappointed. However, we will still be profitable and secure, and we will continue to provide good jobs to our employees and support our community.

Notes

1. PPG Industries: http://www.ppg.com/en/Pages/home.aspx.
2. Murphy, M. E. 2005. The ESOP at thirty: A democratic perspective. *Willamette Law Review*, *41*, 655–705.
3. Atwood, L. February 12, 1990. Buyout keeps paint brush plant open. *Baltimore Evening Sun*, pp. F1 & F12.
4. Maryland Brush Company website: http://www.marylandbrush.com/.
5. Ibid.
6. The Skylouver System website: http://www.skylouversystem.com/.
7. ISO website: http://www.iso.org/iso/home.htm.
8. Maryland Brush Company website: http://www.marylandbrush.com/.

CHAPTER 13

KCI Technologies, Inc.: Engineering the Future, One Employee at a Time

Vera L. Street, Christy H. Weer, and Frank Shipper

Introduction

The company now known as KCI was founded in Baltimore County, Maryland, in 1955 in the basement of one of its cofounders. In 1977, the company was purchased by industrial products conglomerate Walter Kidde & Company and was subsequently merged with three other architectural and engineering firms into an engineering subsidiary that came to be known as Kidde Consultants Inc., or KCI. In 1987, Kidde was purchased by Hanson Trust PLC, a British manufacturing company with diversified holdings worldwide.

Although Hanson favored some of the Kidde businesses, there was a lack of fit between KCI and its new parent company. In particular, being a service-driven firm, as opposed to a product-oriented manufacturing company, KCI's measures of profitability were not consistent with Hanson's expectations. As an example, Terry Neimeyer, KCI's chief executive officer (CEO), explained:

> They had a term called, "Return on Capital Employed,"...and they expected any company that worked for them to have an ROCE of 80 percent...We said, "Well, look, we are an engineering company, we're lucky to do 5 or 6 percent and we think we're doing well at 5 or 6 percent." And they said, "Look, our number's 80 percent."

Even beyond the inconsistencies with respect to financial expectations, the corporate cultures of Hanson and KCI differed drastically. KCI was used to having autonomy in decision-making and authority. Hanson on the other hand, took a much more centralized, top-down approach to management. For example, as Neimeyer remembers, "if you wanted to buy a computer, you would have to go to London and make a presentation."

It was no secret that Hanson's business strategy was to enter the United States, buy a conglomerate, keep what they viewed to be their profitable assets—assets that would be returning 80 percent—and then divest the unprofitable assets. Thus, aware that Hanson would likely want to sooner rather than later divest of KCI, senior managers had an idea. Driven largely by self-preservation, but also with a touch of optimism, the top management team thought, "Hey, let's see what we can do to buy ourselves." And why not? Who knew what would happen if KCI were to be taken over by another company? Indeed, there was a level of excitement over the potential of being a part of, and perhaps even leading, an employee-owned company.

Unfortunately, Hanson was not at all receptive to the idea. As Neimeyer remembers, Hanson's view on selling KCI to its employees was: "Absolutely not. We do not sell to people. We do not sell to former employees. It's just not what we do. We'd like to sell and rid ourselves of this [company] and it's over...and we don't do it [sell to former employees]."

However, by this time, the KCI senior management team was actively seeking a strategy to make a buyout happen. Having determined that alone the senior managers could not come up with enough equity to leverage a deal, they sought the buy-in of the 800 KCI employees. An existing Kidde profit sharing plan, which had accumulated some significant funds, laid the foundation for employee contributions. According to Neimeyer,

> We said, let's look at doing this where we'll ask people [employees] if they'd like to do it. We'll put out perspectives; we'll do a whole pro forma, which we did. And then people [employees] would have the option of contributing whatever they wanted. They could contribute 0 percent, they could contribute 100 percent, they could contribute anywhere in between. So, [based on our calculations as to the value of the company at that time], we basically had the scenario where ballpark figures it was 80 percent employee owned, with 20 percent held by these managers.

However, Hanson refused the offer. They were just not interested in selling the company to former employees.

Disappointed, but ever cognizant of the potential harsh consequences of being purchased by another organization, senior management at KCI went back to the drawing board. They knew the risks of upping the offer, but they also had confidence in their organization and, perhaps even more importantly, in their employees. Ultimately, they presented an increased, leveraged offer Hanson could not refuse. Shortly thereafter, KCI initiated an employee buyout and became a majority employee-owned company on December 15, 1988. On January 1, 1990, KCI established a qualified retirement program for the stock of KCI Technologies, Inc., to be held in trust by an employee stock ownership plan (ESOP). The ESOP initially owned approximately 82 percent of KCI stock, however, in June 1998, the company bought all of the management shares (non-ESOP shares) and became 100 percent employee-owned. Terry Neimeyer is the current chief executive officer and chairman of the board of KCI; Nathan Beil is the president.

Operations and Quality Management

Although most people know an engineer or have at least met one, many may not know exactly what engineers do. To help better understand the nature of KCI, Harvey Floyd, a senior vice president and chief client services officer, offered the following as an explanation of KCI's businesses to outsiders:

> You know what architects do, you know what lawyers do, you know what doctors do, but you have no idea what engineers do...you know when you get up in the morning and you turn the lights on; How do you think that light comes on? It's from the generators that were built by engineers, the power plants, the transmission lines, everything built by, everything was designed by engineers. [To clarify] Not built, but designed by engineers. Then, you walked over and turned the water on, and out came water. Well, where do you think the water came from? From the reservoirs, the towers, the pumps, the pumping stations, all designed by engineers. You flush the toilet. Where do you think it all goes? Pipes, the treatments plants, all designed by engineers. You drove across a road to get here. Where do you think the road came from? The bridge you drove over...who designed the bridges?

In other words, KCI is in the business of designing and coordinating facility and infrastructure projects and improvements for both the public and private sectors. Much of their work, approximately 80 percent, involves public sector work from various Departments of Transportation (e.g., MD DOT, Georgia DOT, PennDOT). Examples of work KCI may become involved with in the private sector includes projects at research parks and universities for contractors and developers. Table 134.1 provides examples of recent projects undertaken by KCI.

The competitive environment facing KCI, as well as the need for precision in the nature of the projects undertaken, drives a quality-focused culture at KCI. In part, there is the recognition that repeat business is critical, and to get that repeat business, projects must be completed to precision. When things do not go as well as expected, it is not uncommon for KCI employees to get out in the field to figure out what could be improved upon for future projects.

Quality is important on both the business side as well as the technical side of the work done at KCI. On the business side there are quality issues with, for example, determining project scope, understanding and negotiating client needs, and understanding regulations. On the technical side, the quality of designs, calculations, and reports and plans must be regulated. Because there are no set products that are being produced, as every project is different, these are challenging tasks.

Obtaining and maintaining ISO certification (verification by the International Organization on Standardization that relevant business standards are met) has been an important quality initiative at KCI.[1] However, obtaining this certification has not been without its challenges. To begin, the standard was initially developed for manufacturing firms. Thus, as a service firm, KCI has had to adopt very broad interpretations of various components of

Table 13.1 Example KCI projects

Project	Discipline	Location	Description
St. Mary's County Courthouse	Construction	Leonardtown, MD	Construction management over renovation and expansion of historic courthouse
Clarice Smith Stormwater Management Pond	Environment	College Park, MD	Designed changes to stormwater management pond
Capitol West Refrigeration Plant Expansion	Land Development	Washington, DC	Survey and layout services for plant expansion
Gettysburg Interchange	Transportation	Cumberland County, PA	Team lead for highway interchange project
Bonita Springs Tower	Telecommunications	Bonita Springs, FL	Worked on repair of tower damaged by hurricane
Verizon	Telecommunications	Varies	On-call to provide engineering services to Verizon
Suwannee Pedestrian Bridge	Transportation	Suwanee, GA	Engineering services for bridge and Boardwalk

Source: Adapted From KCI's website.

the standard. Additionally, as a requirement, KCI had to explicitly write down their business processes. This proved to be somewhat of a hurdle, because, as Floyd put it, "a lot of these things are 'that's just the way we do it.'" Another issue was getting people to exert the extra effort required to obtain the certification. Senior management tried to make this as painless as possible, and they were quick to point out that, although some extra effort was necessary, oftentimes this effort resulted in not only a step toward certification, but also in making business processes easier than they were before.

Logically, they began slowly, just focusing on part of the company. Then as the benefits were seen, it was decided to begin certification for the whole company in order to take the quality of their processes to the next level. The requisite codification of best business and quality control practices has helped to impose a level of discipline in the company's processes that may not have been present prior to the certification. And although it is not necessarily required by all clients, it is looked upon very favorably and helps to win business. At this time, not all of KCI businesses have been certified; however, they are actively seeking ways to do so.

Marketing

Given that KCI is an engineering services firm, marketing is different than in a traditional manufacturing company and is even different from many other types of service firms. Marketing is primarily done through the preparation of proposals and statements of qualification for potential clients. Ultimately, work is secured because of the "expertise and experience of the technical staff at KCI." According to Deborah Boyd, director of proposal preparation, "I would say that 90 percent of our marketing falls within developing project descriptions of work that we've done in the past, employee resumes. Our marketing is very technical in nature, where it revolves around the projects and the staff team qualifications and the qualifications of our sub-consultants." The process begins by finding potential clients who have jobs that need to be done. This primarily happens in two ways. The first, more conventional route is searching for client advertisements. This is usually done by the marketing staff searching online and/or looking in trade publications. A second, perhaps more fruitful route is using a type of networking. Here, the business development staff, as well as other employees working on various projects, keeps in contact with current and past clients to see what other projects they have in the pipeline. Other consultants that KCI has worked with also often prove to be a good source of leads. The marketing staff track these potential projects. Then, a qualified technical lead is brought in to work on the proposal that will be drawn up for the potential client.

The business development staff meets with the potential clients to ascertain information that will help in the proposal writing process. They try to determine what exactly the potential client is looking for, for example, a probable price range, or any "hot buttons." Whereas general advertisements by these clients can be fairly generic and don't always contain everything the client is looking for, the business developers play a critical role in information gathering. The marketing staff then pulls together this information, matches it with the qualifications of KCI and prepares a package to submit to the potential client.

A key to this process is to get shortlisted. This is an area in which KCI may be able to improve. As Boyd put it, "So either we're not qualified to do the job or we're qualified and we didn't show it very well. And if we're qualified and we didn't show it very well, that's a reflection on me because that means my proposal didn't answer the questions in the RFP." An important part of the marketing effort is building project descriptions on prior work and maintaining a database of these descriptions. The project descriptions are like a project "resume." They contain information about the project, including the qualifications of the team that worked on it, and qualifications of any subconsultants.

Additionally, there are efforts aimed at increasing potential clients' awareness of KCI. One way that KCI attempts to build awareness is by standardizing their proposals. Consistency in fonts and colors is maintained so that potential clients can recognize a KCI proposal at a glance. Another example of how KCI attempts to increase awareness is through their corporate website.[2] The website is continually updated to highlight successful projects they are currently working on or have completed. Other corporate communications are also available to interested parties. They produce folders of information including descriptions of successful projects they have completed, indications of awards they've won, and lists of where they are operating. Additionally, presentations at conferences and seminars help to promote the employees of KCI as experts in their respective fields.

HR and Intellectual Capital Development

Clearly, in such a technically focused, service-oriented organization, employee knowledge and expertise are key elements for success, and this is not taken for granted at KCI. There are many ways in which intellectual capital is developed, starting right from the beginning; every attempt is made to hire the right people!

With a focus on shared leadership, hiring managers have a hand in developing realistic job descriptions. Openings are first posted internally, allowing current employees the opportunity to investigate and pursue available positions. After five days, the openings are posted externally. Often, department managers are involved in the entire hiring process, from creating job descriptions to prescreening applicants, to interviewing and making final hiring decisions. Although talent is hard to come by, Tammy Jones, a vice president and HR director, feels that KCI gets high quality applicants due to the company's reputation for doing great work in high profile projects— projects of which employees are proud to be a part.

Once hired, employees have the option to become involved in a year-long formal mentoring program at KCI. This program, launched about seven years ago, was established, in large part, in an attempt to keep the intellectual capital developed at KCI from moving to competitor firms. New hires are paired with more senior employees and move through a 12-month formal mentoring regime. Most senior managers mentor two or three new hires each year and the program appears to be paying off. As indicated by Jones:

> When I came to KCI, which has been almost five years ago, previous employee surveys, and as well as our turnover reports indicated that we were losing employees at two to three years. So thus launched the formal mentoring program. Actually, I was reviewing those statistics recently and we're retaining about 33 percent more than we did prior [to the mentoring program].

Beyond the mentoring program, formal training and development programs are a cornerstone of intellectual capital development at KCI. Perhaps most notable is an extensive set of leadership development programs for which employees at various levels of the organization can be nominated. The series includes three programs: Emerging Leaders, Professional Leaders, and the Advanced Leadership Program.

The Emerging Leaders Program typically consists of 40 to 60 individuals who have been with the company for fewer than five years. Designed by an outside consultant, employees are nominated and accepted into the Emerging Leaders Program based on their leadership potential as noted by their immediate manager. Participants meet every other month for 24 months and have a culminating project focusing on the development of a KCI initiative.

According to Beil:

> On the Emerging Leaders, for example, you have the team building piece as well as training on interpersonal skills, basic management, priority management, conflict management or resolution, stress management, positive reinforcement, and motivation. Sometimes it's hard to motivate even yourself, so expressing yourself in the proper way. And, we actually have a graduation program for these folks.

The Professional Leaders Program is more selective and is typically limited to 20 employees. This program was also designed with the help of an outside consultant and is continuously customized based on survey feedback from KCI middle managers. The program runs for one year—in spring and fall "semesters"—and focuses on topics such as motivating others, coaching and developing others, and relationship management. Participants complete a number of self-assessments, which allows them to better understand themselves and their roles within the organization. With a variety of "credits" to choose from, the program culminates in a three-day off-site Foundations of Leadership Program offered by the University of Maryland.

The third and final component, the Advanced Leadership Program, is facilitated by an outside consultant. This intimate, high-level, high-touch component is composed of only those nominated employees who are deemed as potential vice presidents of KCI. The Advanced Leadership component is an intense development program consisting of deep level soft skills training. This program has not been offered at KCI in a while.

Another development program is the Project Management Academy. This is a one-day, annual event during which participants become deeply involved in project and quality management issues. There are three levels for the program, all focused on project scope, scheduling, and budgeting, but at the highest level the soft skills of management are also honed. Participants in this program are typically those at the project management level or above.

Other types of development are available or supported as well. For instance, there is support for CAD training, safety training, LEED certification, and various software training. KCI hires and supports interns. Additionally, there is a licensure management system to help everyone stay on top of their licenses. And all of this is not to mention the informal training that occurs at KCI on a daily basis. As one can imagine, KCI earmarks significant resources for these training and development programs. Senior management at KCI feels that these career-development initiatives are a necessity to recruit and retain the high quality talent for which KCI is known.

KCI also offers generous benefits to its employees. These vary from a 401K with a company match, to a floating holiday. One benefit that employees find particularly beneficial is tuition assistance. KCI pays 100 percent after an individual has been with the company for more than five years and 80 percent if not. Many employees feel that it is an excellent program. As one employee who recently completed a graduate program put it, "Excellent, excellent program. I mean, I wouldn't have been able to pay for it had it not been for KCI.

So to me, that's another huge benefit. I feel like I owe them [KCI] something because of the benefit. I mean, it's huge." Tuition assistance also enriches the firm by increasing KCI's intellectual capital and qualifications needed to successfully bid on additional projects.

Finance

Given the recent economic downturn, most firms have been faced with financial difficulties. KCI is no exception. This is exhibited by a considerable drop in revenue in recent years. In 2007, total revenues were $142 million, in 2008 revenues stayed constant at $142 million; however, in 2009, revenues dropped to $131 million. Despite this decline, Neimeyer is optimistic, "dealing with this economy—this is my fourth recession, you know—this will pass. I know that it will."

Neimeyer has reason to be optimistic. According to a recent *Business Week* article, one way to help a company overcome an economic downturn is to practice open book management.[3] Open book management is when a company shares its financial and other data with its employees and oftentimes helps these employees to understand how these data relate to their work.[4] And KCI does just this. The financials for the company are open. Employees can ask to see most anything regarding the financial health of the organization. This is important to employees as a portion of their compensation is based on the financial well-being of the company. KCI makes an ESOP contribution based on a percentage of an employee's salary, currently 6.5 percent, which vests in five years. Despite its ups and downs, the ESOP share price is impressive. At inception, one share was worth $1,000 in 1988, now it is valued at over 15 times that amount (see figure 13.1).

As one employee commented, "It was amazing to see over the years how much the ESOP continued to make money over time. One of my coworkers who has been here 12 years now, he has thousands of dollars in this ESOP that he's never had to put any money aside."

To get continued employee buy-in, ESOP education is constant. The company has several events during the year that promote awareness about the program, such as a contest where employees guess the exact value of the stock. Interestingly, and a good sign, many employees' guesses are not too far from the true value. ESOP bingo is another exciting event where employees—even those out in the field—have a chance to play and learn ESOP definitions and terminology.

Sharing in the ESOP is truly that—equal sharing. The largest stock holder is only so because he has been with the company for the longest length of time. No one receives extra perks to make their percentage of stock ownership particularly high, and unlike cash flow issues that can sometime arise when employees leave an employee-owned company, KCI has not had issue with cashing people out. So they know the money from the ESOP is real and truly is the employees'.

Since in service organizations employee compensation is typically such a huge part of the financial outlay, it is worth noting other forms of compensation

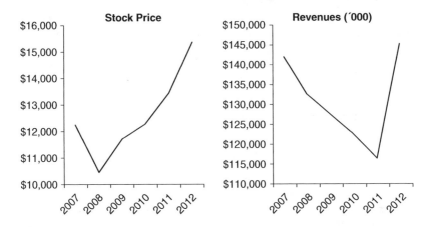

Figure 13.1 KCI Technologies stock price and revenues.
Data for graphs furnished by KCI Technologies, Inc.

here. Aside from the ESOP and regular wages or salaries, top earners at KCI have an "at risk" compensation incentive. A portion, typically 5 to 30 percent of their compensation, is based on the profitability of the business for which they are involved. Additionally, the top 20 earners have a deferred compensation plan. This plan is designed to make the compensation of top employees a bit more competitive with that at rival partnership firms.

The Competitive Marketplace

Considering such a large portion of KCI's projects are public sector projects, it is important to consider this marketplace. There are opposing forces at work here. On one hand, the aging infrastructure in the United States could create great demand for the services of firms like KCI. On the other hand, there are potentially severe budget constraints that could limit the number and profitability of projects requiring those services.

That said, KCI faces fierce competition. Because they are a multidisciplined (e.g., construction, environmental, transportation) engineering firm, the competitors that they meet for a given project depend on the business line(s) needed for that project. Some of their competitors are regional, employee-owned firms of about the same size, like JMT. Others are large, international publically traded firms like Michael Baker Corporation. Additionally, there are many partnerships in the mix, like RK&K, LLP. But, it's important to note that in this field, the competition is not always the competition. Oftentimes firms will be competing with each other for one project and be partners on another. That is, when there is considerable overlap in the skills between two firms, they may compete with one another for a project. However, sometimes the firms will have complementary skills needed to best meet the demands of a potential client, so they will partner with one another.

Two keys to successful competition in this arena are having the proper qualifications for a potential client's project and having relationships built with clients and partners. A company must have the talent available to meet the needs of a potential client's project. This means having available employees with the proper education, experience, and certifications. But just having this talent is not quite enough. As previously mentioned, the company must be able to expertly demonstrate the fit between the company's expertise and the client's needs. Proper coordination of talent and being able to show the fit to the project can be challenging.

Having strong relationships with potential clients and partners is critical to get a leg up on the competition. These relationships are used to both learn about new projects and to find out more detail about potential projects. The earlier a company can start working on a proposal for a potential project and the more specific the proposal is, the more likely they are to beat the competition.

An additional significant area of competition is the competition not for clients, but rather for employees. In the United States, the engineering population is "graying." That is, there is a great shortage of new talent, so firms have to fight over the talent that's out there. According to Beil, KCI relies on their challenging work environment and open culture to capture great talent. Beil also mentioned that they had hoped that the ESOP would be a great recruitment tool, but this has not turned out to be the case. Today's applicant pool is really looking for a job for a couple of years, rather than a career with an organization. As such, they would not be as likely to see the benefits of the ESOP. But that is not to say it is without its recruitment merits. When one employee was asked what brought her to KCI, she commented, "The things I really liked about KCI, besides the staff—we have a great staff here. They had a really good benefits package. The ESOP was very appealing to me."

At the upper management level, a different scenario plays out. Many of KCI's competitors are partnerships, and partnerships allow the partners to have a higher earning potential than that expected of the top executives in an ESOP. As such, it could be difficult to recruit into these positions. But, at least recently, according to Beil, finding upper managers has not been an issue. He believes this due in part to the nature of financial risk differences in the two types of organizations. The financial risk facing the upper managers in an ESOP firm tends to be less than that which faces partners in a partnership.

Shared Leadership

Leadership is about integrity and credibility. Accordingly, Beil feels that letting people know where things stand is important, and never promising more than you feel you can deliver gets real buy in. It's not at all about "just barking orders to employees." The KCI leaders see their role as articulating a vision that resonates with employees.

This mentality is largely derived from the culture at KCI, but it is also a result of being employee owned. Employee involvement resonates through the organization and it is clear that the employees play a large role in the overall direction of the organization. For instance, an employee designee serves on the board of directors. According to Beil, "So our employees actually have a popular election where they elect a member to the Board of Directors...They go out and they have to get ballots and they have to get 35 shareholders sign [the ballot] to say the employee is 'OK.' And then there's this popular election."

Now the true power in any ESOP organization is in its trustees, as trustees control the voting of the stock on all things with the exception of mergers and acquisitions and major changes to corporate bylaws. Interestingly, two non-management employee members are also on the board of trustees at KCI—one elected employee member and one appointed. Having an employee representative involved in governing and approving major decisions for the organization is a true example of shared leadership.

In addition to having formal representation on the board of directors and the board of trustees, it is clear that there are many avenues for open communication that allow ideas to filter from the lower ranks of the organization to the upper echelons. Niemeyer commented,

> One thing about it, and it may be our management style, is that our people have a tendency to speak up. And when they do speak up, they speak up without fear of repercussion. So it's not as if they're worried about saying something in a meeting or to me or to the president and all of a sudden seeing the Grim Reaper come and fire them.

Others in the organization have echoed the idea that there is open and easy communication up the organizational ladder. Indeed, the leaders at KCI provide many avenues through which employees can bring up issues, comment on processes, and make other suggestions to management. As an example, the Companywide Employee Committee (CEC) was formed whereby 36 members, representing each department, meet on a regular basis to discuss issues that are raised by members of their respective departments. In essence, this committee, for which membership rotates on a yearly basis, acts as a sounding board for employee concerns.

In addition, anonymous survey boxes are located in the cafeteria, and an annual survey provides an outlet for employees to provide feedback on a wide range of topics including job satisfaction, human resource issues, compensation, supervisors, and coworkers. Moreover, a blog, to which employees may anonymously post, will soon be available as another mechanism for employee feedback. Town hall meetings, though in practice are primarily a top-down information dissemination tool, provide an additional venue where employees could voice their ideas. Moreover, senior management pride themselves on their availability and openness through an open-door policy.

It is not unusual to hear that organizations are "employee friendly" or have "open door communication"; however, sometimes these espoused views are simply not enacted. However, at KCI, what they preach is exactly what they practice. Employee suggestions do not go unheeded. One key example is the creation of one of KCI's business lines, the Geographic Information Systems (GIS) group. According to Neimeyer,

> The GIS group idea really came up through the organization by some computer folks who weren't in the engineering field, but said, "Look, I think there is going be a business line in geographic information systems. And it's something that we can really deal with the engineering or the planning sector even though it's not typical engineering." And, so one gent came and said, "Hey look, let me take this on. I think I can create a business on this and make a business line." And, that's an example of an idea that came up [through the ranks] and spawned a business.

Another initiative generated from the employees is a technology refresh program, where technology updating is based on technological advancements rather than on a fixed time interval. Neimeyer jokes, "It's not like I come up with all these ideas. I've been here 32 years. My new ideas are limited." These examples make apparent the notion that employee ideas get heard and implemented.

The idea of open lines of communication and continuous implementation of employee ideas is not only an upper echelon perception. Employees do indeed feel like their ideas are respected and welcomed. As one employee put it, "The culture is one where everyone, from the leaders at the top to the newest non-management employees, is in it together."

Information Sharing

Communication of information is critical in any organization, however, in an ESOP, employees have more of a vested interest in understanding, retaining, and utilizing information disseminated to them. Neimeyer and Beil have similar views, "On the ESOP side [as compared to a partnership], communication skills probably have to be a step up. I think your ability to have a vision, and articulate it, then lead the company through it, has to be a step up." Employees' echo this sentiment. For instance, an employee offered,

> I've worked for a partnership before. I had no idea how I was doing on a project, how much money we were making, how much money the company was making, whether my project was a success or not because the profits all went to the partners. In an ESOP culture, we're all owners. We all know what's going on, and because of that, we push information down to our employees.

Another employee added, "We try really hard to communicate what's going on. We have town meetings once a month. The managers are very open to talking to employees. I mean, they'll tell you, 'I can't tell you; it's not for discussion right now,' and they're honest."

KCI has formal approaches to getting important and worthwhile information out to employees. As mentioned earlier, town hall meetings play an important role in information sharing. These open meetings are held by the president once per month at headquarters with those in remote locations tele-, video-, or web-conferencing in. The meetings are also recorded and shared on the company intranet. During these meetings the status of the company is shared, company-wide issues are addressed, like changes to benefits or austerity measures, and exciting new projects are announced. Financial results are also shared quarterly.

In addition to town hall meetings, departmental managers hold monthly meetings with the hope that the information shared will be funneled down through the company ranks. To help facilitate this process, minutes from the meetings are sent out to second tier management.

Beyond these formal approaches, more informal channels of communication exist as well. Even the CEO takes a hands-on approach to information sharing. For example, he attempts to reach out and visit branch offices. On his visit he says his approach is to "just sit with the people and you ask them how things are going and have a little staff meeting and tell them what's going on." Regarding information sharing in general, he comments, "And again, we try and continue to do it. It's a never ending cycle. You can never do enough of it. And in our company we get critiqued for not doing enough of it. No matter what we do, we still have to do more."

Growth and Change through Innovation and Initiatives

It is well understood that KCI cannot simply rest on its laurels and continue to do business as it has always done. Innovation is key to continued growth and development and KCI has been involved in some innovation, forward thinking projects. For instance, Floyd recalls one innovation done to mitigate the impact of a bridge on the environment:

> There were just a number of things that were blocking fish passages, so the fish couldn't go back up the river to spawn, they hadn't for years. So as part of the mitigation effort, the State Highway Administration agreed to create these natural fish passages. They didn't want fish ladders. They didn't want pipes. They wanted natural. Well, this is something that we haven't necessarily done on the East coast, but they're doing it in the West. So some of our guys went out to the West and studied what was being done out there by literature searches, talking with people, and going out visiting.
>
> We saw what they were doing, but what they were doing they were doing in a rural area. We had to do this in an urban area, so our environmental scientists and our hydrologic people actually developed the design method to take that technology and apply it in an urban environment. What they did was they built these natural fish passages in the bottom of the streams, so depending on what type of fish you had, it would determine how strong the fish—what current the fish could swim up, how strong the current could be, and how long they could (swim against) it, their endurance. So what they had to do was they had to design these rock ladders, basically, these fish ladders so that the fish could make it up through the current, and then they had to space boulders to form these little resting areas for the fish so they could get up the stream . . . you would never know that it was a manmade thing. It just looks like it's natural, but in actuality, they

were purposely built and constructed so the fish could get up over the natural blockages. We won a lot of awards for that because that was very innovative.

Providing environmentally friendly solutions to client problems comes natural to KCI, perhaps because the company and its employee owners are invested in sustainability themselves. KCI's headquarters, one of Maryland's newest green buildings, has recently been awarded the US Green Building Council's (USGBC) Leadership in Energy and Environmental Design (LEED) gold certification. The 120,000 square foot building features a white solar reflective roof, which reflects sunlight in the summertime reducing the air-conditioning requirements, a storm-water management pond, and high-performance climate control plumbing and electrical systems, all designed by KCI engineers and LEED specialists. According to Neimeyer, the facility uses resources more efficiently than traditional office buildings and offers employees a healthier and more comfortable work environment.

Indeed, KCI has a forward-thinking mindset. Not being afraid to take on new initiative is another hallmark of KCI's continued growth. In a typical year, 15 to 20 percent of profits are used to fund new corporate initiatives—those that are funded at the corporate level because they tend to be too expensive for an individual division. Usually, an initiative runs upward of $250,000. A prime example is the aforementioned GIS division. This began as a corporate initiative and was funded as such until it reached a critical mass of clients. It now operates on its own with 22 employees. This is not to say that all initiatives work. If an initiative is not on target at year three, funding will be reallocated to other projects, and the initiative will be discontinued. But one cannot expect rewards without taking some risks.

The Reorganization

KCI is in the process of reorganizing. This is a step they have been considering since the mid-1990s. For the most part, KCI has taken a geographic approach to their structure. Now, they are moving to a discipline-based approach. This includes such disciplines as transportation facilities, site management, telecom, and urban planning and development surveys. The headquarters has been somewhat organized by discipline, but the remainder of company has not. The geographic regions were initially established to help promote geographic expansion, and to aid in succession planning at KCI. Unfortunately, particularly during downtimes in the economy, regions would be very protective of their resources and be out for themselves—not for the good of the whole company. It is expected that the new discipline-based approach will be more integrated and less territorial.

The president has vested a great deal of time and effort into trying to facilitate a smooth transition. He has discussed the expectations for the reorganization with individuals, small groups, and large groups. Employee survey data indicate that employees are generally favorably disposed toward the reorganization; however, there are employees who feel that they aren't really affected and that it's mostly a management reorganization. Some believe that people will not quite understand what is happening and why until the official reorganization has taken place and until results start coming in. Additionally, there is some sentiment that the reorganization will be quite challenging because, although senior management realizes that role definition will be important, the lines of authority in the organization may not be as clear after the reorganization. It is expected that there will be more shared and collaborative leadership.

In a follow-up interview in 2013, Terry stated that he believed that the reorganization helped the company to respond to the drop in demand during the recession. He went on to state that it was easier for people to devote their time to where they were needed than under the prior structure.

Looking Forward

With the current economic uncertainty, KCI faces an all too common challenge among businesses—securing enough business to keep their highly talented and committed employees working. According to Beil, "We don't hire for a job and then we fire them later. That's really not our efforts...right now, we're just maintaining it [the firm], finding enough work so that we don't have to tell a good person to find work elsewhere is probably what keeps me awake at night the most." This is not to say that KCI is not constantly looking for good talent. When asked about the future of the organization, Beil was quick to mention that "our challenge will always be finding highly competent people. We're laying people off in a certain sector, but there are other sectors that are strong where we're looking to hire people. And finding talented people is a marathon struggle for us."

Notes

1. http://www.iso.org/iso/support/faqs/faqs_conformity_assessment_and_certification.htm.
2. http://www.kci.com.
3. http://www.businessweek.com/smallbiz/content/jul2009/sb2009077_940499.htm.
4. http://www.nceo.org/main/article.php/id/28/.

CHAPTER 14

W. L. Gore & Associates: Developing Global Teams to Meet Twenty-First-Century Challenges

Frank Shipper, Charles C. Manz, and Greg L. Stewart

I n 2008, W. L. Gore & Associates celebrated its fiftieth year in business. During the first four decades of its existence, Gore became famous for its products and for its use of business teams located in a single facility. To facilitate the development of teams, corporate facilities were kept to 200 associates or fewer. Due to the challenges of a global marketplace, business teams are no longer in a single facility. They are now often spread over four continents. Products are sold on six continents and used on all seven, as well as under the ocean and in space. The challenge of having a successful global presence requires virtual teams to enable a high degree of coordination in the development, production, and marketing of products to customers across the world. As previously, teams are defined primarily by product, but no longer by facility. Team members are now separated by thousands of miles, multiple time zones, and a variety of languages and cultures. Growth and globalization present significant challenges for Gore as it strives to maintain a family-like, entrepreneurial culture. According to Terri Kelly, the president of Gore and a 30-year associate[1]:

> In the early days, our business was largely conducted at the local level. There were global operations, but most relationships were built regionally, and most decisions were made regionally. That picture has evolved dramatically over the last 20 years, as businesses can no longer be defined by brick and mortar. Today, most of our teams are spread across regions and continents. Therefore, the decision-making process is much more global and virtual in nature, and there's a growing need to build strong relationships across geographical boundaries.

The globalization of our business has been one of the biggest changes I've seen in the last 25 years.

The core beliefs are to take the long-term view in business situations, to make and keep commitments, and to drive cooperation among individuals and teams. This is supported by key practices that replace traditional, hierarchical structure with flexible relationships and a sense that all workers are "in the same boat." The ultimate focus is on empowering talented associates to deliver highly innovative products.

Despite substantial growth, the core values have not changed at Gore. The "objective" of the company, "To make money and have fun doing so," set forth by the founder Wilbert (Bill) Gore is still part of the Gore culture. Associates around the world are asked to follow the company's four guiding principles:

1. Try to be fair.
2. Encourage, help, and allow other associates to grow in knowledge, skill, and scope of activity and responsibility.
3. Make your own commitments, and keep them.
4. Consult with other associates before taking actions that may be "below the waterline."

The four principles are referred to as *fairness, freedom, commitment,* and *waterline.* The waterline principle is drawn from an analogy to ships. If someone pokes a hole in a boat above the waterline, the boat will be in relatively little real danger. However, if someone pokes a hole below the waterline, the boat is in immediate danger of sinking. The expectation is that "waterline" issues will be discussed across teams, plants, and continents as appropriate before those decisions are made. This principle is still emphasized even though team members who need to share in the decision-making process are now spread across the globe.

Commitment is spoken of frequently at Gore. The commitment principle's primary emphasis is on the freedom associates have to make their own commitments, rather than having others assign them to projects or tasks. But commitment may also be viewed as a mutual commitment between associates and the enterprise. Associates worldwide commit to making contributions to the company's success. In return, the company is committed to providing a challenging, opportunity-rich work environment that is responsive to associate needs and concerns.

Background

Gore was formed by Wilbert L. "Bill" Gore and his wife in 1958. The idea for the business sprang from Bill's personal, technical, and organizational experiences at E. I. du Pont de Nemours & Co. and, particularly, his involvement in the characterization of a chemical compound with unique properties. The compound, called polytetrafluorethylene (PTFE), is now marketed by DuPont under the Teflon brand name. Bill saw a wide variety of potential applications for this unique new material, and when DuPont showed little interest in pursuing most of them directly, he decided to form his own company and start pursuing the concepts himself. Thus, Gore became one of DuPont's first customers for this new material.

Since then, Gore has evolved into a global enterprise, with annual revenues of more than $3 billion in fiscal year 2013, supported by more than 10,000 associates worldwide. This placed Gore at no. 132 on *Forbes* magazine's 2012 list of the 500 largest private companies in the United States. The enterprise's unique, and now famous, culture and leadership practices have helped make Gore one of only a select few companies to appear on all of the US "100 Best Companies to Work For" rankings since they were introduced in 1984.

Bill Gore was born in Meridian, Idaho, in 1912. By age six, according to his own account, he was an avid hiker in Utah. Later, at a church camp in 1935, he met Genevieve (Vieve), his future wife. In their eyes, the marriage was a partnership. He would make breakfast and Vieve, as everyone called her, would make lunch. The partnership lasted a lifetime.

Bill Gore attended the University of Utah, and earned a bachelor of science in chemical engineering in 1933, and a master of science in physical chemistry in 1935. He began his professional career at American Smelting and Refining in 1936; moved to Remington Arms, a DuPont subsidiary, in 1941; and then to DuPont's headquarters in 1945. He held positions as research supervisor and head of operations research. While at DuPont, he felt a sense of excited commitment, personal fulfillment, and self-direction while working with a task force to develop applications for PTFE.

Having followed the development of the electronics industry, he felt that PTFE had ideal insulating characteristics for use with such equipment. He tried many ways to make a PTFE-coated ribbon cable but with no success until a breakthrough in his home basement laboratory. One night, while Bill was explaining the problem to his 19-year-old son, Bob, the young Gore saw some PTFE sealant tape and asked his father, "Why don't you try this tape?" Bill explained that everyone knew that you could not bond PTFE to itself. After Bob went to bed, however, Bill remained in the basement lab and proceeded to try what conventional wisdom said could not be done. At about 5:00 a.m. Bill woke up Bob, waving a small piece of cable around and saying excitedly, "It works, it works." The following night father and son returned to the basement lab to make ribbon cable insulated with PTFE. Because the idea came from Bob, the patent for the cable was issued in his name.

After a while, Bill Gore came to realize that DuPont wanted to remain a supplier of raw materials for industrial buyers and not a manufacturer of high-tech products for end-use markets. Bill and Vieve began discussing the possibility of starting their own insulated wire and cable business. On January 1, 1958, their wedding anniversary, they founded Gore. The basement of their home served as their first facility. After finishing breakfast, Vieve turned to her husband of 23 years and said, "Well, let's clear up the dishes, go downstairs, and get to work."

When Bill Gore (a 45-year-old with five children to support) left DuPont, he put aside a career of 17 years and a good, secure salary. To finance the first two years of their new business, he and Vieve mortgaged their house and took $4,000 from savings. All their friends cautioned them against taking on such a big financial risk.

The first few years were challenging. Some of the young company's associates accepted stock in the company in lieu of salary. Family members who came to help with the business lived in the home as well. At one point, 11 associates were living and working under one roof. One afternoon, while sifting PTFE powder, Vieve received a call from the City of Denver's water department. The caller wanted to ask some technical questions about the ribbon cable and asked for the product manager. Vieve explained that he was not in at the moment. (Bill and two other key associates were out of town.) The caller asked next for the sales manager and then for the president. Vieve explained that "they" were also not in. The caller finally shouted, "What kind of company is this anyway?" With a little diplomacy the Gores were eventually able to secure an order from Denver's water department for around $100,000. This order put the company over the start-up hump and onto a profitable footing. Sales began to take off.

During the decades that followed, Gore developed a number of new products derived from PTFE, the best-known of which is GORE-TEX® fabric. The development of GORE-TEX® fabric, one of hundreds of new products that followed a key discovery by Bob Gore, is an example of the power of innovation. In 1969, Gore's Wire and Cable Division was facing increased competition. Bill Gore began to look for a way to expand PTFE: "I figured out that if we could ever unfold those molecules, get them to stretch out straight, we'd have a tremendous new kind of material." The new PTFE material would have more volume per pound of raw material with no adverse effect on performance. Thus, fabricating costs would be reduced and profit margins increased. Bob Gore took on the project; he heated rods of PTFE to various temperatures and then slowly stretched them. Regardless of the temperature or how carefully he stretched them, the rods broke. Working alone late one night after countless failures, Bob in frustration stretched one of the rods violently. To his surprise, it did not break. He tried it again and again with the same results. The next morning, Bill Gore recalled, "Bob wanted to surprise me so he took a rod and stretched it slowly. Naturally, it broke. Then he pretended to get mad. He grabbed another rod and said, 'Oh, the hell with this,' and gave it a pull. It didn't break—he'd done it." The new arrangement of molecules not only changed the Wire and Cable Division, but led to the development of GORE-TEX® fabric and many other products.

In 1986, Bill Gore died while backpacking in the Wind River Mountains of Wyoming. Vieve Gore continued to be actively involved in the company and served on the board of directors until her death at 91 in 2005.

Gore has had only four presidents in its 50-year history. Bill Gore served as the president from the enterprise's founding in 1958 until 1976. At that point, his son Bob became president and chief executive officer (CEO). Bob has been an active member of the firm from the time of its founding, most recently as chairman of the board of directors. He served as president until 2000, when Chuck Carroll was selected as the third president. In 2005, Terri Kelly succeeded him. As with all the presidents after Bill Gore, she is a longtime employee. She had been with Gore for 22 years before becoming president.

The Gore family established a unique culture that continues to be an inspiration for associates. For example, Dave Gioconda, a current product specialist, recounted meeting Bob Gore for the first time—an experience that reinforced Gore's egalitarian culture:

> Two weeks after I joined Gore, I traveled to Phoenix for training...I told the guy next to me on the plane where I worked, and he said, "I work for Gore, too." "No kidding?" I asked. "Where do you work?" He said, "Oh, I work over at the Cherry Hill plant."
>
> I spent two and a half hours on this plane having a conversation with this gentleman who described himself as a technologist and shared some of his experiences. As I got out of the plane, I shook his hand and said, "I'm Dave Gioconda, nice to meet you." He replied, "Oh, I'm Bob Gore." That experience has had a profound influence on the decisions that I make.

Due to the leadership of Bill, Vieve, Bob, and many others, Gore was selected as one of the "100 Best Companies to Work For" in the United States in 2013, as compiled by the Great Place to Work Institute and published in *Fortune* magazine for the sixteenth consecutive year. In addition, Gore was included in all three *100 Best Companies to Work For in America* books (1984, 1985, and 1993). It is one of only a select few companies to appear on all 19 lists. Gore is also regularly named a best workplace in France, Germany, Italy, Korea, Spain, Sweden, and the United Kingdom.

As a privately held company, Gore does not make its financial results public. However, it does share its financial results with all associates on a monthly basis. In 2008, *Fortune* magazine reported that Gore sales grew just over 7 percent in 2006, the latest year for which data were available.

Competitive Strategy at W. L. Gore

For product management, Gore is divided now into four divisions— Electronics, Fabrics, Industrial, and Medical. The Electronic Products Division (EPD) develops and manufactures high-performance cables and assemblies as well as specialty materials for electronic devices. The Fabrics Division develops and provides fabric to the outdoor clothing industry as well as the military, law enforcement, and fire protection industries. Gore fabrics marketed under the GORE-TEX®, WINDSTOPPER®, CROSSTECH®, and GORE® CHEMPAK® brands provide the wearer protection while remaining comfortable. The Industrial Products Division (IPD) makes filtration, sealant, and other products. These products meet diverse contamination and process challenges in many industries. The Gore Medical Products Division (MPD) provides products such as synthetic vascular grafts, interventional devices, endovascular stent-grafts, surgical patches for hernia repair, and sutures for use in vascular, cardiac, general surgery, and oral procedures. Although they are recognized as separate divisions, they frequently work together.

Since it has four divisions that serve different industries, Gore can be viewed as a diversified conglomerate. Bob Winterling, a financial associate, described how the four divisions work together financially as follows:

> The thing I love about Gore is that we have four very diverse divisions. During my time here, I've noticed that when one or two divisions are down, you always have one, two or three that are up. I call them cylinders. Sometimes all four cylinders are working really well; not all the time though. Normally it's two or three, but that's the luxury that we have. When one is down—it's good to know that another is up.

Having four diversified divisions not only protects against swings in any one industry, but it also provides multiple investment opportunities. One area where Gore has invested heavily is its Medical Products Division, where the company's unique capabilities align well with very large, attractive market needs. As Brad Jones, a former enterprise leader, said, "All opportunities aren't created equal, and there's an awful lot of opportunity that's screaming for resources in the medical environment." At the same time, the leadership at Gore scrutinizes large investments so those in what Brad Jones refers to as "big burn" projects are not made unless there is a reasonable expectation of a payoff.

Developing Quality Products by Creating and Protecting Core Technology

The competitive objective of Gore is to use core technology derived from PTFE and ePTFE to create highly differentiated and unique products. In every product line the goal is not to produce the lowest cost goods but rather to create the highest quality goods that meet and exceed the needs of customers. Of course, Gore works hard to maintain competitive pricing, but the source of competitive advantage is clearly quality and differentiation. Gore is a company built on technological innovations.

Leaders at Gore often refer to a three-legged stool to explain how they integrate operations. As shown in figure 14.1, the three legs of the stool are technology, manufacturing, and sales. For each product, the legs of the stool are tied together by a product specialist. For instance, a product specialist might coordinate efforts to design, make, and sell a vascular graft. Another product specialist would coordinate efforts related to the creation and marketing of fabric for use in winter parkas. Support functions such as human resources

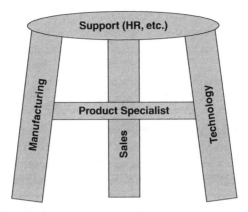

Figure 14.1 Coordinating technology, manufacturing, and sales at Gore.

(HR), IT, and finance also help tie together various aspects of technology, manufacturing, and sales.

Gore's Fabrics Division practices cooperative marketing with the users of its fabrics. In most cases, Gore does not make the finished goods from its fabrics; rather, it supplies the fabrics to manufacturers such as North Face, Marmot, L. L. Bean, Salomon, Adidas, and Puma. On each garment is a tag indicating that it is made using GORE-TEX® fabric. According to a former president of Cotton Inc., Gore is a leader in secondary branding. For example, a salesman in a golf pro shop related how he initially tried to explain that he had GORE-TEX® fabric rain suits made by various manufacturers. After realizing that his customers did not care who manufactured it, only that it was made from GORE-TEX® fabric, he gave up, and just led the customers to the GORE-TEX® fabric rain suits.

Because of its commitment to producing superior goods, Gore emphasizes product integrity. For example, only certified and licensed manufacturers are supplied with Gore's fabrics. Gore maintains "rain-rooms" in which to test new garment designs. Shoes with GORE-TEX® fabric in them will be flexed in water approximately 300,000 times to ensure that they are waterproof.

After all the preventive measures, Gore stands behind its products regardless of who the manufacturer is and even if the defect is cosmetic in nature. Susan Bartley, a manufacturing associate, recounted a recent recall: "A cosmetic flaw, not a fitness for use flaw, was found in finished garments, so we (Gore) bought back the garments from the manufacturer, because we didn't want those garments out on the market." In another incident, it was found that Gore Ride-On® cables if installed on Campagnolo® style brakes could fail. Gore engineered a solution and sent it out to all people requesting a replacement and paid for them to be installed. Such recalls due to either cosmetic or fitness for use flaws happen infrequently. Regardless of the issue Gore is committed to quality of its products and will stand behind them. Strong and clear expectations for such actions are found in Gore's "Standards of Ethical Conduct." Terri Kelly and

Bob Gore in their introduction to the standards state that "given the potential impact to our global reputation and financial success, complying with the legal and ethical issues addressed in the Standards of Ethical Conduct are waterline issues."

Gore's fabrics sales and marketing associates believe positive buyer experiences with one GORE-TEX® product (for instance, a ski parka) carry over to purchases of other GORE-TEX® products (gloves, pants, rain suits, boots, and jackets). Also, they believe that positive experiences with their products will be shared among customers and potential customers, leading to more sales.

The sharing and enhancing of knowledge is seen as key to the development of current and future products. Great emphasis is placed on sharing knowledge. According to Terri Kelly, "There's a real willingness and openness to share knowledge. That's something I experienced 25 years ago, and it's not changed today. This is a healthy thing. We want to make sure folks understand the need to connect more dots in the lattice." Associates make a conscious effort to share technical knowledge. For example, a core leadership team consisting of eight technical associates gets together every other month, reviews each other's plans, and looks for connections among the upcoming products. According to Jack Kramer, an enterprise leader, "We put a lot of effort into trying to make sure that we connect informally and formally across a lot of boundaries." One way associates connect formally to share knowledge is through monthly technical meetings. At the monthly meetings, scientists and engineers from different divisions present information to other associates and colleagues. Attended regularly by most technical associates in the area, these presentations are often described as "passionate" and "exciting."

Even though Gore shares knowledge within the organization, much of its highly technical know-how must be protected for competitive reasons. In a global environment, protection of specialized knowledge is a challenge. Some of the technology is protected by patents. In fact, some of the products are protected by an umbrella of patents. Normally, under US law, patents expire 20 years from the earliest claimed filing date. Thus, the original patents have expired on GORE-TEX® fabric and some other products. Globally, patent procedures, protection, and enforcement vary. Both products and the processes are patentable. To protect its knowledge base, Gore has sought and been granted more than 2,000 patents worldwide in all areas in which it competes, including electronics, medical devices, and polymer processing. However, patents can sometimes be difficult or expensive to enforce, especially globally. Therefore some of the technology is protected internally. Such knowledge is commonly referred to as "proprietary."

Within Gore proprietary knowledge is shared on a need to know basis. Associates are encouraged to closely guard such information. This principle can lead to some awkward moments. Terri Kelly was visiting Shenzhen, China, and was curious about a new laminate that was being commercialized. The development engineer leader kept dodging her questions. Finally he smiled, and he said, "Now, Terri. Do you have a need to know?"

As Terri retold the incident, "He played back exactly what he was supposed to, which is don't share with someone, even if it's a CEO, something that they have no need to know." She laughed and said, "You're right. I'm just being nosy."

Terri continued, "And everyone's—I could see the look in their eyes—thinking, 'Is he going to get fired?' He had taken a great personal risk, certainly for that local culture. We laughed, and we joked and for the next week, it became the running joke." Through stories like this the culture is shared with others in Gore.

The sharing and enhancing of its technology have brought recognition from many sources. From the United Kingdom, Gore received the Pollution Abatement Technology Award in 1989 and the Prince Philip Award for Polymers in the Service of Mankind in 1985. In addition, Gore received or shared in receiving the prestigious Plunkett Award from DuPont—for innovative uses of DuPont fluoropolymers—nine times between 1988 and 2006. Bill and Vieve Gore, as well as Bob Gore, received numerous honors for both their business and technical leadership.

Continuing Globalization and Deliberate Growth

Ever since the company was founded, Gore has recognized the need for globalization. Gore established its first international venture in 1964, only six years after its founding. By 2012, it had facilities in two dozen countries and manufacturing facilities in six countries distributed across four continents (see figure 14.2). One example of Gore's global reach is the fact that it is the dominant supplier of artificial vascular grafts to the global medical community. Gore's Fabrics Division also generates most of its sales overseas.

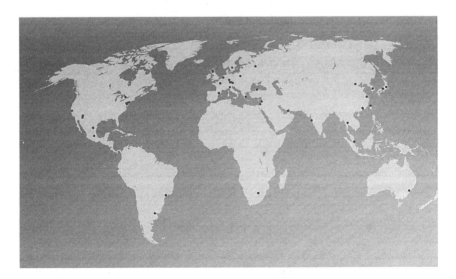

Figure 14.2 Locations of Gore's global facilities. Courtesy of W. L. Gore & Associates.

In addition to globalization, Gore has a strategy of continued growth. Growth is expected to come from two sources. One source will be from Gore associates contributing innovative ideas. The Gore culture is designed to foster such innovation and allow ideas to be energetically pursued, developed, and evaluated. These ideas will lead to new products and processes. Within Gore this form of growth is referred to as organic. Gore encourages both new products and extensions of existing products. To encourage innovation all associates are encouraged to ask for and receive raw material to try out their ideas. Through this process multiple products have come from unexpected areas. For example, the idea for dental floss came from the Industrial and not the Medical Division. Two associates who were fabricating space suits took to flossing their teeth with scraps. Thus, Gore's highly successful dental floss, GLIDE® floss, was born. ELIXIR® guitar strings also came from the Medical Division from an associate who was also a musician. Due to Gore's track record of developing innovative products, *Fast Company* magazine called it "pound for pound, the most innovative company in America."

A second but much less significant source of growth can come from external acquisitions. Gore evaluates opportunities to acquire technologies and even companies based on whether they offer a unique capability that could complement an existing, successful business. The leadership at Gore considers this strategy a way to stack the probability deck in its favor by moving into market spaces its associates already know very well. To facilitate this growth strategy, Gore has a few associates who evaluate acquisition opportunities at the enterprise level. They do not do this in isolation, but in concert with leaders within each division.

By a multibillion dollar corporate standard, the acquisitions made by Gore are small. To date, the largest company acquired employed approximately 100 people. Since Gore is a privately held company, stock swaps are not an option.

A clear issue to any acquisition that Gore considers is cultural compatibility. Gore will consider the leadership style in an acquired company. According to Brad Jones, "If you're acquiring a couple patents and maybe an inventor, that's not a big issue, although if he's a prima donna inventor, it will be an issue." When acquiring a company, the culture that made it successful is closely examined. Issues regarding integrating the acquired company's culture with Gore's, and whether Gore's culture will add value to the acquired company, are just two of many cultural considerations. Gore wants to be able to expand when necessary by buying complementary organizations and their associated technologies, but not at the expense of its culture of 50 years.

Occasionally, Gore must divest itself of a product. One example is GLIDE® dental floss. The product, developed by Gore, was well received by consumers due to its smooth texture, shred resistance, and ability to slide easily between teeth. To meet demand when the product took off, leaders were processing credit cards; human resource people and accountants were out on the manufacturing floor packaging GLIDE® floss, and everybody else in the facility pitched in to make sure that the product got out the door. One associate observed that by rolling up their sleeves and pitching in, leaders built credibility with other associates.

Not long after its introduction, mint flavor GLIDE® floss became the biggest selling dental floss. That attracted the attention of the traditional dental floss manufacturers. Eventually, Procter & Gamble (P&G) and Gore reached an agreement whereby P&G bought the rights to market GLIDE® floss, while Gore continued to manufacture it.

Gore made this agreement with the understanding that no one would be laid off. The announcement of the agreement was made to all the GLIDE® floss team members on a Thursday. It did come as a shock to some. By Monday, however, the same team was working on a transition plan. Associates that were not needed in the manufacturing or selling of GLIDE® floss were absorbed into other fast-growing Gore businesses. In addition, everybody in the enterprise received a share of the profit from the P&G purchase.

Leadership at Gore

Competitive strategy at Gore is supported by a unique approach to leadership. Many people step forward and take on a variety of leadership roles, but these roles are not part of a hierarchical structure and traditional authority is not vested in the roles. Leadership is a dynamic and fluid process where leaders are defined by "followership." Future leaders emerge because they gain credibility with other associates. Gore refers to this process as "natural leadership." Credibility is gained by demonstrating special knowledge, skill, or experience that advances a business objective, a series of successes, and involving others in significant decisions.

Associates step forward to lead when they have the expertise to do so. Within Gore this practice is referred to as "knowledge-based decision-making." Based on this practice decisions are "made by the most knowledgeable person, not the person in charge," according to Terri Kelly. This form of decision-making flows naturally from the four guiding principles established by Bill Gore.

Leadership responsibilities can take many forms at Gore. In an internal memo Bill Gore described the following kinds of leaders and their roles:

1. *The Associate who is recognized by a team as having a special knowledge, or experience* (for example, this could be a chemist, computer expert, machine operator, salesman, engineer, lawyer). This kind of leader gives the team *guidance in a special area.*

2. *The Associate the team looks to for coordination of individual activities in order to achieve the agreed on objectives of the team.* The role of this leader is to persuade team members to *make the commitments* necessary for success (commitment seeker).

3. *The Associate who proposes necessary objectives and activities and seeks agreement and team consensus on objectives.* This leader is perceived by the team membership as having a good grasp of how the objectives of the team fit in with the broader objectives of the enterprise. This kind of leader is often also a "commitment seeking" leader.

4. *The leader who evaluates the relative contribution of team members (in consultation with other sponsors) and reports these contribution evaluations to a compensation committee.* This leader may also participate in the compensation committee on relative contribution and pay and *reports changes in compensation* to individual Associates. This leader is then also a compensation sponsor.

5. The leader who coordinates the research, manufacturing, and marketing of one product type within a business, interacting with team leaders and individual Associates who have commitments to the product type. These leaders are usually called *product specialists.* They are respected for their knowledge and dedication to their products.

6. *Plant leaders* who help coordinate activities of people within a plant.

7. *Business leaders* who help coordinate activities of people in a business.

8. *Functional leaders* who help coordinate activities of people in a "functional" area.

9. *Corporate leaders* who help coordinate activities of people in different businesses and functions and who try to promote communication and cooperation among all Associates.

10. *Intrapreneuring Associates who organize new teams* for new businesses, new products, new processes, new devices, new marketing efforts, or new or better methods of all kinds. These leaders invite other Associates to "sign up" for their project.

Developing a Unique and Flexible Leadership Structure

The leadership structure that works at Gore may have the world's shortest organizational pyramid for a company of its size. Gore is a company largely without titles, hierarchical organization charts, or any other conventional structural arrangement typically employed by enterprises with billions of dollars in sales revenues and thousands of employees.

There are few positions at Gore with formal titles presented to the public. Due to laws of incorporation, the company has a president, Terri Kelly, who also functions as CEO. Terri is one of just a few members of the cross-functional Enterprise Leadership Team (ELT), the team responsible for the overall health and growth of the enterprise.

The real key to the egalitarian culture of Gore is the use of a unique lattice rather than a hierarchical structure. The features of Gore's lattice structure include the following:

1. Direct lines of communication—person to person—with no intermediary
2. No fixed or assigned authority
3. Sponsors, not bosses
4. Natural leadership as evidenced by the willingness of others to follow
5. Objectives set by those who must "make them happen"
6. Tasks and functions organized through commitments

The lattice structure, as described by the people at Gore, is complex and depends on interpersonal interactions, self-commitment to group-known responsibilities, natural leadership, and group-imposed discipline. According to Bill Gore, "Every successful organization has an underground lattice. It's where the news spreads like lightning, where people can go around the organization to get things done."

One potential disadvantage of such a lattice structure could be a lack of quick response times and decisive action. Gore associates say adamantly that this is not the case, and they distinguish between two types of decisions. First, for time-critical decisions, they maintain that the lattice structure is faster in response than traditional structures because interaction is not hampered by bureaucracy. The leader who has responsibility assembles a knowledge-based team to examine and resolve the issue. The team members can be recruited by the leader from any area of the company if their expertise is needed. Once the issue is resolved the team ceases to exist, and its members return to their respective areas. Associate Bob Winterling asserted, "We have no trouble making crisis decisions, and we do it very swiftly and very quickly."

The other response is for critical issues that will have a significant impact on the enterprise's long-term operations. Associates will admit that such decisions can sometimes take a little longer than they would like. Chrissy Lyness, another financial associate, stated,

> We get the buy-in up front instead of creating and implementing the solution and putting something out there that doesn't work for everybody. That can be frustrating to new associates, because they're used to a few people putting their heads together, saying, "This is what we're going to do. This is a solution." That's not the way it works at Gore.
>
> Here, you spend a lot of time at the beginning of the decision-making process gaining feedback, so that when you come out of that process, you have something that's going to work, and the implementation is actually pretty easy.

The associates at Gore believe that time spent in the beginning, tapping into the best ideas and gaining consensus, pay off in the implementation. They believe that authoritarian decision-making may save time initially, but the quality of the decision will not be as good as one made by consensus. In addition, they believe that authoritarian decisions will take longer to implement than those made by consensus.

The egalitarian culture is also supported informally. For example, all associates are referred to and addressed by their first names. This is as true for the president as for any other associate.

Gore's leaders believe that its unique organization structure and culture have proven to be significant contributors to associate satisfaction and retention. *Fortune* magazine reports a turnover rate of 5 percent for Gore. In addition, it reports 19,108 applicants for 276 new jobs in 2008. In other words, it is harder to get a job at Gore than to get accepted at an elite university.

Global Human Resource Practices

The competitive strategy of using cutting-edge technology, empowered teams, and collaborative leadership to create high quality goods is supported by a number of innovative HR practices globally. Many HR initiatives are designed to support the concept that all associates are stakeholders in the enterprise and have a shared responsibility for its success. Parking lots have no reserved parking spaces for leaders. Dining areas—only one in each plant—are set up as focal points for associate interaction. As an associate in Arizona explained, "The design is no accident. The lunchroom in Flagstaff has a fireplace in the middle. We want people to like to be here." The location of a plant is also no accident. Sites are selected on the basis of transportation access, nearby universities, beautiful surroundings, and climate appeal. To preserve the natural beauty of the site on which a production facility was built in 1982, Vieve Gore insisted that the large trees be preserved, much to the dismay of the construction crews. The Arizona associate explained the company's emphasis on selecting attractive plant sites, stating, "Expanding is not costly in the long run. Losses are what you make happen by stymieing people and putting them into a box." Such initiatives are practiced at Gore facilities worldwide.

Getting the Right People on Board

Gore receives numerous applicants for every position. Initially, job applicants at Gore are screened by personnel specialists. Then each candidate who passes the initial screening is interviewed by a group of associates from the team in which the person will work. Finally, personnel specialists contact multiple references before issuing a job offer. Recruitment is described by Donna Frey, former leader of the global human resources function and former member of the Enterprise Leadership Team, as a two-way process. She explained:

> Our recruiting process is very much about us getting to know the applicants and them getting to know us. We are very open and honest about who we are, the kind of organization we have, the kind of commitments we want and whether or not we think that the applicant's values are aligned with ours. Applicants talk to a number of people that they'll be working directly with if hired. We work very hard in the recruiting process to really build a relationship, get to know people and make sure that we're bringing people in who are going to fit this enterprise.

When someone is hired at Gore, an experienced associate makes a commitment to be the applicant's sponsor. The sponsor's role is to take a personal interest in the new associate's contributions, interests, and goals, acting as both a coach and an advocate. The sponsor tracks the new associate's progress, offers help and encouragement, points out weaknesses and suggests ways to correct them, and concentrates on how the associate can better make use of his or her strengths. Sponsoring is not a short-term commitment. When individuals are hired initially, they are likely to have a sponsor in their immediate work area. As associates' commitments change or grow, it is normal for them to change sponsors, or in some cases add a second sponsor. For instance, if they move to a new job in another area of the company, they may gain a sponsor there and then decide whether to keep their former sponsor or not. Because sponsorship is built on the personal relationship between two people, the relationship most often continues even if the official sponsorship role does not.

New associates are expected to focus on building relationships during the first three to six months of their careers. Donna Frey described the first months for a new associate at Gore as follows: "When new associates join the enterprise, they participate in an orientation program. Then, each new associate works with a starting sponsor to get acclimated and begin building relationships within Gore. The starting sponsor provides the new hire with a list of key associates he/she should meet with during the next few months." We encourage the new hire to meet with these associates one-on-one. It's not a phone conversation, but a chance to sit down with them face-to-face and get to know them.

> This process helps demonstrate the importance of relationships. When you're hiring really good people, they want to have quick wins and make contributions, and building relationships without a clear goal can be difficult. Often, new associates will say, "I don't feel like I'm contributing. I've spent three months just getting to know people." However, after a year they begin to realize how important this process was.

To ensure that new associates are not overwhelmed by what is probably their first experience in a nonhierarchical organization, Gore has a two-day orientation program it calls "Building on the Best." New associates are brought together with other new associates after two or three months to participate in the program, which addresses many of Gore's key concepts, who Gore is, and how the enterprise works. The program includes group activities and interactive presentations given by leaders and other longtime associates.

Helping Associates Build and Maintain Relationships

Gore recognizes the need to maintain initial relationships, continuously develop new ones, and cement ongoing relationships. One way this is fostered is through its digital voice exchange called Gorecom. According to Terri Kelly, "Gorecom is the preferred media if you want a quick response." An oral culture is fostered because it encourages direct communication.

To further foster the oral culture, team members and leaders are expected to meet face-to-face regularly. For team members and especially leaders, this can mean lots of travel. As one technical associate joked, "Probably, in the last 12 years, I spent 3 years traveling internationally, a couple weeks at a time."

Gore disseminates its culture internationally through its unique structure. When it sets up a new venture, Gore seeds the new venture with long-term employees who serve as prototypical models for the new hires. As Gore has expanded across continents, this approach is still used, but now also in a virtual manner. Previously, teams at Gore were defined by geographic location. Now, there are many multinational teams, with associates collaborating across regions. A few longer-term associates are often infused into a team and act as mentors to newer hires. Much of the mentoring is done virtually through electronic communication. In addition, some members of a multicultural team travel extensively, as noted previously, to meet other team members face-to-face. Associates at Gore maintain that nothing replaces face-to-face communications. Furthermore, all Gore locations offer intensive training programs to acclimate new hires to Gore's culture.

Another way that Gore facilitates the development of teams and individuals is through training. An associate in Newark noted that Gore "works with associates who want to develop themselves and their talents." Associates are offered a variety of in-house training opportunities, not only in technical and engineering areas but also in leadership development. In addition, the company has established cooperative education programs with universities and other outside providers.

An additional way that Gore facilitates the development of teams and associates is through its unique performance appraisal system. Cohorts of associates who know each other's work are asked to rank everyone in the cohort on "contribution" to Gore in the last year. An associate may be in several cohorts. Committees are set up to take these data and synthesize multiple rankings to arrive at an evaluation for each associate. Separate compensation committees then determine the compensation for that associate. One of the most interesting aspects of the system is that the individual leaders do not determine the evaluation although they contribute their ranking nor do they feedback the evaluation and compensation to their associates. Instead, each associate's designated mentor is responsible for discussing results of this process with the individual and to discuss implications for corrective action and development. This system is designed to create a community of purpose. Michael Beer, professor emeritus of Harvard Business School and chairman of TruePoint, observed: "Peer pressure is obviously strong. This system makes associates aware very quickly that they have to collaborate and think about the good of the whole enterprise. Teamwork and continuous improvement thus become the order of the day."

In many ways, Gore can feel like an extended family for its associates and the communities in which they live. Based on their own interests and initiatives, associates give back to their communities through schools, sports clubs, universities, and other local organizations. Gore encourages their US associates' community outreach activities by providing up to eight hours of paid time off for such efforts. The associates individually or in teams decide to what to commit their time.

Rewarding Associates for Contributions

Compensation at Gore has both short- and long-term equity sharing components. Its compensation goal is to ensure internal fairness and external competitiveness. To ensure fairness, associates are asked to rank their team members each year in order of contribution to the enterprise. In addition, team members are asked to comment on their rationale behind the ranking, as well as on particular strengths or potential areas of improvement for the associates. To ensure competitiveness, each year Gore benchmarks pay of its associates against a variety of functions and roles with their peers at other companies.

Gore also uses profit sharing as a form of short-term compensation. Profits remaining after business requirements are met are distributed among associates as profit sharing. Profit shares are distributed when established financial goals are reached. Every month the business results are reviewed with associates, and they know whether they are on track to meet forecasts. The first profit sharing occurred in 1960, only two years after the founding of the company.

Beyond short-term equity sharing, Gore has an associates' stock ownership program (ASOP).[2] Each year Gore contributes up to 12 percent of pay to an account that purchases Gore stock for associates with more than one year of service. Associates have ownership of the account after three years of service, when they become 100 percent vested. Gore also has a 401K Plan. It provides a contribution of up to 3 percent of pay to each associates' personal investment accounts. Associates are eligible after one month of service. Associates are 100 percent vested immediately.

A particular area where Gore's practices differ from traditional practices at other organizations is in how the majority of the sales force is compensated. They are paid not on commission, but with salary, stock through the ASOP, and profit sharing with all the other associates. When a sales associate was asked to explain this practice, he responded as follows:

> The people who are just concerned with making their sales numbers in other companies usually struggle when they come to Gore. We encourage folks to help others. For example, when we hire new sales associates, we ask experienced sales associates to take some time to help get them acclimated to Gore and how we do things. In other companies where I've worked, that would have been seen as something that would detract from your potential to make your number, so you probably wouldn't be asked to do such a thing.

In other words, they see individual sales commissions as detracting from mentoring and sharing what is at the core of the Gore culture.

The entire package of compensation extends beyond direct monetary payments. As with most companies, associates receive a range of benefits, such as medical and dental insurance. In addition, in *Fortune* magazine's 2008 story about Gore being one of the "100 Best Companies to Work For," onsite fitness centers are listed as benefits. They are part of the Gore's enterprise wellness program.

Facing the Future Together

Associates at Gore believe that their unique organizational culture will allow the company to continue maximizing individual potential while cultivating an environment where creativity can flourish. The unique culture results from an unwavering commitment to the use of cutting-edge technology for developing high quality products. This strategy is carried out through a unique approach to leadership and human resource management. The record of success is demonstrated not only by high financial profitability but also by the creation of a highly desirable workplace. Nevertheless, success in the past cannot be seen as assurance of success in the future. As Brad Jones, former member of the Enterprise Leadership Team, said:

> Twenty or thirty years ago, markets in different parts of the world were still somewhat distinct and isolated from one another. At that time, we could have pretty much the entire global business team for a particular market niche located in a building. Today, as our markets become more global in nature, we are increasingly seeing the need to support our customers with global virtual teams. How do our paradigms and practices have to change to accommodate those changing realities? Those are active discussions that apply across these many different businesses.

The answer of how Gore will evolve to meet these challenges is not something that will be decided by an isolated CEO or an elite group of executives. Critical decisions, those below the waterline, have never been made that way and there is no expectation that this will change.

Notes

1. Throughout this case the word "associate" is used because Gore always uses it instead of "employee." In fact, the case writers were told that the term "associates" evolved early in the company's history because it expressed the belief that everyone had a stake in the success of the enterprise.
2. Gore's ASOP is similar legally to an employee stock ownership plan (ESOP). Again, Gore simply has never allowed the word "employee" in any of its documentation.

About the Authors

Editor & Co-Author

Frank Shipper is professor of management in the Franklin P. Perdue School of Business at Salisbury University. His teaching, consulting, and research interests are managerial/leadership skills development, employee ownership, and collaborative cultures. He has consulted for and studied employee-owned companies for over 25 years. Among other honors, he has received a Regents Award for excellence in research, University System of Maryland's highest faculty honor.

Co-Authors

Stephen B. Adams is associate professor of management in the Franklin P. Perdue School of Business, Salisbury University. His previous books were *Mr. Kaiser Goes to Washington: The Rise of a Government Entrepreneur*, and *Manufacturing the Future: A History of Western Electric*. His next book is on the development of Silicon Valley.

Marvin O. Brown JD, is lecturer of management in the Franklin P. Perdue School of Business at Salisbury University. He is licensed to practice law in the Commonwealth of Virginia and Ohio. Before joining academia, Brown was corporate counsel specializing in employment and labor law in both the electric and telecommunication industries.

Thomas J. Calo is associate professor of management in the Franklin P. Perdue School of Business at Salisbury University. Prior to his university career he was a senior human resources (HR) professional in both public and private sector organizations. His research interests are the aging workforce, the history of HR, and employee ownership.

Wayne H. Decker is professor of management in the Franklin P. Perdue School of Business at Salisbury University. He received his PhD from the University of Pittsburgh. His research interests include humor, ethics, career development, and motivation. His publications include articles in *Journal of Managerial Psychology* and *Journal of Business Ethics*.

Richard C. Hoffman is professor in the Franklin P. Perdue School of Business at Salisbury University. His professional interests include strategic and international management; articles on these topics are published in *Decision Sciences*, *Journal of International Business Studies*, *Journal of Management*, among others. He has served as an interim dean and has held visiting appointments in Asia and Europe.

Charles C. Manz, PhD is an award-winning author of over 200 articles and scholarly papers and more than 20 books. Formerly a Marvin Bower Fellow at the Harvard Business School, he is the Nirenberg Chaired Professor of Leadership in the Isenberg School of Management at the University of Massachusetts Amherst.

Karen P. Manz is a researcher and author of articles and case studies for academic and professional business audiences. Her coauthored books include *For Team Members Only: Making Your Workplace Team Productive and Hassle Free* (Amacom) and *The Virtuous Organization: Insights from Some of the World's Leading Management Thinkers* (World Scientific).

Olivier P. Roche is associate professor of management in the Franklin P. Perdue School of Business at Salisbury University. He holds degrees from Georgetown University (LLM) and McGill University (PhD). He is a licensed attorney in New York. Prior to his academic career, he has worked at the World Bank in Washington DC and as an international investment banker.

Marc D. Street (PhD, Florida State University, 1998) is associate professor of management in the Franklin P. Perdue School of Business at Salisbury University. Dr. Street's research has appeared in journals such as *Organizational Behavior and Human Decision Processes*, *Journal of Business Ethics*, *Journal of World Business*, and *Small Group Research*, among others.

Vera L. Street is associate professor of management in the Franklin P. Perdue School of Business at Salisbury University. Her research interests include competitive dynamics and employee ownership. Her articles have appeared in the *Journal of Management, Academy of Management Executive, Journal of Business Venturing*, and others.

Christy H. Weer (PhD, Drexel, 2006) is an associate professor of management at the Franklin P. Perdue School of Business at Salisbury University. Christy's teaching interests focus primarily on the areas of organizational behavior and the management of change. Her research focuses on the complexities of the work–nonwork interface, career management, and gender and diversity in organizations.

Index